The Wordsworth
Railway Dictionary

–

Alan A. Jackson

Wordsworth Reference

First published 1992 as *The Railway Dictionary*
by Alan Sutton Publishing Ltd, Stroud, Gloucestershire.

This edition published 1997 by Wordsworth Editions Ltd.
Cumberland House, Crib Street, Ware, Hertfordshire SG12 9ET.

ISBN 1-85326-750-3

Printed and bound in Great Britain by Mackays of Chatham PLC.

Contents

Foreword

The objective of this work is to record and define railway terms and phrases, including colloquialisms and slang, by expanding and supplementing rather than repeating the information to be found in standard English language dictionaries. Words adequately defined in standard dictionaries are not normally included here.

While principally concerned with British usage, this dictionary also includes a selective North American, French, German, Spanish, Italian and international European vocabulary. The intention has been to produce a guide to the whole range of specialized language relating to rail transport in all its modes, including tramways and light railways. Explanations of the plethora of railway abbreviations, (including company initials), special names given to certain British lines, the principal named trains, British and overseas, past and present, and the names of many of the major firms involved in the railway industry are all to be found in these pages.

Some books are made because it has not proved possible to find an existing work which fulfils a recurring personal need. This is one.

I would like to record my warm thanks to J.H. Price, formerly the managing editor of Cook's Timetables, and J.N. Faulkner, librarian of The Railway Club, for reading the initial drafts and making many very helpful suggestions which positively contributed to quality, coverage and accuracy; to John L. Brown, for allowing access to manuscript lists of railway words and expressions he has collected over many years, and to J. Diandas FCA MCIT, G.A. Jacobs MCIT, Peter Knottley and S.G. Watts, for valuable assistance.

July 1991

Alan A. Jackson
Dorking

Notes on using the dictionary and on its arrangement

Order of Dictionary Entries: Entries are made in strict alphabetical order by letter, ampersand and the abbreviation 'St' being treated as 'and' and 'Saint' respectively. Company names will be found under their abbreviated titles, including ampersand, where one applies. For example, the *Stratford-upon-Avon & Midland Junction Rly* appears under **S&**MJR not **SMJ**R. Definite articles are ignored for the purposes of placing in alphabetical order. Headwords are printed in bold type, with an initial capital.

Named Trains: With one or two exceptions, only those names bestowed officially by the operating railway are given.

For those named trains operating in Britain, the dates when the name was first and last *officially* used (i.e. in timetables and/or on the trains themselves) are noted, as are any major changes in route. It should, however, be borne in mind that the name may have been applied to a service that already existed and that the service may have continued after the name had been discarded.

In general it may be assumed that named trains ran in both directions between the places given in the entry, but a very small number did work in one direction only.

Again as a general rule, it should be noted that most named trains in Britain and mainland Europe ceased to operate as such during both world wars; where they were resumed afterwards, this is normally clear from the entry. As always there are exceptions, and in Britain, for example, in the Second World War, the Aberdonian, Cornish Riviera, Flying Scotsman and Night Scotsman continued to run as named trains.

Outside Britain, the coverage of train names is less comprehensive but the aim has been to include all the *CIWL* 'Grand Expresses', the *TEE* and EC names and other major named services.

Terms capable of more than one interpretation: Some generic terms such as 'tramway' have had several meanings over the period of their use. In such cases each definition is given a number, and any reference elsewhere in the dictionary to the word repeats the relevant number, e.g. 'tramway (4)' indicates that in the context of the entry it is a tramway of the type defined at 'Tramway (4)'.

National Variations: Unless otherwise noted by the presence of an abbreviation such as '(US)' or '(Fr)', the definition given relates to British/Irish usage. Where an entry is annotated '(US)', the usage explained can generally be taken to flow over into Canada. Foreign words and phrases are given in italics.

British and Irish Railway Companies: These normally appear in the main dictionary under their *full initials*, including any '&' in the title (see Order of Dictionary Entries above).

No attempt has been made to list every railway company that ever existed in Britain and Ireland, but all the major companies are shown, as well as all others owning rolling stock. In addition, many other companies have been included, particularly those whose title offers little or no indication of the location of their lines. An effort has been made to include all jointly-owned or jointly-worked lines of significant length.

The notes against each company entry do not attempt to summarize its history and geography but merely give the date of incorporation (normally that of the first act of parliament or LRO), the extent of the main system, the opening date of the first lines and the date of any disappearance into the maws of a larger concern. In the case of those small companies which remained independent after the grouping of 1923, and light railways, closure dates are normally given.

Gauge: This is noted only when it differs from the British standard (4 ft 8½ in or in Ireland 5 ft 3 in).

Slang, colloquialisms and nicknames: In some cases usage did not, and does not, stray far from the place of origin, but it is always difficult to be dogmatic about this, so no regional distinctions are noted other than those for the London Underground system (marked '(LTRS)'), and even some of these may have gained currency in parts of the main railway system. Some very localized and transient terms have been omitted. For these, the user is referred to the three works on railway slang noted in the list of sources below.

Difficulty also arises in distinguishing between the language of railway officers and staff and that of railway amateurs or enthusiasts. This occurs partly because so many of the latter are to be found in the ranks of the former but also because there has always been a certain cross-fertilization. For this reason, although we began with the intention of distinguishing between these two categories of slang, colloquialisms and nicknames, it soon appeared that the boundary was too often ill-defined and it has therefore all been classified as '(RS)'. As well as distinguishing slang words peculiar to the London Underground, we have also annotated the often colourful North American railway expressions as '(USRS)'.

The derivations of slang, colloquialisms and nicknames are often obvious but where they are not, the origins can frequently be obscure. If a derivation is of particular interest or can be given with reasonable certainty it has been noted; but on the whole, we have preferred not to make intelligent guesses. It should also be noted that certain terms which may now be considered offensive are included in the dictionary because of their historical and specific relevance to railways. Their inclusion in no way reflects the views of either author or publisher.

Obsolete and obsolescent terms: The annotation '(obs)' has been omitted where the entry makes it clear that the company etc. no longer exists. Although most of the telegraphic codes noted are no longer in daily use on BR, these words do remain alive among modellers and others and in many cases have survived to become the convenient accepted names of the type of rolling stock mentioned in the entry. In all other cases, although many words, abbreviations and expressions have fallen out of everyday use on the main railway systems, they do remain current among those fascinated by railways, most notably among modellers and those working with old railway and tramway equipment in museums and on preserved lines, both in the UK and overseas. For these reasons the annotation '(obs)' has been used sparingly.

Place-names: These are usually given in the form used at the time to which the entry relates, e.g. Portmadoc rather than Porthmadog, but should always be recognizable. For most of the period covered by this dictionary it was customary to use Anglicized versions of some foreign place names, e.g. Venice and not Venezia; Cologne, not Köln; Hook of Holland, not Hoek van Holland etc. Again these English forms have been used and should offer no difficulty.

Other proper names, companies, periodicals, societies etc.: These usually appear under their initials when consisting of more than one word.

Trade and proprietary terms: Inclusion in this dictionary of some words or trade marks does not imply that they have acquired non-proprietary or general significance; no judgment of any kind concerning the legal status of these words is intended by such inclusion.

Abbreviations

BR	British Rail
cctv	closed circuit television
Co	company
Fr	France/French language
Ger	Germany/German language
h	hours
inc	incorporated
Ire	Ireland (usually Republic of Ireland)
It	Italy/Italian language
Junc	Junction
loco	locomotive
LT	London Transport and predecessors (London Underground railways)
LTRS	slang or colloquialism used by staff of London's underground railways
m	miles
min	minutes
NI	Northern Ireland
obs	obsolete
qv	*quod vide* – refer to the main entry under this name, term or word
rly	railway
RR	Railroad
RS	railwaymen's or railway amateurs' slang or colloquialism
S	general British slang or colloquialism, not specially confined to railwaymen or railway amateurs
Sp	Spain/Spanish language
TC	telegraph code
US	United States of America
USRS	railway slang or colloquialism in the US and Canada
vdu	visual display unit

All other abbreviations used are defined in the main dictionary.

Sources

Of the wide variety of sources consulted, the following proved particularly helpful:

Books and Articles

Anon., *British Railways Glossary of Terms*, 1966 (limited circulation).

Anon., *The Railroad Dictionary of Car and Locomotive Terms*, USA, 1980.

Anon., *The Railway Yearbook/Railway Directory & Yearbook,* various issues.

Beck, James H., *Rail Talk: A Lexicon of Railroad Language*, USA, 1978.

Beebe, Lucius, *Mixed Train Daily*, USA, 1961.

Behrend, G., *The History of Wagons-Lits 1875–1955*, 1959.

Body, G., *The Railway Language*, 1972, and *Supplement* [on slang] (n.d.).

Botkin, B.A., and Harlow, Alvin F. (eds.), *A Treasury of Railroad Folklore*, USA, 1954.

Charlton, E. Harper, *Railway Car Builders of the United States & Canada*, USA, 1957.

Cole, W.H., *Permanent-Way Material, Platelaying and Points and Crossings with a few remarks on Signalling and Interlocking*, 8th edn., revised by Lt.-Col. G.R. Hearn, 1920.

Davies, W.J.K., *Light Railways, their Rise and Decline*, 1964.

Gale, P.R., *The Great Western Railway*, 1926.

McKenna, F., *The Railway Workers 1840–1970*, 1980.

Marshall, J., *A Biographical Dictionary of Railway Engineers*, 1978.

——, *Guinness Book of Rail Facts & Feats*, 1979.

Mitchell, N.H.G., 'A Dictionary of Underground Slang', published in *Underground*, no. 6 (July 1980).

O'Dell, A.C., *Railways and Geography*, 1956.

Price, J.H., *A Source Book of Trams*, 1980.

Rowsome, Frank, *Trolley Car Treasury*, 1956.

Sekon, G.A., *Sekon's Dictionary of Railway Words & Phrases*, 1901.

Sheppard, H., *Dictionary of Railway Slang*, 2nd edn., 1970.

Periodicals

Various issues of the following:

Modern Railways
Modern Tramway

Modern Transport
Railroad Magazine [USA]
The Railway & Travel Monthly
The Railway Magazine
Railways/Railway World
Trains Illustrated
Transport & Travel Monthly
La Vie du Rail [France]

A

A&BR

1. Aylesbury & Buckingham Rly:
Aylesbury–Verney Junction (junc
with L&NWR) inc 1860, opened
1868, worked by GWR, part of
Metropolitan Rly, 1891, worked by
Metropolitan from 1894.

2. Antofagasta (Chile) & Bolivia Rly
(FCAB): First section opened 1873,
2 ft 6 in/762 mm gauge; completed
1892; converted to metre gauge
1928.

A&N Jt

Ashby & Nuneaton Joint, Nuneaton to
Overseal & Moira/Coalville, inc 1866,
1867, opened 1873, jointly vested in
Midland and L&NWR, part of
LM&SR from 1923.

A&ST

Alford & Sutton Tramway, Alford to
Sutton-on-Sea, 2 ft 6 in gauge steam
tramway (*4*), inc 1880, opened 1884,
renamed Great Northern Steam
Tramways Co. 1886, closed 1889.

A&TER

Athenry & Tuam Extension Rly (Ire),
inc 1890, opened 1894, worked by
GS&WR, part of GSR 1924.

A&WCR

Aberystwyth & Welsh Coast Rly,
Machynlleth–Aberystwyth/Pwllheli/
Dolgelley, inc 1861, opened 1863,
1864, 1865, 1867, 1869, part of
Cambrian from 1865.

AAR

Association of American Railroads;
established 1934, a consolidation of
the American Railway Association and
other organizations dating back to
1867. The central co-ordinating and
research agency of the US rly
industry. Canadian and Mexican rlys
also participate.

ABAC

*Association Belge des Amis des Chemins
de Fer*; formed 1929, published
Ferrovia from October 1931. Now
known as *ARBAC* (qv).

Abadan (RS)

Loco driver who makes excessive use
of oil. From the Iranian oil port.

Abbey Tanks (RS)

GCR 4–6–2T.

ABC

ABC or Alphabetical Railway Guide; a
rly timetable set out in alphabetical
order of towns served from London,
showing services from and to London;
first published in 1853. Guides
arranged on similar lines were also
published for some other British cities
and towns. 'I would sooner lose a train
by the *ABC* than catch it by
Bradshaw'— Oscar Wilde.

ABCs

Booklets of loco numbers published by
Ian Allan for the use of train spotters
(qv). When a loco was seen, the user
crossed out the printed number. *See
also* Number cruncher; Ref.

ABCL

Automatic Barrier Crossing Locally-
monitored (BR); similar to AOCL (qv)
but fitted with road barriers.

Aberdares (RS)
GWR inside-cylinder 2–6–0 locos of
1900. From their use on coal trains
between Aberdare and Swindon.

Aberdonian, The
Express between London (Kings
Cross) and Aberdeen, introduced
1927, name dropped 1971.

Abermule
Station on the Cambrian Rlys near the
scene of a 1921 head-on collision
caused by the issue of the wrong
tablet, which was not checked by the
driver. Some locos in India
subsequently carried the injunction
REMEMBER ABERMULE inscribed in
their cabs.

Abonné (Fr)
Season ticket holder, commuter.

ABP
Associated British Ports (formerly
BTDB (qv)).

ABS
1. Automatic Brake System.
2. Air Braked Service.

Absent rider (RS)
An engineman who has failed to report
for duty.

Absolute block
see Block system.

ACC
American Car Co., St Louis, Mo, US,
established 1891, bought by Brill (qv)
1902. Builders of all types of electric
traction rolling stock. Plant closed 1931.

Accelerato (It)
Stopping Train; 'Somewhat faster than
the Treno Omnibus' — Baedeker.

Accommodation crossing
A private level crossing provided for
the use of the landowner or his tenants
when a parcel of land under single
ownership has been severed by
construction of a rly.

Accommodation train (US)(obs)
A slow or local train.

ACE
Area Civil Engineer (BR).

Ace, The (RS)
The Atlantic Coast Express (qv).

ACF
American Car & Foundry Co.,
manufacturers of rly and tramway
rolling stock, established 1899
following a merger of thirteen
companies. British works functioned at
Trafford Park, Manchester 1904–9.
Later known as ACF Industries Inc.

ACFI
A form of feed-water heater (qv)
evolved by the French organization
*Association des Chemins de Fer
Industrielles. See also* Hikers.

ACI (US)
Automatic Car Identification. A set of
nodules on each side of locos and
rolling stock which, when read by an
optical scanner as the train passes (at
up to 80 m.p.h.), identifies ownership,
number, classification etc.

ACL (US).
Atlantic Coast Line RR Co.

A–Co–Tra–L
Operators of the *Rome Metro* and
Rome–Ostia Rly.

ACPF
*Asociacion del Congreso Panamericano
de Ferrocarriles*; Pan-American Railway
Congress Association.

Adex (obs)
TC for an advertised excursion.

Admiraal de Ruyter
Daytime EC service between London
(Liverpool St.) and Amsterdam via
Harwich–Hook of Holland sailings,
introduced 1987, ceased 1989.

Adriatic (US)
A steam loco with 2–6–4 wheel
arrangement.

Adriatico
TEE Milan–Bari, introduced 1973, IC
1987.

Advance, in
Signalling term denoting anything beyond a given point on the rly when facing the direction of travel.

Advanced starter
Stop signal placed more than a train length in advance (qv) of the starting signal, indicating a point to which trains can draw up after completing station platform work if the block section ahead is not clear, thus allowing a following train to use the platform.

Advertised, on the (USRS)
see On the Advertised.

AEC
Associated Equipment Co., a subsidiary of the UERL (qv), formed in 1912, became independent in 1933.

AEE
American–European Express (qv).

AEG
Allgemeine Elektrizitäts Gesellschaft. Founded 1881 as German Edison Co., became AEG 1887, merged with *Union Elektrizitäts Gesellschaft* 1903 as *AEG-Union*, later *AEG* again.

AEI
Associated Electrical Industries Ltd, successors to BTH (qv) and MV (qv) 1959–67; part of GEC (qv) 1967.

Aero
GWR TC for an aircraft propeller wagon.

AET
Automatic Equipment Technician (LT).

AFAC
Association Française des Amis [originally *Amateurs*] *des Chemins de Fer;* founded 1929; has published *Chemins de Fer* since 1933.

AFC
Automatic Fare Collection [system].

African Village, The (RS)
Muddle of buildings in the forecourt area of Kings Cross Station, London, not finally cleared away until 1972–3.

Agent (obs)
Scottish alternative term for stationmaster (which was also used).

Aguila Azteca
Express between Mexico City and Nuevo Laredo.

AHB
Automatic Half Barriers; barriers obstructing the nearside half of the roadway at a level crossing, raised and lowered automatically by the passage of trains.

AICCF
Association Internationale des Congrés des Chemins de Fer; International Railway Congress Association, established 1885 to facilitate the progress and development of rlys by holding periodical congresses and by means of publications.

AIR
Association of Independent Railways. A retitling of AMRC (qv).

Air artist (USRS)
A driver skilful in the use of the air brakes.

Air brake
A braking system in which brakes are held off by compressed air acting on a piston and applied by the controlled release of pressure.

Air cans (RS)
Air conditioned coaches.

Air dump (US)
A car which tips its body by use of air pressure to ease loading or unloading.

Airey's Maps and Junction Diagrams
Published by John Airey and Zachary Macaulay of the RCH (qv) from 1854; they show the distances between stations and junctions and the ownership of each section of rly. They became official publications after the RCH purchased the business in 1895.

Air giver (USRS)
Brakeman.
Air jammer/jumper (USRS)
Rlyman who connects train air hoses.
Air line (US)
Term indicating a rly providing the most
direct route between two places, e.g.
Seaboard Air Line, following the
Atlantic coast from Richmond to Florida
by the shortest and straightest route.
Air monkey (USRS)
Air brake fitter/mechanic.
Air slide (US)
Car whose contents can be unloaded
by use of air pressure and a sliding
interior section.
Aisle (US)
Gangway through a coach.
AJR
see Axholme.
Akropolis
Through service between Munich and
Athens via Salzburg and Belgrade,
introduced 1968.
AL
Chemin de Fer de l'Alsace-Lorraine
[France]; part of *SNCF* (qv), 1938.
Aladdin (LTRS)
A handlamp.
ALAF
*Asociacion Latino Americana de
Ferrocarriles*; Latin American Railways
Association.
Albert Schweitzer
TEE Dortmund–Strasbourg,
introduced 1980, ceased 1983.
Alco
American Locomotive Co.
Ale
GWR TC for a wagon used for
carrying casks.
Alice
The service between Sydney and Alice
Springs (Australia).
Alignment
The course of a rly as determined by

the final surveys; a ground plan of a
rly route.
Allegheny (US)
A loco with 2–6–6–6 wheel
arrangement.
Alleluia! (RS)
A signal to shut the tap when
washing out the boiler of a steam
locomotive.
Alley (USRS)
An unobstructed track in a
marshalling or shunting yard.
All system timetable
A single volume containing details of
all BR passenger services, first issued
by BR in 1974.
Alpazur
A seasonal diesel railcar service
between Nice and Digne, 1974–89.
Alpen Express
Through service between Copenhagen
and Rome via Brenner, introduced
1957, became a day train Munich to
Rome. *See also* Michelangelo.
Alps/over the Alps
1. (RS) Several routes with
   pronounced undulations received
   this description, notably Alton to
   Alresford, Carlisle to Stranraer via
   Castle Douglas, and Barnstaple to
   Torrington.
2. (LTRS) The raised sidings at
   Neasden and Ealing Common
   depots.
ALR
Ashover Light Rly, Ashover to Clay
Cross, 60 cm gauge, opened 1925,
closed to passengers 1936, to freight
1950.
Alsace-Lorraine, Chemin de Fer de l'
see AL.
Alstholm
Société Alsacienne–Thomson–Houston,
formed 1928, successor to *CFTH* (qv)
and *SACM* (qv). Now part of GEC–
Alstholm.

Alternate layout
Parallel tracks arranged in pairs, Up
and Down, Up and Down.

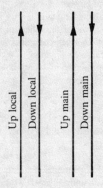

Up local | Down local | Up main | Down main

AM
1. Area Manager.
2. (obs) BR prefix for alternating
current mu sets (AM6 etc.).
Amain (RS)(NE England)
Runaway (qv). A usage derived from
the normal meanings 'at full speed; in
or with full force' (*Shorter Oxford
English Dictionary*).
Ambrosiano
TEE Milan–Rome, introduced 1974,
lost *TEE* status 1987.
Ambulance (USRS)
A caboose (qv).
Ambulance Train
A train specially equipped to carry
invalids, principally soldiers wounded
in battle, or taken sick at the front.
Accommodation is provided for
stretcher cases, doctors and nurses.
There is usually a dispensary,
operating room and kitchen etc.
First used in the American Civil War
and much refined and extensively
deployed in the First and Second
World Wars.

Ambulant (Fr)
A postal sorter on a mail train.
Américain, chemin de fer
see Chemin de fer Américain.
American
A loco with 4–4–0 wheel arrangement.
From its wide adoption by American
rlys in the nineteenth century.
American devils (RS)(obs)
Steam-driven excavators used in rly
construction, originally developed in
the US in the 1840s. *See also* Steam
navvy.
American–European Express
Luxury club, sleeper and dining cars
available at supplementary fares,
attached to Amtrak expresses and
segregated from the rest of the train.
First adopted on the Capitol Limited
(qv) in 1989.
American Express
An express freight (qv) company,
formed in US 1850, a consolidation of
competing operators. *See also* Wells
Fargo.
**American Specials/American Boat
Specials**
L&NWR trains between London
(Euston) and Liverpool connecting
with Atlantic liner sailings and
arrivals.
AMRC
Association of Minor Railway
Companies, founded 1938 to replace
ARLI (qv). Now known as AIR (qv).
Amshack (USRS)
A contraction of Amtrak (qv) and
shack – a small station.
Amtrak
Brand name for the US National
Railroad Passenger Corporation
(NRPC), a public corporation set up
in 1970 with authority to support the
operation of inter-city and some other
passenger trains using federal funds.
Began to operate train services May

1971. A contraction of 'American Track'.

Anadolu Express
Service between Istanbul (Haydarpasa) and Konya.

A(N&SW)D&R
Alexandra (Newport & South Wales) Dock & Rly Co., inc as dock and dock rlys undertaking 1865, renamed A(N&SW)D&R, 1882. Pontypridd to Penrhos, opened 1884, absorbed 1897. Part of GWR from 1922.

Anatolie Express
A *CIWL* all-sleeper service between Istanbul (Haydarpasa) and Ankara, introduced 1927.

Anchor (USRS)
1. A handbrake
2. A caboose (qv)

Anchors, to release (USRS)
To release handbrakes.

Anchor them, to (USRS)
To set handbrakes.

Ancient lights (RS)
Modern rly employees' term for semaphore signals (qv).

Andalucia Pullman Express
A Pullman car train between Seville and Granada operated by the *CIWL* 1929–39 (Malaga was also served in 1929–30).

Angel's seat, the (USRS)
The cupola (qv) in a caboose (qv).

Angle bar (US)
Fishplate (qv).

Anglia
BR region formed in 1988 out of Eastern region and embracing all lines east of the axis London (Fenchurch St.)–Hertford East–Meldreth–Whittlesea–Kings Lynn (all inclusive).

Anglia Electrics
NSE brand name from 1989 for services between London (Liverpool St.) and Cambridge, Kings Lynn, Southend, Southminster, Braintree, Colchester, Clacton/Walton, and Harwich.

Anglo-Scottish Car Carrier
A restaurant car train for motorists and their cars between London (Holloway), Newcastle and Edinburgh, introduced 1960. Name dropped in 1966 when the London terminal became Kensington (Olympia) and the term Motorail (qv) came into use.

Animal car (USRS)
A caboose (qv).

Ankara Express
Service between Istanbul (Haydarpasa) and Ankara.

Annett's Key
Key and lock for little-used siding connections, invented by J.E. Annett, L&SWR signal superintendent, in 1875. When the siding is out of use the key is kept in the controlling signal box and cannot be removed from its housing in the signal locking frame until all conflicting signals are set at danger. These signals remain locked until the key is replaced. At the siding, the key unlocks the lever controlling the access points and cannot be removed until that lever is relocked. On single lines, the key is normally incorporated in the train staff (qv).

Ann Arbor (US)
Toledo, Ann Arbor & North Michigan RR, eventually known as the Ann Arbor Co.

Annunciator
A device giving a remote audible indication of the passage of a train at any given point.

ANR or AN Rail
Australian National Rlys, formed 1975. An amalgamation of Commonwealth Rlys, Tasmanian Government Rlys and the non-

metropolitan lines of South Australian Rlys.

Ant
GWR TC for six-wheel composite coach.

Antwerp Continental
see Continental Express.

AOCL
Automatic Open Crossing Locally-monitored; a level crossing without road barriers and fitted with flashing lights for road users. Correct operation of the road lights is shown by white lights exhibited to the train driver at the approach to the crossing. *See also* ABCL.

AOCR
Automatic Open Crossing Remotely-monitored; a level crossing without road barriers and fitted with flashing lights for road users. Correct operation of the road lights is proved in the controlling signal box.

Ape wagon (USRS)
A caboose (qv).

Apex
Special cheap InterCity return fares only available if purchased seven days in advance of travel, introduced 1990.

Appendix [to the Working timetables]
An official publication containing instructions on the working of sidings, stations etc., also particulars of signal boxes, gradients, tunnels and other matters not varying frequently enough to justify inclusion in the Working timetables (qv).

Applesauce (US)
Nickname for New Orleans, Opelousas & Great Western RR, later part of Southern Pacific RR.

Apply the rule, to (LTRS)
To pass a signal at danger under 'stop and proceed' rule (qv).

Approach locking
Electric locking effective while a train is approaching a signal displaying a clear (proceed) aspect and designed to prevent alteration to the route set should the signal be replaced to danger in face of the train.

Approach release
A system of electrical control preventing clear or caution aspects being displayed by a signal until the approaching train is within a predetermined distance.

Apron (US
A metal platform between loco and tender or between passenger cars.

APT
Advanced Passenger Train. An unsuccessful BR tilting train project of 1969–86 designed to achieve high speed running without the expense of altering existing track alignments. APT-E was the APT-Experimental gas-turbine train completed in 1972; this was followed by the electrically-propelled APT-P (APT-Prototype).

APTA
American Public Transit Association; formed 1974, incorporating the American Transit Association and the Institute for Rapid Transit.

APTIS
All Purpose Ticket Issuing System (BR); introduced from 1984. *See also* PORTIS; SPORTIS.

Aquilon
Express between Paris and Marseilles, introduced 1959. Now an un-named *TGV* service.

Aquitaine
TEE Paris–Bordeaux, introduced 1971, journey time 4 h and then the fastest train in Europe, lost *TEE* status 1984, ceased 1990.

ARBAC
Association Royale Belge des Amis des

Chemins de Fer. Renaming of *ABAC* (qv) following its receipt of a royal charter.

Arbalète
TEE Paris–Basle–Zurich, introduced 1957, lost *TEE* status 1979, EC from 1987.

'Arbour lights (RS)
Junction route indicators or lunar lights (qv).

ARC
1. Automatic Revenue Control (BR).
2. Amey Roadstone Co.

Argyle Line
Partick to Rutherglen via Glasgow Central (LL). Former steam underground service, reopened with electric trains in 1979.

Ark, The (RS)(obs)
The loco lifting shop at Stratford, London.

Arlberg Express/Arlberg–Orient Express
A *CIWL* service of through sleepers from Paris to Athens and Bucharest with Calais–Bucharest portion, running via Basle, Zurich, Vienna and Arad, introduced 1924. Re-introduced after the Second World War. Paris to Vienna only from 1962, when it became known as the *Arlberg Express*.

ARLI
Association of Railways of Local Interest; formed 1912 as the Association of Railways; an organization of those fifty or so small companies not parties to the RCA (qv). Replaced by AMRC (qv).

Armada
An express between Leeds, York and Plymouth, introduced 1988.

Armistice Coach
A 1913 *CIWL* dining car in which the Armistice marking the end of the First World War was signed on 11 November 1918. After exhibition at the Invalides Museum in Paris, it was moved back to a building on the site of the signing in the Forest of Compiègne in 1927. On 22 June 1940 Hitler obtained a French surrender in the same coach, after which it was exhibited in Berlin. It was destroyed by the Germans in 1944 probably to prevent its use for a third time. A replacement car of the same type was installed at Compiègne in 1950.

Armourclads (RS)
SR Merchant Navy and West Country 4–6–2 locos in their original form. From their outer casing.

Armstrong (USRS)
Any manually operated device for which there is no power-driven alternative.

Armstrong gear (RS)(obs)
A combined lever and screw loco reversing gear introduced by William Bouch, loco superintendent of the S&DR in 1865. It required considerable effort to operate, hence the name.

Armstrongs (RS)
LM&SR 4F class locomotives used on the S&DJR. From the builders, Armstrong, Whitworth.

Armstrong, Whitworth
Sir W.G. Armstrong, Whitworth & Co. Ltd, Newcastle, loco and railcar builders, 1919–37.

ARPS
Association of Railway Preservation Societies, founded 1960.

Arrêt pipi (FrRS)
A comfort stop (qv).

Arrow of Indecision
A cynical nickname for BR double arrow logo introduced in 1965, arising from a wilful misinterpretation of its meaning.

ARS
Automatic Route Setting. First

installed by BR at Three Bridges 1983. Operated by train describers (qv) on SDS (qv).

Articulated stock
Rolling stock in which vehicles share one bogie at adjacent ends. *See also* Quad-arts.

Asbestos (USRS)
Poor quality loco coal.

Ashbury
Ashbury Railway Carriage & Iron Co. Ltd, 1862–1902, became part of MCW (qv).

Ashcat/ash eater (USRS)
A steam loco fireman.

Ash pit engineer (USRS)
A steam loco fitter.

Asia Express
A streamlined steam train introduced 1935 by South Manchuria Rly between Dairen and Changchun. Ceased *c.* 1944.

ASLEF
Associated Society of Locomotive Engineers & Firemen, founded 1880. Now the trade union for all types of train driver.

ASLRA
American Short Line Railroads Association.

ASM
Assistant Station Master/Manager.

Asmo
GWR TC for covered motor car carrying wagon.

Aspect
The position of a signal at any given time; its indication.

ASRS
Amalgamated Society of Railway Servants; the first enduring rly trade union in the UK, founded 1871, registered as a trade union 1872, amalgamated with UP&SS (qv) and GRWU (qv) to form NUR (qv), 1913.

Astrodome
Upper deck section of a passenger car with large glazed areas to allow passengers to view scenery.

ASTT
All System Timetable, BR.

ATA
Advanced Transport for Avon; light rail transit system in and around Bristol.

ATAC
Azienda Tramvie e Autobus del Commune di Roma; Tramways and Bus Agency for the Commune of Rome, formed 1929.

AT&SF (US)
Atchison, Topeka & Santa Fe Railway Co. *See also* Santa Fe (*1*).

ATC
1. Automatic Train Control. A general term for any system designed to check the driver's reaction to signals etc, ranging from cab warning systems to complete automatic control. *See also* ATO; ATP; AWS.
2. Army Transportation Corps, US Army. Its rly battalions functioned in all theatres of war in the First and Second World Wars. In 1945 there were 43,306 officers and men engaged in ATC rly activities.

ATCS
Advanced Train Control Systems; incorporating a radio data link between an on-board controller unit and a central computer.

ATH
American Thomson–Houston Co.; became part of the General Electric Co. of America.

ATIS
Advance Traffic Information System for freight services, fully operational on BR from 1970. Eventually included in TOPS (qv).

Atlantic
US, and later British, term for steam loco with 4–4–2 wheel arrangement. From the Atlantic Coast RR, which ordered the first one.

Atlantic Coast Express, The
An express between London (Waterloo) and Padstow, also serving Ilfracombe, Bude, Torrington and Plymouth, introduced by the SR in 1926. Re-introduced 1947, ceased 1964. Name revived by BR for London (Paddington) to Newquay summer service, 1988.

Atlantic Line
BR name (1980) for Victoria to Peckham Rye section of the South London Line (qv). From the Atlantic Bridge over Atlantic Road, Brixton.

Atmospheric railway
A system of traction, also known as pneumatic rlys, which was tried in the first half of the nineteenth century. Trains were drawn by a small four-wheeled vehicle fitted with a piston which engaged in a continuous pipe between the rails. As air was exhausted from the pipe by stationary steam engines, the vacuum created was sufficient to pull the truck and its train forward. The problems encountered could not be overcome by the technology of the period and were not in any case pursued after *c.* 1850 owing to the successful development of the steam loco. Atmospheric propulsion for tube rlys (qv) was, however, considered as possibility for a further thirty years or so.

ATO
Automatic Train Operation. Term used by LT for system in which all train movement control is automatic apart from door operation and starting from stations. Safety information is continuously transmitted to the train in the form of electrical codes in the running rails which tell the train its permitted speed. If codes are absent or incorrect, the brakes are applied. For signal stops, a brake command signal in the running rail causes the brakes to be applied and restarts the train automatically when the signal is cleared. Similarly, speed reduction and braking instructions are given by electrical impulses as the train approaches a station. Lineside signals are not provided except at junctions and for station starters. After trials in 1963–4, the new Victoria Line tube rly was equipped with ATO from 1968 onwards.

ATP
Automatic Train Protection. A system which will stop a train automatically or regulate its speed if a driver fails to respond to signal indications or speed restrictions.

ATS
Automatic Train Supervision. A system for maintaining adherence to timetable and headways, and imposing coasting to save electrical energy, over-riding the driver's manual controls in these respects.

Attika
A sleeping car service between Munich and Athens, introduced 1989.

Aurora
1. *TEE* Rome–Reggio di Calabria, introduced 1974, lost *TEE* status 1975, continued as Rapido service, extended to Syracuse 1979, name dropped 1987.
2. A fast day service between Moscow and Leningrad, so named 1964–77.

Ausbaustrecken (Ger)
DB lines upgraded for high speed operation in the 1980s and '90s.

Austerities (RS)
Second World War Ministry of Supply

steam locos; also Bulleid Q1 0–6–0 locos.

Austin Sevens/Austins (RS)
LM&SR Fowler 7F 0–8–0 locos, introduced 1929 when the famous 'baby car' was becoming popular.

Austria Express
An express between Hook of Holland (connections with sailings to and from Harwich), Amsterdam and Klagenfurt, introduced 1953. Hook portion withdrawn 1989.

Austrian Goods (RS)
G&SWR 2–6–0 locos of 1915, built by North British, which incorporated parts originally intended for an Austrian contract.

Auto (LTRS)
Automatic signal/ticket/machine/internal telephone.

Autobuffet (obs)
A BR coach fitted with self-service coin-in-the-slot machines dispensing snacks, cigarettes and drinks, introduced 1962.

Auto-cars (obs)
Auto-train (qv).

Automatic brakes
Continuous brakes (qv).

Automatic signal[ling]
A system in which signals, normally in the 'clear' mode, are activated and changed to 'stop' by the passage of the train itself, affording protection to the track section it occupies while it remains on it. Treadle devices were formerly used but these were superseded by the use of track circuits (qv).

Automatic train
Train without an active driver, entirely controlled by electronic systems during normal operation. *See also* ATO.

Autorail (Fr)
A railcar (qv).

Autos-Express
SNCF motorcar-carrying service, using fast freight trains.

Auto-train
1. (obs) A semi-permanently coupled train of one to six coaches, capable of being driven from either end, usually with steam tank locomotive at one end and at the other a control driving cab fitted with connections to the loco regulating handle, reversing gear, brake valve and whistle. In some cases there were control driving cabs at each end with the steam loco in the centre of the train. Also known as 'auto-cars' and 'motor trains'.
2. A sleeping car train, carrying the passengers' cars; US equivalent of Motorail (qv).

Autowagon (obs)
A BR experimental project of 1971 involving self-propelled, unmanned container wagons operating over the rly system in a computer-planned movement pattern. It included automatically-controlled transfer of the containers from road to rail vehicles and vice versa.

Auxiliary signal (obs)
Old name for distant signal (qv)

AVE
Alta Velocita Española; Spanish High Speed Trains/Rlys. First section Madrid–Seville, 1992.

Aveling & Porter
Established 1850 at Rochester as Messrs Aveling; works located at Strood from 1861; became A&P 1862. Manufactured small industrial locos from 1866. Later merged with Barford & Perkins to become Aveling–Barford of Grantham.

Average throughout trainload
The number of passengers averaged over the complete journey or train

service; usually calculated by dividing passenger miles by loaded train miles.

AVIS
Automatic Vehicle Identification System; introduced 1989–91 for MGR (qv) trains. Each wagon is fitted with a transponder coded to represent its number and as it moves around the rly system, it is detected by lineside reading equipment which passes the data to TOPS (qv) and the computer installations of British Coal and the electricity generating undertakings. *See also* ACI.

Avon Metro
Light rail system in and around Bristol. *See also* ATA.

Avonside
Avonside Engine Co., 1866 (formed from Stothert, Slaughter & Co., loco builders, established at Bristol in 1841, name changed to Slaughter, Gruning & Co. 1858). Goodwill purchased by Hunslet (qv) 1935.

Avon Valley
A preserved rly on former BR Bath–Bitton–Bristol line, opened from 1991.

Awayday (obs)
Former BR brand name for cheap day return ticket, hence (LTRS) a day's unauthorized absence from duty.

AWS
Automatic Warning System (BR); gives driver an audible confirmation of clear and caution indications of signals and applies brake if the caution warning is not acknowledged.

Axholme
Axholme Joint Rly, Haxey Junc to Marshland Junc/Fockerby/Hatfield Moor, promoted as Goole & Marshland Light Rly and Isle of Axholme Light Rly (LROs 1898). Opened 1900, 1903, 1904, passenger traffic from 1905. Hatfield Moor branch (freight only) opened 1909. Purchased by L&YR and NER jointly 1902 and renamed AJR; owned by L&NWR and NER 1922, LM&SR and L&NER 1923, BR from 1948.

Axle counter
Equipment placed at entrance and exit to a block section which electrically records the number of axles which have passed over it. Signalling apparatus which is locked to protect a train in the corresponding block section is not unlocked until the exit counter has registered the same number of axles as leaving the section.

B

B
BR gangwayed bogie brake coach.

Babe/Baby (RS)
Baby Scot (qv).

Baby Bongos (RS)
L&NER Thompson K1 2–6–0 steam locos.

Baby Deltics (RS)
English Electric BR type 23 1,100 hp diesel-electric locos, 1959.

Baby lifter (USRS)
A brakeman on a passenger train.

Baby load (USRS)
Freight load requiring great care in handling.

Baby Scots (RS)
LM&SR 4–6–0 5XP steam locos Patriot class of 1930 rebuilt from LNWR 1913 'Claughton' class. Also known as Babes or Babies.

Bacchus
TEE Munich–Dortmund, introduced 1979, ceased 1980, replaced by Albert Schweitzer (qv).

Back board (RS)
A distant signal (qv). So called because it is the signal at the back of others (Home and Starter) in the section, in the direction of running.

Back down, to
To move a loco backwards towards its train.

Backhead (US)
Back plate (qv).

Backing signal
A distinctive semaphore arm controlling wrong direction working within station limits.

Back light
The light shown by a semaphore signal lamp at the back allowing signalman to check whether signal is 'on' or 'off' and whether lamp remains lit.

Back plate
The plate at the back of the boiler and firebox of a steam loco on which the regulator, gauges and other controls are mounted.

Back porch yardmaster (USRS)
A switchman in a yard.

Back shift (RS)
Late turn (14.00 to 22.00).

Back shunt, to (LTRS)
To propel a train.

Back signal (RS)
see Back board (qv).

Back slotting
A GWR signalling system controlling stop and distant signals with one lever.

Back stick (RS)
see Back board (qv).

Back tripped (LTRS)
A train irregularly tripped by operation of rear tripcock (qv).

Back 'un (RS)
see Back board (qv).

Bacon slicer (RS)
A large wheel in a signal box for manual operation of level crossing gates. From its resemblance to the bacon slicing machines formerly seen in grocers' shops.

Badge porter (obs)
A man working at a rly station, under supervision of the rly staff but paid by the passenger, according to an agreed scale, for carrying luggage outside the station area. Also known as an outside porter.

Bad Order (USRS)
A vehicle or loco in need of repair or attention.

Bad order track (USRS)
A siding reserved for bad order (qv) stock.

Bag (RS)
1. The leather sleeve of a water crane (qv).
2. A flexible vacuum hose used for connecting brake pipes between vehicles.

Bag, to (RS)
see Cop, to (qv).

Baggage (US)
Luggage.

Baggage car (US)
Luggage van.

Baggage master
An official at US rly stations, usually in the baggage room, who takes charge of passengers' luggage, issuing a 'check' in exchange which is used to reclaim the item(s) at the destination.

Baghdad Rly
(Also known as Berlin–Baghdad Rly.) Planned to connect Mesopotamia (now Iraq) then part of the Turkish Empire, with the main European network. Originally a German expansionist project, aimed at securing influence over Turkey and pushing out towards British imperial interests, it was financed mostly by the *Deutsche Bank*. The line was completed under German auspices as far as Aleppo (Syria) by 1918. In 1928 the Turkish government purchased the rights of the old company. Further extensions were made in Syria by the French and the Iraqi frontier was reached in 1935. Iraq Rlys motor services meanwhile covered the gap still existing in that country. A continuous rly between the Bosphorus and Baghdad was finally achieved in July 1940. *See also* Taurus/Toros Express.

Bagnall
W.G. Bagnall & Co. Ltd, Stafford, loco builders, established 1875. Part of EE (Vulcan Foundry) (qv) 1961.

BAGS
Buenos Ayres & Great Southern Rly; a British co. formerly operating in Argentina.

Baguley
Baguley Cars Ltd, loco and railcar builders, Burton on Trent from 1911, became Baguley Engineers Ltd 1923, E.E. Baguley Ltd 1932. Amalgamated with Drewry (qv) as Baguley–Drewry Ltd 1967. Ceased production 1984.

Bahnhofsmission (Ger)
A German organization similar to Travelers' Aid (qv).

Bail, to (USRS)
To fire a steam loco.

Baileys (RS)
see Bill Baileys.

Bailing out (Ire RS)
Stopping a train between stations to raise steam from poor quality fuel (current in the Second World War).

Bait (RS)
A rlyman's packed lunch.

Bake a cake, to (USRS)
To build up a good head of steam on a loco.

Bakehead (USRS)
A fireman on a steam loco.

Bakerloo
A London tube rly owned by a US co., so called by the journalist G.H.F. Nichols ('Quex') because it linked Baker St. and Waterloo

stations. The tag was adopted officially from 1906. '. . . for a railway itself to adopt its gutter title, is not what we expect from a railway company. English railway officers have more dignity than to act in this manner.' — The editor of the RM (Sekon), 1906. *See also* BS&WR.

Balaclava Rly
The first military rly, built out of Balaclava port by the British, to serve the Crimean Front in 1855.

Bala Lake
Bala Lake Rly, a 1 ft 11½ in/597 mm gauge pleasure rly over the former BR line between Bala Junction and Llanuwchllyn. First section opened 1972.

Bald facing (USRS)
Propelling a train.

Bald wheels (USRS)
Loco wheels without flanges, to facilitate negotiation of sharp curves.

Baldwin (US)
Baldwin Locomotive Works, Philadelphia; founded by Matthias W. Baldwin in 1832.

Balkan Express/*Balkanzug*
A service between Vienna, Graz, and Belgrade, with coaches for Athens and Istanbul, introduced 1955, ceased 1965.

Balkanzug (Ger RS)
Any lengthy East European international train made up with vehicles from several countries or a train carrying migrant workers to or from Germany.

Ballast
Small stones used as a bed for sleepers (*1*) (qv). Clinker, slag, shingle and other substitutes are sometimes used.

Ballast scorcher (USRS)
A loco driver fond of high speed.

Ballast train
A train designed for bringing in new ballast and from which ballast is distributed over the formation. On LT, the term was formerly used to describe any type of engineer's train.

Ballet master (USRS)
A section foreman, in charge of gandy dancers (qv).

Ball of fire (USRS)
A very fast run.

Balloon (RS)
Foreman. ('Don't let me down, lads!')

Balloon stack (USRS)
The wide chimney of a wood-burning loco.

Balloon stock (RS)
LB&SCR coaches with very high arched roofs.

Ball the jack, to (USRS)
To build up the speed of a loco or train.

Ballycastle
see BR (2).

Baltic
US, and later British, term for steam loco with 4-6-4 wheel arrangement.

Baltimore & Ohio (US)
A steam loco with 4-4-4-4 wheel arrangement, after the first had been delivered to that rly.

Balt–Orient Express
A service from Stockholm to Bucharest, introduced 1948; operated between Stockholm and Sofia via Bucharest from 1950. From 1954 the name was applied to the Berlin–Bucharest–Sofia service with its connecting Stockholm–Sassnitz–Berlin sleeping cars. From 1956 the train again ran to Sofia via Belgrade. Later ran Berlin–Bucharest.

BAM
Baikal–Amur–Magistral; a relief line for the Transiberian Rly (qv), completed 1974–89.

Banalisation (Fr)
A double track line in which each

track is available for reversible working (qv), thus allowing a one-way, double capacity flow in either direction according to traffic requirements.

Banana boats (RS)(obs)
IC 125 HST sets in their original livery.

Bananas (RS)
see Flying Bananas.

Banana van (RS)
A coach or van with distorted frame, sagging in the middle.

B and B gang (USRS)
Building and bridge maintenance men.

B&CDR
Belfast & County Down Rly, NI, Belfast–Downpatrick–Ardglass; Downpatrick–Newcastle–Castlewellan; Comber–Donaghdee; Ballynahinch; Belfast–Bangor, inc 1846, first section opened 1848. Purchased by UTA 1948. All except Belfast–Bangor and Newcastle–Castlewellan closed 1950, latter closed 1955.

B&ER
Bristol & Exeter Rly, inc 1836, opened 1841, 1842, 1843, 1845, 1847, 1848, 1853, part of GWR from 1876.

B&FT
Blackpool & Fleetwood Tramroad, inc 1896, electric tramway (3), opened 1898, taken over by Blackpool Corporation 1920 and then connected to that town's tramway system.

B&LR
Ballymena & Larne Rly, inc 1873, 3 ft gauge, opened 1877, 1878, part of B&NCR from 1889.

B&M (US)
Boston & Maine RR. See also GTI.

B&MTJR
Brecon & Merthyr Tydfil Junction Rly, Bassaleg–Rhymney; Bargoed–Dowlais–Brecon; Pontsticill–Merthyr,

inc 1859, first section opened 1863. Merthyr line joint with L&NWR from 1875. Part of GWR from 1922. See also BMR.

B&NCR
Belfast & Northern Counties Rly, Belfast to Larne, Ballymena, Coleraine, Portrush, Londonderry etc., inc as Belfast & Ballymena Rly 1845, opened 1848, B&NCR 1860, amalgamated with Midland Rly of England from 1903. See also NCC.

B&NSR
Bristol & North Somerset Rly, Bristol to Radstock and Camerton branch, inc 1863, opened 1873, 1882, part of GWR 1884.

B&NT
Bessbrook & Newry Tramway (NI), inc 1884, 3 ft/914 mm gauge, electric tramway (4) on private right of way, opened 1885, closed 1948.

B&NWR
Bengal and North Western Rly, India, formed 1882.

B&O (US)
Baltimore & Ohio RR.

B&PCR
Brompton & Piccadilly Circus Rly, London, tube rly inc 1897, part of GNP&BR, 1902.

B&SWUR
Bristol & South Wales Union Rly, Bristol (Lawrence Hill) to New Passage with steam ferry across River Severn and line from Portskewett Pier to P. Junc, inc 1857, opened 1863, worked by GWR, part of GWR from 1868. New Passage Ferry discontinued 1886 on the opening of Severn Tunnel. Part reopened by GWR 1900 for use as a section of its new Pilning–Avonmouth line.

Bandwagon (USRS)
A coach from which men are paid.

B&WR
see Bodmin & Wenford Rly.

B&WVR
Brynmawr & Western Valleys Rly,
Nantyglo Junc to Brynmawr, inc
1899, opened 1906, vested in
L&NWR & GWR 1902, LM&SR &
GWR 1923, BR 1948.

Banger (RS)
Detonator placed on the line as a
warning.

Bang road (RS)
Wrong line, opposite to normal
direction of working.

Bang them up, to (LTRS)
To shunt loose-coupled or uncoupled
vehicles.

Banjo (RS)
Anything vaguely banjo shaped, thus:-
1. Fireman's shovel on steam loco.
2. Vacuum brake handle in loco cab.
3. (LTRS) A shunt signal.
4. Tripcock (qv) on steam loco.

Banjo player
A fireman on a steam loco: *see* Banjo
(*1*).

Bank
1. A steep incline (usually in northern
   England).
2. A raised platform in parcels or
   goods depot or goods shed.

Banker, banking engine
An additional loco attached at front or
rear of a train to assist it up a bank
(qv).

Banner, to carry the (USRS)
To flaunt Brotherhood (qv) emblems.

Banner repeater
A small illuminated centrally-pivoted
semaphore arm in a circular glass case
or a similar electronic representation,
showing the indication of a signal
which may be hidden from view when
a train is at a station platform; usually
placed 50–200 yards in rear of the
relevant signal.

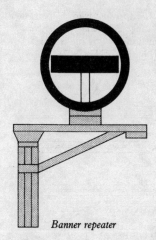

Banner repeater

BAR (Ger)
Berlin Aussenring; a belt line around
Berlin. *See also GAR*.

Bar boys (RS)(obs)
Slim and nimble youths able to enter a
steam loco firebox to clean the firebars
and remove clinker.

Barcelona Express
A *CIWL* night train, Paris to Port Bou
with connection to Barcelona, 1903–
14, re-introduced 1929, renamed
Paris–Côte Vermeille 1974.

Barcelona TALGO
A sleeping car express between Paris
and Barcelona with *TALGO* (qv)
stock, introduced 1974.

Barclay
Andrew Barclay, Sons & Co. Ltd,
Kilmarnock. Loco and rolling stock
builders established 1859. Merged
with Hunslet (qv) 1972 to form
Hunslet–Barclay.

Barefoot (USRS)
A loco with brakes on tender only.

Barlow rails (obs)
Rails with profile which enabled them
to be supported continuously on the

ballast, dispensing with sleepers, the exact gauge maintained by tie bars. Patented in 1849 by the engineer W.H. Barlow (1812–1902).

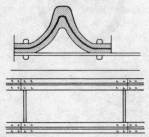

Barn (USRS)
A loco shed. *See also* Carbarn.

Barn, railroad in a (USRS)
A line protected by snow sheds (qv).

Barneys (RS)
Highland Rly Drummond 0–6–0 locos.

Barnums (RS)
1. GWR double-framed Dean 2–4–0 locos of 1889 after Barnum's Circus appearing in London that year.
2. GCR 1910 excursion open saloons with matchboarded straight sides, resembling vehicles in Barnum's Circus train.

Barracks (RS)(obs)
An engineman's overnight hostel.

Barred train
Any train on which rly employees' passes and privilege tickets are not usable.

Barrel (USRS)
A cylinder on diesel-electric loco.

Barrier vehicles
Vans, empty coaches or wagons placed between a dangerous load and the loco or between the loco and the brake van, or at each end of a passenger train.

Barry
Barry Dock & Rly, inc 1884, Barry–

Bridgend/Coity; Barry–St Fagans–Pontypridd/Trehafod; Cadoxton–Cardiff (Cogan); St Fagans–Penrhos Junc with B&MJR. First section opened 1888, renamed Barry Rly 1891, part of GWR from 1922.

BART
1. Bay Area Rapid Transit; rail system, linking San Francisco with Oakland and other communities on the east side of the Bay, opened 1972.
2. Belfast Area Rapid Transit [proposed].

BASA (Ger)
Bahn-Selbst-Anschluss; the internal rly telephone network.

Base plate
A plate fixed under a sleeper (*1*) to form a bearing pad and locating device for flatbottom (qv) rail. The rail is secured to the base plate by spring clips.

Bash, to (RS)
To visit a loco depot or other rly facility, usually without permission.

Basher (RS)
Abbreviated form of haulage basher (qv) or track basher (qv).

Basic rly
A BR concept for lightly-used lines featuring unmanned stations stripped of all structures except bus type shelters, tickets issued on trains by conductors, minimal signalling, automatic level crossing systems etc. First introduced on ER rural lines in 1966.

Bathgate Line
Edinburgh (Waverley)–Bathgate–Airdrie–Glasgow.

Bat out, to (USRS)
To shunt or classify wagons and vans very quickly.

Battering
Rail wear caused by wheels skidding on curved track.

Battery end (RS)
A buffer stop.
Bat the stack [off her], to (USRS)
To work a loco hard, making fast time.
Battlefield Line
Preserved operation on former BR Coalville–Nuneaton line between Shackerstone, Market Bosworth and Shenton. First section reopened (as The Shackerstone Rly), 1978.
Battleship (USRS)
Any very large and ponderous loco or interurban car.
Battlewagon (USRS)
A coal wagon.
Bavaria
TEE Zurich–Munich, introduced 1969, lost *TEE* status 1977, EC from 1987.
Bay
A short platform with buffer stops at one end, usually in a through station and normally set into opposite side

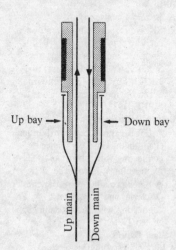

Up bay → ← Down bay

Up main

Down main

(and sometimes at opposite ends) of a full length platform. Used for branch line or stopping services terminating at the station. *See also* Dock.
Bay line
A track in a bay (qv).
BB&CIR
Bombay, Baroda & Central India Rly, formed 1855, taken over by government 1905. Mostly part of Western Rly of India from 1951.
BB&TJR
Birmingham, Bristol & Thames Junc Rly, inc 1836, became WLR (qv) 1840.
BC
British Coal. *See also* NCB.
BC&RR
Ballymena, Cushendall & Red Bay Rly (NI), inc 1872, 3 ft/914 mm gauge, Ballymena–Retreat, opened 1875, 1876, part of B&NCR 1884, closed 1940.
BCK
BR Brake Corridor Composite coach.
BCM
Ballast Cleaning Machine.
BCR
1. Bishop's Castle Rly, inc 1861, Craven Arms & Stokesay (Stretford Bridge Junc) to Lydham Heath and Bishop's Castle, opened 1866, closed 1935.
2. Border Counties Rly, inc 1854, 1859, Riccarton Junc–Bellingham–Hexham. First section opened 1858, part of NBR 1860.
BD&R
see Barry.
BDM
Battery Driving Motor [car]
BDT/BDTS
Battery Driving Trailer/Standard Class
BDZ
Bulgarian State Rlys.
Beaches, the (LTRS)
Roads at the back of Neasden depot.

Beanery (USRS)
Mess room. Hence beanery queen, a
waitress in a mess room.
Beans, to go to (USRS)
To go for a meal.
Bear law (USRS)
A federal law limiting loco and train
crews to a maximum of twelve hours'
continuous duty. *See also* Dog law;
Hog law; Monkey, caught by the.
Bearcat (USRS)
Any rlyman disliked by his colleagues.
Beardmore
William Beardmore & Co. Ltd,
Glasgow, loco builders 1919–30.
Beardmores (RS)
GER/L&NER N7 0–6–2T locos. From
the builders, William Beardmore &
Co. Ltd.
Beaver
GWR TC for flat trucks of various
types (Beaver A, B, C, D & E).
BEC
British Electric Car Co. Ltd, Trafford
Park, Manchester, suppliers of electric
tramcars, established 1900. Production
ceased 1904. Purchased by Castle Car
Syndicate on behalf of UEC (qv).
Bedbug (USRS)
A Pullman car porter.
Bed house (USRS)
A caboose (qv).
Bedpan Line (obs)
A name used jokingly by Sir Peter
Parker (BR chairman) for the
BEDford to London (St PANcras) line
at the opening of the electric services,
an 'own goal' enthusiastically
embraced by the media and public but
subsequently subsumed in
Thameslink.
BEE
see Brush (2).
Beeching/Beeching Era
The traumatic period (1961–5) in
which BR was drastically 're-shaped',

reduced, modernized and 'rationalized'
under the chairmanship of Dr (from
1965 Lord) Richard Beeching
(1913–85). The cuts made in mileage,
services and staff were referred to as
the 'Beeching Axe'. The associated
'Beeching Report', *The Reshaping of
British Railways*, was published in
1963.
Beedler (USRS)
A driver who works his loco to the
limits of its performance.
Beehive (USRS)
A yard or control office.
Beer trains (RS)(obs)
The Garden Cities & Cambridge
Buffet Car expresses (qv).
Beetle crusher (RS)(Scottish)
Shunting loco; from its slow,
ponderous movements.
Beetles
1. GWR TC for continuously-braked
   cattle wagons or boxes, with
   attendant's compartment.
2. (RS) LM&SR Sentinel 0–4–0 locos
BEL
1. Battery Electric Locos.
2. SR five-car all-Pullman emu open
   corridor sets for Brighton BELle
   (qv); two motor brake parlour
   Second/Standard class cars, two
   kitchen First class cars, and one
   Second/Standard class parlour car;
   5-BEL, 1933.
Belfast Boat Express
1. A GWR express between London
   (Paddington) and Birkenhead,
   connecting with Liverpool–Belfast
   night sailings, introduced 1928.
2. A BR express between Manchester
   (Victoria) and Heysham,
   connecting with Belfast sailings,
   ceased 1976.
Belfast Express
A Londonderry–Belfast service
introduced 1950.

Bellowers (RS)
Football supporters, or gricers (qv)
who windowhang (qv) and shout at all
and sundry from trains.

Bell ringer (USRS)
A loco fireman.

Bells (RS)(obs)
see On the bells.

Belpaire
A type of steam loco firebox invented
in 1860–64 and refined in 1884 by the
Belgian engineer Alfred Jules Belpaire
(1820–93).

Belt line (US)
A rly around or within a city or town
linking up different companies' lines
and facilitating interchange of freight
etc.

Bench, the (RS)(obs)
The cab road side of the old South
Station at London (Waterloo). So
named from the steps leading down to
the cab road which formed a seat for
the waiting cab drivers.

Bend the iron/the rails/the rust, to
(USRS)
To change the position of points.

Benguela Rly
Lobito (Angola) via Benguela to the
Belgian Congo (now Zaire) frontier at
Dilolo (838.23 m/1,349 km); opened
throughout 1928.

Benjamin Britten
An EC service between London
(Liverpool St.) and Harwich,
connecting with overnight sailings
to and from Hook of Holland
(for Amsterdam). The NS connecting
service was given the same
name. Introduced 1987, ceased
1989.

Bent dart (RS)
Long steel poker with an arrow head
and a bend at its centre, used for
dislodging clinker from the firebox of
a steam loco.

BEP
BR (SR) four-car emu corridor sets
with Buffet car and Electro-Pneumatic
brakes, 1956 and 1958–9; two motor
brake Second/Standard Class, one
trailer composite, and one buffet
trailer; 4-BEP.

Bergbahn (Ger)
Any type of mountain climbing rly.

Berks & Hants
Inc 1845 as Berkshire & Hampshire
Rly, Hungerford to Reading and
Basingstoke, opened 1847, 1848,
amalgamated with GWR 1846.

Berks and Hants Extension
Hungerford to Devizes, inc 1859,
opened 1862, worked by GWR, part
of GWR 1882.

Berks & Hants Line
Reading–Newbury–Westbury.

Berkshire (US)
A steam loco with 2–8–4 wheel
arrangement. The first were made for
the Boston & Albany RR which
traversed the Berkshire Mountains of
New England.

Berliner
The unofficial name for the British
military restaurant car train operated
daily from 1945 until 1990 to and
from Braunschweig across the former
German Democratic Republic
territory, to serve the British zone in
Berlin.

Berlin–Baghdad Rly
see Baghdad Rly.

Berne [Convention] Gauge
A standard loading gauge (qv) for all
European rlys specified by the UIC
(qv), originally at a Berne Convention
but subsequently modified. Currently
set at maximum height 4.28 metres,
maximum width 3.15 metres.

Berolina
A service between Berlin and USSR
frontier at Brest Litovsk, introduced

1950. Now runs Berlin to Warsaw only.

Berth track circuit
A track circuit (qv) on the approach side of a stop signal.

Berts (RS)
Ordinary passsengers, those interested only in getting from A to B, not in the rly as such. From 'Bert 'n' Ada'.

BET
British Electric Traction Co. Ltd.

Bexleyheath Line
London (Charing Cross/Cannon St.)–Bexleyheath–Dartford.

Beyer–Garratt
A Garratt (qv) steam loco built by Beyer, Peacock.

Beyer, Peacock
Beyer, Peacock & Co. Ltd, Gorton Foundry, Manchester, loco builders 1853–1956.

BFK
BR Brake Corridor First class compartment coach.

BG
BR bogie brake van, gangwayed, with open stowage area and guard's brake compartment.

BGZ
BG (qv) with six wheels.

BHC
Belfast Harbour Commissioners.

Bhf (Ger)
Bahnhof; rly station.

BHR
Bexley Heath Rly, inc 1883, opened Blackheath (London) to Slades Green, 1895, part of SER 1900.

Bh rail
Bullhead rail (qv).

Bible (RS)
The rule book for rly employees.

Bicester route
London (Paddington)–High Wycombe–Bicester–Banbury.

Bicycle (RS)
A steam loco with 4–2–2 wheel arrangement.

BIG
BR (SR) four-car emu sets with Buffet car and Interconnecting Gangway, 1965–6, for London to Brighton services. Formation as CIG (qv) but with buffet car instead of Second/Standard Class trailer, 4-BIG.

Big Bertha (RS)
Midland Rly 0–10–0 no. 2290 built 1920 for use as a banking engine on the Lickey Incline.

Big Boys (USRS)
Union Pacific RR articulated Mallet (qv) 4–8–8–4 locos of 1941–4.

Big brain (RS)
Control (qv).

Big dipper (RS)
An exceptionally tall semaphore signal to give visibility over the tops of bridges etc.

Big-E (USRS)
Brotherhood of Locomotive Engineers, hence any loco driver.

Big Emma (RS)
Another name for Big Bertha (qv).

Big end
The end of a connecting rod (qv) of a steam loco, adjoining the crank axle or pin.

Big Four, the
1. The companies formed in the 'grouping' of 1 January 1923, i.e. LM&SR, L&NER, GWR, SR.
2. (US) Nickname of Cleveland, Cincinnati, Chicago & St Louis RR.
3. (US) Brotherhood of Locomotive Engineers; Brotherhood of Railway Conductors; Brotherhood of Railway Firemen and Brotherhood of Railway Trainmen.

Big handle man (RS)(obs)
A steam loco driver using mainly two positions on the regulator – wide open and slammed shut.

Big hole
1. (RS) The Severn Tunnel.
2. (USRS) The emergency position (qv) of a Westinghouse brake control lever.

Big hook (USRS)
A breakdown train. From the hook on its large crane.

Big Lizzies (RS)
LM&SR 4–6–2 locos of 1937. After the name of one, Princess Elizabeth.

Big Mets (RS)
L&NER N2 O–6–2T used over the Metropolitan Rly CWL (qv).

Big–O (USRS)
Order of Railway Conductors (a guards' trade union).

Big ox (USRS)
A conductor (*3*).

Big penny (RS)
Overtime or bonus payment.

Big pike (USRS)
A major rly co. or system.

Big smoke (USRS)
A loco fireman.

BIL
SR two-car emu sets of 1935 for semi-fast services, with side corridors to give access to lavatory but no gangway connection between cars, hence BI-Lavatory; one motor brake Second/Standard Class and one driving composite; 2-BIL

Bill Baileys (RS)
L&NWR four-cylinder compound 4–6–0 locos 1400 class. After the contemporary song 'Come Home, Bill Bailey'.

Billy (RS)
A ground signal.

Binder (USRS)
A hand brake.

Bionics (LTRS)
LT 1973 stock.

Birdcage
1. (RS) A signalbox resting on a gantry or girders.
2. (RS) A spark arrester on a loco chimney.
3. (USRS) A brakeman's oil lamp.

Birdcage brake/coach (RS)
1. A coach design incorporating an open air verandah type side corridor protected by ironwork.
2. A passenger train brake van or brake composite coach with raised glazed section in guard's compartment projecting above roof level to allow observation of signals etc.

Birds, to join the (USRS)
To jump from a moving train.

Birkenhead Joint
Inc as Birkenhead Rly 1859, Chester to Birkenhead, opened 1840, 1848, 1850. Vested in L&NWR and GWR jointly 1861, LM&SR & GWR from 1923, BR from 1948.

Birmingham
BRCW (qv).

Birmingham Pullman
A BR eight-car dmu air-conditioned Pullman train painted medium blue, introduced between London (Paddington), Birmingham and Wolverhampton in 1960. Withdrawn 1967. Also a BR Pullman service between Birmingham (New St.) and London (Euston) introduced 1988.

Birney car
A tramcar design patented by Charles O. Birney, first produced in USA, 1916. A lightweight, one man operated, single truck, single deck car with important safety features which included door interlocks which prevented the car from moving when the doors were open and also a dead-man's handle (qv).

Birth control hours (RS)
Night work after midnight.

Birth Controllers (RS)
LM&SR Beyer–Garratt locomotives
(2–6–6–2T) of 1927–30. From the
supposed effect of their rough riding
on the enginemen.

Biscuit (RS)
A single line token.

Bissell truck
A two- or four-wheel radial truck in
which the pivoting point is located at
some distance from its transverse
centre. Invented in US in 1857 by
Levi Bissell.

Blackboard (RS)
An oblong ground signal.

Black diamonds (USRS)
Company coal.

Black Eights (RS)
LM&SR Stanier class 8F 2–8–0 freight
locos.

Black Fives (RS)
LM&SR Stanier class 5 4–6–0 mixed
traffic locos.

Black hole (USRS)
A tunnel.

Blackies
1. (RS) Another name for Black Fives
(qv).
2. (USRS) Loco firemen.

Black Isle branch
Muir of Ord to Fortrose.

Black light (RS)
An empty electric light bulb socket;
also a lamp unlit at night.

Black Motors (RS)
L&SWR Drummond 700 class 0–6–0
locos of 1897, rebuilt 1923–9. Name
probably derived from the
contemporary arrival of the motor car.

Black oil (RS)
An unlit semaphore signal lamp.

Black Pigs (RS)
1. GCR 4–6–0 locos, L&NER class
B7.

2. LM&SR class 4MT 2–6–0T of
1947.

Black Princes (RS)
Steam loco cleaners.

Black snake (USRS)
A train consisting entirely of coal
wagons.

Black Staniers (RS)
Another name for Black Fives (qv).

Black Tanks (RS)
LB&SCR Stroudley E1 tank locos.

Blackwall
see L&BR (*3*).

BL&CJR
Birkenhead, Lancashire & Cheshire
Junction Rly, Chester to Walton
Junction (Warrington), inc 1846,
opened 1850, name changed to
Birkenhead Rly (qv), 1859.

Blanketing
Excavation and dumping of an existing
track bed to a depth of about 1.5
metres, with renewal of the drainage
system and the laying down of a blanket
of stone dust before reballasting.

Blanket stiff (USRS)
A vagrant who steals rides on trains.

Blauer Enzian
A service between Hamburg and
Munich, *TEE* from 1965, extended to
Klagenfurt 1970, lost *TEE* status
1979, EC Dortmund–Klagenfurt 1987.

Blazer (USRS)
A hot axle box which has set the
packing alight.

Bleed, to (USRS)
To drain air from a brake reservoir.

Bleeders (RS)
Bulleid Leader class 0–6–6–0T of
1948. Rhyming slang, referring to the
very poor operating environment
afforded to the fireman.

Blind baggage (USRS)
Any vehicle at the front of a train
without through gangway access to
rest of train.

Blind rider (USRS)
A vagrant riding in a blind baggage car.
Blind tires (USRS)
see Bald wheels (qv).
Blinkers (RS)(obs)
Smoke deflectors; fitted to front end of
steam locos to lift smoke away from
the cab windows and sides.
Blister (RS)
Any request from management for
information; also drivers' report form
explaining lateness etc.
Blizzard lights (USRS)
Auxiliary lamps on a loco.
Bloater
GWR TC for fish van.
Blockade
1. TC for 'all lines blocked'.
2. (USRS) A yard so choked with
   wagons that shunting is almost or
   completely impossible.
Blockall Junction (RS)
Watford.
Block book (RS)
A signalbox train register.
Blockhead (USRS)
A brakeman.
Blocking back
Trains queueing behind a congested
junction or an obstruction on the line.
Block instruments
see Block system.
Block load (obs)
A group of wagons, less than a
trainload, remaining in the same
formation between point of origin and
destination which may be marshalled
as a unit in different trains en route.
Block man
British Army term for a rly signalman.
Block, on the (RS)
see Blocking back (qv); On the block.
Block post
British army term for signal box. Also
any signal box equipped with block
instruments. *See also* Block system.

Block section
see Block system.
Block signals
Signals used to operate the block
system (qv).
Block system
Widely adopted signalling arrangement
in which the rly is divided into
absolute intervals of space known as
'block sections'. Only one train is
allowed into each block section at a
time. The sections are controlled by
signal boxes at each end. A block
section extends from the most
advanced starting signal (qv) under the
control of one box to the first
(outermost) home signal (qv)

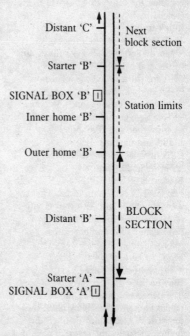

controlled by the next. In the traditional system, signalmen communicate with colleagues in adjacent boxes regarding all train movements using electric block telegraph instruments which indicate 'train on line', 'line clear' or 'line blocked', and by single stroke bell signals (bell codes) which are sent forward in conjunction with the block telegraph indications to describe the type of train. Also known as 'Absolute Block'. *See also* Moving block; Permissive block; Station limits.

Block switching

The operation of a switch in a signal box which brings together the block circuits of the boxes on each side of it, enabling the intervening box to be closed.

Block train

1. A train which is not normally uncoupled, i.e. always runs as an integral unit.
2. A freight train whose formation remains unaltered between point of origin and destination. Often a complete consignment between consignor and consignee.

Blood and custard (RS)

BR's first passenger coach livery (crimson and cream).

Bloomers (RS)

L&NWR 2–2–2 steam locos. They were contemporary with the activities of Mrs Amelia Bloomer, a US propagandist for feminine dress reform.

Blow, to give it/her a (LTRS)

To apply the air brake.

Blowback

The dangerous situation in which flames and hot gases blow on to the footplate of steam loco through the firehole. Usually the result of a sudden closure of the regulator when the engine is steaming hard and the blower is not turned on.

Blower (S)

A telephone.

Blow her down, to (USRS)

To reduce the amount of steam pressure or water in the loco boiler.

Blowing off (RS)

A safety valve releasing a jet of steam.

Blow off, at (USRS)

A steam loco ready to start, its boiler at full pressure, safety valve about to blow off.

Blow through (RS)(obs)

A wagon lacking continuous brakes but equipped with pipes to connect up the braking system through the train.

Blow up, to (RS)

1. To stop to raise more pressure in a badly-steaming loco.
2. To create a vacuum for braking.
3. (LTRS) To sound train whistle/hooter.

BLS

Branch Line Society; formed 1955, publishes *Branch Line News*.

Bluebell Line/Rly

A name given by a journalist *c*. 1955 to former LB&SCR line between East Grinstead and Culver Junc near Lewes, closed 1958. The section between Horsted Keynes and Sheffield Park was reopened in 1960 by the Bluebell Railway Preservation Society, which from 1990 extended its operations northwards towards East Grinstead over the old alignment. The name 'Bluebell & Primrose Line' was also current in the 1960s but has now fallen out of use.

Bluebottles (RS)

GWR 14XX 0–4–2T locos.

Blue Danube

A train between Ostend, Vienna and Budapest chartered by Dean & Dawson Ltd for holiday travel, 1933.

From 1934 it was replaced by special reserved coaches in the Ostend–Vienna express.

Blue Electrics (RS)(obs)
Glasgow suburban electric trains and services of BR when first introduced. From the livery. *See also* Blue Trains.

Blue Engine
see Red Engine.

Blue flag/light (US)
Displayed at each end of a loco, car or train when receiving attention from workmen and not able to be moved.

Blue Flashes (RS)(obs)
25 kV 50 Hz BR electric locos, when first introduced.

Blue Lagoons (RS)(obs)
Nightrider (qv) coaches. From the dimmed lighting.

Blue liner (USRS)
A rly employee who steals from trains.

Blue One/'un (RS)
A green signal indication.

Blue Pullmans
see Blue Streaks.

Blue Streaks (RS)(obs)
BR 'Blue Pullman' dmu trains introduced in 1960 (Midland Pullman, Bristol Pullman, Birmingham Pullman (qv)). From the contemporary Blue Streak rocket.

Blue Train
1. Colloquial term (also, in Fr, *le Train Bleu*) for the *CIWL* Calais–Méditerranée Express and Paris–Méditerranée Express to San Remo and Ventimiglia. These trains were combined in the 1930s and the title was adopted officially in 1949 for the Calais/Paris–Ventimiglia sleeping car service. The service was reorganized in 1980, when the name was transferred to a new overnight Paris–Ventimiglia service.
2. Name given to new blue and cream coaches introduced on the SAR

Union Express (Cape Town–Johannesburg) when introduced in 1939. In 1946 the name was officially adopted for the luxury service between Cape Town, Johannesburg and Pretoria. New stock was introduced in 1972, featuring accommodation entirely in private rooms, some with en suite bathrooms.

Blue Trains (RS)(obs)
1960 emu sets for Glasgow area suburban services. From the original livery. *See also* Blue Electrics.

Blue 'uns (RS)
L&NER A4 4–6–2 locos. From the livery.

Blunderbuss (RS)
A train incorrectly signalled.

BM (obs)
BR Braked Milk van.

BMR
Brecon Mountain Rly.
A pleasure line on a section of B&MJR from Pant (Merthyr) to Pontsticill, 1 ft 11¾ in/603.25 mm gauge, opened 1980. *See also* B&MJR.

BN
1. Burlington Northern Inc. (US), a 1970 merger of CB&Q, GN, NP and the Spokane, Portland & Seattle Rly.
2. Belgian rly and tramway equipment manufacturers, originally *La Brugeoise*, Bruges. Merged with *Nicaise et Delcuve* of la Louvière, 1913, to form *La Brugeoise et Nicaise et Delcuve* (*BND*). Merged with *les Ateliers Métallurgiques* of Nivelles, 1956, to form *La Brugeoise et Nivelles* (*BN*). Sold to Bombardier group (qv) 1986–88. *See also Bombardier–Eurorail*.

BND
see BN (2).

BNR
Bengal–Nagpur Rly, formed 1887, taken over by Government of India 1944. From 1952 part of ER (5).

BNW&SR
Birmingham, North Warwickshire & Stratford-upon-Avon Rly, Birmingham (Tyseley) to Bearley, inc 1894, powers transferred to GWR 1900, opened 1907, 1908.

BO (US)
Bad Order (qv).

'Bo (USRS)
Abbreviation of hobo (qv).

Board
1. (RS) Originally the arm of a semaphore signal, but later any type of signal.
2. (USRS) Any fixed signal, e.g. slow board, order board, clear board etc.
3. (USRS) A list of employees available for service.

Boarding card
see Regulation [of passenger traffic].

Boat train
A train operated exclusively for passengers travelling by shipping services, connecting with the sailings and arrivals of specific services at ports.

Bobbing signal (RS)
A defective colour-light signal with aspects repeatedly changing.

Bobby (RS)
A signalman. From Sir *Robert* Peel, founder of the police force; signalling was originally a responsibility of the rly police, so the popular nickname adhered.

Bob hole door (RS)
A wagon door which only opens halfway.

Bobol
TC for bogie bolster wagon.

Bobtail bounce (USRS)
A short train.

Bobtails
1. (RS) LC&DR Kirtley 'R' Class locos of 1891.
2. (US)(obs) Colloquial term for tramcars without a rear platform and designed for one-man operation and haulage by a single horse or mule.
3. (USRS) A shunting loco.

Bocar
GWR TC for van with canvas cover used for carrying motor car bodies.

'Bo chaser (USRS)
A rly policeman or security man.

Bodmin & Wenford Rly
Bodmin & Wenford Rly plc; preserved rly on former BR Bodmin (Parkway)–Bodmin–Boscarne Junc line, first section opened to passengers and freight 1990. Operates a freight service in connection with BR.

Boff vans (RS)(obs)
L&NWR guard's vans of *c.* 1900 fitted with cycle racks designed by a guard named Boff.

Bogie
1. A short wheelbase four-wheeled vehicle.
2. An alternative term for truck (3) (qv).
3. A trolley manually propelled along the line by track maintenance staff.
4. In India, a term for any passenger coach fitted with bogies (2).

Bogie blocks (RS)
L&SWR four-coach suburban sets of *c.* 1906.

Bogie man (RS)
Passenger stock repair man. Pun on bogie (qv).

Bog unit (RS)
A dmu with lavatory/wc (bog = (S) for wc).

Boiler ascension (RS)(obs)
A loco boiler explosion.

Boiler head (USRS)
A steam loco driver.
Boiler header (USRS)
Any person riding in a steam loco cab.
Boiler wash (USRS)
A nervous, ultra-cautious steam loco driver.
Boiler washer
A steam loco driver.
Bolster
A transverse member of a truck normally carrying the weight of the car body and usually separated from the bogie frames by springs and other shock-absorbing devices.
Bolster wagon
An open wagon with raised transverse beams to hold a load clear of the floor, thus easing loading and unloading.
Bolt hole (RS)
1. A refuge (qv).
2. (LTRS) A cross passage between running tunnels on underground rlys.
Bombardier–Eurorail
Rly and tramway/LRV manufacturers, formed 1991, incorporating BN (2) (qv), *ANF Industrie (Ateliers du Nord de la France)* and *Bombardier–Rotax*, Vienna. *See also* Bombardier Inc.
Bombardier Inc
Manufacturers of rly rolling stock etc., based at Montreal, Canada and Barre VT, US. *See also Bombardier–Eurorail*; Bombardier Pro Rail.
Bombardier Pro Rail
New name of Procor (qv) after its purchase by Bombardier Inc, in 1990.
Bombs (RS)
BR class 20 diesel electric locos.
'Bo money (USRS)
Money collected by freight train crews from vagrants allowed to ride on the train. Usually a fixed amount for each division traversed.

Bon Accord
An express between Glasgow (Buchanan St.) and Aberdeen, introduced 1937, ceased 1939, re-introduced 1949.
Bone out, to (RS)
To carry out a survey of a section of rly to adjust levels.
Bone yard
1. (RS) British Army (Royal Engineers) term for a cripple (qv) siding.
2. (USRS) A rip track (qv) or scrap yard.
Bongos (RS)
L&NER B1 4–6–0 locos.
Boning rods (RS)
Boards used for sighting when surveying.
Book, the (RS)
The Working Timetable (qv).
Booked service
A train appearing in the Working timetable (qv), for which loco, rolling stock and crew are diagrammed.
Booking clerk
An employee who issues passenger tickets. From the early practice of entering each passenger transaction in a book. *See also* Booking office.
Booking constable (obs)
In the early days of rlys, a rly policeman who acted as the sole member of staff at a small station, performing all duties including that of booking clerk.
Booking lad
A trainee signalman, employed in busy signal boxes to enter information in train register (qv).
Booking office
A ticket office. From the road coaching and early rly practice of entering each passenger transaction separately in a book.
Booking on (RS)
Reporting for duty.

Boomer
1. (USRS)(obs) Rly worker who wandered from system to system and job to job at will, staying only a short time, and often going south in the winter. From boom camps.
2. (USRS) Any item of rolling stock which has been owned by more than one rly co./ system.

Boomerang (RS)
A return ticket.

Boomer pike (USRS)
A rly using a high proportion of boomer (qv) labour.

Booster
A small steam engine driving the wheels of a loco tender or the bogie between the footplate and the tender. Originally manufactured by Franklin Railway Supply Co. Inc, USA.

Booster/retarder
A device which automatically accelerates or slows down wagons, moving by gravity in a marshalling yard. It works by reference to a pre-arranged (latterly computer-calculated) optimum speed, acting to bring the wagon to rest at the correct position in the sorting siding.

Bootlegger (USRS)
A train running over more than one rly system.

Boozer (RS)
Any late night train. *See also* Vomit Special.

'Bo park (USRS)
Any place at which vagrants (hobos) assemble to seek illicit free rides on freight trains, usually a rly yard.

Boplate
TC for bogie freight wagon.

Border Counties Line
Riccarton Junc to Reedsmouth and Hexham.

Bord-na-Mona
Irish Turf Board, operators of narrow gauge rlys in peat bogs.

Bosh (RS)
A mixture of water and chemicals used to clean grease and oil from locomotive underframes.

Boss key (LTRS)
Driver's control switch key (with raised boss).

Boss man (LTRS)
A station manager.

Bostwick gates
Lattice steel folding gates used for lifts, at entrances to platforms etc.

BoT
Board of Trade; the government department with responsibility for rly and tramway matters from 1840 until formation of the MoT (qv) in 1919.

Bouncer (USRS)
A caboose (qv).

Bourbonnais (US)
Term for loco with 0–6–0 wheel arrangement.

Bournemouth Belle
A Pullman car express between London (Waterloo) and Bournemouth (West), introduced 1931, reintroduced 1946, ceased 1967.

Bournemouth Limited
A service between London (Waterloo) and Weymouth, non-stop to Bournemouth, introduced 1929, ceased 1939.

Bow collector
A uni-directional sliding current collector in the form of a bow, sprung to press its top surface against the overhead wire carrying the traction current. Used for both rlys and tramways (3).

Bowes Rly
From near Pontop to Jarrow, first
section opened as Springwell Colliery
Waggonway 1826, incorporating rope-
worked inclines; operated by colliery
owners John Bowes & Partners from
1850, renamed Bowes Rly 1932.
Worked by NCB until 1974. Section
between Blackhams Hill and
Springwell operated as a preserved rly
since 1981.
Bowled (LTRS)
An employee run down by train.
Bowler hats/bowler hat brigade (RS)
Inspectors and foremen not
in uniform. Until recent years,
the bowler hat was a symbol of
middle-management authority on the
rlys.
Bowling alley (USRS)
A manually-fired loco. From the
motion of throwing lumps of coal
through the fire hole.
Bowling green (RS)
A line laid out for fast running, the
fast roads.
Box car (US)
A covered freight wagon.
Box car tourist (USRS)
Vagrant (hobo (qv)) who hitches illicit
free rides on freight trains.
Boxer (RS)
1. Any untimetabled train proceeding
   at short notice from one signal box
   to the next.
2. Message passing between signal
   boxes.
Boxing (RS)
1. The effect on rails of sideways
   movement of bogies.
2. Completion of work on track.
Boxing-in (obs)
The practice of covering the sleepers
with fine ballast.
Box on wheels (RS)(obs)
Derogatory term used by steam

loco enthusiasts for early diesel
locos.
Boy driver (LTRS)
A newly-passed out guard/motorman
or motorman.
Boys' club (LTRS)
British Transport Police.
Boys' Line (LTRS)
Metropolitan Line.
BP (obs)
A bogie gangwayed brake vehicle
with racks for racing pigeon baskets
(BR).
BP&GVR
Burry Port & Gwendraeth Valley Rly,
inc 1865 as Kidwelly & Burry Port
Rly, first section, Burry Port to
Cwmmawr opened 1869. Part of GWR
from 1922.
BPR&P
Bristol Port Rly & Pier; Bristol
(Hotwells) to Avonmouth Dock, inc
1862, opened 1865. Clifton Extension,
Bristol (Ashley Hill Junc) to
Avonmouth (Sneyd Park Junc), inc
1867, vested in GWR and Midland
1871, opened 1874. GWR & LM&SR
1923–47. Original line vested in GWR
and Midland 1890, closed 1922.
BR
1. British Rail/ways. General title of
   the nationalized rly system from its
   formation on 1 January 1948.
   Operated initially by the Railway
   Executive (qv) as an agent of the
   BTC (qv) and divided into six
   regions (London Midland;
   Western; Southern; Eastern; North
   Eastern and Scottish). From 1963
   managed by the BRB (qv). Short
   title 'British Rail' and double arrow
   logo in use from 1 January 1965.
   Regional organization discarded in
   favour of 'business sectors' and
   'profit centres' from 1990–92. *See
   also* BRB.

2. Ballycastle Rly (NI); Ballymoney–Ballycastle, 3 ft/914 mm gauge, inc 1878, opened 1880, absorbed by NCC 1924, closed 1950.
3. Buckinghamshire Rly; formed 1847 as an amalgamation of Buckingham & Brackley Junction (Claydon–Brackley) and Oxford & Bletchley Junction Rlys (both inc 1846) opened 1850, 1851, Bletchley–Banbury/Oxford. Worked by L&NWR, part of L&NWR from 1879.
4. Barry Rly: *see* Barry.
5. Bangladesh Rlys; part of former Bengal Assam Rly and subsequently Pakistan Eastern Rly, renamed BR 1972.
6. Bowes Rly: *see* Bowes.
7. Burma Rlys; metre gauge, nationalized 1948.
8. Berwickshire Rly; inc 1862, opened Duns to Earlston 1863 and to Ravenswood Junc 1865. Part of NBR 1876.

Brabant
TEE Paris (Nord)–Brussels, introduced 1963, lost *TEE* status 1984, became EC 1987.

Bracket arm
A straight or curved tubular steel arm fixed at right angles to a traction pole to suspend the overhead wire of a tramway (*3*).

Bradford Executive
An express between London (Kings Cross) and Bradford, introduced in 1973.

Bradford Pullman
BR Bradford–Leeds–London (Kings Cross) service, introduced 1991.

Bradshaw
Bradshaw's General Railway & Steam Navigation Guide for Great Britain and Ireland. A comprehensive volume of public rly timetables, published monthly from December 1841, originally compiled by George Bradshaw (1801–53), Quaker printer and engraver of Salford. Publication ceased after the issue of May 1961. Also *Bradshaw's Continental Railway Guide*, from June 1847 until August 1914 and *The General Directory & Shareholders' Guide*, 1849 until 1923. *Bradshaw's Air Guide* was published from November 1934 until May 1961 and *Bradshaw's Manchester ABC Railway Guide* from 1861 until May 1961. An Indian *Bradshaw* is still published ten times a year by Newman of Calcutta. However, to the British public in general, *Bradshaw* signified the monthly national rly timetables. 'The vocabulary of *Bradshaw* is nervous and terse, but limited.' — Sir Arthur Conan Doyle.

Brain plate (USRS)
A badge worn by a rly employee.

Brains
1. (RS) Traffic Control Office/staff.
2. (USRS) A conductor (*3*) of a passenger or freight train (qv).

Brains car (USRS)
A caboose (qv).

Brake club (USRS)
A hickory stick about 3 ft/914 mm in length used to tighten hand brakes on freight trains.

Brake compo[site]
A coach with accommodation for two classes of passengers and also compartment for guard, luggage etc.

Brakeman (US)
An auxiliary working with a train crew or in a yard.

Brake pin
An iron pin holding wagon brake secure after brake lever handle has been pushed down.

Brake road
A siding allocated to storage of brake vans.

Brakes (RS)
A fully-fitted (qv) freight train.

Brakesman
A freight train guard.

Brake stick/pole
Used by shunters for forcing down wagon brake handles.

Brake tender (obs)
A four-wheeled 35-ton vehicle equipped with continuous brakes temporarily used by BR in the 1960s and '70s to provide adequate braking power on unfitted or partly-fitted trains hauled by diesel-electric locos.

Brake tri-compo[site] (obs)
Coach with accommodation for three classes of passenger and compartment for guard, luggage etc.

Brakie (USRS)
A brakeman (qv).

Brass (USRS)
A bronze bearing on which the weight of a rly vehicle rests.

Brass buttons (USRS)
A tramcar conductor or a member of a passenger train crew. From the uniform.

Brass collar/hat (USRS)
A middle ranking rly official. From the gold braid on uniform collar and brass plate worn on cap.

Brass pounder (USRS)
A rly telegraph operator.

Braunhaus (RS)
BR Headquarters. A distortion of the Nazi Party headquarters (*Das Braunes Haus*).

BRB
British Railways Board. Formed 1963 under Transport Act, 1962, to take over from the BTC (qv), with virtually complete commercial freedom, the responsibility for running the nationalized rly system.

BRCW
Birmingham Rly, Carriage & Wagon Co., Smethwick, 1855–1963.

BR (E)
British Railways, Eastern Region. Absorbed former BR (NE) from 1966. *See also* Anglia; BR (NE).

Bread & Onion Line (RS)(obs)
Wansford to Stamford branch.

Bread Bins (RS)
GCR 4–6–2 locos.

Breakaway
A train accidentally divided.

Breakdown train
A train with heavy lift crane, tool vans, kitchen and other accommodation for breakdown gang, maintained in a state of readiness at depots for attendance at any accident, breakdown or derailment.

Breaker (RS)
A circuit breaker.

Breast beam (US)
A buffer beam.

Breather (RS)(obs)
An evening excursion working to the seaside.

Breeze (USRS)
Service air in the brake system.

BREL
Formerly British Rail Engineering Ltd; a subsidiary of BRB, but in 1989 sold off as an independent undertaking. Manufactures all types of rly rolling stock.

BRE–Metro Ltd
A joint sales co. set up by BREL and Metro–Cammell in 1971.

Brenner Express
A night service Munich–Milan/Venice/Florence, introduced 1954.

BRH
British Rail Hovercraft Ltd; formed 1966, brand name 'Seaspeed'. Initial service was to the Isle of Wight. A subsidiary of BRB until merged with

Hoverlloyd Ltd as Hoverspeed (qv) 1981.

BRI

1. British Rail International Inc; a BTC subsidiary formed to sell technical advice to overseas administrations. Taken over by BRB 1963. *See also* Transmark
2. British Rail International. Specialized marketing and promotional organization for rail travel between Britain and mainland Europe.

Brick, the (RS)(obs)
Bricklayers' Arms loco depot, Bermondsey, London.

Bridge hog (USRS)
A bridge maintenance engineer/worker.

Bridge rails (obs)
Bridge-shaped in cross section, with wide bottom flanges or wings, these rails were secured to longitudinal sleepers by fang spikes and bolts. Used by the GWR in its early years.

Brigade of cars (US)(obs)
An early expression for a rly train. *See also* Car.

Brighton, the (RS)
LB&SCR (qv).

Brighton Belle
1934 renaming of Southern Belle (qv) all-Pullman car express between London (Victoria) and Brighton, re-introduced 1947, ceased 1972.

Brighton [Pullman] Limited
A Sunday all-Pullman car train

between London (Victoria) and Brighton, introduced 1898, running October to June. Name dropped 1908. *See also* Southern Belle.

Brill
J.G. Brill, Philadelphia, established 1868, J.G. Brill Co. 1887, Brill Corporation 1926. Builders of rly and tramway (*3*) cars. Ceased rail vehicle production 1941.

Bristol
Bristol Wagon & Carriage Works Ltd, 1866–1920.

Bristolian
An express between London (Paddington) and Bristol, introduced 1935, ceased 1939. Name restored 1951, dropped 1965, restored 1971, dropped 1973.

Bristol Pullman
BR eight-car dmu air-conditioned Pullman trains painted medium blue, introduced between London (Paddington) and Bristol in 1960, withdrawn 1973.

Britannia
A service between Harwich (Parkeston Quay) and Manchester (Piccadilly) in connection with Continental sailings, introduced 1989.

British Railway Journal
see BRJ.

British Railways
see BR (*1*).

British Railways Magazine
see BRM.

British Westinghouse
see Westinghouse.

BRITRA
British Road/Rail Intermodal Trunk Route Association.

Brits (RS)
BR standard class 7P 4–6–2 locos. The first in the class was named Britannia.

Brittany Express
A summer service between London

(Waterloo) and Southampton Docks in connection with St Malo sailings, 1954–64.

BRJ
British Railway Journal, an illustrated magazine devoted to rly history, first published 1983.

BRM
British Railways Magazine, issued in monthly regional editions from 1950 until 1963. *See also Railnews.*

BR (M)
British Railways, London Midland Region.

BRML
British Rail Maintenance Ltd. A division of BREL (qv) retained in BR ownership.

BR (NE)
British Railways, North Eastern Region. Merged with BR (E) 1966.

Broad gauge
Any rail gauge wider than standard (qv). The early lines of the GWR were 7 ft/2,134 mm gauge, later altered to 7 ft 0¼ in/2,140 mm. A broad gauge of 5 ft 6 in/1,676 mm is used in India, Pakistan, Sri Lanka, Spain, Portugal, Argentina, and Chile; 5 ft 3in/1,600 mm in Ireland, South Australia, Victoria, and Brazil; and 1,520 mm (orginally 5 ft) in Russia.

Broadlands Line
Brand name adopted in 1990 for BVR (qv).

Broadsman
An express between London (Liverpool St.), Norwich, Cromer and Sheringham, so named 1950. Name dropped 1962.

Broad Street Rattlers (RS)
NLR 4–4–0T.

Broadway Limited
An overnight Pennsylvania Railroad express between New York and Chicago, via Pittsburgh. Began 1902 as all-Pullman Broad Way Limited, the name arising from the six-track formation between New York and Philadelphia, not the famous New York street, although that was soon changed. 18 h in 1932. New loco and train designs by Raymond Loewy and a 16 h schedule began in 1938. After wartime relaxation, the 16 h timing was resumed in 1946 and reduced to 15 h 30 min in 1954. Name dropped 1967. Name adopted by an Amtrak New York–Chicago service from 1972.

Broca rail
A grooved rail designed for street tramways.

Brogden joint
A joint used in laying long rails, in which a vertical cut is made along the centre line of the rail for about 9 in (228 mm) and half the rail cut away, the other half overlapping the corresponding half of the adjoining rail, thus preserving a continuous bearing surface for the wheel tread. Each rail end is supported by a 'joint chair'.

Broken rail (USRS)
An experienced, long service rlyman.

Brotherhood (US)
Equivalent of trade union.

Brownie box (USRS)
A coach used by the superintendent of the railroad.

Brownies/Brownie points (USRS)
Demerit points recorded in a rlyman's personal career record and graded according to the seriousness of the offence. From the surname of the originator of the system.

Brown, Marshalls
Brown, Marshalls & Co. Ltd, Birmingham, rolling stock manufacturers 1870–1902. Became part of MCW (qv).

Brown one/'un (RS)
A distant signal showing yellow.

BRPB
British Rail Property Board. Set up in 1969 to control all property matters for the whole of the BRB undertakings, notably commercial development and sales of rly land, exploitation of space over stations etc. *See also* RSL.

BR (S)
British Railways, Southern Region.

BR (Sc)
British Railways, Scottish Region. *See also* Scotrail.

BRT
1. British Railway Traffic & Electric Co., established 1902 as rolling stock hirers. Acquired by Procor (qv), 1974.
2. BR Telecommunications; BR subsidiary formed 1990 to operate BR's telecommunications network and to market and develop surplus capacity and offer facilities on a commercial basis.

Brugeoise, la
see BN (*2*).

Bruiteur (Fr)
Paris Métro equivalent of hustler (qv).

Brunel
An express between London (Paddington) and Plymouth, introduced 1984. Became Brunel Executive, 1986.

Brush (RS)
1. A guard.
2. Brush Electrical Engineering Co. Ltd, Falcon Works, Lough-borough. The original co. was established in 1879 by Charles F. Brush; became Brush Electrical Engineering following a merger with Falcon (qv) in 1889. Manufacturers of steam, electric and diesel locos, rly coaches, electric tramcars, wagons and road transport vehicles. Steam loco production ceased 1912.

Amalgamated with Bagnall (qv) as Brush–Bagnall Traction Ltd, 1951. Renamed Brush Traction 1956. Part of Hawker Siddeley Group (qv), 1957.

BRUTE
British Railways Universal Trolley Equipment; large manually-propelled or tractor-hauled open wire net-sided trucks (for parcels, luggage etc. at stations), introduced 1964.

BR (W)
British Railways, Western Region.

BS (obs)
BR Brake Second/Standard class compartment coach, non-gangwayed, with luggage and guard's sections.

BS&WR
Baker Street & Waterloo Rly, inc 1893. A tube rly connecting these two London stations, eventually extending from Elephant & Castle to Queens Park. First section opened 1906. Part of LER from 1910. *See also* Bakerloo.

BSK (obs)
BR Brake Corridor Second/Standard class Compartment coach.

BSO
BR Brake Second/Standard class Open coach.

BTA
British Transport Advertising Ltd; BTC subsidiary, handling commercial advertising rights on stations etc. A wholly-owned subsidiary of BRB and THC 1963; sold to a group of BTA managers, Ironlook Ltd, 1987.

BTC
British Transport Commission; formed under Transport Act, 1947, as a public authority to control and administer all nationalized inland transport, including the rly system. Took over the rlys of Great Britain from 1 January 1948; first chairman Sir Cyril (from 1950 Lord) Hurcomb.

Reorganized 1953–4 with the abolition of the Railway Executive (qv). Management then designated to the LTE (qv) and (from 1955) to BR Area Boards for the six rly regions, whose CROs (qv) became General Managers. The BTC was effectively dissolved in 1963 though did not peter out formally until 1 January 1964. The rlys then passed to BRB and LTB (qv).

BTDB
British Transport Docks Board. Originated as Docks & Inland Waterways Executive of the BTC, inheriting the rly companies' docks and ports in 1948. Reorganized 1953 as a division of the BTC. BTDB formed under Transport Act 1962 as a separate undertaking, 'privatized' as ABP (qv) 1982.

BTFU or BTF
British Transport Films Unit. Formed by the BTC in 1949 to make documentary films for general distribution and instruction films for the staff of the BTC undertakings. Soon abbreviated to British Transport Films (BTF). Wound up 1986.

BTH
1. British Thomson–Houston Company Ltd, Rugby, established 1894, manufacturers of electric traction equipment for rlys and tramways (*3*). Controlled by International General Electric Co. (USA) 1929–58. Part of AEI (qv) from 1959.
2. British Transport Hotels. Originated 1948 as the Hotels Executive of the BTC, which inherited the rly companies' hotels. From 1953 became BTH & Catering Services, a division of the BTC, responsible in 1958 for 36 hotels, 350 refreshment rooms and 700 daily restaurant and buffet car

services. Registered as BTH Ltd 1962 with continuing responsibility for station catering facilities, restaurant car services, and rly and hotel laundry services. In this capacity it became a wholly-owned subsidiary of the BRB from 1963. Following the 'privatization' policy of the 1980 Conservative administration, by the end of 1983 all the rly hotels had been sold to private companies outside the BRB. Station catering was separated from BTH in 1982 (*see* Travellers-Fare) and train catering became a direct responsibility of the BRB at the same time. These changes enabled BTH to be dissolved in 1984.

BTHR
British Transport Historical Records. Responsible for the care of the archives of the constituents of the BTC undertakings and for making them available for historical research. The records were transferred to the Public Record Office in 1972 and BTHR ceased to exist.

BTP
British Transport Police [Force]. Formed 1948 to take over the responsibility of policing all BTC undertakings and assuming the duties of the former rly company and LPTB police forces. Responsibility for the BTP was transferred to the BRB in 1963 with a separate area force designated for London Transport, the final reorganization dating from January 1965. BTP ceased to police the former rly docks and ports after 30 June 1985.

BTU
Breakdown Train Unit.

Bubble cars (RS)
BR diesel railcars capable of running as a single unit.

Buchan Line
Dyce to Fraserburgh.

Bucharest Express
A service between Zagreb and
Bucharest via Subotica, 1967–78.

Bucket (USRS)
The piston of a diesel-electric loco.

Buckeye
A vertical plane automatic knuckle
coupling invented by Eli H. Janney,
in which the coach ends are bow-
shaped and thus brought close
together, allowing the steel jaws of the
couplers to engage firmly with each
other when the vehicles are pushed
close. These couplers were the
recommended practice of the MCB (*1*)
(qv) from 1899 and in the US are
therefore known as MCB (later AAR)
couplers. They were introduced in
Britain in 1897. Named after the
Buckeye Steel Castings Co. of
Columbus, Ohio, USA (Ohio is the
'Buckeye State').

Buckingham Palace (RS)
The former NER headquarters
building, York, which remains in BR
use. From its palatial and dignified
architecture.

Buck Jumpers (RS)
GER J67, J68 and J69 0–6–0T locos.

Budd
Established by Edward G. Budd in
Philadelphia, US, in 1912 but did not
produce rail vehicles until 1932.
Holders of patents for stainless steel
bodywork construction for which
licences have been granted to French
and Portuguese firms.

BUF
SR four-car emu corridor set with
BUFfet car, provided for 1938 Mid-
Sussex line electrification; two motor-
brakes Second/Standard class, one First
class trailer, one buffet trailer, the last
two with open seating areas, 4-BUF.

Buffer beam/plank/plate
The horizontal component of locos
and rolling stock to which the buffers
and coupling gear are fixed.

Buffer kissing (RS)
see Track bashing.

Buffet car
A coach with a counter from which
snacks, hot and cold drinks and
alcoholic refreshment are served.
There is a small kitchen unit and the
coach may also contain benches or
seats and tables. *See also* Autobuffet;
Mini[ature] buffet.

Buff, rly/steam (US)(S)
Term for anyone particularly
interested in rlys or steam locos. Has
some currency in UK, usually among
those who are not.

Bug, the
1. Combined inspection saloon and
   loco (F9 4–2–4T) built 1899 for the
   personal use of the L&SWR
   mechanical engineer, Dugald
   Drummond.
2. (USRS) A high speed telegrapher's
   key.

Bug box (RS)(obs)
A four-wheel passenger coach.

Bug dust (RS)(obs)
Coal in very small pieces.

Buggy (USRS)
A caboose (qv).

Bugler (RS)(obs)
A driver who uses the whistle
excessively. From the bugles
used before the invention of the steam
whistle. *See also* Captain
Hornblower.

Bug letter (USRS)
A standard form of words used by rly
co. head offices in reply to any
complaint regularly received from
passengers. From the response to
complaints about insects in the
upholstery of rly cars.

Bug torch (USRS)
A shunter's lamp. From the insects its light attracts at night.

Bulkhead
A partition extending over the full width of a vehicle at some point between the ends, usually fitted with a door.

Bull
see Railroad bull.

Bulldogs (RS)
1. GWR 4–4–0 locos class 3300 (1898).
2. L&SWR 415 class Adams 4–4–2T of 1882.
3. Midland Rly Johnson 3F 0–6–0 locos used on the S&DJR.

Bulldozer (RS)(obs)
A steam loco used for ECS working.

Bullet trains
Trains used on Japanese Shinkansen (qv) high speed lines.

Bullhead rail
A development of parallel rail (qv), it has a larger upper surface over which the train wheels run. The lower bulge is supported in chairs which are fastened to the sleepers. In Britain bullhead rail is now largely superseded by flat-bottom rail (qv).

Bullnose (USRS)
1. The front drawbar of a loco.
2. A clerestory (qv) sloped down at each end of a coach.

Bull pen (USRS)
A crew room.

Bull's Eye (RS)
A signal light.

Bump, to (USRS)
To gain another man's position by exercising seniority.

Bumper (RS)(obs)
Another word for a bunk (qv).

Bunk (RS)(obs)
A train working a short branch line, hence the line, or its traffic. Possibly from bunker (2) (qv).

Bunk a shed, to (RS)
To trespass in a loco depot in order to cop (qv) locos. Current in 1920s, if not earlier.

Bunk car (USRS)
A car fitted up with sleeping accommodation for train crews.

Bunker
1. A coal container at back of tank loco.
2. (RS) Any small tank loco.

Bunker first
A tank loco travelling backwards.

Bunny (RS)
A locally-experienced driver conducting another over an unfamiliar stretch of line. *See also* Pilotman.

Bun trains (LTRS)(obs)
Tube trains adapted in the Second World War to carry refreshments to people sheltering in tube stations during air and missile raids.

Bure Valley
Bure Valley Rly, 15 in/381 mm gauge light rly between Aylsham and Wroxham, Norfolk, over former BR Wroxham–County School line. Opened 1990.

Burlington
CB&Q (qv). *See also* Q, The
Burlington Zephyr
Streamlined three-car articulated diesel-powered stainless steel sets introduced 1934. First used on Lincoln (Nebraska)–Omaha–Kansas City service, 250 m in 4 h 55 min. Later operated between Chicago and Minneapolis–St Paul, also Chicago and Denver. Renamed Pioneer Zephyr (qv).
Burma Rly/ Burma–Thailand Rly
see Railway of Death.
Burma Road (RS)(obs)
Halwill to Torrington line. Also the CIE line from Claremorris to Cooloney (ex WL&WR). From their bleak, inhospitable situation.
Burrowing junction
A formation in which a diverging line is carried beneath a main line to avoid conflicting movements.
Burst (RS)
A loss of air pressure or vacuum in the braking system, usually from a fault or severance in a pipe.
Bury
Edward Bury & Co., Clarence Foundry, Liverpool, machinery manufacturers, established by Edward Bury (1794–1858); built steam locos from 1829, later known as Bury, Curtis & Kennedy. Ceased production 1850.
Bus (USRS)
A loco.
Business car (US)
A car for use by rly officials travelling round the system, fitted out with office, cooking, eating and sleeping accommodation, lavatories etc.
Bus line
A multi-core cable providing an electrical connection between the collecting shoes of an emu (qv) train and between them and the master controller.
Bustitution
The replacement of rly passenger service by buses; rarely a satisfactory substitute and therefore often followed after a short interval by complete withdrawal of the service. A term first used in the 1960s.
Butlin's Expresses (obs)
Special trains between London (Kings Cross) and Skegness, and between London (Liverpool St.) and Clacton and London (Victoria) and Bognor, introduced 1950 to carry traffic generated by Butlin's Holiday Camps.
Butterfly
1. (RS) Indicator and re-set valve at ends of passenger carriages. From its shape.
2. GWR TC for six-wheel tri-composite coach.
3. (USRS) A notice passed by a train crew member to a rlyman at lineside or vice versa. From the shape of the note, when tied or weighted at the centre.
Butterfly cock (LTRS)
An external door valve cock. From the shape of the handle.
Button (LTRS)
The master controller in an electric train.
Button pusher (LTRS)
A guard. From the door control buttons.
Buzzard's roost (USRS)
The yard office.
BVG (Ger)
Berliner Verkehrs Betriebe; Berlin Public Transport Authority, formed 1928 to manage and operate the city's trams, buses, and *U-bahn*.
BVR
Bure Valley Rly (qv).

BW (Ger)
Bahnbetriebswerk; motive power
depot.

BWH&AR
Bideford, Westward Ho! & Appledore
Rly, inc 1896; its line, opened 1901
and 1908, was not connected with
main rly system. Closed 1917.

BY (obs)
BR four-wheeled passenger brake
vehicle.

BZ (obs)
BR six-wheeled passenger brake
vehicle, non-gangwayed.

C

C
BR Composite Compartment coach, non-gangwayed.

Cab, to (RS)
To ride by invitation with the driver.

Cab hop (USRS)
Abbreviation of caboose hop (qv).

Cabin car (US)(obs)
Early term for caboose (qv).

Caboose (US)
Since *c*. 1855 the accepted term for last vehicle on a freight train, accommodating the train crew and providing a vantage point (*see* Cupola) for inspection of the moving train. Probably from the Greek *kabuse* meaning little room or hut.

Caboose bounce (USRS)
see Caboose hop.

Caboose hop (USRS)
Train consisting only of loco(s) and caboose(s) (qv).

Cab rank (RS)(obs)
Siding at Stratford, east London, on which Buck Jumpers (qv) lined up to work the Jazz Service (qv).

Cad (USRS)
A conductor (*3*) (qv).

CAF (obs)
BR Cafeteria car (qv).

Cafeteria car (obs)
A coach fitted out to dispense self-service hot meals and other refreshments; introduced by BR 1952.

Cage (USRS)
A caboose (qv).

Cairn Valley
Cairn Valley Light Rly, Dumfries–Moniave, LRO 1899, opened 1905, worked and owned by G&SWR and from 1923 by LM&SR. Closed 1943 (passengers), completely closed 1949.

CAL (obs)
Carted Across London; freight moved across London by rly-owned road transport.

Calais–Bruxelles Pullman Express
A *CIWL* express providing Brussels connection with cross channel sailings to and from Dover; ran 1927–39.

Calais–Méditerranée Express
see Blue Train.

Calais–Nice–Rome Express
A *CIWL* service, 1883–1914.

Calder Valley Line
Normanton–Wakefield–Sowerby Bridge–[Todmorden–Manchester].

Caledonian
Express between London (Euston) and Glasgow, 1957–1964.

Caledonian Rly (Brechin)
A preserved rly between Brechin and Bridge of Dun on former BR Forfar–Bridge of Dun line.

Caley (RS)
Caledonian Rly: *see* CR (*1*).

Caley-stop (RS)
see Euston stop.

California car
A single deck tramcar in which half

the passenger accommodation has open sides and the other half is fully glazed and protected from the weather.

California Zephyr
A Chicago–Denver–San Francisco service of CB&Q, D&RGW and WPRR. Introduced 1949 with Vista-Dome cars (qv), withdrawn 1970. Re-introduced 1983 as Amtrak service. *See also* San Francisco Zephyr.

Call a train over, to (obs)
To walk along a train making an announcement to all passengers in each coach.

Caller (US)(obs)
A boy employed to rouse train crews for duty.

Caller-up (obs)
Employee who roused train crews for duty by knocking at their bedroom windows.

Callie (RS)
Caledonian Rly: *see* CR (*1*).

Calling-on arm/signal
A small semaphore signal fixed to the post carrying a starting or home signal. In the 'off' position it authorizes a movement at caution to the next stop signal when the block section ahead is not clear. When fixed to a distant signal post, the 'off' indication allows a cautious advance beyond the home signal (which will also be 'off') up to the starting signal (which will be 'on'). The calling-on signal usually shows no light when 'on', green when 'off'. Such signals were also used at termini to call on light engines after the train they had brought in had left, allowing the loco to follow the train out and attach itself to another train. These signals also allow a train to enter a platform already partly occupied.

Calliope (USRS)
Steam loco. From (US) calliope = a steam organ (Greek for a beautiful voice).

Call point examiners
Rolling stock examiners located at specified points on LT rlys where they are 'on call' to attend to defects arising on trains in service.

Calmac
Caledonian Macbrayne shipping services to and from the islands off the west coast of Scotland, many of them operating in connection with rail services.

Calumet (US)
A steam loco with 2–4–2 wheel arrangement, after these had been supplied to the Chicago & Calumet Terminal Co.

Camber
Raising of one rail above the other to allow higher speeds round curves. *See also* Super-elevation.

Cambrian
Cambrian Rlys Company, inc 1864, from Oswestry, Ellesmere & Whitchurch Rly (opened 1863, 1864), Oswestry & Newtown Rly, (opened 1860, 1861, 1863), Llanidloes & Newtown Rly (opened 1859) and the Newtown & Machynlleth Rly (opened 1863). The Aberystwyth & Welsh Coast Rly (opened 1863, 1864, 1865, 1867 and 1869) was absorbed from 1865. The company operated 295 route miles by 1914, mainly in central Wales. Amalgamated with GWR 1922.

Cambrian Coast Express
GWR summer express between London (Paddington) and Aberystwyth/Pwllheli, introduced

1927. Re-introduced by BR 1951.
Pwllheli working withdrawn
1966, ceased 1967. Re-introduced
1987 as London (Euston) to
Aberystwyth all year round service,
ceased 1991.

Cambrian Coast Line
Dovey Junction–Barmouth–Pwllheli.

Cambrian Radio Cruise
see Land cruise.

Camels/Camelbacks
1. (USRS) Steam locos in which the
driving controls and driver's cab
were placed centrally, on top of the
boiler, with firing cab in the
normal position.
2. Any electric or diesel loco with cab
in the centre.

Cammell Laird
Cammell Laird & Co. Ltd, Sheffield,
manufacturers of locos and rolling
stock and parts, established 1903.
Rolling stock activities transferred to
Metro–Cammell (qv), 1929.

Camp car (US)
Outfit car (qv).

Camping coaches
Rly coaches adapted as holiday
accommodation and placed in sidings
at suitable locations. Introduced 1932,
withdrawn 1939, restored 1946,
finally withdrawn as a public service
1971.

Can (USRS)
A tank wagon.

Canadian
A CPR express between Montreal
and Toronto and Vancouver
via Calgary, with 'scenic dome' cars,
introduced 1955, scheduled at
70 h 20 min eastbound. Withdrawn
1990.

Canal Line
Glasgow–Paisley(Canal)–Elderslie.

C&D (obs)
Collection & Delivery; parcels and

freight 'smalls' collected from
consignor and delivered after rail
transit to the consignee's address,
using the rly's road vehicles at each
end of the journey.

C&GWUR
Cheltenham & Great Western Union
Rly, Swindon–Gloucester–
Cheltenham, inc 1836, opened 1841,
1844, absorbed by GWR 1844.

C&LR
Cavan & Leitrim Light Rly, (Ire) inc
1883 as Cavan, Leitrim & Roscommon
Light Rly, Dromod–Ballinamore–
Belturbet and Ballinamore–Arigna,
3 ft gauge, opened 1887, 1888.
Renamed C&L Light Rly 1895, part
of GSR from 1925. Closed 1959.

C&MR
1. Cork & Muskerry [Light] Rly,
inc 1883, 3 ft/914 mm gauge,
Cork–Blarney–Donoughmore–
Coachford, opened 1887, 1888.
Donoughmore–St Annes opened by
separate co, worked by C&MR,
1893. Part of GSR from 1925,
closed 1934.
2. Campbeltown & Machrihanish
Light Rly, 2 ft 3 in/686 mm gauge
line between these two places, inc
1905, opened 1906, partly a
conversion of 1875 industrial line.
No connection with main rly
system. Closed 1932.

C&MDR
Cork & Macroom Direct Rly, inc
1861, opened 1866, part of GSR 1925.
Regular passenger services ceased
1935, closed 1953.

C&NW
Chicago & North Western Rly Co.
Purchased in 1972 by C&NW
Transportation Co., which also
included the CGW (qv).

C&O
Chesapeake & Ohio Rly Co.

C & O Hotel Express
A Caledonian Rly weekend express
between Glasgow, Callander and
Oban, 1905–14.

C&O Joint
Croydon & Oxted Joint Committee,
inc 1878 (part of Croydon, Oxted &
East Grinstead Rly) South Croydon–
Oxted– Crowhurst Junc East.
LB&SCR and SER (later SE&CR)
Joint from opening in 1884. Partly
built on the abandoned works of the
S&SJR (qv).

C&OVR
Cardiff & Ogmore Valley Rly,
Llanharan–Blackmill, inc 1873,
opened 1876, amalgamated with
L&OR 1876.

C&SLR
City & South London Rly. London
tube rly, inc 1884 as City of London
& Southwark Subway, name changed
1890. Opened Stockwell to King
William Street, City, 1890. Extended
from Borough to Moorgate and also
from Stockwell to Clapham Common
1900, from Moorgate to Angel 1901,
from Angel to Euston 1907. Became
part of UERL from 1912. *See also*
Northern Line.

C&T indicators
Illuminated lineside indicators showing
the commencement and termination of
temporary speed limits.

C&VBT
Castlederg & Victoria Bridge
Tramway (NI), inc 1883, 3 ft/914 mm
gauge tramway (*4*), opened 1884,
closed 1933. Ordinary steam rly locos
were used from 1904.

C&W
Carriage & Wagon [Department/
Examiner].

C&W Jc
Cleator & Workington Junction Rly,
inc 1876 Cleator/Rowrah to

Workington and Linefoot, first section
opened 1879, part worked by FR. Part
of LM&SR from 1923.

C&WT
Cavehill & Whitewell Tramway, inc
1881, opened 1882, Chichester Park,
Belfast to Glengormley. Steam and
horse-worked tramway (*4*). Electrified
1906 and in 1910 became part of the
Belfast tramway system. Closed 1949.

Candy butchers (USRS)
Peripatetic salesmen offering
confectionery etc. at stations.

Candy run (USRS)
An easy trip.

Cannonball Express (USRS)
Any fast, high priority train working.

Cant
see Super-elevation.

Cantrail
A supporting longitudinal member in
a coach or tramcar roof.

Canteen Cowboys (RS)
Men on duty but awaiting work.

CAP
BR four-car emu sets formed from two
2-HAP units permanently coupled and
used for 'Coastway' services east and
west of Brighton, 4-CAP.

Cape
TC for 'cancel'.

Cape gauge
3 ft 6 in/1,067 mm gauge, as used in
South Africa (beginning in Cape of
Good Hope).

Cape to Cairo Rly
The dream of Cecil Rhodes – a
continuous line of rails under the
British flag from Capetown to Cairo. By
the end of 1928 it had become possible
to make this journey by rail and public
bus and lake steamer services, but even
today there remain two gaps in the rail
link, one fairly short (El Shellal
(Egypt)–Farriq (Egypt)) and the other
lengthy (Waw (Sudan)–Kindu (Zaire)).

Capitals Limited
An express between London (Kings Cross) and Edinburgh introduced 1949, renamed The Elizabethan (qv), 1953.

Capitals United Express
An express between London (Paddington) and Cardiff, so named 1956, name dropped 1965.

Capitole
A First class only express between Paris and Toulouse, introduced 1960, a *TEE* from 1970–84. The first European express timed at 200 km/h (from 1967).

Capitol Limited
A B&O express between Washington, New York and Chicago, introduced 1923. An Amtrak service since 1971.

Captain (USRS)
A train conductor (3) (qv). *See also* Train captain.

Captain Hornblower (RS)(obs)
A driver using whistle excessively. *See also* Bugler.

Capuchon
A raised lip at front of a steam loco chimney intended to prevent down draught and to deflect exhaust steam and smoke, lifting it clear of the front windows of the driving cab.

Car (US)
Term for any passenger or freight rail vehicle, adopted in UK, from early 1900s, at first mainly for electric rly passenger coaches. Also used in UK from *c.* 1895 as an abbreviated term for tramcar (qv).

Carbarn (US)
Tram/interurban shed or depot.

Car carrier
Train carrying motorists and their cars, later known as Motorail (qv).

Cardeans (RS)
Caledonian Rly 4-6-0 locos.

Cardiff Valleys [Lines]
Cardiff–Pontypridd–Treherbert/ Merthyr Tydfil; Cardiff– Caerphilly– Rhymney.

Car hop (USRS)
A brakeman (qv).

Car knocker (USRS)
A carriage and wagon fitter.

Carline
Transverse members supporting the roof of a wagon or car.

Carman (US)
A fitter who maintains rolling stock.

Car mile
A measurement unit equalling one car, loaded or empty, moved over one mile of track.

Carpati Pullman Express
A *CIWL* express between Bucharest and Brasov, 1929–31.

Carriage dock
A short platform with an end ramp to road level abutting on to a dead-end siding and designed to facilitate loading of road and military vehicles on to rly flat wagons or end-door vans.

Carriage lines
Tracks used solely or mainly for movement of ecs (qv) to and from large passenger stations.

Carriage truck (obs)
A flat open wagon designed to convey private horse carriages or motor cars.

Carry a white feather, to (RS)
see White feather.

Carry green, to (USRS)
To run under green flags (day) and green lights (night), indicating that a

second part of the train is following
immediately behind.
Carry the banner, to (USRS)
To use flags for signalling (usually
applied to brakeman).
Carry the mail, to (USRS)
To bring train orders (qv).
Carry white, to
To run under white flags (day) and
white lights (night), indicating that the
train is an extra working.
Car Sleeper Limited
A summer express with
accommodation for cars and their
passengers, between London (Kings
Cross) and Perth, introduced 1955.
The first BR service of this kind.
Subsequently many other similar
services were added under the brand
name Motorail (qv).
Cartage (obs)
The transport of goods, parcels etc.,
using the rly's own road vehicles for
collection and for delivery at each end
of the rail transit; also use of rly road
vehicles between rly stations/depots in
large towns and cities. *See also* C&D.
Cartic
A BR articulated wagon for
transporting motor cars in quantity.
Cartic 4s, introduced in 1964, carry
up to thirty-four cars on two decks.
Car-tink/tonk (USRS)
A carriage & wagon inspector.
Car toad (USRS)
A carriage & wagon fitter or carman
(qv).
Car whack (USRS)
A carman (qv).
Cascade
1. TC for 'rearrange timings'.
2. The process which follows the
   injection of new rolling stock on to
   the rly, allowing older but still
   serviceable stock to be moved
   'down' to other duties and in turn,

at the bottom of the 'cascade', the
withdrawal from service of outdated
and worn out stock.
Casey Jones
John Luther Jones, a loco driver on
the Illinois Central RR (US) who was
killed in a head-on collision between
his Cannonball Express and a freight
train on 30 April 1900. Although his
fireman jumped clear, Jones stayed on
to sound his whistle, giving the crew
of the freight time to escape. His
sacrifice was commemorated in a folk
song written by the black loco cleaner
Wallace Saunders. 'Casey Jones' was
then adopted to describe any loco
driver in the US.
Casseyway (obs)
A Scottish term for waggonway/
tramroad. Derived from 'causeway'.
Castle (USRS)
A rly station.
Castleman's Corkscrew/Snake
The Southampton & Dorchester Rly,
inc 1845, opened 1847, part of
L&SWR 1848. From its sinuous
course through the New Forest to
avoid stands of timber and the name
of its promoter, a Wimborne solicitor.
Catalan TALGO
Originated as a Geneva–Port Bou
(connection to/from Barcelona) diesel
service 1955–69. This was replaced by
the *Catalan TALGO*, a through
service between Geneva and
Barcelona, a *TEE*, in 1969. Lost *TEE*
status 1982, became EC 1987.
Catch points
Trailing points arranged to derail
harmlessly any vehicle running in the
wrong direction. Inclines are usually
protected in this manner and
catch points are an official requirement
where the gradient exceeds 1 in
260; a second pair is also required
if the gradient is lengthy. A runaway

or catch siding may also be provided.

Catch the water, to (RS)
The priming of a steam locomotive with excess of water in boiler.

CATE
Computer Assisted Timetable Enquiries; a BR computer system.

Catenary
The supporting cable and hangers for the conductor wire used in overhead wire electric traction current feeder systems.

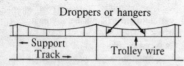

Catenary (side view)

Catford Loop
Nunhead–Catford–Shortlands [London].

Cathcart Circle
Glasgow (Central)–Langside– Cathcart – Glasgow (Central).

Cathedral jig
A large frame within which the body sides, roof and floor of a rail vehicle are assembled for final welding.

Cathedrals Express
A service between London (Paddington), Oxford, Worcester and Hereford, introduced 1957. Name dropped 1965, re-introduced 1985.

Cat's eyes (RS)
A calling-on signal (qv).

Cattle arch/creep
A form of occupation crossing (qv), a subway provided beneath a rly when the fields of a farm are severed by its construction.

Caught for a job (LTRS)
Spare trainmen given running work to do.

Cauliflowers (RS)
LNWR Webb 0–6–0 locos. From the L&NWR crest on the wheel splashers which was thought to bear a resemblance to the vegetable.

CB&PR
Cork, Blackrock & Passage Rly, (Ire), inc 1846 as Cork, Blackrock, Passage & Monkstown Rly, opened Cork to Passage 1850. Converted from 5 ft 3 in/1,600 mm to 3 ft/914 mm gauge 1900–4 and extended to Crosshaven. Part of GSR 1925. Closed 1932.

CB&Q
Chicago, Burlington & Quincy RR. Co. *See also* Burlington; Q, The.

CB&SCR
Cork, Bandon & South Coast Rly, (Ire), Cork to Bantry, branches to Baltimore, Clonakilty, Courtmacsherry and Kinsale. Inc 1845 as Cork & Bandon Rly, first section opened 1851. Part of GSR 1925.

CCC
Cincinnati Car Co., Cincinnati, Ohio, US, established 1903. Builders of cars for tramways (*3*) and interurbans. Ceased production 1931.

CCE
Chief Civil Engineer.

CCE&HR
Charing Cross, Euston & Hampstead Rly. London tube rly inc 1892, opened Charing Cross (SER) to Golders Green and Highgate (now Archway) 1907. Part of LER from 1910. *See also* Northern Line.

CCF
Canadian Car & Foundry Co., Montreal, established 1909, manufacturers of all types of rly, tramway and interurban equipment.

CCSC
Carlisle Citadel Station Committee, formed 1857. The station and approaches north and south were the

joint property of CR (*1*) and L&NWR. The NER, M&CR, G&SWR, NBR and Midland were tenants. The L&NER and LM&SR shared ownership 1923–47.

CCT
1. Covered Carriage Truck, BR; similar to PMV, with end doors and end flaps so that motor cars could be driven on board. Non-gangwayed.
2. Cook's Continental Timetable *see* Cook's Timetables.

CDRJC
County Donegal Railways Joint Committee, Londonderry–Strabane–Donegal–Killybegs/Ballyshannon, with branches to Glenties and Letterkenny. Opened 1863 as Finn Valley Rly, 5 ft 3 in/1,600 mm gauge, Strabane–Stranorlar. West Donegal Rly, Stranorlar–Donegal, inc 1879, 3 ft/914 mm gauge, opened 1889. Both rlys amalgamated as Donegal Rly 1892. System completed and Finn Valley line converted to 3 ft/914 mm gauge 1893–1905. Taken over by GNR (I) and Midland Rly of England 1906 and CDJRC formed. Strabane–Londonderry was wholly-owned by Midland but worked by Joint Committee. Midland interests passed to LM&SR 1923. CDRJC also worked the Strabane & Letterkenny Rly, opened 1909. All CDRJC-worked lines were closed 1947–59.

CEH
Conference Européen des Horaires; European Timetable Conference.

Ceinture, Grande, la
Outer belt line around Paris, linking all radial trunk lines.

Ceinture, Petite, la
Inner belt line around the centre of Paris. Now exists only in part.

CEJ
Clifton Extension Joint Rly: *see* BPR&P.

Cenotaph (RS)(obs)
A mechanical coaling plant in a steam loco depot. From the shape, like a giant version of the famous London war memorial.

Centipede (US)
A steam loco with 2–12–0 wheel arrangement.

Central/Central London
see CLR.

Central Wales
Central Wales Rly, inc 1859, Llandrindod Wells–Craven Arms, opened 1865, part of L&NWR 1868, LM&SR 1923. Also Central Wales Extension Rly, Llandrindod Wells–Llandovery, inc 1860, opened 1866, 1867, 1868, part of L&NWR 1868, LM&SR 1923. *See also* Heart of Wales Line.

Central Wales Line
Shrewsbury–Craven Arms– Llandrindod Wells– Llanelly– [Swansea].

Centre, The (RS)
BRB headquarters.

Centre the key, to (LTRS)
To move the reverser key of an electric train into the central or 'off' position (this is against the rules when coasting).

Centro
The brand name of West Midlands Passenger Transport Executive, adopted 1990.

CEP
BR four-car all-steel Corridor emu sets with Electro-Pneumatic brakes, of 1956 and 1958–9; two motor brake Second/Standard class, one Second/ Standard trailer and one composite trailer, 4-CEP.

CERTS (obs)
Cheap Evening Return Tickets, LT.

Cess
That part of the track formation beyond the outermost edges of the sleepers.

Cévenol
A diesel railcar service between Clermont Ferrand and Marseilles, introduced 1955. 'Panoramique' railcars with Vistadome (qv) from 1959, name transferred to Paris–Clermont Ferrand–Marseilles service 1979.

CFC
Chemins de Fer de la Corse; Corsican Rlys.

CFD (Fr)
Chemin de Fer Départementale; Departmental Railway, a secondary rly (qv), authorized and largely financed by the *département* (local authority). Usually, but not necessarily, a light rly.

CFE (Fr)
Chemin de Fer Économique; term for a light rly.

CFF
Chemins de Fer Fédéreaux Suisses; Swiss Federal Rlys. Also known as *SBB* and *SFF* (qv).

CFL
Société Nationale des Chemins de Fer Luxembourgeois; Luxembourg National Rlys Authority.

CFR
Căile Ferate Romane; Roumanian State Rlys.

CFTA
Compagnie Générale des Chemins de Fer et des Transports Automobiles. A company operating various minor rlys, road services etc. on behalf of the *SNCF* (qv).

CGR
Cape Government Rly. Became part of SAR (qv).

CGTC
Carlisle Goods Traffic Committee, formed 1873 with representatives of CR (*1*), L&NWR, Midland and G&SWR to manage and control the jointly-owned goods loop from south of Citadel station, Carlisle, to Caldew and Willowholme Juncs. LM&SR was sole owner from 1923.

CGW (US)
Chicago Great Western RR Co.

CH
Hellenic [Greek] State Rlys.

Chafer
GWR TC for invalid coach.

Chain gang (USRS)
A relief train crew.

Chair
A cast iron fitting fastened to a sleeper which supports bullhead rail secured in it by a key (qv).

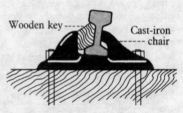

Wooden key ---- Cast-iron ----- chair

Chair, in the (RS)
At the controls of a loco.

Chaix
The French equivalent of 'Bradshaw' (qv), *l'Indicateur Chaix*, showing the times of all trains running in France. First published April 1847. Ceased publication 1976. By the 1930s, the style of *Chaix* was standard for all French rly timetable matter and the train service posters displayed at stations were enlarged photographic reproductions of pages in the main volume. Named after the *Imprimerie Chaix*, its printers and publishers.

Challenger (US)
A steam loco with 4–6–6–4 wheel arrangement.

Chamber maid (USRS)
A fitter at a loco depot.
Champs Elysées
Paris–Lausanne *TGV*, introduced
1984.
Channel trains
BR (SR) term adopted in 1989 for
trains connecting with cross-Channel
hovercraft, jetfoils and car ferries.
Chaos in Excelsis (obs)
Nickname for CIE (qv).
Chariot
1. (RS)(obs) A GWR shunters'
wagon.
2. (USRS) A caboose (qv).
Charlies (RS)
SR Bulleid Q1 0–6–0 locos.
Charnwood Forest
Charnwood Forest Rly, Hugglescote to
Loughborough (Derby Rd), partly on
site of a canal and canal tramway (1)
opened 1794, closed 1799; inc 1874,
opened 1883, worked by L&NWR,
part of LM&SR 1923.
Charterail
A RfD (qv) and private sector
business formed 1990 to provide door-
to-door freight services exploiting
road/rail intermodal vehicles and
containers, with Rfd acting as
subcontractor.
Chartex
TC for chartered excursion train.
Chaser (RS)(obs)
Rly worker who braked wagons being
shunted in a marshalling yard.
Chase red, to (USRS)
To go to the rear of a train stopped on
the running line with a red flag or
light to protect it.
Chatham, The
LC&DR or SE&CR (qv).
Chat Moss Line
Manchester–St Helen's–Liverpool.
Cheap, The (RS)(obs)
A parliamentary train (qv).

Check down, to (LTRS)
To reduce speed.
Checking back (LTRS)
Blocking back (qv).
Check rail
An additional rail placed inside and
parallel to running rails to guide wheel
flanges at road and rail crossings and
also on curves, viaducts, bridges etc.
to hold wheels to rails.
Check system (US)
Method of handling rly passengers'
luggage. *See also* Baggage master;
Transfer agent.
Cheltenham Flyer
An express between London
(Paddington) and Cheltenham
Spa, introduced 1923. The name never
enjoyed full official status, but
appeared on loco headboards from
1931. This train soon became the
fastest regular service in Britain and
by 1931 was officially claimed by the
GWR as 'The World's Fastest Train',
attaining speeds of around 90 m.p.h.
at times. A year later, the average
booked speed between Swindon and
Paddington was raised to 71.35 m.p.h.
In 1933 its record was taken by the
Fliegende Hamburger (qv).
Cheltenham Spa Express
A BR express between London
(Paddington) and Cheltenham Spa,
introduced 1956, name dropped 1973.
Name revived 1985.
Chemin de fer Américain (Fr)(obs)
Tramway (*3*). By the 1870s it had
been replaced by the English word.
Chemin de fer secondaire (Fr)
Secondary rly (qv).
Chemin de fer vicinal (Fr)
Local light rly line/lines, usually
narrow gauge. The term is also used
in Belgium and Switzerland.
Cheminots (Fr)
Rly workers.

Cherries (LTRS)
Current rail gap indicators.
Cherry picker (USRS)
A pointsman. From the red lights on
his signals.
Chesapeake (US)
A steam loco with 2–8–8–2 wheel
arrangement. First used on the C&O
(qv).
Chessie
Nickname for the C&O (qv).
Chicago Bears (RS)
BR class 59 3,300 hp diesel-electric
freight locos owned by Foster Yeoman
and ARC. Built by General Motors at
La Grange, Illinois, USA.
Chief, The
An express running daily between Los
Angeles and Chicago, introduced
1926. 50 h 25 min in 1936. Ceased
1967. *See also* Super Chief.
Children's Railways
Miniature rlys (qv) established in
communist countries, to serve the dual
purpose of providing amusement and
serious training for a rly career.
Chiltern Lines
NSE brand name introduced 1989 for
London (Marylebone)–Aylesbury/High
Wycombe and Banbury dmu services.
Chinese Fours (RS)
BR Class 4 2–6–0 freight locos.
Chinese labour (RS)(obs)
Part-time luggage porters at large
stations, making a living solely from
gratuities.
Chintz
GWR TC for family saloon.
Chip bin (RS)
A lineside ballast container.
Chippies (USRS)
Narrow gauge rolling stock.
Chipstead Valley
Chipstead Valley Rly, Purley to
Tadworth, inc 1893, opened 1897,
1900, part of SER from 1899.

Chopin
A Warsaw–Vienna service with
seasonal through coaches to and from
Moscow, introduced 1961.
Chopper
A thyristor, used in electric train
control, which 'chops' electric current,
providing variable ac voltage by
interrupting the fixed voltage supply
in a controlled manner.
Choppers (RS)
1. L&NWR Webb 4 ft 6 in 2–4–2T,
   some of which were fitted with
   'chopper valves' in the smokebox to
   divert the exhaust into the side
   tanks to condense it when working
   through London Underground
   tunnels.
2. BR diesel locos class 20, from a
   sound effect resembling the
   intrusive row created by
   helicopters.
Christmas card (LT rhyming S)
A guard.
Christmas tree (RS)
1. Colour light signals on a gantry.
2. A loco or vehicle pillaged of parts
   or elements (i.e. cannibalized) to
   keep others of same type in service.
Chub
GWR TC for an eight-wheel Third
class saloon with table and end
compartment.
Chunnel
The Channel Tunnel.
Churchills (RS)
1. French rlymen's term for GWR
   Dean Goods locos imported into
   France during the Second World
   War.
2. LM&SR class 8F 2–8–0s used
   overseas in the Second World War.
Church interval
The suspension of certain London
local train services for 2–3 hours
during Sunday morning church

services, a practice first adopted by the London & Greenwich Rly in 1836, with the intention that employees should attend church. The custom was broken by the CLR from its opening in 1900 but did not finally disappear from all London lines until 1926.

Churnet Valley Line
North Rode–Leek–Rocester.

CIE
Córas Iompair Eireann; Transport Company of Ireland, formed 1945, assuming responsibility for managing and operating rlys in the Republic of Ireland. The rlys passed to *IE* (qv) in 1986.

CIG
BR (S) four-car emu sets of 1964–72 for London–Brighton services with Corridor throughout and Interconnecting Gangway. Two driving trailer composites (compartments in First class only), one trailer Second/Standard class and one non-driving motor brake Second/Standard, 4-CIG.

CIM
Convention Internationale sur le Transport de Marchandises par chemin de fer; international convention regulating rly freight transport.

Cinder cruncher (USRS)
A pointsman.

Cinder dick (USRS)
A rly policeman.

Cinderella (RS)
An electric train or loco on a third or fourth rail system (qv) which has discarded a current-collecting shoe.

Cinderella's coach (RS)
A special coach with an observation platform, used by District Engineers and other senior officers.

Cinder snapper (USRS)
Brakesman. Also a passenger riding on the open end platform of a passenger coach.

Circle/Circle Line
see Inner Circle.

Circus (USRS)
A rly.

Circus train
A train composed of vehicles suitable for carrying all the animals, equipment, staff, performers etc. of a circus, particularly in North America.

Cisalpin
An electric *TEE* Paris–Milan, introduced 1961, ceased 1984. Name used for Paris–Lausanne TGV 1984 and connecting EC Geneva–Milan, 1987.

CIT
1. International Rail Transport Committee, founded 1902.
2. SR six-car emu sets 1933, for London Bridge–Brighton commuter services with one Pullman car and a high proportion of First class accommodation, 6-CIT.
3. *Compagnia Italia Turismo*; Italian Tourism Co., owned by *FS* (qv).

City Express
An express between London (Holborn Viaduct) and Ramsgate, introduced 1896. To and from Cannon St. 1904, ceased 1905. In 1921–7 the name was used for various services between London and Ramsgate, some with Pullman cars.

City Limited
Businessmen's express between Brighton and London Bridge, introduced 1921, name dropped 1934.

Cityrail
Brand name of the urban/suburban rail network in Sydney, Australia.

City to City
An L&NWR service for businessmen between London (Broad St.) and Birmingham (New St.), 1910–14. A typist was available on the train.

City Widened Lines
A second pair of tracks between Kings Cross and Moorgate, Metropolitan Rly (London), mostly used by passenger and freight services to and from Midland Rly and GNR (LM&SR and L&NER from 1923–47, then BR (M) and BR (E)). Used by BR NSE Thameslink cross-London passenger services since 1988.

CIV
Convention Internationale sur le transport des Voyageurs par chemins de fer; international convention for regulating rail passenger transport.

Civilink
A generic term, introduced 1990, for BR Civil Engineers' services and their dedicated rolling stock and locos.

CIWL
Compagnie Internationale des Wagons-Lits; International Sleeping Car Company, founded 1876, '*et des Grands Express Européens*' added to title 1883. Title altered to *CIWL et du Tourisme* (*CIWLT*) in 1967. Until 1970–1 *CIWL* operated and staffed international sleeping, dining and Pullman car services in Europe, Asia and Africa (and Russia until 1917). The last Pullman service on the European mainland (Milan–Rome) ran in 1971. National sleeping car and on-train catering services continue in Europe and Morocco as well as hotel and catering services at airports etc. 'Discretion is the better part of *Wagons-Lits*'— Robertson Hare in the 1932 film *Rome Express*.

CK (obs)
BR Corridor Composite Compartment coach.

CK&PR
Cockermouth, Keswick & Penrith Rly, inc 1861, opened 1864, 1865,

worked by L&NWR and S&DR/ NER, part of LM&SR 1923.

CL (obs)
1. Carted Luggage; system by which luggage brought to a station is carried by rail and then delivered to destination by rly road vehicle.
2. BR composite compartment coach, non-gangwayed, with lavatory reached by a side corridor, this being on opposite sides for each class.

Clacton Sunday Pullman
A L&NER service from London (Liverpool St.) to Clacton, introduced 1928.

Clag (RS)
A pronounced display of exhaust steam and smoke by a steam loco.

Clan Goods (RS)
Highland Rly Cummings 4–6–0 locos.

Clankers (RS)
L&NER K2 2–6–0 locos. From the distinctive noise made by their nickel chrome steel connecting rods.

Clansman
An express between London (Euston), Birmingham and Inverness, introduced 1974.

Clarence Rly
Inc 1828, Port Clarence to S&DR at Simpasture, first section opened 1834, absorbed by WHH&R, 1852.

Class, to (RS)
The train spotter's triumph – to see and note all the locos in a particular class.

Class 1 railroads (US)
A classification embracing those undertakings with operating revenue above a certain minimum level.

Clauds/Claud Hammies (RS)
GER 4–4–0 locos, one of which was named after Lord Claud Hamilton, GER chairman from 1893 to 1923. L&NER class D15/16. *See also* Super Clauds.

Clay & Knocker
Nickname for LD&ECR.

Clay hoods (obs)
Open wagons with tarpaulins
supported by a central rail, formerly
used for carrying china clay.

Clayliner
A BR wagon designed for carriage of
china clay, replacing clay hoods (qv).

Clayton
Clayton Wagons Ltd, Lincoln, later
Clayton Equipment Co.,
manufacturing locos and railcars.

Claytons (RS)
BR type 1 900hp centre cab diesel
locos built by Clayton.

CLC
Cheshire Lines Committee, Liverpool/
Southport–Warrington–Manchester;
Glazebrook–Baguley–Stockport–
Godley Junc; Altrincham–Northwich–
Chester. Constituted 1865, with GNR
and MS&LR as owners. Midland
became third partner in 1866.
LM&SR and L&NER joint 1923–47.
First section opened 1862. The CLC
possessed passenger and freight stock,
but the owning companies supplied
locos.

Clearance/depression bar
A bar fixed on track at junctions or
platforms, interlocked to signals,
which cannot be put to 'off' until the
bar is lifted, thus ensuring no vehicles
are present, since the bar cannot be
raised when a vehicle is on it. These
bars are used to define the fouling
point between diverging tracks. *See
also* Fouling bar; Fouling point.

Clearance card (US)
An authority to operate on the main
line.

Clearing House
see RCH.

Clearing point
In absolute block working, the point

ahead of the first stop signal/outer
home signal, usually a quarter of a
mile distant, to which the line must be
clear of obstruction before a signalman
can give permission for another train
to approach.

Clear pop (RS)
A clear signal, i.e. one showing 'off'
indication.

Clee Hill
Ludlow & Clee Hill Rly, inc 1861,
Ludlow–Clee Hill (Corley), including
1 m rope incline, opened 1864,
worked by L&NWR and GWR from
1877, vested in L&NWR and GWR
1893. Used only as a mineral line.
Incline closed 1960, remainder closed
1962.

Clerestory
A raised central section of a coach roof
fitted with ventilators and deck lights,
intended to give extra daylight and
ventilation.

Cleveland Executive
An express between London (Kings
Cross) and Middlesbrough, introduced
1981, withdrawn 1990.

Clickety, The (RS)
Grimsby & Immingham Electric Rly,
GCR/L&NER/BR. From the sound
made by its electric cars running at
high speed.

Clifton Extension Joint
see BPR&P.

Cliftonville Express
A summer service London (Victoria/
Holborn Viaduct)–Ramsgate, 1894
only. Re-introduced 1911, Victoria–
Ramsgate, ceased 1915. Re-introduced
1921, name dropped 1927.

Clinker link (RS)(obs)
Men who cleaned out loco fires in loco
depots.

Cloakroom/Cloakroom business
A facility at stations to deposit luggage
and other items for a small fee.

Clock (USRS)
A loco steam gauge.

Clockface service
A regular interval service providing departures from stations at the same minutes past each hour in the same sequence throughout the day (with the possible exception of peak hours). Introduced for the first L&SWR electric services (1915) and subsequently adopted for the SR electric network, and for many BR services. 'People don't like timetables, make it easy for them' — Sir Herbert Walker, general manager L&SWR.

Clock train, (RS)(obs)
The LB&SCR 'Southern Belle', from the clocks in its Pullman cars.

Clockwork engines (RS)
Midland Rly 0–6–4T with a motion access aperture in the side tank which suggested the key hole of a toy clockwork engine.

Clockwork Orange (RS)
Glasgow Underground Rly as modernized in 1980. From the novel and film of that title and suggested by the new livery and circular nature of the service.

Clockworks (LTRS)
District Line trains.

Clodhoppers (RS)
LM&SR class 4 MT 2–6–0 locos of 1947.

Clog & Knocker (RS)
GCR, or GCR main line.

Clogs on (RS)
A loco or vehicle with flat wheel(s).

Close the gate, to (USRS)
To move points back after a train has passed.

Clown (USRS)
A brakeman or switchman.

Clown wagon (USRS)
A caboose (qv).

CLR
1. Central London Rly, a tube rly, inc 1891, opened Bank to Shepherds Bush 1900, extended to Wood Lane 1908, to Liverpool St 1912. Part of UERL (qv) from 1912.
2. Corringham Light Rly, LRO 1899, Corringham to Coryton (Kynoch Town) and Thames Haven, opened 1901. Closed to passengers 1939, reopened 1945, closed entirely 1952 except for Coryton–Thames Haven section, which was relaid to main line standards and remains in use for oil tanker traffic.

Club (US)
see Brake Club.

Club car (obs)
A special car for men, equipped for service of alcoholic drinks and light refreshments. Cuspidors were placed within convenient range of leather armchairs. Such cars were a regular feature of Pullman accommodation in the US for many years and were also found in British club trains (qv).

Club Train (obs)
A long distance commuter train which included private club cars, in which regular travellers (predominantly if not exclusively male) enjoyed segregation from other passengers and were provided with special facilities such as armchairs, tables, hairdresser/barber, private bar, personal lockers etc. in return for payment of a premium over the season ticket rate. Until the Second World War, club train services operated between Manchester and the North Wales coast, Manchester and the Fylde coast, Manchester and the Lake District etc.

Club Trains, The
First class supplementary fare services between London and Dover (for Calais and Paris) inspired by the Paris

Exhibition of 1889 and operated by the LC&DR, SER and *CIWL*, 1889–1893. 'I'm leaving this afternoon by the Club Train'— Mrs Erlynne in Oscar Wilde's comedy *Lady Windermere's Fan*.

Club winder (USRS)
A brakeman. From brake club (qv).

Clyderail
Brand name for the reopened and electrified Glasgow Central Low Level or Argyle line, Partick to Rutherglen and Cambuslang, linking north and south bank suburban lines, in use from 1979.

CM&GIR
Croydon, Merstham & Godstone Iron Rly, inc 1803, opened from SIR at Croydon to Merstham only, 1805. Closed *c.* 1842.

CME
Chief Mechanical Engineer.

CMP
Chemin de Fer Métropolitain de Paris; Paris Métro or underground rlys. First section opened 1900. Part of *STCRP* (qv) from 1942.

CMR
Cornwall Minerals Rly, Newquay to Fowey and branches, inc 1873, and included existing tramways (*1*) dating from 1847, which were to be converted to rlys. First section opened 1874, worked by GWR from 1877. Absorbed Lostwithiel & Fowey Rly (opened 1869) from 1892. L&FR was closed in 1880 and reopened by GWR 1895. CMR became part of GWR from 1896.

CNR
Canadian National Rlys, inc 1919, to enable various rlys under federal control (including Canadian Northern, Inter-Colonial & National Transcontinental) to be operated by one company for the government.

Amalgamated with Grand Trunk Rly of Canada 1923. All capital owned by the government.

CNW (US)
Chicago & North Western RR.

Coach (or Day Coach) class (US)
The cheapest type of accommodation on trains, broadly equivalent to British Third (later Second and Standard). Reclining seats were often provided for night use.

Coaching stock
Vehicles used in passenger trains, including those not designed to carry passengers.

Coaching traffic (obs)
Any traffic carried by passenger train (including parcels, fish, mail, perishables etc.).

Coal engines (RS)
L&NWR Webb 0–6–0 locos.

Coal heaver (USRS)
A steam loco fireman.

Coal pusher
A steam piston device to push coal forward in the loco tender, thus easing the fireman's task.

Coal stage
A platform from which locos are loaded with coal.

Coal tanks (RS)
L&NWR Webb 0–6–2T; these locos were not confined to coal traffic and were also used on passenger trains.

Coastway
BR brand name for Portsmouth–Brighton–Hastings services, introduced 1972.

Cobbinshaw Line
Cowlairs Junc, Glasgow, to Edinburgh. From the Cobbinshaw summit, west of Kirknewton.

Cobblers (RS)
Electric services between London (Euston) and Northampton.

Cock-loft (USRS)
A cupola (qv).

Cockneys (RS)(obs)
1. GWR men's name for Midland Rly lines and trains in South Wales.
2. Train crews from NLR.
3. NLR 0–6–0T locos.

Cod's mouth, the (RS)(obs)
The effect of the streamlined front casing of L&NER A4 Pacific locos when opened up to give access to the smoke box.

COFC (US)
Container on flat car.

Coffee Pot (RS/USRS)
Any vertical-boilered steam loco; any antiquated loco, especially one with tall chimney.

Coffee Pots (RS)
GER 0–4–0T locos (L&NER class Y5).

Coligny–Welch signal lamp (obs)
Equipment fixed alongside signal lamps of distant signals when these signals had green and red indications, to show a white arrow at night, thus enabling a driver or fireman to distinguish the distant from other signals. From the names of the inventors. Replaced from 1924 by the use of yellow light for distants in the 'on' position.

Coffin (RS)
Any BR air-conditioned coach with sealed windows. The term arises from the frustration of those inclined to indulge in windowhanging (qv).

Collar work (RS)
Any very heavy task for a steam locomotive.

College Boy (LTRS)
An area manager imported from head office.

College of knowledge (RS)
A trade union representative.

Collieries route
Huyton–St Helen's–Tyldesley–Eccles.

Colonel Stephens Rlys
Light rlys associated with Lt.-Col. H.F. Stephens RE (TR) (1868–1931) and managed from 23, Salford Terrace, Tonbridge until 1948, viz EKR, K&ESR, WC&PR, HofM&ST (WSR) and S&MLR (qv).

Color blind (USRS)
A dishonest employee unable to distinguish between his own money and property and that of his employer.

Colosseum
TEE Milan–Rome, introduced 1984, the Settebello (qv) re-equipped. Lost *TEE* status 1985, became EC Frankfurt–Rome, 1987.

Colour-light signal
A signal employing a powerful beam of electric light by day and by night, capable of penetrating fog and providing easy visibility in sunshine. *See also* Multi-aspect signal; Searchlight signal.

Columbia (US)
A steam loco with 2–4–2 wheel arrangement.

Combination train (US)
Mixed traffic train (qv).

Combine Harvesters (RS)
BR Class 9F 2–10–0 steam locos. From their ungainly appearance.

Comeng
Loco and rolling stock builders, Sydney, New South Wales, formerly the Commonwealth Engineering Co.

Comet
1. A steam loco with 0–4–0 wheel arrangement.
2. An express between London (Euston) and Manchester, 1932–39. Re-introduced by BR 1949–62.

Comfort stop
A scheduled stop to allow train crew to use station or depot lavatories.

Comic (RS)

Any newspaper or magazine produced officially for consumption by rly employees.

Common carriers

Until 1962 the rlys of Great Britain were so described because they were obliged to carry any type of freight traffic offered to them. This obligation was removed by the Transport Act 1962.

Common user

1. Any vehicle which can be used for traffic purposes on any part of the rly system irrespective of its ownership.
2. (RS) A female child.

Commonwealth Rlys

see CR (7).

Commuter/commute, to

Originally a US term for the holder of a rly commutation ticket (i.e. season ticket) and the associated travelling. Adopted in UK to describe rly season ticket holders *c.* 1950 and subsequently extended (principally by journalists) to cover all those travelling regularly to and from their daily workplace, by any form of transport, including private motor cars, and the action of so doing.

Company Bible (USRS)

Rly employees' rule book.

Company jewelry (USRS)

Hat badges, points keys, carriage keys etc.

Company notch (USRS)

The position of the steam loco regulator handle most likely to lead to economical coal consumption.

Company train

A freight train worked regularly for full trainload traffic associated with one customer.

Compartment

A partitioned-off section of a coach,

with seats facing and opposite to direction of travel, accommodating on standard gauge two to six passengers each side, according to class and the need to provide space for a side corridor. On corridor stock there may be a door on the outside in addition to the door into the side corridor.

Compensated gradient

An easing of gradient over curves so that resistance offered by curve and gradient together does not exceed that due to the gradient on a straight road.

Compensators

An attachment which allows for contraction or expansion of point rodding.

Composite/compo

A coach containing accommodation for two classes of passenger. *See also* Tri-composite/compo.

Composteur (Fr)

Self-service ticket-validating machine in use on the *SNCF*.

Compound

A design of steam loco in which the expansion of steam is divided into two stages. Two types of cylinders are fitted in various combinations, the high pressure ones taking steam direct from the boiler and then passing it in partially-expanded state into low pressure cylinders, which complete the expansion. If the compounding is well designed, the work done in relation to the amount of coal burnt is high.

Con (US)

Abbreviation for conductor (*3*) (qv).

Concertina (RS)(obs)

A GWR 70 ft/21.34 metre coach of 1906 with recessed doors.

Concrete Bob

Nickname for Robert (later Sir Robert) McAlpine arising from his extensive use of concrete construction when building the West Highland Rly.

Concrete cavern, the (RS)
Birmingham New St. station as rebuilt
in 1967 with a low roof over all
platforms to carry station amenities,
shops etc.

Condensing loco
A loco fitted with arrangements to
divert exhaust steam by means of flap
valves to the upper parts of the water
tanks to provide some improvement in
the atmosphere when working over
tunnel rlys, principally in London,
Liverpool and Glasgow.

Condor
A BR express door-to-door freight
container service, London (Hendon)–
Glasgow, introduced 1959 and
Birmingham–Glasgow, introduced
1963. Both withdrawn 1967.

Conductor
1. An engineman accompanying a loco
   hauled by another.
2. An engineman or guard
   accompanying staff working on an
   unfamiliar line.
3. (US) The official in sole charge of a
   passenger or freight train,
   responsible for its safe operation,
   its administration, care of
   passengers, ticket checking,
   documentation etc. The title was
   also current in Britain in the 1840s
   but was superseded by 'guard' in
   the 1850s. From 1988 all BR
   InterCity guards became known as
   'conductors' or 'senior conductors',
   the latter undertaking a range of
   duties broadly equivalent to those
   of the US passenger train
   conductor.
4. Guards on London Underground
   electric rlys were so described from
   1905 to *c*. 1920 as a consequence of
   US management.
5. The second crew member of a
   tramcar, responsible for collecting

fares, turning the trolley at the end
of the line etc.

Conductor-guard
Term first used by GER in 1921 to
describe guards on branch line and
other local services who were also
required to issue and check tickets on
the trains and assist passengers using
steps at ground-level halts. BR
adopted the term in 1963 to describe
guards given ticket-issuing and
revenue protection responsibilities.

Conductor rail
A rail placed in the centre or at the side
of running rails to carry the positive
traction current, which is collected by
shoes on the locos or emu trains.

Conductor's van (US)(obs)
A caboose (qv).

Conduit blanche (Fr)
White pipe; a through pipe on an
unbraked vehicle or a vehicle
differently braked from the main part
of the train; or a pipe conveying steam
for coach heating.

Conduit track (obs)
Traction system for tramways (3) in
which rails carrying the positive and
return traction current are placed in a
trench and below the running rails.
Traction current is collected and
returned by ploughs fixed to the tramcars
and designed to pass through a
continuous slot above the trench. In the
1900s and 1910s this method, though
more costly to install and maintain, was
favoured as more aesthetically acceptable
than overhead wire trolley systems.

Cone
GWR TC for gunpowder van.

Confederation (US)
A steam loco with 4–8–4 wheel
arrangement.

Conflat
GWR TC for a container flat wagon
with four wheels.

Congressional
A long-lived express between New York and Washington DC, introduced 1885. Scheduled at 3 h 35 min in 1936.

Conker (RS)(obs)
Any motor vehicle used only on rly premises, and not licensed for running on public roads.

Connecting rod
This connects the crosshead on the piston rod of a loco with the crank pin or axle. Pivoted to the crosshead, it converts the backward and forward motion of the piston into the circular motion of the wheels or crank axle.

Conqueror
A London (Charing Cross)–Hastings service, so named in 1987, for that year only.

Conrail
Abbreviation for Consolidated Rail Corporation, a US government enterprise formed on 1 April 1976 to take over some 15,000 m of rly from seven bankrupt private rly companies (B&M; Penn–Central; Erie–Lackawanna; LVR (3); Central of New Jersey; Reading Lines; and Lehigh & Hudson River). A private company from 1987.

Con rod (RS)
Connecting rod (qv).

Consigne (Fr)
A left luggage office.

Consist (US)
Train make-up/formation; also the report sent ahead with this information so that yardmasters can make plans for marshalling. Adopted by BR in 1955.

Consolidated Signal
Consolidated Signal Co., originally the Pneumatic & General Engineering Co.; acquired majority interest in Saxby & Farmer (qv) and Evans O'Donnell & Co. Ltd (qv) in 1901–2,

operating from the latter's Chippenham Works from 1903. Later acquired a controlling interest in McKenzie, Holland & Westinghouse Power Signal Co. (qv). Became part of Westinghouse Brake & Saxby Signal Co. (qv) from 1920.

Consolidation (US)
A steam loco with 2–8–0 wheel arrangement.

Container
A large storage box or tank which can be lifted on and off rail and road vehicles to facilitate transits using both modes.

Conti (obs)
Nickname for the former through service from Birkenhead to Dover (for the Continent) via Reading and Tonbridge.

Continental Club Train
see Club Trains, The.

Continental Express
A GER service between London (Liverpool St.) and Harwich in connection with Antwerp and Rotterdam sailings, introduced 1864; daily from 1882. Separate trains for the Antwerp and the Hook of Holland services 1893; all year round services, 1896. Withdrawn 1914. Restored 1921, with Pullman cars, as 'Continental Restaurant & Pullman Car Expresses', one for each service. The L&NER renamed the services respectively 'The Antwerp Continental' and 'The Hook Continental' in 1927. Amalgamated as one train, 'The Hook & Antwerp Continental', in 1932. From 1938 separate trains again, both ceasing in September 1939. 'Hook Continental' restored 1945, name dropped 1987.

Continental notation
A system of classifying steam locos by enumerating from left to right the

number of axles in any leading truck, the coupled driving wheels and any trailing truck; thus 2–2–1 in Continental notation corresponds to 4–4–2 in Whyte's notation (qv).

Continental services/traffic (obs)
A generic term for rail and sea services/traffic between UK and European mainland current until *c*. 1970.

Continuous blowdown valve
A device to allow a limited amount of water to be continuously blown out of a loco boiler while the regulator is open, thus prolonging the period between boiler washouts.

Continuous [automatic] brakes
Any system of braking all the vehicles in a train simultaneously under the control of driver or guard which is also self-applying in the event of severance of the train or other failure in continuity of brake action. Vacuum and compressed air systems were both formerly employed but the latter is now standard on BR. Continuous automatic brakes have been a government requirement for passenger trains in the UK since 1889.

Contract (obs)
Term used in northern Britain for a season ticket.

Control/Train or Traffic Control
A system of controlling, organizing and reorganizing train and loco movements, staff duties, vehicle provision etc. over a large defined area of rlys, working from a central point, using telephones, diagrams etc. Information on the state of traffic is received from selected signal boxes, depots etc. Controllers have wide powers to adjust timetables in emergencies. First introduced on Midland Rly in 1907–12. Not to be

confused with Automatic Train Control (*see* ATC).

Contrôleur de route (Fr)
Travelling ticket inspector.

Controlled train
see Regulation [of passenger traffic].

Controller
1. A staff grade employed in Control (qv).
2. Apparatus used to control the current applied to the motors of electric locos, emu motor cars and control trailers, and tramcars, allowing regulation of speed by varying the voltage, and also controlling starting, stopping and reversing.

Control orders
Orders issued by Control (qv) arranging special trains, alterations to timetables or staff rosters, or for allocating tasks to spare locos and crews, or rearranging crew duties.

Control trailer
Unmotored car in an mu train containing driving cab and driving controls.

Convertible car
A tramcar design in which the glazed body sides can be fully or partly (semi-convertible) removed for summer operation. Popular in the US from *c*. 1890 until *c*. 1914.

Conveyor car (US)
A motorized freight car used for freight movements on wharves etc.

Conwy/Conway Valley Line
Llandudno Junction–Blaenau Ffestiniog.

Cook (USRS)
A brakeman.

Cook's
see Cook's Timetables; Thomas Cook.

Cook shack (USRS)
A caboose (qv).

Cook's Timetables
Cook's Continental Timetables and Tourists' Handbook, first published 1873, with the aim of providing a handy summary of European train services which could be carried by the traveller. Cook's was the first British timetable to adopt the 24-hour clock system, in 1919. *Cook's Overseas Timetable*, first published in 1981, offers a similar useful abstract of train times for all countries outside Europe.

Coolie (RS)(obs)
A loco fireman.

Coon, to (USRS)
1. To operate a train at low speed.
2. To walk along the tops of cars.

Coordonnée, une ligne (Fr)
A line open for freight but whose passenger traffic is entrusted to a 'co-ordinated' road service shown in the rly timetable, calling at the rly stations and making convenient connection with other rly services.

Cop, to/cop, a (RS)
To see and record a loco for the first time. Also used as a noun. In use in this sense in the 1920s if not earlier. From northern English dialect, to cop = to capture, to catch. *See also* Train spotter.

Cop book (RS)
Notebook containing details of cops (qv).

Coppernobs (RS)
Furness Rly Bury 0–4–0 locos.

Coppertops (RS)
SE&CR Wainwright D class 4–4–0 locos.

Copypit Line, The
[Leeds–]Halifax–Burnley–Blackburn [–Preston–Blackpool]. *See also* Roses Line, The.

COR
SR four-car emu CORridor sets of 1937–8 for Portsmouth and Mid-

Sussex electrifications, two motor brake Second/Standard class cars, one Second/Standard trailer and one composite trailer, 4-COR. Also BR six-car emu sets of 1965 made up from 6-PUL and 6-PAN units, 6-COR.

Corail
Inter-city VTU 75 centre-aisle passenger stock with two-tone grey livery used on accelerated internal services introduced by the *SNCF* from 1975 onwards. First *SNCF* standard stock with air-conditioning. Name derived from *COnfort et RAIL*.

Coral
GWR TC for four-wheel glass-carrying truck.

Cordon
GWR TC for gas reservoir truck.

Cork Express
Dublin to Cork non-stop service introduced 1953.

Corks (RS)(obs)
Boiler tubes choked with ashes.

Corner, to (USRS)
To move a car or wagon in a siding to a position in which it fouls another line.

Cornfield meet (USRS)
A head-on collision of two trains on a single line.

Cornishman
1. Unofficial name for an express introduced in 1890 between London (Paddington) and Penzance via Bristol. Not used after 1904.
2. A relief to The Cornish Riviera, running only in 1935.
3. An express between Wolverhampton and Torquay/Penzance, introduced in 1952 and later extended to Leeds and Bradford. Name dropped 1975.
4. An express between Edinburgh and Penzance, introduced 1986.

Cornish Riviera Express/Limited
An express between London

(Paddington) and Penzance via
Westbury, introduced 1904 as Cornish
Riviera Limited. 'Limited' dropped
1977.

Cornish Scot
An Edinburgh, Glasgow and Penzance
service, introduced 1987.

Cornwall Rly
see CR (*4*).

Coronation
A L&NER supplementary fare
streamlined express with 'beaver-tail'
observation car, and meals served at
seats; ran between London (Kings
Cross) and Edinburgh in 6 h, 1937–9.

Coronation Land Cruise
see Land cruise.

Coronation Scot
A LM&SR streamlined express
between London (Euston) and
Glasgow, 1937–9. It carried a
maximum of only 232 passengers;
journey time 6 h 30 min.

Correo, tren (Sp)
A stopping train conveying mails.

Corridor
A passageway between the outer side
of a coach and compartments, allowing
passengers access to lavatories and, via
corridor connections, to other parts of
the train. *See also* Vestibuled [train/
coach].

Corridor, The
West Coast Corridor Express (qv).

Corridor tender
A loco tender vestibuled to its train
and incorporating a side corridor
which allowed engine crews to change
over during non-stop runs. Introduced
on the L&NER in 1928.

Corris Rly
see CR (*3*).

Corrugation
A regular pattern of alternate ridges
and hollows appearing on the running
surface of rails. Caused by various

factors, not properly understood, and
most frequently encountered on
electric rlys. When present, the
passage of a train is marked by a
characteristic roaring noise. Cured by
use of rail-grinders (qv). Also a
problem on tramways (*3*).

Cosh it, to (LTRS)
To make an emergency brake
application using driver's brake
handle.

Côte d'Azur Pullman-Express
A *CIWL* service between Paris, Nice
and Ventimiglia, introduced 1929,
ceased 1939.

Cotswold & Malvern Express
A service between London
(Paddington), Worcester and Great
Malvern introduced 1985. Extended to
Hereford and renamed Cotswold
Express, 1988. Renamed Cotswold &
Malvern Express, 1989.

Cotswold Line
Oxford–Worcester.

Cotter
A wedge used for tightening the ends
of the connecting rod of a loco.

Cotton Belt
Nickname of the St Louis
Southwestern RR.

Couchette (Fr)
A coach with low cost double or triple
berth sleeping accommodation
arranged in compartments opening on
to a corridor.

Count ties, to (USRS)
To reduce speed to the point at which it
becomes possible to count the sleepers.

Country end
The end of a station opposite to the
London end (qv).

County tanks
GWR 4–4–2T rebuilt from County
Class 4–4–0 locos.

Coupé
A half-compartment; also the private

compartment at one end of the classic British Pullman cars.

Coupling rod
The exterior rod which couples together the driving wheels of a loco.

Coupling screw
Two iron links with right and left hand screw between them and a lever in the centre allowing the couplings of passenger coaches and fitted wagons to be screwed taut until buffers press into one another, so preventing oscillation at high speed.

Coupling stick (obs)
A shunter's pole fitted with a hook at one end, used to couple and uncouple wagons.

Coupon ticket
A ticket for a long journey valid for travel over two or more rly systems, with detachable coupons covering different sections of the journey.

Cowboy Line (LTRS)
The East London Line.

Cowcatcher
A metal grid fixed to buffer beam of loco, railcar or interurban car and designed to push aside any obstruction on the track.

Cow crate (USRS)
A cattle wagon.

Cow puncher (USRS)
A derisive term for a cowboy riding stock trains (qv) and prodding cattle when loading and unloading.

Cow Shed, The (RS)
The Waterloo Area Signalling Centre, Wimbledon. From its featureless, utilitarian appearance.

Cow's horn (RS)
A hook shaped like a cow's horn on which single line tokens, usually enclosed in a pouch with a loop attached, are deposited by train crews without stopping the train.

Cow's udder (RS)
A plastic sleeve for twin connections between vehicles.

CP
Companhia dos Caminhos de Ferro Portugueses; Portuguese Rly Authority.

CPR
Canadian Pacific Rly, inc 1881, completed Montreal–Vancouver trans-Canada line in 1887, absorbed many smaller companies and became the largest ocean-steamship owning rly in the world, operating trans-Atlantic and trans-Pacific routes.

CR
1. Caledonian Rly, inc 1845, first section opened 1847, 1,117 route miles by 1914, mainly in central Scotland. Became part of LM&SR from 1923.
2. Cardiff Rly, inc 1897, lines in Cardiff Bute Docks; also Heath Junc, Cardiff to Rhydyfelin Halt near Treforest (intended junc with TVR not completed). Opened freight 1909, passengers 1911. Part of GWR from 1922.
3. Corris Rly, Machynlleth to Aberllefeni and Ratgoed Quarry 2 ft 3 in/686 mm gauge, inc 1858 as Corris, Machynlleth & River Dovey Tramroad, opened 1859, name changed to CR 1864, relaid and operated by locos from 1878, passenger service from 1883, absorbed by GWR 1930, passenger service ceased 1931, closed 1948. Preservation project in progress.
4. Cornwall Rly, Plymouth to Falmouth, inc 1846, leased to GWR, B&ER and SDR 1859, opened 1859, 1863. Part of GWR from 1889.
5. Cambrian Rlys: *see* Cambrian.

6. Central Rly [of India], formed 1951.
7. Commonwealth Rlys [Australia]. Part of ANR (qv) from 1975.

Crab (RS)
LM&SR Hughes Class 5 2–6–0 steam locos of 1926. From the appearance of the outside motion in action.

Crab and Winkle
Nickname for GER Brightlingsea and Tollesbury branches and possibly for other branches to coastal towns.

Cracker (RS)
A detonator.

Cradle (USRS)
A gondola or hopper wagon.

Crampton
A type of loco designed by Thomas Russell Crampton (1816–88) in which a low centre of gravity was obtained by placing the driving wheels behind the boiler and firebox.

Crampton, prendre le, (Fr)(obs)
Expression for taking the train, after Thomas Russell Crampton, locomotive engineer, whose designs were very popular in France. Also *M'sieu' Crampton*, (obs) colloquial Fr term for a rlyman.

Crankex
TC for a special train chartered by rly enthusiasts.

Cravens
Cravens Railway Carriage & Wagon Co. Ltd, Darnall, Sheffield, established 1867. Rolling stock activities taken over by Metro–Cammell (qv) in 1965.

CRC
Continental Railway Circle. Catering for those interested in European mainland rlys.

Creep
Rail creep (qv).

Creeper (LTRS)
A three-aspect draw-up signal which can be passed at low speed.

Crescent Limited
A Southern Rly System express between New Orleans and New York, introduced 1925. Became an Amtrak service in 1971, renamed Southern Crescent, later renamed The Crescent.

Crested Goods (RS)
Another name for cauliflowers (qv).

Crewe goods (RS)
Early L&NWR 2–4–0 locos.

Crewe type
A loco with inclined outside cylinders set between two deep iron frames. Known in France as *le Buddicom* after its introduction there by William Buddicom.

CRI&P
see Rock Island.

Crib (USRS)
A caboose (qv).

Cricket
GWR TC for eight-wheel composite coach.

Crimea
Name given (e.g. Crimea Sidings) to any rly installation broadly contemporary with the Crimean War (1853–6).

Crime sheet (RS)
The personal record of an employee, including a note of any disciplinary offences.

Criminal link (RS)(obs)
A link (qv) incorporating much trip (qv) and shunting work, to which top link drivers were posted after committing disciplinary offences.

Crimson Ramblers (RS)
Midland Rly 4–4–0 compound locos. From their use all over the LM&SR system.

Cripple (RS/USRS)
Any defective, damaged or worn
vehicle.
Cripple train (USRS)
A breakdown train (qv).
CRO (obs)
Chief Regional Officer, in charge of
BR regions under the BTC regime
1948–55. In the latter year they
became general managers under the
Area Boards.
Crocodile
GWR TC for long low truck ('trolley')
for conveying rolling stock, lofty road
vehicles, boilers etc. There were
thirteen types (A to M).
Cromer Express
A service between London (Liverpool
St.) and Cromer, by-passing Norwich,
introduced in 1897, renamed Norfolk
Coast Express (qv) 1907.
Crompton Parkinson
Crompton Parkinson (Chelmsford)
Ltd. Established as Crompton & Co.
Ltd 1888, became CP Ltd 1927
after amalgamation with E. & A.
Parkinson Ltd. Manufacturers of
electric traction equipment. Taken
over by Hawker Siddeley Group 1967,
rail traction business transferred to
Brush (qv).
Cromptons (RS)
BR diesel locos class 33, from
the manufacturer, Crompton–
Parkinson.
Cronks (RS)
BR diesel locos class 08.
Cross, The (RS)
Kings Cross Station, London, and
associated depots.
Crossing
The place in a set of points or
diamond crossing (qv) where two lines
of rail first come into contact and
the wheels following one rail cross
over another. In points, the type of

crossing in general use is the 'V' or
frog.
Crossing place or loop
The point on a stretch of single line at
which double track is provided to
allow trains or tramcars proceeding in
opposite directions to pass. On rlys
usually sited at a station, for
convenience.
Crossover/crossover road
A pair of rails leading from one line to
another to allow trains to be moved
from up to down line or vice versa.
Term also used on tramways (3) to
denote a connection allowing reversal
on double track lines.

CrossRail
see East–West CrossRail.
Crow
A sequence of five loco whistle signal
blasts, imitating a cock's crow.
Crown, to (USRS)
To complete a train by attaching the
caboose. Until this is done the train is
referred to as a cut (qv) of cars .
Crow's nest (USRS)
A cupola (qv).
CRS
Computerized Reservations System
(BR).
Crummy (USRS)
The commonest slang term for a
caboose (qv).
Crumpet line (LTRS)(obs)
A diagonal stripe to denote season
ticket issued to a female commuter,
thus assisting detection of fraudulent
use. From (S) crumpet = the female
sex.

Crystal Palaces (RS)
GER '1300' (L&NER F7) 2–4–2T,
from their disproportionately large
side-windowed cabs.

CS
Carriage sidings; also carriage/coaching
stock.

CS&TE
Chief Signals & Telegraphs/
Telecommunications Engineer.

ČSD
Československé Státní Dráhy;
Czechoslovakian State Rlys.

CSX Transportation Inc
A conglomerate of shipping, rly and
other companies which from 1980
included the B&O (qv) and SCL (qv).

CT
Control Trailer (qv).

CTAC
Creative Tourist Agents' Conference.
A consortium of nine UK travel
agencies and firms formed in 1932 and
reconstituted in 1946. It chartered
special trains for Continental holidays
from 1933–9 and from 1946–68, also
from the Midlands and the North to
Scotland from 1952–65. Disbanded
1969.

CTC
Centralized Traffic Control. A system,
first used in the US in 1927, in which
the signalling of a long section of rly is
undertaken from one control point,
using illuminated diagrams which
show the position of any trains on the
line, and push buttons which can
operate the signals and points and set
up non-conflicting routes for any train
movement. First used in Great Britain
on the Metropolitan Rly's new
Stanmore branch, 1932.

CTCC
Central Transport Consultative
Committee, established 1948 under the
1947 Transport Act, reconstituted

1962. Represents the interests of users
of BR and investigates complaints,
taking a national view. Its remit
excludes fares and charges. There are
eight separate Transport Users'
Consultative Committees (TUCC) for
designated areas of Great Britain
including one for London (the London
Regional Passengers' Committee).
These have a similar function but
concentrate on local matters; they also
have the duty of considering and
reporting to ministers upon proposed
withdrawals of passenger services.

CTO (obs)
BR open carriage truck.

CTRL
Channel Tunnel Rail Link, the new
rly between London and the Channel
Tunnel.

CTT
Cook's Time Tables: *see* Cook's
Timetables; Thomas Cook.

Cuckoo line
Nickname for Eridge–Polegate line,
LB&SCR.

Cuffley Loop
Hertford Loop (qv).

Culemeyer (Ger)
A road vehicle designed to carry a
loaded rail wagon.

Culm Valley
Light rly from Tiverton Junc to
Hemyock, inc 1873, opened 1876, part
of GWR from 1880.

Culvert
Pipe or small tunnel beneath a rly
embankment carrying water from one
side to the other.

Cu Na Mara
A service between Dublin and Galway,
introduced 1960, name dropped 1975.

Cunarder
A boat train between London
(Waterloo) and Southampton Docks,
introduced 1952, to connect with

sailings of RMS *Queen Mary* and *Queen Elizabeth*. Ceased 1968.

Cunard Firsts
GWR 70 ft/21.34 metres eight-compartment corridor First class coaches built for Atlantic liner boat trains to and from Fishguard 1909–14.

Cupboard, The (RS)
Coppermill Junction, GER (Walthamstow, East London).

Cupboard, in the (RS)
Placed in a layby or loop to allow another train to pass on the running line.

Cupola (US)
A covered lookout cabin raised above the roof of a caboose (qv).

Cushions (RS/USRS)
Passenger vehicles. *See also* On the cushions.

Customer
BR term for a passenger, introduced 1988.

Customer train
Company train (qv).

Cut
1. (US) A cutting.
2. (USRS) Two or more cars coupled together without a caboose.
3. (RS)(obs) A part of a train; a set of two or more wagons in a yard bound for the same destination or for the same siding in the yard.

Cut and cover
A method of building tunnels and underground rlys by cutting out a trench and roofing it with girder work.

Cut back, to
To remove a service, or all services, from the outer end of a branch or route. Mostly used of tramways (*3*).

Cut card (obs)
A document showing in code the cuts (*3*) (qv) into which a train must be split for marshalling, the destination siding of each cut, the number of

wagons in each, and other information.

Cut-off
1. The period of steam admission to the cylinders of a loco as controlled by the driver when using the valve gear. At the moment of starting, cut-off is about 75 per cent but it can be reduced until the loco is cutting off in the cylinders at 25 or 20 per cent of piston stroke.
2. Term used by shunters, guards etc meaning to uncouple vehicles.

Cutter-up (RS)(obs)
An employee in a marshalling yard who divides a train into cuts (qv) for various destinations.

CV&HR
Colne Valley & Halstead Rly, Chappel & Wakes Colne to Halstead and Haverhill, inc 1856, 1859, opened 1860, 1861, 1862, 1863, part of L&NER 1923. Short section at Castle Hedingham now preserved as 'Colne Valley Rly'.

CV&YR
Cheddar Valley & Yatton Rly, Yatton Junc to Wells (S&DR Junc), inc 1864. In 1865 powers transferred to B&ER who built it; opened 1869, 1870. Built to broad gauge, converted 1875.

CVLR
Cairn Valley (qv).

CVR
1. Clogher Valley Rly, NI, Maguiresbridge–Tynan, 3 ft/914 mm gauge, inc 1884 as a tramway. Much of it was built as a tramway (*4*). Opened 1887, title changed to CVR 1894, closed 1941 (officially, but actually in the early hours of 1942, delayed deliberately 'to get the better of the Government').
2. Chipstead Valley Rly (qv).
3. Colne Valley Rly: *see* CV&HR.
4. Culm Valley Rly (qv).

CWE
Carriage and Wagon Examiner.
CWR
Continuous Welded Rail over
distances exceeding half a mile. *See*
also LWR/LWT.
Cycnus
TEE Milan–Ventimiglia, introduced
1973, lost *TEE* status 1978.

D

DA
Disturbance Allowance.

Dagger
TC instructing signalman to 'cease accepting [trains] without assent'.

Daisies (RS)
The 0–8–4 locos used at Wath Yards.

Daisy chain (USRS)
The type of derailment that can occur as a train negotiates a very sharp curve.

Dales Rail
A scheme started in 1975 to sponsor and organize rail services in the Yorkshire Dales area, also connecting buses for ramblers using the Settle & Carlisle and other rly services.

Dalmatia Express
A service between Ostend and Rijeka, introduced 1958, renamed Rijeka Express 1969. Dalmatia Express then became a Stuttgart–Split service, later combined with Stuttgart–Sarajevo services as Mostar–Dalmatia.

Damo
GWR TC for covered motor car truck.

Damper
A cover fixed to the ash pan of a steam loco to regulate the supply of air to the firebox.

Dance the carpet, to (USRS)
To be the subject of a disciplinary investigation or interview in a manager's or supervisor's office (cf. British (S) 'On the carpet').

Dancing (RS)
Loco wheels slipping on the rails and preventing movement.

D&A Joint
Inc as Dundee & Arbroath Rly, 1836, 5 ft 6 in/1,676 mm gauge, opened 1838, 1839, 1840. Converted to standard gauge 1847. Vested in Scottish North Eastern Rly 1862, part of CR (1) 1866, jointly vested in CR (1) and NBR from 1880, including the Carmyllie mineral branch, opened 1854 by Lord Panmure. LM&SR & L&NER Joint 1923–47. Carmyllie branch became Carmyllie Light Rly (LRO 1898), providing a passenger service 1900–29; freight services ceased 1965.

D&B Joint
Dumbarton & Balloch Joint Rly, inc 1891 (see L&DR), opened 1896, joint NBR, CR (1) and L&DR. Vested in CR (1) and NBR from 1909. LM&SR & L&NER joint 1923–47.

D&BJR
Dublin & Belfast Junction Rly, inc 1845 Drogheda to Portadown. Opened 1849, 1850, 1852. Part of GNR (I) from 1876.

D&BT
Dublin & Blessington Tramway, steam tramway (4) between Dublin (Terenure) and Blessington, opened 1888. Extension to Poulaphouca opened 1890, closed 1928. Physical connection at Terenure with Dublin electric tramway system. Main line closed 1932.

D&CR
Devon & Cornwall Rly, a renaming of

OR (2) (qv), inc 1865. Yeoford–North Tawton opened 1865, extended to Sampford Courtenay 1867, to Okehampton 1871, to Lydford 1874. Leased to L&SWR, part of L&SWR from 1874.

D&D
Dean & Dawson Ltd, a travel agency owned by the GCR/L&NER/BTC/ THC. Part of Thomas Cook (qv) from 1969.

D&H (US)
Delaware & Hudson Rly Co. Acquired by CPR (qv) 1991.

D&KR
Dublin & Kingstown Rly, inc 1831, opened 1834, Dublin to Dun Laoghaire, first rly in Ireland, 4 ft 8½ in/1, 435 mm gauge. Part of Waterford, Wexford, Wicklow & Dublin Rly (see D&SER), 1846. Converted to 5 ft 3 in/1,600 mm gauge, 1857.

D&LST/D&LER
Inc as Dublin & Lucan Steam Tramway 1880, opened 1881, 1883, 3 ft/914 mm gauge, tramway (4). Extension to Leixlip inc as Lucan, Leixlip & Cellbridge Steam Tramway 1889, opened to Leixlip only 1890. Renamed D&L Electric Rly 1897 and gauge changed to 3 ft 6 in/1,067 mm. Leixlip–Lucan steam tramway closed 1897. D&LER electrically worked with double and single deck overhead trolley wire tramcars from 1900, freight wagons hauled by electric loco. Leixlip extension reopened as electric tramway by Lucan & Leixlip Electric Rly, 1910, worked by D&LER. Line closed 1925. The two undertakings became part of the Dublin United Tramways from 1927 and the tracks were rebuilt to 5 ft 3 in/1,600 mm gauge to Lucan only. Reopened as part of the Dublin city tramways system in 1928, closed 1940.

D&RGW (US)
Denver & Rio Grande Western RR Co.

D&SER
Dublin & South Eastern Rly, Dublin, Wicklow, Waterford and Wexford, inc 1846 as Waterford, Wexford, Wicklow & Dublin Rly, and including D&KR (qv) which had been opened in 1834. Generally known as Dublin, Wicklow & Wexford Rly. Opened 1854, 1856, 1864, 1872, 1887, 1891, 1904. Name changed to D&SER 1907. Part of GSR from 1925.

D&SR
Devon & Somerset Rly, inc 1864, Norton Fitzwarren to Barnstaple, opened 1871–3, worked by B&ER and then GWR, absorbed by GWR 1901.

Dandy (RS)(obs)
A small four-wheeled coach hauled by a horse, especially that on the Port Carlisle branch of the NBR.

Dandy cart (obs)
A wagon in which a horse travelled to descend an incline, behind a train going down under gravity, after having hauled a train up.

Danger ticket
A ticket handed to a driver by a pilotman or by a signalman controlling a swing bridge. Until the ticket is personally collected by the signalman or pilotman, the train is not allowed to proceed.

Danubiu
A CIWL Pullman service between Bucharest and Galatz, 1932–9, a renaming of the Dunarea.

Dare Valley
Aberdare to Nantmelyn and Bwllfa Dare Colliery, inc 1863, opened 1866, worked by TVR, leased to TVR 1871, part of TVR 1889.

Dark money (LTRS)
Unsocial hours allowance.

DART
Dublin Area Rapid Transit; name
adopted for Dublin suburban electric
services when introduced in 1984.

Dart
A catch on the inside of the smokebox
door of a steam loco.

Dartford Loop
London (Charing Cross/Cannon St.)–
Hither Green–Sidcup–Dartford.

Dart Valley
Totnes to Ashburton line. Section
between Buckfastleigh and a point
near Totnes now operated as a
preserved line, first section opened
1969, under various names: Dart
Valley Light Rly, Buckfast Steam Rly,
Primrose Line, and (1990) the South
Devon Rly.

Dating press
A device invented in 1837 by Thomas
Edmondson (1792–1851) to stamp
the date of issue on the small
cardboard passenger tickets of
his design, printed on a machine of his
design. Tickets were consecutively
numbered and kept in racks.
This combined system, which replaced
the laborious arrangement of
writing out an individual ticket for
each passenger, and recording the
issue in a book,was virtually universal
on British rlys for many years,
not finally disappearing until the
late 1980s. *See also* Edmondson
ticket.

Day Coach (US)
see Coach (or Day Coach) class.

Day Continental
A BR boat train between London
(Liverpool St.) and Harwich
(Parkeston Quay) introduced 1947,
name dropped 1987.

Daylight sidings
Tracks on which engine movements
are forbidden after dark.

DB
1. *Deutsche Bundesbahn*; formed 1949
   to take over *DR* lines in Western
   Germany following the formation of
   the Federal Republic.
2. *Deutsche Bahn*; German Rlys, an
   amalgamation of *DB* (*1*) and *DR*
   following the 1990 reunification of
   Germany.

DB (LT)
Disciplinary Board. Also (LTRS) 'to
be DB'd' – to appear before a DB.

DBSO
A BR driving brake Second/Standard
class open coach.

DC, The (RS)
Any section of BR or LT operated by
direct current (dc) electric traction,
usually to distinguish it from a nearby
line operated by alternating current
(ac).

DCR
Dorset Central Rly, inc 1856,
Wimborne to Blandford. Opened
1860, 1862. part of S&DJR (qv) 1862.

DD (obs)
BR (S) Double Deck four-car units
introduced 1949, two driving motor
cars and two trailers, 4-DD.

Dead (RS)
A train or loco suffering loss of power.

Dead buffers
Buffers consisting of nothing more
than square wooden beams.

Dead centre
The position in which a steam loco
comes to a stand and in which,
when the regulator is opened to
re-start, the valves are covering the
steam ports, preventing steam from
entering the cylinders. Overcome by
reversing.

Dead early (LTRS)
A duty covering first train of the day.

Dead end kid (RS)
An employee refusing promotion.

Dead end siding
A siding with access at one end only.
Dead engine (RS)
A loco not in steam.
Deadhead (USRS)
1. Empty stock or other unproductive working
2. An employee travelling free on a pass or any other non-revenue-earning passenger.
3. A brakeman.
Dead late (LTRS)
A duty covering last train of the traffic day.
Dead load
The tare weight of a wagon or coach including all its permanent fixtures.
Deadman's handle/button/control
A safety device incorporated in the master controller of an electric train which requires the driver to exercise a continuous pressure to prevent interruption of current supply and the application of the brakes. Invented in 1902 by the American Frank J. Sprague. Originally (RS), but later adopted officially. *See also* DSD.
Dead signal (RS)
Signal permanently at the danger or 'on' position, often lettered 'STOP'.
Dean and Dawson
see D&D.
Dean Forest Rly
A preserved line from Lydney to Park End over part of former S&WJR. *See also* S&WR&C.
Dean Goods (RS)
GWR 0–6–0 locos, designed by William Dean, introduced 1883–99. Many saw service in war zones overseas in both World Wars.
Dearness Valley
Dearness Valley Rly, NER Waterhouses branch, inc 1855, part of NER 1857, opened 1858, passenger service 1877.

Dearne Valley
DVR (*1*) (qv).
Death chamber (RS)
The high voltage cubicle in a diesel loco.
Death, Railway of
see Railway of Death.
Deauville Express
CIWL Pullman train between Paris and Deauville; ran only in 1927.
DEBG (Ger)
Deutsche Eisenbahn Betriebs-Gesellschaft; a co. owning secondary rlys, mainly in southern Germany.
Decapod
Any steam loco with ten coupled driving wheels.
Decauville line
Any light rly of narrow (usually 60 cm) gauge. From Decauville track (qv).
Decauville track
Pre-fabricated narrow gauge (usually 60 cm) track, produced in unit lengths to facilitate ease of transport and fast laying. Much used in France and French Empire for military and other light rlys. After its inventor, Paul Amand Decauville.
Deccan Queen
An express between Bombay and Poona.
Decency board (obs)
A screen placed below the upper deck rails of an open-topped tramcar to protect ladies' ankles and legs from the vulgar masculine gaze.
Deck
1. (US) Footplate (qv) and also the footwalk on the roofs of freight cars.
2. *see* Bank (*2*).
Deck, to
see Decking.
Deckhand (USRS)
Vagrant (US = hobo) who steals a free ride on the roof of a freight car.

Deckies (RS)(obs)
Persons working on goods loading
decks in depots and warehouses.
Usage confined to the GWR.

Decking (USRS)
Riding on the roof of a freight wagon.

Decklights
Long and narrow windows in the
clerestory (qv) of a passenger coach.

Decorate, to (USRS)
To climb to the roof of a freight car.

Deeside Line/Rly
Aberdeen to Ballater.

Déferée, une ligne (Fr)
see Déposée, une ligne (qv).

Deiseach
A service between Waterford,
Kilkenny and Dublin, introduced
1970, name dropped 1975.

Delayer (USRS)
A train dispatcher; *see* Train order.

Dels (RS)
Deltics (qv).

Deltics (RS)
BR class 55 3,300hp diesel-electric
locos introduced 1961. From the
profile of their diesel engines.

Demi-car
A small single deck tramcar designed
or adapted for one-man operation.

DEMU
Diesel-electric multiple unit.

Demurrage
A charge raised for the detention by
consignor or consignee of wagons, wagon-
sheets or containers held beyond a pre-
scribed free period, also for wagons held up
in transit to meet a trader's convenience.

Den (USRS)
A caboose (qv).

Denver Zephyr
An express diesel set running between
Chicago and Denver, introduced 1936.

Déposée, une ligne (Fr)
A line which has been closed and
completely lifted.

Depot (pronounced *deepo***)** (US)
A station; now largely superseded by
'train station'.

Depression bar
see Clearance/depression bar.

Derail (US)
Catch points (qv).

Derailer
A device which can be moved into
position on top of a running rail to
derail a loco attempting to back on to its
train before the road is set. It
requires less space than catch or trap
points.

Derby (RS)
Midland Rly, later London Midland
Region, BR.

Derrick car (US)
A crane wagon.

Derry Express
A Belfast–Londonderry service,
introduced 1950.

Derwent Valley
see DVLR (*1*).

Describer
see Train describer/indicator.

Desert Driver (RS)(obs)
A steam engineman in fear of running
short of water and/or sand.

DESG (Ger)
*Deutsche Eisenbahn Speisewagen
Gesellschaft*. A pre-1914 subsidiary of
CIWL (qv) which operated restaurant
cars in Germany.

Desk Jockey (RS)
A clerk.

Det (LTRS)
A detonator.

Detainer (USRS)
A train dispatcher; *see* Train order.

Detector bar
The part of a signal interlocking
mechanism which warns the signalman
that points are not properly home.

Detectors, point
A mechanical system which aligns signal

wire slides and point slots to ensure that signals cannot be cleared unless point blades are fully home and have correctly responded to the lever movement.

Detonator
see Fog signal.

Devils (RS)
Coal braziers.

Devil's Arrow, The (RS)
BR double arrow logo.

Devon & Cornwall Special
A Third-class-only express between London (Paddington) and Falmouth with through coaches to Torquay, Paignton and Newquay, operated in 1913–14.

Devon Belle
An all-Pullman summer-only express, with rear observation car, between London (Waterloo) and Ilfracombe/Plymouth, introduced 1947, Plymouth section withdrawn 1950, ceased 1954.

Devon Great Consols Mineral Rly
A mining rly running north from the River Tamar and Tavistock Canal at Morwellham, 1858–1901.

Devonian
A summer express between Bradford and Leeds and Torquay and Paignton, introduced 1927, ceased 1939. Re-introduced by BR 1949. Name dropped 1975. Revived 1987 as Leeds–Paignton.

Devon Scot
A through service between Aberdeen and Plymouth via Birmingham, introduced 1988.

Devon Valley
see DVR (*2*).

DGS
BR driving trailer with guard's accommodation (Driving Guard Second/Standard class).

DH
Diesel-hydraulic.

DI
District Inspector. Still used on LT

rlys, after the correct title became Area Manager.

Diagram
A schedule designed to obtain the best working arrangements for train crews, rolling stock and locos over a given period of time, showing the routes and services to be covered, times etc.

Diamant
A Paris–Brussels–Amsterdam service introduced 1954, became Antwerp–Bonn 1962. Name then given to *TEE* Antwerp–Dortmund, introduced 1965, reduced to Brussels–Dortmund 1966, Cologne–Brussels 1968–70, Hanover–Brussels 1970–6. Name revived 1979 for a Hamburg–Munich service. Lost *TEE* status 1981.

Diameter
For rly purposes the diameter of a wheel is measured across the tread at its centre, ignoring the flange.

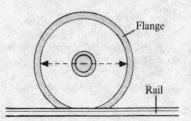

Diamond cracker/pusher (USRS)
A loco fireman. From black diamonds = coal.

Diamond crossing
A track crossing another track diagonally, the rails so forming a diamond or lozenge shape.

Dice train (USRS)
A fast train.
Dick
1. W.B. Dick & Co., Kilmarnock,
builders of locos, and tramway and
narrow gauge rly equipment
(including cars) from 1881. Became
Dick, Kerr & Co., 1883 (DK (qv)).
2. (LTRS) District Line, LT.
Diddly Dike (RS)(obs)
Cheltenham–Andover line, M&SWJR.
Diddy box (LTRS)
A small disconnection box used with
signalling equipment.
Dido (RS)(obs)
A GCR and L&NER train service for
rlymen, Bulwell Common to
Annesley, The 'Annesley Dido'. Dido
is obs (S) for a prank, a shindy.
Die, to (USRS)
To bring a train to a stop on a hill, or
to stall or lose motive power.
Diggle Route
Huddersfield–Stalybridge.
Dike, to (RS)
To signal a train into a refuge siding.
Dilly (LTRS)
Piccadilly Line, LT.
Dilly road (USRS)
A spur line.
Diner (USRS)
A restaurant car.
Dinger (USRS)
A yardmaster or a conductor (3) (qv).
Dinky (USRS)
A four-wheel tramcar; also a small loco.
Dinting (RS)
Digging out old ballast.
Dip (LTRS)
A flyunder.
Diploducus (Fr)
A large rail-mounted crane used by
French Army Engineers.
Dippers (RS)
LM&SR Hughes 2–6–0 locos. From
the 'dip' in the footplate.

Direct-Orient Express
A *CIWL* service between Paris, Milan
and Belgrade, introduced 1921. Re-
introduced 1950, extended to Istanbul
1962–7. Ceased to run beyond Venice
1977 and name dropped. This was the
last through Paris–Istanbul service and
the last of the long distance *CIWL*
European international sleeping and
dining car services. *See also* Marco
Polo; Marmara Express; Orient
Express.
Directors (RS)
GCR 4–4–0 locos named after the
company's directors.
Direct Portsmouth
see PR (*4*).
Direttisima (It)
FS lines built to give faster and more
direct routes between the major Italian
cities.
Direttisimo, treno (It)
An express train. Originally a mail
train with accommodation restricted to
First and old Second class.
Diretto, treno (It)
A semi-fast train or 'ordinary express'.
Dirt, in the (RS)
Derailed or driven into a sand drag.
Dirt, to hit the (USRS)
To jump or fall from a moving
train.
Dirt relief (LTRS)
Trainmen's physical needs relief.
Dirty, Ragged and Greasy, The
Nickname for D&RGW (qv).
Disc
A ground signal.
Dishwasher (USRS)
A loco cleaner.
Dispatcher/dispatching
see Train order.
Display board
A white board fixed behind a
semaphore signal to enhance its
visibility.

Distant signal

The first signal of a set seen from
approaching trains, usually sited one-
quarter to three-quarters of a mile
before the first stop signal (home or
outer home) to which it applies. If at
danger, it indicates that the home or
stop signal ahead is likely to be in that
position and the driver may pass it at
reduced speed until he can see the
indication of the stop signal. If 'off'
(clear), it indicates that the subsequent

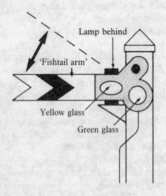

signal is also 'off' and it can only be
cleared if this is so. Semaphore distant
arms are fish-tailed in shape (i.e. a vee
notch cut into the outer end of the
arm). At night such signals originally
showed a white light when 'on' but
c. 1900 this was altered to red. From
1924 the 'on' light was again changed,
this time to orange/yellow. *See also*
Warning boards.

District

Abbreviation for MDR (qv) or, after
1933, the equivalent District Line of
LT.

DIT (US)

Dead In Train; the movement of an
inactive loco as part of a train.

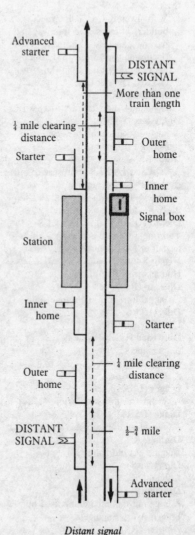

Distant signal

Ditch, to (USRS)
1. To derail a train [often putting it in the drainage ditch at the side of the track].
2. To throw a vagrant (hobo) off a train.

Ditch, in the (USRS)
Wrecked or derailed; *see* Ditch, to.

Division (LTRS)
Divisional Manager's Office.

Dixie (US)
A steam loco with 4–8–4 wheel arrangement.

DK
Dick, Kerr & Co. Ltd, Britannia Works, Kilmarnock. Formerly Dick (*1*) (qv); founded 1883, builders of steam tramway locos and suppliers of equipment for tramways (*3*). New works set up at Preston in 1899 for the manufacture of electric tramcars etc. under the control of a subsidiary, ER&TCW (qv). New works built at Preston in 1900 for manufacture of electric traction and power station equipments by a subsidiary, English Electric Manufacturing Co. Ltd, which was absorbed into DK in 1903. All taken into EE (qv) in 1919.

DL&W (US)
Delaware, Lackawanna & Western RR Co.

DLR
Docklands Light Rly (London), inc 1984,1985, Tower Gateway–Poplar–Stratford/Island Gardens [North Greenwich], largely over formation of L&BR (*3*) and MER (*2*). Opened 1987, Britain's first fully-automatic computer-controlled passenger rly, with driverless trains; also London's first LRT line. Under-contact third rail traction supply. Extension to Bank 1991; also (under construction) to Beckton and (proposed) to Lewisham.

DM
1. Driving Motor car in an mu set.
2. Diesel Mechanical.

DMB
BR Driving Motor Brake power car.

DMBS
BR Driving Motor Brake Second/Standard class car.

DMC
BR Driving Motor Composite car.

DMLV
BR Driving Motor Luggage Van.

DMMU
Diesel-Mechanical Multiple Unit.

DMO
Divisional Manager's Office.

DMR
Deferred Meal Relief allowance, paid to LT trainmen if meal relief is delayed.

DMS
BR Driving Motor car Second/Standard class.

DMU
Diesel Multiple Unit.

DN&GR
Dundalk, Newry & Greenore Rly, NI/Ire. Inc 1863, capital raised by L&NWR, who were virtual owners, supplied the locos and rolling stock and operated a steamer service to Greenore from Holyhead. Became part of LM&SR 1923. Dundalk–Greenore opened 1873, Greenore–Newry 1876. Taken over by GNR (I) 1933. Closed 1951.

DN&SR
Didcot, Newbury & Southampton [Junction] Rly, Didcot to Shawford Junction, Winchester, inc 1873, opened 1882, 1885, 1891. Worked by GWR, name changed to DN&SR 1883. Absorbed by GWR 1923.

Dock
A short length of track, usually a dead end, accommodating coaches or other vehicles, usually with platform

alongside and used for loading and unloading parcels, milk and other freight. Adopted from canal usage. *See also* Bay.

Dockers' umbrella
Nickname for the Liverpool Overhead Rly, whose continuous viaduct afforded shelter for dockers in wet weather.

Dod (RS)
A ground or shunt signal.

Dodger (RS)(obs)
1. A shunting track.
2. A branch line train.

Dog (USRS)
A freight train operating for a short distance only; also 'short dog'.

Dog catcher (USRS)
A member of a relief crew.

Dog collector (obs)
A large dog with a collecting box for a rly charity strapped to its back, which patrolled station premises unsupervised, seeking contributions from passengers.

Doggy (RS)
A platelayer (qv). Possibly from dog spike (qv).

Doghouse (USRS)
1. A caboose (qv) (usually a four-wheeler).
2. A cupola (qv).
3. A brakeman's shelter on a loco tender.

Dog law (USRS)
A federal law restricting train crews to a maximum of twelve hours' continuous duty. *See also* Bear law; Hog law; Monkey, caught by the.

Dogs (RS)
A tool for pulling up sleepers.

Dog Spike
A spike with a dog-like head.

Do-it-yourself kit (RS)(obs)
A contemptuous term for a badly-maintained steam loco – steam enginemen were expected to carry out minor running repairs and adjustments.

Doll (RS)
A signal post with one or more semaphore arms

Dolly (RS)
1. A dwarf ground or shunt signal.
2. A small shunting loco.
3. A roll of cotton waste.

Dome car
see Vistadome.

Donegal
see CDRJC.

Donegan (USRS)
An old rly coach converted to an office or residential accommodation. From the name of a man who specialized in such conversions.

Donkey (RS)
1. A Westinghouse pump.
2. (obs) A branch line, or the branch line train, e.g. Marlow Donkey, Delph Donkey.

Donkeys (RS)
LM&SR 350 hp diesel shunting locos.

DOO
Driver-Only Operation (i.e. train in sole charge of driver, no other train crew).

Doodlebugs (RS)
1. (RS) BR 4–6–2 locos. After the German Second World War missile.
2. (RS) S&DJR 430XX 2–6–0 locos. After the missile.
3. (USRS) A petrol railcar, especially the small type used to transport track maintenance workers.

Dope, doping it (USRS)
A chemical compound used to prevent boiler water foaming when the loco was being worked hard; the insertion of this material.

Dope monkey (USRS)
A car inspector.

Dormientes (South American Sp)
Track sleepers.

Dorset Scot
An Edinburgh–Poole service,
introduced 1990.

Dortoir (Fr)
A staff dormitory/hostel.

DoT (US)
Department of Transportation.
Formed in 1966, it includes the
Federal Railroad Administration. For
the UK Department of Transport, *see*
DTp.

Double, to (USRS)
To take a train over a steeply-graded
section by dividing it into two
parts.

Double bedroom
A private compartment in a US long
distance train consisting of wide settee
across the width for day use,
convertible to a bed at night, when a
second bed is let down from the
compartment wall. Introduced *c.* 1938.

Double berth
The upper or lower 'half section' in a
US Pullman sleeping car.

Double Breasters (RS)
L&SWR '443' T14 class 4–6–0s.
Notorious for oscillation; their drivers
were alleged to wear double-breasted
coats for protection.

Double bubble (LTRS)
A double shift (sixteen hours of duty).

Double bucket (RS)
Two class 20 diesel locos running
together, chimney to chimney.

Double crossing
Another name for scissors crossover
(qv).

Double docking
Allowing a second train into an
occupied platform at a terminus, thus
trapping the first.

Double end, to (LTRS)
To use two crews, one at each end of
a train, to obtain quick turnarounds.
The term is also current on the

Toronto metro, where two drivers are
used, one acting as guard in one
direction.

Double-ended tank/double ender
(RS)
A tank loco with symmetrical wheel
arrangement, e.g. 2–4–2T.

Double headed/ing
Two locos hauling one train.

Double home turn (RS)(obs)
A lodging turn (qv).

Double peg[ged] (RS)
Both signals in the 'off' position on a
single post, indicating that two
sections in advance are clear.

Double quad (RS)(obs)
Two quad-arts (qv) coupled together.

Double rest (LTRS)
Two rest days in one week.

Double shovelling (RS)
Bringing the coal forward towards the
footplate.

Double shunt
A loco propelling two sets of wagons,
from one line to another, each set
coupled together but not to each
other, or to the loco.

Double singles (RS)
Locos with two sets of driving axles,
each connected to its own set of
cylinders.

Double slips
A diamond crossing with connections
between both tracks in both
directions. *See also* Slips.

Double yellow
see Double yoke.

Double yoke (RS)
A colour-light signal showing the

double yellow preliminary caution indication.

Doubling back (LTRS)
Changing to an earlier shift with no intervening rest day, thus obtaining short rest period between shifts.

Doves (RS)
LB&SCR 2–4–0 and outside-framed 0–6–0 locos built by Dübs & Co., Glasgow.

Down
1. The line carrying trains away from London or the location of the rly's headquarters, or, in lines wholly in Scotland, away from Edinburgh. A train moving in that direction. Adopted from road stage coach usage, dating from the seventeenth century. *See also* Up (*1*).
2. (RS) Late, e.g. 'ten down' = ten minutes late. *See also* Up (*2*).

Down siding
A siding trailing off the Down (*1*) (qv) line.

Downstairs (LTRS)
East London Line, LT.

Down the hole (LTRS)
In the deep level tube system.

Down the nick (RS)(obs)
A loco short of steam.

Down the pipe (LTRS)
see Down the hole.

Down the plug (RS)(obs)
A loco running short of water.

Down the road, to go (LTRS)
To see a manager over a misdemeanour.

Down the slot/put down the s., to (RS)
To divert a freight or slow passenger train to a loop or siding to make way for a fast train.

DPU
BR diesel parcels unit.

DR
1. District Rly: MDR (qv).

2. (LTRS) District Line.
3. *Deutsche Reichsbahn*; German State Rlys, formed 1923. Continued in East Germany (GDR) after the Second World War but part of system located in West Germany (FRG) became *DB* (*1*) (qv). Now part of *DB* (*2*) (qv). *See also* DRG.
4. Donegal Rly *see* CDRJC.

Drag (USRS)
1. A very slow or heavy freight train.
2. A train of empties.

Drahtseilbahn (Ger)
A funicular (cable) rly.

Drain, The (RS)
1. The Waterloo & City platforms at Waterloo station, London, or the whole rly. Originally (RS), but since it was suitably deprecatory, subsequently adopted by journalists and commuters.
2. Tunnels between Metropolitan City Widened Lines and surface lines at Kings Cross.

Dram road
The original (eighteenth-century) term for tramroad (*1*).

Drapeau
An express between Paris and Bordeaux, introduced 1945. Replaced by unnamed TGV 1990.

Drawbar
The hooked bar fixed to the centre of the end frame of a vehicle for coupling purposes.

Drawbar pull
The force exerted on a train at the loco/tender drawbar after taking account of all resistance losses of loco and any tender. Sometimes known as 'drawbar tractive effort'. 'Equivalent drawbar pull' includes correction for gradient and acceleration on the weight of the loco and tender; on the level and at

uniform speed it is the same as
drawbar pull.

Drawing room

1. A private compartment on US long
   distance train accommodating up to
   four passengers; furnished with
   settee and two loose armchairs for
   day use and transverse upper and
   lower beds and a longitudinal bed
   for night use.
2. (USRS) A caboose (qv).

Draw up to the peg, to (RS)
To approach and stop at a signal.

Dreadnoughts (RS)

1. GWR 70 ft/21.34 metre corridor
   coaches of 1905.
2. L&YR 4–6–0 locos of 1908–9.
3. Metropolitan Rly compartment
   coaches with round-topped doors,
   introduced 1910–12.

All were named after the
contemporary Royal Navy battleships.

Drewry
Drewry Car Co. Ltd, Burton on
Trent, railcar and loco builders from
1911. Amalgamated with Baguley (qv)
as Baguley–Drewry Ltd, 1967.

DRG
Deutsche Reichbahn–Gesellschaft. Full
title of DR (3) (qv) from 1923–45.

DRICO (obs)
DRIver to COntroller tunnel wire
communication system formerly used
on LT Rlys.

Drift, to (USRS)
To run a loco downhill without
working steam.

Drifting throttle (USRS)
Running with the regulator cracked
open to keep air and dust from being
sucked into the steam cylinders.

Drill (USRS)
Operations in a shunting yard.

Driving Trailer
A car devoid of traction equipment
but fitted with a driving cab.

Drone
GWR TC for six-wheel Third class
coach.

Drone A
GWR TC for Third class bogie coach
with luggage compartment.

Drone B
GWR TC for four-wheel Third class
coach with luggage compartment.

Drone cage (USRS)
A private rly car (qv).

Drop, to (USRS)
To shunt by uncoupling wagons from
the loco and allowing them to roll into
position by their own momentum.

Drop a track, to (LTRS)
The process whereby a train de-
energizes a track circuit (qv) on
entering a section.

Drop coach (obs)
The early term for slip coach (qv).

Drophead Buckeye Coupler
A form of central automatic coupler
adopted by BR consisting of a drawhook
and drophead. When one coach is shunted
against another, the claw of one coupling
passes and engages with the claw of the
other. In the engaged position, the
coupling is secured with a pin.

Droplight
That part of a coach door window
which can be lowered and secured
with leather strap, or in more modern
stock by a spring clutch.

Drop off, to (of a signal) (RS)
To change from 'on' to 'off' (clear)
indication.

Drop off–Drop on signal (LTRS)
A signal that illuminates and clears as
a train approaches it.

Drop on, to (of a train) (LTRS)
To appear on the signalman's track
diagram or train describer.

Drop out, to (of train motors) (LTRS)
To cease to function owing to action of
circuit breakers.

Dropped ends (LTRS)
Ends of cars bent downwards by
clumsy shunting or coupling up.

Droppers (USRS)
Brakemen riding on a wagon and
jumping off during shunting
operations.

Dropping a short (LTRS)
Evading fares by buying two short
distance season tickets covering only
the end sections of a long journey.

Dropping back (LTRS)
1. see Doubling back (qv).
2. see Stepping up/back (qv).

Dropping the consist (USRS)
Passing down a consist [form] (qv) to
a telegraph operator from a train.

**Drop the button/the deadman's/the
handle, to** (RS)
To release pressure on the deadman's
handle, so stopping the train.

Drop the lever, to (RS)
To advance the cut-off on a steam loco
to provide more power when starting,
accelerating or climbing.

Drop the lot, to (LTRS)
To make an emergency stop.

Druid (RS)
A Welsh rlyman.

Drumm battery cars
Battery electric railcars using an
improved alkaline battery with high
rates of charge and discharge, patented
by Prof. James Drumm in 1929. Ran
on the GSR/CIE 1930–49.

Drunkard (USRS)
A late Saturday night service carrying
drunks home from a town or city.

Dry turn (LTRS)
A duty with a guard or driver who
rarely, if ever, brews tea.

DSB
Danske Statsbaner; Danish State Rlys.

DSD
Driver's Safety Device, ensuring that
the train stops if the driver collapses.

Usually a plate depressed by a foot.
See also Deadman's handle/button/
control.

DSG
*Deutsche Schlafwagen und Speisewagen
Gesellschaft*; German Sleeping Car and
Restaurant Car Company, formed
1950 to undertake all internal sleeping
and restaurant car services on the *DB*.
Renamed *Deutsche Service Gesellschaft
der Bahn*, 1990.

DTBS
BR Driving Trailer Brake Second/
Standard class.

DTC
BR Driving Trailer Composite.

DTp
Department of Transport. Re-formed
1976 as a separate department of state
(between 1970 and 1976 the relevant
rly and road functions had been the
responsibility of the Department of the
Environment). Sometimes cynically
known as the 'Department of Road
Transport' since it is predominantly
concerned with road building and road
transport matters. For earlier history
see MoT.

DTS
BR Driving Trailer Second/Standard
class.

DTSL
DTS with lavatory.

Dual-fitted (obs)
A loco or vehicle equipped with both
air and vacuum brake systems.

Dub Ds (RS)
BR 2–8–0 locos ex Ministry of Supply
and War Department (hence WD,
'Dub D'), introduced 1943.

Dublin Express
A Cork–Dublin non-stop service,
introduced 1937.

Dübs
Dübs & Co., loco builders, Glasgow
from 1863. Amalgamated with Neilson

(qv) and Sharp (qv) to form North British (qv) in 1903.

Duchesses (RS)
LM&SR 4–6–2 locos introduced in 1937.

Duckbill roof
US version of royal clerestory (qv). *See also* Bullnose.

Duck eggs (RS)(obs)
Coal in ovoid form.

Duck eights (RS)
L&NWR 0–8–0 locos.

Ducket
A small projecting window at the side of a coach to provide the guard with view along the train and the line.

Dud (LTRS)
A defective train.

Dudding Hill Loop
Acton to Cricklewood (London), N&SWJR.

Dude (USRS)
A passenger train conductor, especially on the more important trains. From his smartly-uniformed presence (dude = dandy).

Dude wrangler (USRS)
Brakeman on a passenger train, apt to wrangle (argue) with the dude (qv).

Duffield Bank
Pioneer 15 in/381 mm gauge rly built by Sir Arthur Heywood on his estate on the outskirts of Duffield, near Derby, to demonstrate the potential of the gauge. This line was operated from 1874 until 1916.

Duff (RS)(Ire)(obs)
A coal dust mixture used to fire steam locos in Ireland during the Second World War.

Duffs (RS)
BR class 47 diesel electric locos.

Dukedogs (RS)
GWR class 90XX 4–4–0 locos, built with parts from Duke and Bulldog classes.

Dukeries Route
Brand name of the LD&ECR line from Chesterfield to Lincoln.

Dulas Valley
see DVMR.

Dumb buffer
A buffer which does not compress when in contact with another buffer.

Dumb end
Head shunt (qv).

Dummy
1. (obs) A small steam loco used to haul tramway (*3*) trailer cars; often disguised as a passenger car to avoid frightening the horses in the streets.
2. (obs) A grip car (qv).
3. (RS) A ground or shunt signal. Mainly SR and BR (S) usage.
4. (USRS) (obs) A shunting loco.

Dummy chucker (RS)
A shunter.

Dummy coach
An empty vehicle placed between loco and train for safety reasons.

Dump car (US)
A wagon designed to discharge its load through doors or by tipping of its body.

Dumpling
A method of construction under streets in which trenches are first excavated on both sides of the street and the side walls of the rly tunnel are built in them. The road surface is then replaced by timber baulks and the area below these dug out to enable steel cross girders to be inserted, to rest on the walls and form the permanent roof of the tunnel. The remaining soil (the 'dumpling') is then removed to complete the tunnel.

Dunalastairs (RS)
McIntosh Caledonian Rly 4–4–0 locos, introduced 1896–1914.

Dunarea
A *CIWL* Pullman train between

Bucharest and Galatz, introduced
1929. Renamed the *Danubiu* (qv) in
1932. Ceased 1939.

Dunnage
Straw pads or other packing materials
used to protect freight in transit.

Duorail
A term used by planners and
architects to distinguish the
conventional rly from monorail or
other unconventional forms. Not
found in the vocabulary of those
professionally involved in rly transport.

Duplex
A development of the Roomette (qv);
a private compartment on a US long
distance train with corridor at one side
and transverse beds, upper and lower.
The several duplex sections in a coach
are arranged to dovetail into each
other to make the optimum use of
available space.

Duplex fog signal
A single detonator with two sets of
explosives providing two fog signals in
one case.

Duplex ticket
A two-part ticket divided by
perforation.

Duplicate locos (obs)
Locos replaced in the capital accounts
of a rly company were entered on the
'duplicate list'. As such they received
no further heavy repairs but often
remained in service for several years
until thoroughly worn out. They could
usually be identified by special
numbers or a prefix to their original
number.

Duster (USRS)
A loco.

Dust her out, to (USRS)
To put sand through the fire door of
an oil-burning steam loco while
working it hard, to reduce soot in the
flues and assist steaming.

Dust raiser (USRS)
A loco fireman.

Dusty bin (RS)
BR class 321 emu.

Dutch clock (USRS)
A speed recording device on a loco.

Dutch drop, to (USRS)
To shunt a wagon from the front of a
loco to behind it.

Dutchman
Flying Dutchman (qv).

Dutton
Dutton & Co.; manufactured
signalling equipment at Worcester
from 1888. Dissolved 1899, assets
passing to J.E. Pease & Co.

DVLR
1. Derwent Valley Light Rly,
   standard gauge line from York
   (Layerthorpe) to Cliffe Common,
   LRO 1907, opened 1913. Passenger
   service ceased 1926, finally closed
   1980.
2. Dart Valley Light Rly: *see* Dart
   Valley.

DVMR
Dulas Valley Mineral Rly, inc 1862,
Cadoxton (Neath) to near Drim
Colliery (Onllwyn), opened 1864,
name changed to N&BR (qv) 1863.

DVR
1. Dearne Valley Rly, Black Carr
   Junction (south of Doncaster)–
   Cadeby–Grimethorpe–Brierley
   Junction (east of Barnsley). Inc
   1897, opened throughout, 1909,
   passenger service began 1912;
   worked by L&YR, part of
   L&NWR 1922, LM&SR from
   1923.
2. Devon Valley Rly, inc 1858,
   Tillicoutry–Kinross, opened 1863,
   1869, 1871. Worked by NBR. Part
   of NBR 1875.

DVT
Driving Van Trailer. A guard's van

with driving cab designed for BR main line push-pull working in combination with electric locos, introduced 1989.

DW&WR
Dublin, Wicklow & Wexford Rly, formed 1860, became D&SER (qv) 1907.

Dwarf (RS)
A ground or shunt signal.

Dwarf frame
A small frame for working points and signals, set apart from normal signalbox.

Dynamiter (USRS)
A coach or wagon with defective air brakes which have locked into the full emergency position.

Dynamometer Car
A coach specially adapted to carry instruments and recording devices for measuring loco performance when working a train on the line. When in use, it is marshalled between the loco and the rest of the train.

D-Züge (Ger)
Durchgangszüge; fast corridor trains, usually with supplementary fare, on *DB*, *DR*, *OBB*.

E

Eagle eye (USRS)
A loco driver.

Eagle stock (RS)
L&SWR coaches for American Line boat trains, 1892.

E&CHR
Easton & Church Hope Rly, Easton and Inmosthay Quarries to Church Hope Cove and Portland (junction with Admiralty Portland Breakwater Rly). First section inc 1867, further acts 1884, 1887, 1890. Opened 1900. Worked by GWR and L&SWR jointly, as were the Admiralty line (opened for through running 1900) and the Weymouth & Portland Rly (inc 1862, opened 1865), the whole forming a continuous line. Passenger traffic (Weymouth–Portland) 1902. GWR and SR joint from 1923–47. BR 1948.

E&CVR
Ely & Clydach Valleys Rly, Penycraig to Clydach Vale, Blaenclydach, inc 1873, opened 1878, worked by GWR, part of GWR from 1880.

E&HR
Edgware & Hampstead Rly (London), inc 1902, Edgware to junction with CCE&HR at Golders Green, part of LER 1912, opened 1923, 1924 as an open air extension of the CCE&HR tube rly.

E&MR
Eastern & Midlands Rly, inc 1882, amalgamation of Lynn & Fakenham, Yarmouth Union and Yarmouth &

North Norfolk Rlys. Opened Melton Constable–Norwich 1882, Melton–Cromer (Beach) 1887. Absorbed M&ER and Peterborough, Wisbech and Sutton Bridge Rlys, 1883. Became M&GNJC 1893.

E&NR
Edinburgh & Northern Rly, inc 1845, Burntisland to Perth, purchased Edinburgh, Leith & Granton Rly 1847 and renamed Edinburgh, Perth & Dundee Rly. Opened 1847, 1848. Part of NBR 1861.

E&SBR
Ealing & Shepherds Bush Rly, Ealing Broadway to junction with WLR near Kensington (Olympia). Inc 1905 (part of GWR), connections with CLR at Shepherd's Bush authorized 1911 and built by GWR. Opened to freight traffic 1917, passenger service of CLR electric tube trains between Wood Lane Junction and Ealing Broadway started 1920.

E&SHR
Ealing & South Harrow Rly (London), inc 1894, North Ealing to South Harrow [Roxeth], part of MDR 1900, completed 1901 but not opened. Used as test bed for MDR electrification 1903 and public electric services begun. Piccadilly Line tube service was extended over it in 1932.

E&WID&BJR
East & West India Docks & Birmingham Junction Rly, inc 1846, Camden Town (London &

Birmingham Rly) to West India Docks
at Blackwall, opened 1850, 1851,
1852; became NLR (qv) 1853.

E&WJR
East & West Junction Rly, inc 1864, from
junction with N&BJR near Towcester to
Stratford-upon-Avon. Opened 1871,
1873. Part of S&MJR from 1909.

E&WYJR
East & West Yorkshire Junction Rly, inc
1846, Poppleton Junction to
Knaresborough, opened 1848, 1851,
worked by the York, Newcastle & Berwick
Rly. Absorbed by Y&NMR 1851.

E&WYUR
East & West Yorkshire Union Rly,
Stourton Junc (Leeds)–Rothwell–
Robin Hood–Lofthouse/Newmarket
Collieries (Silkstone), inc 1883,
opened 1891, part of L&NER 1923.

EAR
1. East Anglian Rly, Ely–Kings Lynn/
   Wisbech–Dereham; St Ives–
   Huntingdon; an 1847 amalgamation
   of Lynn & Dereham, Lynn & Ely
   and Ely & Huntingdon Rlys, all inc
   1845. Worked by ECR from 1852,
   part of GER 1862.
2. East African Rlys and Harbours
   Administration (operating all rlys in
   Kenya, Uganda, and Tanganyika),
   formed 1948, EA Rlys Corporation
   1969; split into separate national rly
   organizations 1975.

Ears
Metal components suspending
tramway (*3*) overhead wires.

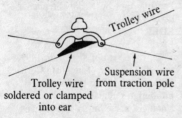

Trolley wire
soldered or clamped
into ear

Trolley wire

Suspension wire
from traction pole

Easingwold
see ER (*1*).

Eason's Specials (obs)
Cheap excursion trains organized
by the Grimsby travel agent,
J.W. Eason over the GNR and
L&NER, 1905–39: Eason's slogan was
'Good for the Public. Good for the
Railway'.

East Anglian
An express between London
(Liverpool St.) and Norwich,
introduced 1937, ceased 1939, re-
introduced 1946, name dropped 1962.
Name used in 1980 for a London
(Liverpool St.)–Norwich–Yarmouth
service. From 1987 a London
(Liverpool St.)–Norwich service.

Eastbound (US)
Term for a train or train service
travelling in a generally easterly
direction. 'Northbound', 'southbound'
and 'westbound' were similarly used.
This terminology was adopted on
London underground rlys from 1905
in place of the traditional British
'Down' and 'Up' (qv). Later adopted
on certain BR lines and more recently,
for motorways.

Easterling
A summer-only express between
London (Liverpool St.) and
Yarmouth, so named 1950. Name
dropped from 1959.

Eastern Belle [Pullman Limited]
L&NER all-Pullman excursion
trains from London (Liverpool St.)
to East Anglian resorts, introduced
1929.

Eastern and Western Valleys Line
Newport to Blaenavon, South Wales
[Eastern]; Newport–Aberbeeg–Ebbw
Vale/Blaina [Western].

East Fife Line
Leuchars Junc–St Andrews–Leven–
Thornton Junc.

East Gloucestershire
see EGR.
East Lancashire
see ELR (*1*) and (*2*).
East Lincs Line
Peterborough–Boston–Grimsby.
East Norfolk Line
see ENR.
East Somerset
see ESR (*1*).
East Suffolk Line
Ipswich–Beccles–Lowestoft. *See also*
ESR (*2*).
East–West CrossRail
A main line-loading gauge tube rly
under London, linking existing BR
lines and carrying BR services.
Extending from Royal Oak, just west
of Paddington via Tottenham Court
Road to a point just east of Liverpool
St. Also known as CrossRail. Planned
to open *c*. 1999.
Easy sign (USRS)
Any signal requiring reduction of
speed.
EC
Euro-City Express (qv).
EC&TJR
Eastern Counties & Thames Junction
Rly, inc 1844, Stratford (London) to
Thames Wharf and Canning Town,
opened 1846. Part of ECR from 1847.
ECJS
East Coast Joint Stock; passenger
coaches jointly owned by NBR, NER
and GNR and operating between
London (Kings Cross) and Edinburgh/
Aberdeen, introduced 1860.
ECML
East Coast Main Line, London (Kings
Cross) to York, Newcastle,
Edinburgh, Dundee and Aberdeen.
ECMR
East Cornwall Mineral Rly, inc 1869
as Callington & Calstock Rly, 3 ft
6 in/1,067 mm gauge, Calstock Quay,

Gunnislake and Callington. Name
changed to ECMR 1871, opened 1872.
Part of PD&SWJR from 1891.
Converted to standard gauge and
connected to PD&SWJ at Bere Alston,
1908, with wagon lift from Calstock
Quay to the new connecting line.
ECR
Eastern Counties Rly, inc 1836,
London to Norwich and Yarmouth via
Colchester and Ipswich, first section
opened London (Devonshire St.) to
Romford, 1839, 5 ft/1,524 mm gauge,
converted to standard gauge 1844.
Part of GER from 1862.
ECRJC
East Coast Rlys Joint Committee
(NER, NBR, GNR).
ECS
Empty Coaching/Carriage Stock.
ED
Engineering/Engineers' Department.
Edelweiss
1. A *CIWL* Pullman express between
   Amsterdam and Zurich, 1928–39.
   There were modifications at each
   end of the route over the life of this
   train.
2. A railcar service Brussels–Basle
   1955, Brussels–Zurich 1956.
3. *TEE* Amsterdam–Zurich 1957;
   electric working throughout,
   completing electrification of *TEE*
   services, 1974. Lost *TEE* status
   1979, IC/EC 1979, name dropped
   1987.
Eden Valley Line
Penrith–Appleby–Kirkby Stephen. *See
also* EVR (*3*).
EDER
Epsom Downs Extension Rly, inc
1892, 1897, part of SER from 1899,
opened Tadworth–Tattenham Corner
1901. *See also* Chipstead Valley.
Edinburgh Pullman
Unofficial name for an all-Pullman

service between London (Kings
Cross), Leeds, Harrogate, Newcastle
and Edinburgh, introduced 1925
(extension of Harrogate Pullman).
Became Queen of Scots (qv) 1927.

Edinburgh Suburban Line
Gorgie–Duddingston.

EDL
Electro-Diesel Loco.

Edmondson ticket
A cardboard ticket, in Britain 1$\frac{3}{16}$ in by
2$\frac{1}{4}$ in/5.7 cm by 3 cm, numbered
consecutively, pre-printed with
journey details, station of issue and
price, date-stamped at moment of
issue by a dating press (qv). Named
after its inventor, Thomas Edmondson
(1792–1851). In general use on British
rlys for some 150 years, the
Edmondson ticket system was finally
displaced on BR in 1989. It survives
on some British preserved lines and
overseas rlys.

EDS (Ger)
Eisenbahndienstsache: see OCS.

EE
English Electric Co. Ltd, an
amalgamation in 1918–19 of DK (qv),
Siemens (qv), Phoenix Dynamo
Manufacturing Co. Ltd and Willans
Robinson. Suppliers of large electrical
generating plant and switchgear,
electric and diesel-electric locos and
railcars, tramcars, buses and
trolleybuses, also radio valves. Electric
traction activities were concentrated at
Preston. Merged with GEC (qv), 1968.

EFB
Electric Fouling Bars. Provided on the
track to protect places where light
engines and other vehicles may stand.

EFCR
East Fife Central Rly, inc 1893, from
a point near Cameron Bridge to
Lochty, opened 1898. Part of NBR
from 1895.

EFE
Empresa de los Ferrocarriles del Estado;
Chilean State Rlys.

EFK
Initials of German title of European
Timetable Conference. *See also CEH.*

Egg Timers (RS)
BR class 58 diesel electric locos.
Suggested by their outlines.

EGR
1. East Gloucestershire Rly, Witney to
    Fairford, inc 1862, opened 1873,
    worked by GWR, part of GWR
    from 1890.
2. East Grinstead Rly, inc 1853,
    Three Bridges to EG, opened 1855,
    worked by LB&SCR, part of
    LB&SCR from 1865.

EH&LR
Edgware, Highgate & London Rly,
inc 1862, Edgware to Finchley and
Finsbury Park; Barnet to Finchley inc
1866; part of GNR from 1867; opened
Finsbury Park–Edgware 1867,
Finchley to Barnet 1872.

EHLR
Edge Hill Light Rly, Burton Dassett
S&MJR to ironstone workings on
Edge Hill, including $\frac{1}{2}$ m cable-
worked incline, LRO 1919, opened
1920, closed 1925.

EHO
Extra Heavy Overhaul.

Eight Freights (RS)
LM&SR Stanier class 8F 2–8–0 locos.
From the power classification. Also
abbreviated to 'Eight Fs'.

Eight wheel switch[er] (US)
A steam shunting loco with 0–8–0
wheel arrangement.

Eilzug (Ger)
A train stopping at most stations on its
route.

EIR
East Indian Rly; purchased by the
government 1879.

Ejector
A part of steam loco which, by means of a continuous jet of steam, creates the vacuum for keeping the brakes released.

EKLR
East Kent (Light) Rly: Canterbury Road (Wingham)–Shepherdswell/ Sandwich Road. Sandwich Road– Richborough extension built but not opened. LROs 1911, 1912. Opened 1912, passengers 1916. Part of BR (S) and closed to passengers 1948. Last section out of use 1984. There is a preservation project, based at Shepherdswell.

EKR
East Kent Rly; St Mary Cray– Chatham–Faversham–Canterbury– Dover; inc 1853, first section opened 1858. Renamed LC&DR (qv) 1859.

El, The (US)(S)
Elevated rly (qv).

Elan Valley
A construction rly for building Birmingham Corporation Reservoir; ran west from Mid-Wales Line near Rhayader to Craig Gôch, inc 1892, opened 1894, 1896, closed 1917.

Electric Railway and Tramway Journal
see LR&TJ

Electric Scots (obs)
Brand name for Anglo-Scottish WCML services when first electrified, 1974.

Electric train staff/tablet
see Train staff/tablet/token and ticket.

Electrotren (Sp)
A fast emu service.

Electrotreni (It)
The fastest services, electrically-worked, usually First class only, with supplementary fare.

Elephant car (USRS)
A passenger coach marshalled behind

the loco for the use of the front brakesman.

Elephant's ears (RS)
Loco smoke deflectors (qv).

Elevated [rly]
An urban passenger rly rapid transit system running over and along the line of city streets on elevated steel structures. Such systems were built in New York, Chicago, Boston, Hamburg and Berlin. *See also* LOR.

Elevated Electric (obs)
Brand name for LB&SCR electric services on South London Line (qv) when introduced in 1909. Derived from the route, which is largely on viaducts and embankments.

Elham Valley Line
Cheriton Halt–Canterbury. *See also* EVLR.

Elizabethan
A renaming of Capitals Limited, 1953. Name dropped 1963.

Elk (LTRS)
A device on a flat wagon, used for lifting rails.

Ellen
Nickname for the Louisville & Nashville RR (US). *See also* Old Reliable, The.

Ellofamess
Nickname for LM&SR .

Elmer (RS)
A North American travelling on BR, usually with a Britrail go-as-you-please ticket.

ELNA
Engerer Lokomotiv–Normen–Ausschuss.
A committee set up to design standard steam locos for German rlys after the First World War.

ELR
1. East Lancashire Rly; Manchester (Clifton Junc)–Bury– Blackburn/ Burnley/Colne/Bacup. Inc 1844 as Manchester, Bury & Rossendale

Rly, renamed ELR 1845, opened 1846. Absorbed Blackburn & Preston; Blackburn, Burnley, Accrington & Colne Extension; and Liverpool, Ormskirk & Preston Rlys in 1846. Extended to Bacup 1852, part of L&YR 1859.

2. A preserved rly operating over parts of (*1*) from 1987.

3. East London Rly, inc 1865, opened 1869 Wapping to New Cross (LB&SCR) via the existing Thames Tunnel. Worked by LB&SCR. Extended to Shoreditch and Liverpool St. (GER) 1876. SER services 1880 and connection at New Cross in use. Metropolitan and MDR through services to New Cross SER and LB&SCR via connection at Whitechapel, 1884. GER services from 1887. MDR services ceased 1905, Metropolitan 1906. LB&SCR, SER and GER passenger services ceased 1913. Electrified 1913 with passenger services operated by Metropolitan Rly. Managed by Metropolitan from 1921 and maintained by it from 1924, vested in SR 1925. Managed and operated by LPTB from 1933. Part of BTC 1948 but managed and controlled by LT. With the cessation of through freight and parcels traffic over the ELR in 1966, all connections with BR were severed (the last, in sidings at New Cross Gate, in 1975), and the line became a part of the London Underground system. *See also* ELRJC.

4. East Lincolnshire Rly, inc 1846, Grimsby to Louth and Boston, opened 1848. Leased by GNR 1846. Part of L&NER from 1923.

ELRJC
East London Rly Joint Committee, inc 1882 to lease ELR in perpetuity, lease operated from 1884. Composed of Metropolitan, MDR, LB&SCR, LC&DR, SER (later SE&CR). The GER joined in 1885. SR, Metropolitan, MDR and L&NER were the lessees from 1923, the SR, L&NER and LPTB from 1933. The Committee was dissolved in 1949 following formation of the BTC, which became the owner.

Ely Valley
see E&CVR; EVER; EVR.

Em (USRS)
One thousand tons load. From the Roman M = 1,000.

Embsay
see ESR (*5*).

Emerald Isle Express, The
Express between London (Euston) and Holyhead, in connection with Dunlaoghaire (Dublin) night sailings, introduced 1954, name dropped 1975.

Emergency application
A brake application at maximum reduction in air pressure, to stop a train as quickly as possible. Occurs automatically if a brake pipe is severed.

EML
BR (S) term for a train combining emu and loco haulage.

Emmett
GWR TC for Third class six-wheel brake coach.

Emmett A
GWR TC for Third class bogie brake coach.

Emmett B
GWR TC for Third class four-wheel brake coach.

Empire Builder
A Great Northern RR express between Chicago, Tacoma and Seattle, introduced 1929. Now an Amtrak express of double-decker 'Superliner'

cars between Chicago and Seattle, introduced 1980, covering the 2,287 m in 46 h.

Empire State Express/Limited
An express between New York and Buffalo, introduced 1891 and later extended to Cleveland and Detroit. Featured on a US postage stamp in 1901. In 1947 it was covering the 637½ m from New York to Detroit in 13 h 15 min. Later withdrawn but the name has been adopted by Amtrak for its New York–Buffalo–Niagara Falls service.

Empress Voyager
A boat train between London (Euston) and Liverpool(Riverside) in connection with Canadian Pacific sailings, 1953–66. Name was also used for the contemporary Glasgow(Central)–Gourock (Princes Pier) boat trains for Canadian Pacific.

EMU
Electric Multiple Unit.

End dock
A dock (qv) which provides end as well as side loading/unloading facilities.

Endeavour
An express between Wellington (NZ) and Napier, introduced 1972.

End man (USRS)
The rear end brakeman on a freight train.

Engadine Express
An express between Calais (connections with UK) and Chur for St Moritz, introduced 1901. Revived after the First World War as a winter sports train. Ceased 1939. Revived 1946–7 only.

Engineer (US)
Loco driver, adopted in UK by ASLEF (qv), but not generally.

Enginemen
Collective term for loco driver and fireman/second man.

Engine turner
see Turner, engine.

ENR
East Norfolk Rly, inc 1864, Whitlingham to North Walsham, inc 1872 to Cromer, inc Reepham to County School 1879. Opened 1874, 1876, 1877, 1882. GER running powers Norwich to North Walsham 1874, part of GER 1881.

Enterprise
An express between Dublin and Belfast, introduced 1947. Extended to Cork 1950–3 only.

EofFR
East of Fife Rly, inc 1855, 1856 , Leven to Kilconquhar; opened 1857, worked by Edinburgh, Perth & Dundee Rly. Amalgamated with LR as Leven & East of Fife Rly 1861, extended to Anstruther 1863, part of NBR 1877.

EP
Electro-Pneumatic [brake].

EPB
BR (S) emu two and four-car Second/Standard class sets of 1951–5 and 1960 with EP Brakes. Motor brake open and driving trailer open cars, 2-EPB. Two motor brake open cars, one open trailer and one trailer with compartments, 4-EPB.

EP Blow (LTRS)
Audible warning of an electrical defect in ep brake.

EPSL
European Passenger Services Ltd, a BR subsidiary formed 1990 to provide international passenger services via the Channel Tunnel.

ER
1. Easingwold Rly, inc 1887, opened 1891, closed passengers 1948, closed 1957.
2. Exeter Rly, inc as Exeter, Teign Valley & Chagford Rly, 1883,

Exeter to Christow (junction with
TVR (2)) and branch to Chagford.
Name changed to ER 1898, and
Chagford branch dropped; opened
1903, worked by GWR, part of
GWR from 1923.
3. Eyemouth Rly, inc 1884,
Burnmouth to Eyemouth, opened
1891, worked by NBR. Part of
NBR from 1900.
4. Eastern Region, BR.
5. Eastern Rly [of India], formed
1952. Part of it became SER (2) in
1955.

ER&SJR
Evesham, Redditch & Stratford-upon-
Avon Junction Rly, inc 1873, from
E&WJR at Stratford to Midland Rly
at Broom, opened 1879, completing
the cross country link between Broom
and Blisworth. Worked by E&WJR.
Part of S&MJR from 1909.

ER&TCW
Electric Railway & Tramway Carriage
Works Ltd, a subsidiary of DK (qv),
established at a new works at Preston
for the manufacture of electric
tramcars and rly rolling stock, 1898.
Name changed to UEC (qv), 1905.

Erasmus
TEE The Hague–Munich, introduced
1973. Amsterdam–Frankfurt 1979.
Lost *TEE* status 1980. EC
Amsterdam–Munich 1987, extended
seasonally to Innsbruck.

Erie
New York, Lake Erie & Western
RR, eventually renamed Erie RR Co.,
then Erie Lackawanna RR Co. from
1960 following merger with DL&W
(qv).

Erewash Valley
Trent–Clay Cross (Midland Rly).

ERR
Egyptian Republic Rlys, a renaming
of ESR (4) (qv) from 1954.

ERS
Electric Railway Society, established
1946. Published *The Electric Railway*,
until 1955 and from 1956 the *Electric
Railway Society Journal*.

ERTO
European Rail Traffic Organization
(BR).

ES&SR
Edinburgh Suburban & Southside
Rly, inc 1880, St Leonards Junc to
Haymarket and Niddrie spur, opened
1884. part of NBR from 1885.

Eskdale
see R&ER.

Esk Valley Line
Whitby–Grosmont–Battersby. *See also*
EVR (4).

ESL (LT)
Electric sleet loco.

Espee
Nickname of Southern Pacific RR.
From initials.

ESR
1. East Somerset Rly, Witham
Junction to Wells, inc 1856, opened
1858, 1862, worked by GWR,
absorbed by GWR 1874 and in
same year converted from broad to
standard gauge. *See also* (2).
2. A steam rly preservation centre at
Cranmore on part of (1), opened
1973.
3. East Suffolk Rly, inc as Halesworth,
Beccles & Haddiscoe Rly 1851,
opened Beccles to Haddiscoe 1854,
worked by ECR. Name changed to
ESR 1854. Extension to Woodbridge
and branches to Leiston,
Framlingham and Snape inc 1854,
opened 1859. Leiston–Aldeburgh
opened 1860. All worked by ECR.
Yarmouth & Haddiscoe and
Lowestoft & Beccles Rlys absorbed
1858. Leased to Sir Morton Peto
1855–61. Part of GER 1862.

4. Egyptian State Rlys, formed 1905. Retitled ERR (qv) 1954.

5. Embsay Steam Rly. A preserved rly on part of former BR Embsay Junc–Ilkley line. First section opened (as Yorkshire Dales Rly), 1979. Name changed to ESR 1988.

Essex Coast Express
A commuter express between London (Liverpool St.) and Clacton, 1 h 26 min, introduced 1958. Name dropped 1968.

Essex Continental
A service between London (Liverpool St.) and Harwich in connection with sailings to the Continent, calling at principal intermediate stations, 1986–8.

Est
Chemin de fer de l'Est, France. Part of *SNCF* (qv) from 1938.

Estate agent (RS)
Second man (qv).

État, Chemins de Fer de l'
French State Rlys, incorporating from 1909 the former *Chemin de fer de l'Ouest*. Part of *SNCF* (qv) from 1938.

ETD
Electric Traction Department.

Étendard
An express between Bordeaux and Paris, introduced 1968. *TEE* from 1971 with 4 h 25 min timing. Extended to Irun, with Madrid connection, 1973–5. Lost *TEE* status 1984. Fastest train in Europe 1973–81 (jointly with *l'Aquitaine* (qv) 1973–6). Ceased 1990.

ÉTG (Fr)(obs)
Élément de Turbine à Gaz. The second type of *SNCF* gas turbine train.

ETH
Electric Train Heating (i.e. heating of train by electricity).

ETHEL (obs)
Electric Train Heating Locos; mobile

generators, converted from BR class 25 diesel locos, to supply power for ETH.

Étoile du Nord
A *CIWL* Pullman express between Paris (Nord), Brussels and Amsterdam, 1927–39. Revived 1946, *TEE* 1957. Lost *TEE* status 1984, EC 1987.

ETS
Electric Train Staff, patented 1888; *see* Train staff/tablet/token and ticket.

ETT
1. Electric Train Tablet, patented 1878; *see* Train staff/tablet/token and ticket.

2. (obs) Experimental Tube Train, LT. Two three-car sets of 1973 stock used in 1983 to try out chopper (qv) control. Later converted to standard 1973 stock.

EUR
1. Eastern Union Rly (Colchester–Ipswich–Norwich/Bury St Edmunds) inc 1844, opened 1846. Absorbed Eastern Union & Hadleigh Rly 1848 and Ipswich & Bury St Edmunds Rly 1849. Extended to Norwich (Victoria) 1849. Worked by ECR from 1854, part of GER 1862.

2. East Usk Rly, Newport along east bank of River Usk to Uskmouth, inc 1885, opened 1898, part of GWR 1892, completed 1901.

Eurailpass
A ticket available for a period of unlimited First or Second class travel on all railways in Western Europe except BR. Sold only outside Europe and North Africa. Introduced 1959.

Euro-City Express
A brand name introduced 1987 for two-class, high quality international trains in Europe which meet criteria set by the UIC (qv). Replaced most

TEE (qv) and international IC (qv) services.

Eurofima
European Company for the financing of rly rolling stock, founded 1956.

Euro-400
Brand name for BR marketing arrangement relating to international rail journeys to popular destinations originating in the UK. Provides information and fares to facilitate ticket issue. Introduced 1990.

European
A service in connection with Continental sailings, Glasgow/ Edinburgh–Manchester–Sheffield– Harwich (Parkeston Quay), introduced 1983. Replaced 1947 by Rhinelander (qv).

Européen
A Luxembourg–Metz–Paris service, 1956. Name dropped 1985.

Europ Wagon Pool
Established 1951; formed of common user wagons to UIC standards circulating on European rail systems.

Eurorail
A consortium (Trafalgar House and BICC) formed in 1989 to develop and operate with BR a new direct rail link between the Channel Tunnel British terminal at Cheriton and London.

Euro-Scot
An Edinburgh–Harwich–Felixstowe Freightliner service introduced 1968.

Euston Square Confederacy, The
L&NWR, Midland Rly and MS&LR acting in concert.

Euston Stop (RS)
A rough, jolting stop, often said to consist of three applications; the first to lift the passenger to his feet, the second to jerk his luggage on to his head, and the third to assist him unceremoniously through the door. Also known as a 'Caley Stop'.

Evans, O'Donnell
Evans, O'Donnell & Co. Ltd, established a signalling equipment works at Chippenham in 1894. Effectively taken over by the Pneumatic & General Engineering Co., later the Consolidated Signal Co. (qv), in 1901–2.

Even time
Sixty miles an hour.

EVER
Ely Valley Extension Rly, inc 1863 from junc with EVR (*1*) near Hendreforghan to Gilfach, opened 1865, part of OVR 1865.

EVEX (obs)
TC for evening excursion train.

EVLR
Elham Valley Light Rly, inc 1881, Cheriton–Elham–Canterbury, part of SER from 1884, opened 1887, 1889.

EVR
1. Ely Valley Rly, Llantrisant to Pen-y-Craig, with branches, inc 1857, opened 1860,1862,1865. Leased to GWR 1861, part of GWR 1903.
2. Exe Valley Rly, inc 1874, opened Tiverton–Stoke Canon 1885, part of B&ER from 1875.
3. Eden Valley Rly, inc 1858, Kirkby Stephen–Clifton (near Penrith). Opened 1862, worked by S&DR, part of S&DR from 1863.
4. Esk Valley Rly, inc 1863; Esk Valley Junc NBR to Polton. Opened 1867, leased by NBR, part of NBR from 1871.

EWP
Europäische Wagenbeistellungsplan; European through coach working book. Issued twice yearly to regulate balancing mileage between the various railway systems on a basis of axle-kilometres.

Excursion [trains]
Traditionally these were special

advertised passenger workings at very low fares, usually made up of old rolling stock or suburban stock and subject to special conditions of travel (e.g. no luggage allowed). They were normally classified as 'Day', 'Half-Day' or 'Evening'. Although special cheap trains are still occasionally provided by BR, using normal rolling stock, the traditional excursion train faded away in the late 1960s and early 1970s. The term is also applied to very cheap tickets available on specified regular trains and to chartered trains for private parties.

Executive
Express between London (Euston), Birmingham and Wolverhampton, 1967–72.

Exe Valley Line
[Exeter]–Stoke Canon–Tiverton–Morebath Junction[–Dulverton]. *See also* EVR (2).

Exhibition train
A train equipped with coaches fitted out to display products and services, demonstrate processes, techniques etc., which tours round the rly system.

Expansion switch
A long scarfed joint, allowing considerable longitudinal movement between adjacent lengths of long or continuously-welded rails to allow for thermal movement.

Expreso, tren (Sp)
Fast trains, sometimes restricted to First class.

Express fares (obs)
Fares above normal rates charged for travel on the fastest trains of the day. Largely abolished in the UK by the end of the nineteenth century but survived on SR boat trains until 1940.

Express freight
A system, unique to North America, and first established in 1839, by which private companies independent of the rlys undertook the care and handling of luggage and many types of freight consignment, using fast passenger train services and collecting and delivering at each end of the journey. Special trains were also operated by the rly companies for this traffic, running at passenger train speeds. Express freight companies included Wells Fargo (qv) and American Express (qv). *See also* REA.

Express, trains (Fr)(obs)
Fast trains, although not so fast as *trains rapide*. Originally restricted to First and old Second class passengers, but latterly all three classes were admitted on trains so classified.

Extended London Area (obs)
All stations within 80 m radius of London termini.

Extension Line (LTRS)
The section of the Metropolitan Line between London (Baker St.), Harrow and beyond.

Extra board (USRS)
see Board (3).

Eye (USRS)
A fixed signal at the side of the running line.

E-Züge (Ger)
Eilzüge; semi-fast trains on the *DR* and *OBB*.

F

F
First class (BR).

FA
Ferrocarriles Argentinos; Argentinian Rlys.

Face
That part of a platform alongside a track.

FACETS
Fully Automated Customer Enquiry and Travel System (BR).

Facing point bar
A lifting or clearance bar (qv) arranged to prevent movement of facing points when a train is passing over them.

Facing point detector
A device which ensures that the relevant signals cannot be moved to the 'off' indication unless the point movement has been fully and properly completed.

Facing point locks
Bolts securing points to be run over in the facing direction before the signal for a train or route can be placed in 'off' indication.

Facing points
Points facing a train in its direction of travel, giving a choice of route, and over which the train will move from

the toe to the heel of the points before reaching the crossing. Facing points are 'like good dinners, the fewer one has of them, the better.'— Henry Oakley GNR general manager.

FACS (Fr)
Fédération des Amis des Chemins de Fer Secondaires; League of Friends of Secondary Railways.

FACT
Full Automatic Control of Trains (LT).

Factory, The (RS)
Swindon Works, GWR, BR (W).

Faidherbe
TEE Paris–Tourcoing, introduced 1978. The last *TEE*, with Watteau (qv).

Failte
A service between Dublin and Cork, so named 1960, name dropped 1975.

Fairlie
An articulated steam loco invented in 1863 by Robert Francis Fairlie (1831–85).

Fair Maid
An express between London (Kings Cross), Edinburgh and Perth; an extension and renaming of Morning Talisman from 1957.

Fairy glen (RS)
A wc.

Fairyland (RS)
Multiple-aspect colour light signals; also such signals when malfunctioning.

Falcon
Falcon Engine & Car Works Ltd,

Loughborough, originally Henry
Hughes, and Hughes' Locomotive &
Tramway Works Ltd, manufacturers
of rly and steam tramway locos.
Loughborough Foundry (Falcon
Ironworks) established 1874. Falcon
Engine & Car Works Ltd established
1882. Merged with Brush (qv), 1889.

Fall-plate

A hinged steel plate covering the gap
between loco and its tender; also a
similar plate between two coaches with
open end balconies.

Falmouth coupé (obs)

A type of GWR non-corridor coach
designed to be detached from main
line trains at junctions to serve branch
lines (e.g. Falmouth). Self-contained
with accommodation for First and
Third class, lavatories, and luggage
compartment.

Family Saloon (obs)

A type of coach which could be hired
for exclusive use by a family or small
private party. These vehicles usually
had a large central compartment with
longitudinal seats and a fixed table
with folding flaps, the seats fitted with
bolsters at each end for sleeping
purposes. There were also smaller
compartments for smoking and the
accommodation of servants, a lavatory
and luggage storage space.

Fan

1. A complex of sidings diverging
   from one track.
2. (USRS) The blower on a steam
   loco.

F&BR

Formartine & Buchan Rly, inc 1858,
Aberdeen (Dyce)–Peterhead/
Fraserburgh, opened 1861, 1862,
1865, worked by GNofSR, part of
GNofSR 1866.

F&CJR

Forth & Clyde Junction Rly, inc 1853,

Stirling to Balloch, opened 1856,
worked by NBR, leased by NBR
1875, part of L&NER 1923.

F&KR

Fife & Kinross Rly, inc 1855,
Ladybank to Kinross, opened 1857,
part of NBR from 1862.

F&MJR

Furness & Midland Joint Rly, inc
1863, Wennington Junc–Carnforth,
opened 1867, part of LM&SR from
1923.

F&RR&H

Fishguard & Rosslare Rlys &
Harbours Company, inc as Fishguard
Bay Rly & Pier, 1893, name changed
to F&RR&H 1894 and Waterford &
Wexford Rly and Rosslare Harbour
Commissioners taken over. Waterford–
Rosslare and Fishguard & Goodwick
station to Fishguard Harbour lines
opened 1906 together with connecting
steamer service, giving a 13 h timing
London to Cork. Rlys worked by
GWR (later BR) in Wales, by
GS&WR (later GSR, CIE, IE) in
Ireland. Steamer service suspended
1941–7. F&RR&H remained a
separate company, jointly owned
by the BTC and CIE, from 1948.
British properties vested in BRB
1967.

F and S

Full and Standing; the official
description of a well-loaded train.

Fang bolt

A screw bolt which passes through the
lower flange of an FB rail and is
secured to the sleeper by a nut.

Fang spike

A metal spike driven into a sleeper to
secure FB rail.

Fat box (RS)(obs)

An axle grease box.

'Father of British railways'

George Stephenson (1781–1848). The

term has also been applied to the
L&MR (qv) and to its secretary,
Henry Booth.

'Father of Railways'
William James (1771–1837), solicitor,
surveyor and first protagonist of rly
construction.

Fat Nancy (RS)
A saddle tank (qv).

Fat Nannies (RS)
L&YR 0–6–0 saddle tank locos.

Fayle's Tramway
An industrial rly, 3 ft 9 in/1,143 mm
gauge, operated by Messrs Fayle to
carry excavated ball clay from Norden,
Corfe Castle, to Goathorn Pier and
Middlebere Wharf on
Poole Harbour. First lines opened
with animal haulage *c.* 1806. Lines to
Poole Harbour closed by 1936. Some
remaining trackage at Norden
converted to 1 ft 11½ in/597 mm
gauge 1948. Finally closed 1972.
See also Middlebere Plateway.

FBR
Forth Bridge Rly, inc 1873 and 1882,
opened 1890, worked by NBR and,
from 1923, L&NER. Part of BR,
1948.

FB rail
Flat Bottom rail (qv).

FCAB
see A&BR (2).

FD&R
Felixstowe Dock & Rly, inc 1879,
opened 1886. Still an independent
company.

FD-Züge (Ger)
Ferndurchgangzüge or *Fernschnellzüge*;
long distance fast trains usually
serving holiday resorts not on the
IC-netz (qv).

Feathers (RS)
1. Lunar lights (qv).
2. Crossed bars placed over signals to
indicate they are not in use.

FEBA
Full Emergency Brake Application.
See also Emergency application.

FEC
Florida East Coast Rly, formed 1892.
See also Flagler's Folly.

Feeder (RS)
An oil can, usually one with a long
and thin spout.

Feed pipe
The means of conveying water from
tank or tender to the boiler of a steam
loco. *See also* Injector.

Feed-water heater
A device for heating water to a high
temperature before it enters the boiler
of a steam loco.

Feldbahn (Ger)
A military narrow gauge light rly, or a
contractor's narrow gauge temporary
line using similar equipment.

Fell
A system for mountain rlys employing
the friction between a wheel of the
specially-designed locos and an
additional central rail. Invented by
J.B. Fell (1815–1902). First used for
line over Mont Cenis Pass,
Switzerland, in 1868.

Fell loco
BR experimental 2,000hp 4–8–4 diesel-
mechanical loco no. 10100 of 1950.
Named after Lt.-Col. L.F.R. Fell,
inventor of the transmission and various
ancillary features.

Fenman
An express between London
(Liverpool St.) and Hunstanton/Bury
St Edmunds, introduced 1949. Name
dropped 1968.

Ferrophiliac (US)
Term for a person seriously interested
in rly matters.

Festival
A Belfast–Londonderry service which
ran in 1951 only.

Festival land cruise
see Land cruise.

FIC
Freight Integration Council, formed 1968.

Field (USRS)
A classification (freight marshalling) yard.

Fielder (USRS)
Brakeman in a field (qv).

Field to field crossing
Accommodation crossing (qv).

Fife Coast Express
Summer service between Glasgow (Queen St.) and St Andrews, 1949–51.

Fife Coast Line
Thornton Junc–St Andrews–Leuchars Junc.

Fifeshire Coast Express
A summer service between Glasgow (Queen St.) and St Andrews, 1912–39.

Fifty Five Broadway
Headquarters offices of the Underground Co., London, and later of the LPTB, LTE, LTB, and now LRT. Situated at 55 Broadway, Westminster, London, SW1 and completed in 1929 to the designs of the architect Charles Holden.

Figurehead (USRS)
A timekeeper.

Fill (US)
An embankment.

Fireboy (USRS)
A steam loco fireman.

Fire devil
A brazier lit at water cranes in cold weather to prevent the supply freezing; or one used by fogmen.

Fireless loco (obs)
A small steam loco without firebox, fed with steam from an external source and therefore suitable for use in high fire risk locations.

Fireman
The second member of crew of a steam loco, with the duty of maintaining the fire to produce the required quantity of steam; also attends to injectors and coupling up loco with train etc.

Fire train (obs)
A train equipped with steam pumps, water tank wagons etc., maintained at loco depots in a state of readiness to fight fires on or alongside the rly.

First A
GWR TC for eight-wheel First class coach.

First Reader (USRS)
A conductor's train book.

Fish
GWR TC for fish van.

Fish and chip van (RS)(obs)
A Sentinel steam railcar.

Fish bellied rails (obs)
An early form of cast iron rail with concave under-section to add strength.

Fish engines (RS)
GCR 4–6–0 locos (L&NER class B5), often seen on fast fish trains.

Fish horn (USRS)
An electric horn on a railcar.

Fishing
Placing rails together end to end.

Fishplates
Steel or wrought iron plates placed in

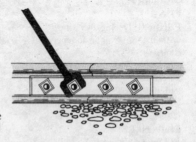

pairs at rail joints to bring the rail heads together, strengthen the joint and form a continous running surface. In their original form, when the two halves were held together, the shape suggested that of a fish. The patentee, William Bridges Adams used this name when describing his invention in 1847.

Fish tail (RS)
A distant signal. From the notched arm, resembling a fish's tail.

Fish Tanks (RS)
BR standard 2–6–4T locos.

Fitted freight/goods
A freight train with continuous brakes.

Fitted head (obs)
A group of continuously-braked wagons or vans at the head of an otherwise unfitted freight train.

Fitter's cap (RS)
A type of fault caused by unnecessary or over-conscientious interference. From the apocryphal blocking of the feed to a loco's injectors by a cloth cap left behind by a fitter when inspecting a tender water tank.

Fixed distant
An unworked distant signal permanently in the 'on' mode. Located to mark a speed restriction or the approach to a passenger platform or a passing loop on a single line.

FK
BR Corridor First class Compartment coach.

Flag docket (obs)
A document handed to a guard by booking clerk or other official indicating that passengers have been booked to stations at which his train stops 'conditionally', i.e. only when there are passengers to be set down on request (or waiting to be picked up).

Flagging
Controlling train movements by means

of red and green flags during signal failure, track repairs etc.

Flaggy (RS)
A flagman or look-out man.

Flagler's Folly
FEC (qv) between Miami and Key West, across the Florida Keys, a chain of small islands. Completed 1912 and destroyed by a hurricane in 1935. After its builder, Henry M. Flagler.

Flagman
An employee engaged in flagging (qv).

Flag halt/station/stop (obs)
An optional stop at which trains called only when there were definite indications of passengers wishing to be picked up or set down (the guard would be notified of the latter at the previous station (*see* Flag docket). Also known as a conditional stop. To indicate to the driver that he should stop, a red flag was exhibited (or at night, a raised lamp). In some cases the train was stopped by placing a semaphore signal in the 'on' position.

Flaman
A design of speedometer and speed recorder for locos. Its use has long been a legal requirement on French rlys. After its inventor.

Flamer (RS)
A hot box (qv), well alight, usually when seen at night.

Flandres–Riviera
A Calais–Ventimiglia service, avoiding Paris. So named 1970.

Flange lubricators
Equipment fixed to the rails to lubricate wheel flanges and reduce rail wear on curves.

Flannel Jackets (RS)
SR Bulleid Merchant Navy 4–6–2 locos of 1941 (rhyming slang: the first locomotive of this class was 'Channel Packet').

Flashbox (RS)
An emu (qv).

Flashing blade (RS)
A fireman's shovel.

Flat
1. (USRS) A flat wagon.
2. (USRS) A rail carrying wagon.
3. (RS) A wheel surface partly worn flat by harsh braking or skidding.

Flat bottom rail
Rail with flat section at base, so enabling it to be fastened direct to the sleepers.

Flat car (US)/**wagon**
Freight wagon with a flat floor, no sides, ends or roof.

Flatcase
GWR TC for a wagon designed to carry goods in cases.

Flat crossing
Tracks crossing on the level.

Flat irons (RS)
Midland Rly 0–6–4T. From their shape.

Flat yard
A yard in which all movements require use of locos.

Fleabox (RS)
Guard's van.

Flèche d'Or, La (Fr)
Golden Arrow; a *CIWL* all-Pullman service between Calais and Paris, in connection with Dover sailings and UK Golden Arrow (qv) service. Introduced 1929, ceased 1939, re-introduced 1946. Pullmans withdrawn 1969, ceased 1972.

Fliegende Hamburger
Flying Hamburger; *DR* service Berlin–Hamburg using pioneer streamlined articulated two-car diesel-electric sets, introduced 1933. Became the world's fastest train at that time.

Fliegende Kölner
A *DR* service Berlin–Hannover–Cologne using four-car streamlined

articulated diesel-electric sets, introduced 1935.

Fliegende Münchener
A *DR* service Berlin–Leipzig–Munich, using streamlined articulated diesel-electric units, introduced 1935.

Flighting
Grouping of trains travelling at similar speeds to increase line capacity.

Flimsy (USRS)
A train order (qv). From the thin paper used.

Flip, to (USRS)
To board a moving train, hence 'flipper', a hobo stealing a ride.

Flirt, The
Nickname for MS&LR. From its many overtures to other companies.

Floater (USRS)
Boomer (qv).

Florence Nightingale (RS)(obs)
A shunter carrying his oil lamp after dark.

Florida Special
A long-established winter season express between New York and Miami, introduced 1887. In the 1930s its consist included a bathing pool and a gymnasium. In the 1970s its passengers enjoyed fashion shows, colour television and bingo sessions.

FLT
Freightliner (qv) Terminal.

Fluff (RS)
Gratuities.

Fluffer (LTRS)
A tube rly tunnel cleaner, usually a female.

Fluffing
1. (LTRS) The work of a fluffer (qv).
2. (RS)(obs) An off duty porter picking out wealthy passengers at a large station and offering to carry their luggage in the hope of receiving fluff (qv).

Fluffy link (LTRS)(obs)
Neasden train crews on a separate
duty roster from which men were
drawn to cover all the odd jobs such
as stock transfers, stores trains, test
runs, sick absences etc. 'Like a piece
of fluff, they never settled down
anywhere . . .' — Harry Luff.

Flushing Continental
An express between London
(Liverpool St.) and Harwich
(Parkeston Quay) in connection with
sailings to Vlissingen (Flushing),
introduced 1926.

Fly
1. (RS)(obs) GWR and BR (W)
   shunter's truck.
2. GWR TC for six-wheel slip coach.
3. (RS)(obs) A pick up goods train
   (qv).

Flyers (RS)
L&SWR Adams 4–4–0 locos.

Flying Angel (RS)
A travelling ticket inspector.

Flying Bananas
1. (RS)(obs) GWR diesel railcars.
   From their shape.
2. (RS) BR HST/IC 125 trains, from
   their shape and their livery.

Flying Bedsteads (RS)
SE&CR Wainwright rebuilt Stirling
4–4–0 locos.

Flying Bufferbeam (RS)
A Peckett tank loco with low overall
height, giving prominence to buffer
beams.

Flying Duck (RS)
A section insulator.

Flying Dutchman
The unofficial title of GWR expresses
between London (Paddington) and
Exeter, after a famous racehorse.
Particularly applied to the 11.45
'Down', introduced 1862, which from
1871–84 was claimed to be the fastest
train in the world. Obs by the 1900s.

Flying Hamburger
see Fliegende Hamburger.

Flying junction
A branch line carried over main lines
by a bridge, thus avoiding the
conflicting movements of a flat
junction.

Flying Sausage (RS)(obs)
Early form of BR station name totem.

Flying Scotsman
The unofficial title (sometimes
expressed as 'Flying Scotchman' or
'Flying Scot') for the principal day
express between London (Kings Cross)
and Edinburgh (Waverley), current
from soon after its inauguration in
1862. Adopted officially by the
L&NER in 1923 and still in use. Ran
non-stop to Newcastle from 1927 and
non-stop to Edinburgh with corridor
tender (qv) from 1928. The journey of
392.7 m took 8 h 15 min in 1901, 8 h
8 min in 1927, 7 h in 1937, and 3 h
59 min with electric traction in 1991.

Fly[ing] shunt (obs)
A prohibited method of shunting, in
which the loco spurts ahead into one
track after the wagons it was hauling have
been uncoupled, leaving them to run on,
switched into another siding. Also
incorrectly applied to any form of loose
shunting (i.e. with uncoupled wagons).

Flying Snail (RS)(obs)
The CIE emblem as adopted in 1943.

Flying Squad (RS)
Travelling ticket inspectors.

FO
BR First class open coach with 2 + 1
seating.

Fog
1. (RS) A detonator.
2. (USRS) Steam.

Fogger (LTRS)
A fog repeater (qv).

Foggeys (RS)
Fogmen (qv).

Fogging (RS)
Fog signalling duty.

Fogging machine
A device which automatically places detonators on the rail surface when a signal is 'on', removing them when it changes to clear.

Fog gongs
Electric gongs attached to signal posts to warn drivers of the location of signals in foggy weather and to prevent overrunning should they be 'on'.

Fogmen
Rlymen called out in foggy weather to signal trains by flags and hand lamps and place detonators on tracks when fog is obscuring semaphore signals in the 'on' position.

Fog pit
A pit between rails in which a fogman stands to place detonators on the line.

Fog repeater
A colour-light signal only switched on during periods of poor visibility to repeat the indication of the next normal signal in advance.

Fog signal
Disc-shaped detonators with pliable metal clips which are placed on the surface of the rails in pairs to warn drivers that a signal obscured by fog is at danger or that there is an obstruction ahead.

Fog signalmen
Fogmen (qv).

Footboard yardmaster (USRS)
A freight conductor (3) acting as a yard switchman.

Footex
TC for football supporters' excursion or special train.

Footplate
The platform behind the firebox of a steam loco on which the enginemen stand.

Footplate staff
Enginemen.

Footwarmers (obs)
Metal cylinders filled with very hot water or chemicals at stations and placed on the floor of coaches not fitted with any form of heating system. Steam and electric heating had rendered them obsolete by the mid 1920s.

Fordell Rly
St David's Harbour to Inverkeithing, 4 ft 4 in/1,321 mm gauge, opened *c*. 1770, horse-worked, carrying coal from pits to harbour. It had three self-acting inclined planes and wooden rails. Rebuilt with iron rails 1833–8 and again relaid, for steam locos, in 1867. Closed 1947.

Foreign (obs)
Any rly other than that of the person using the term; the locos and rolling stock of such a rly; traffic arrived from or despatched to such a rly.

Foreign engine (RS)
A loco from another depot, even one on the same rly system.

Foreign Legion (RS)
Men on loan outside their usual base.

Forest of Dean Central Rly
Awre to Howbeach Slade and New Fancy Colliery, inc 1856, opened 1868. Worked by GWR. Part of GWR from 1923.

Forest of Dean Rly
Bullo Pill Junc to Churchway/ Cinderford Junc. Inc 1809 as Bullo Rly (horse), Churchway Hill–Bullo Pill, renamed FofD Rly 1826, purchased by SWR 1847, opened with loco traction 1854, Cinderford Loop 1908.

Forever Amber (RS)
A signal showing yellow indication consistently (fixed distant). After the title of a 1940s novel and film.

Formation
1. The earthworks and track bed of a rly.
2. Composition of a train. *See also* Consist.

Formsignal (Ger)
A semaphore signal.

Forney/Forney Engine (US)
Term for 0–4–4T steam loco type widely used on suburban and city elevated rlys. After its designer, M.N. Forney (1835–1908), US inventor and rly engineer. Came to be used for any tank loco without a leading truck.

Forth & Clyde
see F&CJR.

Fouling bar
A bar placed alongside a rail which is depressed by the weight of a vehicle or loco, and is connected with the signals, which it prevents from being put to 'off' indication when it is pushed down.

Fouling point
The point on converging tracks beyond which a vehicle on one line will obstruct anything passing on the other line.

Four (RS)
LM&SR class 4F 0–6–0. From its power classification. Also 'Four F'.

Four-foot
The space between the two running rails. *See also* Six-foot [way].

Fourteen wheelers (RS)
LB&SCR 4–6–4T locos.

Fourth class
The most inferior type of passenger accommodation, introduced on certain services of the Manchester & Leeds Rly, Edinburgh & Glasgow Rly and GNR in the 1840s and 1850s, but withdrawn after a few years. On the European mainland, Fourth class accommodation, with very cheap fares

and more standing space than seats, survived into the twentieth century, not being abolished in Germany, for example, until 1928.

Fourth rail
The negative or return current rail in a ground conductor insulated return system of electrification, usually placed in the centre between the running rails and is near earth potential.

Four wheel switch[er] (US)
A steam loco with 0–4–0 wheel arrangement.

Fowler's Ghost
Nickname of the unsuccessful prototype steam loco designed by Sir John Fowler to eliminate steam and smoke as far as possible when running in the Metropolitan Rly tunnels. Built by Robert Stephenson & Co. in 1861.

Foxfield Rly
A preserved industrial line from Blythe Bridge, Staffs to Dilhorne Park, opened 1968.

FR
1. Ffestiniog Rly, Portmadoc–Blaenau Ffestiniog. Inc 1832, for transport of slate from quarries to port, 1 ft 11½ in/597 mm gauge. Opened 1836, passenger service 1865. Closed passengers 1939, freight 1946. Reopened as preserved/ tourist line from 1955.
2. Furness Rly, inc 1844, Barrow to Lindal, opened 1846, subsequent extensions made to Carnforth, Whitehaven, Lakeside, Coniston. 158 route miles in 1914. Part of LM&SR 1923.
3. Fairbourne Rly, Fairbourne (Cambrian Rlys)–Penrhyn Point (Barmouth Ferry), 2 ft/609 mm gauge horse tramway, opened 1890 for freight, passengers carried from *c.* 1895. Converted to 15 in/ 381 mm gauge steam miniature rly

1916 by NGR (qv). Closed 1940, reopened 1947. Converted to 12 in/ 305 mm gauge 1986 and renamed F&Barmouth Steam Rly.

FRA (US)
Federal Railroad Administration; that part of the DoT (qv) which coordinates US federal government business relevant to rail safety, research and development etc.

Frame, mechanical
The apparatus, usually within a signal box, but occasionally found on station platforms or elsewhere, which includes the levers and interlocking for manual operation of points and signals.

Franco-Crosti boiler
A loco design incorporating a bank of tubes in a secondary drum or drums through which the exhaust gases pass before being released from a final chimney, the heat being used to raise the temperature of the feed water to a level almost as high as that in the main boiler. The chimney in the normal position is used only for lighting up when the loco is being steamed. Developed by *SA Locomotive a Vapore Franco* (It). Originally designed by A. Franco and built in Belgium in 1932 but improved by Ing. Piero Crosti and first built in Italy in 1940 and 1954. BR introduced ten 9F 2–10–0 locos with this feature in 1955.

FR&P
Felixstowe Rly & Pier, inc 1875, Westerfield–Felixstowe, opened 1877, worked by GER 1879, part of GER 1887. *See also* FD&R.

Franz Liszt
An EC between Dortmund and Budapest, introduced 1989.

Freaks (RS)
L&YR 4–6–0 locos.

Free-hauled traffic
Rly service materials carried on revenue-earning trains.

Free trucking
Free conveyance of scenery, stage properties and costumes for theatrical companies travelling by rail. Withdrawn after 1964.

Freezer (USRS)
A refrigerator wagon.

Freight
A generic term for all types of non-passenger traffic; originally US but imported to UK by the NER in the 1900s. By *c.* 1960 the term had replaced the former UK usage of 'goods' and 'minerals'.

Freightliner
A system for moving marine and road transport containers in dedicated trains of low-platform bogie wagons, with related transfer facilities from road to rail vehicles and vice versa. Developed by BR from 1963, the first service ran in 1965. Transferred in 1969 to Freightliners Ltd, a separate self-accounting company jointly owned by the NFC (qv) and the BRB. By 1974 there were 150 daily services carrying over 500,000 containers annually, including those to and from container ports. In 1978 this activity was returned to direct BR control. It was merged with Speedlink (qv) to form Railfreight Distribution (qv) in 1988. *See also* Speedfreight.

French notation
Continental notation (qv).

Frequency
The number of trains, or tramcars/ LRVs in a service per unit of time, e.g. 5 tph (trains per hour). Not to be confused with headway (*1*) (qv).

Fresh, The
Nickname for FY&NR (qv).

Fresher (RS)
Station refreshment rooms/buffet.
Fried eggs (RS)
Poached eggs (qv).
Friedrich Schiller
A winter season *TEE* Stuttgart–
Dortmund, 1979–82.
Frog
1. The 'V' type of crossing (qv) in
general use. In the US, a crossing.
2. The fitting placed at junctions of
overhead trolley wires on tramways
(*3*) to guide the trolley wheel. At
facing junctions the frog is fitted with
a moveable tongue. The tongue of a
two-way switch frog is maintained in
one position by a spring and moved
to the other by a wire operated by the
pointsman or point controller.
Automatic frogs are designed so that
their tongue is set for the branch line
by the trolley pole engaging a
weighted lever at the side of the frog
which is then released to allow the
tongue to return to its normal
'through line' position.
Front coupled (RS)
A loco with 0–4–2 wheel arrangement.
Frontier Mail
An express between Bombay, Delhi and
Peshawar, so named from 1928. Bombay
to Delhi, 950 m in 23 h in 1968. Now
runs between Bombay and Amritsar.
Front shift (RS)
An early turn, as opposed to back shift
(qv).
Frost devil (RS)
A brazier used for melting ice in a water
crane or to prevent a water crane from
freezing. *See also* Fire devil.
Frothblower (RS)
LM&SR Fowler 2–6–0 locos.
Fruit
GWR TC for fruit van.
FS
Ferrovie dello Stato; Italian State Rlys,

formed 1905–7.
FTA
Freight Transport Association.
Fudge, to (RS)
The action of a fudger or deceitful train
spotter – to count a loco as 'spotted' or
'copped' when it has not been seen.
Fulger Regele Carole 1er
A *CIWL* Pullman service between
Bucharest and Constantza, introduced
1933.
Fully-fitted train
A train in which there is a continuous
air or vacuum brake pipe connection
throughout and on which at least 90
per cent of the vehicles are equipped
with continuous brakes.
Funnel
A less usual alternative to chimney (of
a loco); at one time used officially by
GWR. *See also* Smokestack.
Further North Express
An express between Inverness,
Dornoch and Wick, introduced 1906.
See also John o' Groat.
Furzebrook Tramway
An industrial rly, 2 ft 8½ in/825 mm
gauge, operated by Pike Bros for
carriage of fire clay from Furzebrook
to Ridge on Poole Harbour, opened
1840, extended west from Furzebrook
to Povington 1920, main lines all
closed by 1957.
FY&NR
Freshwater, Yarmouth & Newport Rly
(Isle of Wight), inc 1881, opened
1888, 1889, worked by IofWCR until
1913. Part of SR from 1923.
Fylde Coast Express
A service between London (Euston)
and Blackpool with through coaches
for Blackburn/Colne, introduced 1934.
F-Zug (Ger)(obs)
Fernschnellzug; express train, usually
First class only. Replaced by IC (qv).
See also FD-Züge.

G

Gadfly
GWR TC for flat wagon used for carrying small aircraft.

Gadgets (RS)
L&NWR Webb 0–6–2T.

Galileo
A Paris–Venice–Florence service introduced 1989. Paris–Florence 1990. *See also* Rialto.

Gallery (US)
1. A signal gantry.
2. The upper deck of a double deck suburban coach with upper seating in galleries flanking the high ceiling of the central aisle of the lower deck.

Gallery car (US)
A freight car with two or three floor levels or decks.

Galloping Goose (USRS)
Any improvised rail vehicle, especially a self-propelled van.

Galloping rod (USRS)
The connecting rod of a diesel-electric loco.

Galvaniser (USRS)
A car inspector.

Gambrinus
A Munich–Hamburg service introduced 1952, *TEE* 1978. Stuttgart–Bremen from 1980, Münster–Stuttgart 1981, Dortmund–Stuttgart 1982–3. Lost *TEE* status 1983.

G&AR
Greenock & Ayrshire Rly, inc 1865, Greenock to Bridge of Weir, opened 1869. Part of G&SWR from 1872.

G&DFR
Gloucester & Dean Forest Rly, inc 1846, Gloucester to Grange Court, opened 1851, leased to and worked by GWR. Part of GWR from 1874.

G&KER
Garstang & Knot (*sic*) End Rly, inc 1864, Garstang to Pilling, opened 1870. Closed 1872, reopened 1875; Knott End Rly inc 1898, Pilling to Knott End, opened 1908, acquired the G&KER 1908, absorbed by LM&SR 1923.

G&LT
Glenanne & Loughgilly Tramway (NI). Tramway (*4*) 1 ft 10 in/559 mm gauge, horse traction. Opened 1897, closed 1919.

G&P Jt
Glasgow & Paisley Joint (CR & G&SWR), Glasgow (Central)–Cardonald–Paisley and branches to Govan, Shieldhall and Renfrew, formed 1837, main line opened 1840, LM&SR from 1923.

G&SWR
Glasgow & South Western Rly, inc 1850, a fusion of Glasgow, Paisley, Kilmarnock & Ayr Rly and Glasgow, Dumfries & Carlisle Rly, many other lines built subsequently; 492 route miles by 1914, serving south-west Scotland. Part of LM&SR from 1923.

G&WR
Gloucestershire & Warwickshire Rly. Preserved rly on former BR line between Cheltenham and Broadway. First section opened 1984.

Gandy dancer (USRS)
A track surfaceman. From the motion of men using track tongs or claw bars supplied by the Gandy Manufacturing Co. of Chicago when carrying rails from stockpiles to the track formation.

Gane
GWR TC for 40-ton bogie bolster truck used by Engineers' Department.

Ganger (obs)
A man in charge of a track maintenance gang, chargehand. Now known as track chargeman.

Gang road (obs)
A horse-worked plateway (qv).

Gangway
A metal plate or deck providing access between loco and tender or between one car and another. *See also* Fall plate.

Gangwayed
A coach with a means of access from one end to the other and to adjacent vehicles.

Ganz Electric
A Hungarian state enterprise manufacturing rly electrical equipment, founded as the Ganz Electrical Co. and by 1901 the largest industrial firm in Hungary, with 6,400 employees.

Ganz–Hunslet
An Anglo Hungarian firm partnering the Telfos-owned Hunslet (qv) and Ganz–Marag (qv).

Ganz–Marag
A Hungarian state enterprise manufacturing rly mechanical equipment.

Gapped (RS)
An electric train unable to move because its collector shoes are over a gap in the conductor rail.

GAR (Ger)
Güteraussenring; a freight belt line round Berlin.

Garda
An EC service between Munich and Verona, introduced 1989.

Garden
1. (RS)(obs) Ashpit and fire cleaning area in a loco depot.
2. (USRS) A freight yard.

Garden Cities & Cambridge Buffet Car Expresses
A L&NER service between London (Kings Cross), Welwyn Garden City, Letchworth and Cambridge, introduced 1932, restored 1948, withdrawn 1978.

Garden seats (obs)
Transverse slatted seats on open-top tramcars.

Garex
TC for guaranteed excursion.

Garratt
A steam loco type invented in 1907 by H.W. Garratt (1864–1913). It has two independent sets of driving wheels, carrying wheels, cylinders and motion, each mounted on a separate chassis, and each chassis carrying at its inner end one end of a central heavy girder frame supporting the boiler, which supplies steam to both sets of motion. This central unit also contains the controls and driving cab. Pivoting at each end of the central section allows negotiation of sharp curves and the general arrangement spreads the weight over a considerable length of track. The Whyte notation copes by using a plus sign, thus a Garratt might be a 4–8–2 + 2–8–4 or a 2–8–0 + 0–8–2.

Gas (RS)
Steam.

Gas buggy (USRS)
Any petrol or diesel-driven rail vehicle.

Gas house (USRS)
A yard office.

Gas up, to (RS)
To raise steam on a loco.

Gate (USRS)
A set of points.

Gate box
A signal box with the sole purpose of controlling a level crossing.

Gatwick Express
Regular and frequent non-stop service between London (Victoria) and Gatwick Airport, using air-conditioned Inter-City stock, introduced 1984.

Gauge
The distance between the rails of a track; measured from inside edge to inside edge of the rail heads. *See also* Broad gauge; Loading gauge; Narrow gauge; Standard gauge.

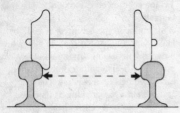

Gauge glass
A tube in the cab of a steam locomotive which shows the height of the water in the boiler; also a similar device showing the water level in tender.

Gauntletted track/Gauntletting
In which rails of parallel tracks are arranged so that the inner rail of one set is between the rails of the other. Normally adopted to allow additional working space on a viaduct or in a tunnel under lengthy repair. Effectively reduces the section concerned to single track without the expense of installing full points but must be signalled accordingly. Also used on tramways (*3*) when street width becomes insufficient for double track for a short distance. Also known as interlaced track or interlacing.

Gayant
TEE Paris–Tourcoing 1978. Lost *TEE* status 1983.

GB&K Jt
Glasgow, Barrhead and Kilmarnock Joint, G&SWR and CR, formed 1869, LM&SR from 1923.

GC&DR
Glasgow City & District Rly, inc 1882, first section opened 1886, worked by NBR, part of NBR 1887. Popularly known in Glasgow as 'The Underground', from its Finnieston–Queen St. (Low level)–High Street underground section, it comprised at its fullest extent a circular line from Queen St. via Great Western Road, Maryhill, Springburn and Bellgrove back to Queen St., with branches to Hyndland, Bridgeton Cross and Victoria Park.

GC & Midland Rly Joint Committee
Formed 1869 and inc 1872 as Sheffield [MS&LR] & Midland Committee, to administer jointly vested lines Manchester & Stockport, Hyde to Marple, and Marple, New Mills and Hayfield Junction; became GC & Midland JC 1897, LM&SR and L&NER joint 1923–47.

GC&NS Rlys Joint Committee
Formed 1871 as Macclesfield Committee, to administer the jointly vested MS&LR and NSR line Marple to Macclesfield. Name changed 1897, LM&SR and L&NER joint 1923–47.

GC, H&B & Midland Rlys Joint Committee
Inc 1907, Aire Junc–Doncaster–Braithwell Junc–Thurcroft–Brantcliffe Junc/Don Bridge Junc; became LM&SR and L&NER joint 1923–47.

GCP&BVR&T
Giant's Causeway, Portrush & Bush
Valley Rly & Tramway, inc 1880,
Portrush–Giant's Causeway, 3 ft/
914 mm gauge, opened 1883, 1887
with electric traction. First rly to use
hydro-electric power. Closed 1949.

GCR
1. Great Central Rly; an 1897
   renaming of the MS&LR (qv), 824
   route miles by 1914, mainly in
   central England, but also between
   Sheffield and London. Became part
   of L&NER from 1923.
2. Great Central Rly; a preserved
   section of (*1*) between
   Loughborough and Leicester. First
   section opened 1973.
3. Glasgow Central Rly; Inc 1888,
   part of CR (*1*) 1889, opened
   1894,1895,1896, Dalmarnock
   (Strathclyde Junc)–Stobcross–
   Maryhill and Dawsholm via Central
   (Low Level), almost all
   underground. Part of LM&SR
   1923. Closed 1964, reopened with
   electric trains 1979 (*see* Clyderail).

GE
1. The GER (qv).
2. General Electric Co. [of America]
   formed 1892, absorbing Thomson–
   Houston Electric Co.

GEC
General Electric Co. Ltd [UK], 1889
to date. Used initials WT (qv).
Absorbed AEI (qv) 1967, absorbed EE
(qv) 1968.

GEC stock (RS)(obs)
GEC-built emu stock for LM&SR
London suburban services, 1927.

General, The
Name of a 4–4–0 loco built for
Western & Atlantic RR (US) in 1855.
On 12 April 1862, during the Civil
War, it featured in a raid into
Confederate territory led by Capt.

James J. Andrews, and was recaptured
by Capt. W.A. Fuller after an exciting
100-mile chase. The loco, which has
been the subject of films, ballads and
books, has been preserved.

General merchandise (obs)
Freight traffic other than coal and
minerals; usually divided into
wagonload (qv) and sundries (qv).

Generators (RS)
BR class 47 diesel-electric locos.

Genevois
A Paris–Geneva *TGV*, introduced
1982.

Genial menial (RS)(obs)
A labourer in loco depot.

Geordies (RS)(obs)
NER locomotives and men.

GER
Great Eastern Rly, formed 1862 of the
ECR, EAR, NR, EUR, Newmarket
Rly, and ESR together with some
smaller companies. 1,191 route miles
by 1914, mainly in East Anglia. Part
of L&NER from 1923. *See also* Great
Eastern.

Germans (RS)
SE&CR L 4–4–0 locos built by Borsig,
Berlin.

Get Wets (RS)
GWR 2–4–0T and 0–6–0T without
cabs.

Ghan, The
Rly between Maree, Australia and
Alice Springs, 3 ft 6 in/1,067 mm
gauge, completed 1929. Rebuilt to
standard gauge on new route from
Port Augusta, via Tarcoola 1980.
Also a train running over these lines,
between Adelaide and Alice
Springs. From the Afghan immigrants
who operated camel trains over
the route before the rly was
completed.

Ghost (LTRS)
Pop-up (qv).

Ghoul (RS)
A buckeye coupling (qv).

Ghoul, to (RS)
To couple a train by use of automatic couplers.

Giant
GWR TC for 50 ft/15.24 metres bogie van.

Giesl ejector
An oblong ejector invented by Dr Adolph Giesl-Gieslingen of Vienna for the front end of steam locos. First used in Britain on the Talyllyn Rly in 1958.

Gigs (RS)(obs)
GWR shunter's wagons.

Ginger 'un (RS)
A distant signal showing cautionary yellow.

Gippo (LTRS)
An outside telephone, as distinct from rly internal system. From GPO (General Post Office), the former telephone monopoly.

GIPR
Great Indian Peninsula Rly; formed 1853. Purchased by Government 1900. Part of the Central Rly of India from 1951.

Girl/old girl (USRS)
An affectionate term for a loco or train. *See also* She.

GJR
Grand Junction Rly, inc 1833, Birmingham–Warrington (Newton) (junction with L&MR), opened 1837, freight 1838; amalgamated with other companies to form L&NWR (qv) in 1846.

Glacier Express
A metre-gauge service between Zermatt and St Moritz, introduced 1930. Summer only until 1981; all year round (Zermatt–Chur) from 1982.

Gladstone's Act
see Parliamentary fares/trains.

Gläserne–Zug
Glass Train; an electric observation railcar with roof, sides and ends largely of safety-glass, introduced by *DR* in 1935, rebuilt by *DB* 1949 and based at Munich.

Glasgow District Subway
A circular underground 4 ft/1,219 mm gauge cable rly in centre of Glasgow with fifteen stations, inc 1890, opened 1896, renamed GDS Rly 1914, purchased by Glasgow Corporation 1922, electrified 1935, modernized 1980. *See also* Clockwork Orange.

Glasgow Executive
An express between London (Euston) and Glasgow, introduced 1984, name dropped 1985.

Glassback (RS)
A lazy fireman, not happy about bending his back.

Glass car (USRS)
A passenger coach.

Glass Coach (RS)
The District Engineer's Inspection Saloon.

Glasszug
see Gläserne–Zug.

Glimmer (USRS)
A loco headlight.

Globe strainers
Spherical insulators hung between bracket arms and ears (qv) of tramway

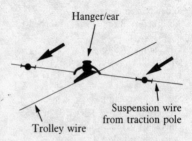

Hanger/ear

Suspension wire from traction pole

Trolley wire

(3) overhead to prevent electric current from passing between the two.

Glory (USRS)
A string of empty vehicles.

Glory hunter (USRS)
A reckless driver.

Glory wagon (USRS)
A caboose (qv).

Glossies (RS)
Weekly traffic and working notices.

Gloucester
Gloucester Wagon Co., founded 1860. Also manufactured signalling equipment from the 1870s. Became Gloucester Railway Carriage and Wagon Co. Ltd, 1888. Ceased production of rly equipment, apart from trucks, 1968. Merged with PDWCL (qv), 1986.

Glow worms (LTRS)
Circle Line trains (from their headlights).

GLV
Gatwick Luggage Vans, BR (S), fitted with gangway at one end. *See also* MLV.

GM
General Manager.

GM(EMD)
General Motors (Electromotive Division); US loco builders.

GMML
Greater Manchester Metro Ltd. Founded 1990 as the operating company for Metrolink (qv).

GMPTA/E
Greater Manchester Passenger Transport Authority/Executive.

GN (US)
Great Northern RR.

GN&CR
Great Northern & City Rly, main line loading gauge tube rly between Moorgate, London and a terminus under Finsbury Park (GNR). Inc 1892, opened 1904, absorbed by

Metropolitan Rly 1913. Passed to LPTB 1933 and was operated by its successors (normal LT tube rly stock used from 1939). Closed 1975. Reopened 1979 and integrated with BR Great Northern suburban lines by new connections at Drayton Park/Finsbury Park, BR taking over operation.

GN&GEJC
Great Northern & Great Eastern Joint Committee, formed 1879 to manage existing lines Huntingdon–St Ives–March–Spalding and Lincoln–Doncaster. Spalding–Lincoln opened 1882. Ramsey & Somersham Rly purchased 1896. All part of L&NER from 1923.

GN&L&NWR JC
Great Northern and L&NWR Joint Committee, inc 1874, to manage lines between Welham and Drayton Juncs near Market Harborough and Melton Mowbray and Bottesford/Saxondale Junc nr Nottingham, opened 1879. L&NER & LM&SR joint 1923–47.

GN&SR
Great Northern & Strand Rly, tube rly, London, inc 1899, Finsbury Park–Aldwych, absorbed (before opening) into GNP&BR (qv) 1902.

GN&WR
Great Northern & Western Rly, Athlone to Westport, inc 1857. Opened 1860, 1861, 1862, 1866. Branch Manulla to Ballina opened 1868, 1873. Part of M&GWR from 1890.

Gnat
GWR TC for slip coach (three types).

Gnat's blood (RS)
Tea.

GNofE, C&HJR
Great North of England, Clarence and Hartlepool Junction Rly, inc 1837, Wingate–Ferryhill, opened 1839, 1846,

leased to York, Newcastle & Berwick Rly 1848 and lease passed on to NER from 1854. Became part of L&NER 1923.

GNofER

Great North of England Rly, inc 1836, 1837, Darlington to York, opened 1841. Worked by Newcastle & Darlington Junction Rly from 1845 and purchased by it 1846, becoming the York & Newcastle Rly. Latter amalgamated with Newcastle & Berwick to form York, Newcastle & Berwick Rly in 1847, this forming part of the new NER from 1854.

GNofSR

Great North of Scotland Rly, inc 1846, Aberdeen to Huntly, first section opened 1854. Other lines added and absorbed; 334 route miles by 1914. Became part of L&NER from 1923.

GNP&BR

Great Northern Piccadilly & Brompton Rly, tube rly, London, inc 1902, an amalgamation of the B&PCR (qv) and GN&SR (qv). South Kensington–Hammersmith section used powers of District Railway Deep Level scheme of 1897 between South Kensington and Earls Court, then rising to surface near West Kensington to run along the MDR alignment into separate platforms at Hammersmith. Opened Finsbury Park–Hammersmith 1906, Holborn to Strand (now Aldwych) 1907. Became part of LER from 1910.

GNR

Great Northern Rly, inc 1846, London to York etc., first sections opened 1848, 1849, 1850, 1852. Many other lines subsequently built and absorbed; 1,032 route miles by 1914. Became part of L&NER from 1923. *See also* Great Northern.

GNR (I)

Great Northern Rly (Ireland), inc 1876 as Great Northern of Ireland Rly but usually referred to as GNR (I). An amalgamation of the Ulster Rly (opened 1839 with 6 ft 2 in/ 1,879.6 mm gauge) and the Northern of Ireland Rly (a combination of the Dublin & Drogheda Rly (opened 1844) and the Dublin & Belfast Junction Rly) and other smaller lines. 616 route miles by 1914. Purchased by Northern Ireland and Republic of Ireland Governments 1953 and managed by Great Northern Rly Board. In 1958 the trackage in the Republic became part of the CIE, and that in Northern Ireland part of the UTA (qv).

GO/GO Transit

Government of Ontario-financed scheme for development of the CNR suburban services in the Toronto area, inaugurated 1967.

Goat (USRS)

Any shunting loco. Also 'yard goat'.

Goat herder (USRS)

A loco driver in a shunting yard.

Go back, to (of a signal) (LTRS)

To change from green to red. When the driver of an approaching train sees this, he will describe the signal as having 'gone back in my face'.

Gobblers (RS)

GER Worsdell '650' 2–4–2T locos, from their large appetite for coal when first fitted with Joy valve gear.

God (LTRS)

The Line Controller.

Go dead, to (USRS)

To work twelve hours continuously.

Go devil (USRS)

A manually-operated rail car.

God's Wonderful Railway (RS)

Nickname for the GWR. The term persisted into the early days of BR (W).

Goethe
TEE Paris–Frankfurt, introduced
1970. Lost *TEE* status 1975. Name
used for *TEE* Dortmund–Frankfurt
1979–83 and an EC Paris–Frankfurt
1987. Extended to Dresden 1991.

Golden Arrow
A Pullman express between London
(Victoria) and Folkestone/Dover in
connection with sailings for Calais and
La Flèche d'Or (for Paris) (qv).
Introduced 1929, ceased 1939,
restored 1946, withdrawn 1972.

Golden Hind/Executive/Pullman
An express between London
(Paddington), Plymouth and, from
1972, Penzance, introduced 1964. 3 h
50 min London–Plymouth in 1964,
3 h 13 min in 1982. Renamed GH
Executive 1986, GH Pullman 1987.

Golden Mountain Pullman Express
A *CIWL* service Montreux–
Zweisimmen (metre gauge) and thence
to Interlaken by standard gauge train
with same name, ran summer 1931
only.

Golden Rail
BR holiday packages, introduced
1971, renamed Gold Star Holidays
1988, sold outside BR, 1989.

Golden Sands Express
A Llandudno–Rhyl summer service,
introduced 1930.

Golden Spike
A ceremony on 19 May 1869 at
Promonotory, Utah, when the final
sections of the UP and Central Pacific
Railroads were laid, establishing a
continuous rly across the USA
between the Atlantic and Pacific
coasts. A spike of California gold and
another of Nevada silver were driven
home by distinguished officials.
The original Golden Spike is now
displayed at Stanford University,
California.

Golden Valley
Golden Valley Rly, inc 1876, Hay-on-
Wye to Pontrilas, opened 1881, 1889.
Closed at various periods, part of
GWR from 1899, reopened 1901.

Golfers' Express
A Belfast–Portrush service, introduced
1934.

Goliath
GWR TC for 50-ft open theatrical
scenery wagon.

Gon (USRS)
A gondola (qv).

Gondola (US)
Any type of open freight wagon.

Gone Completely
The latter day nickname for the GCR,
the only large pre-grouping company
whose main line has been closed.

Gone to bed (LTRS)
A stabled train.

Good Old England! (RS)
Exclamation uttered at a derailment.

Goods line
A line normally used only by freight
trains and maintained to a reduced
standard accordingly. Usable by
passenger trains at slow speeds in an
emergency.

Goose
TC for 'Stop accepting [trains] until
further notice'.

Goose, to (USRS)
To make an emergency stop.

Got Nowhere
Nickname for GNR, because its main
line from London ended nowhere in
particular, at Shaftholme Junc, with
the NER, north of Doncaster.

Gottardo
TEE Zurich–Milan, introduced 1961,
extended to Basle 1965–82; extended
to Geneva 1974–80. Lost *TEE* status
1988, and was the last of the *TEE*
international services. Name used for a
Zurich–Milan EC 1988.

Gotthard Oberland Pullman Express
A *CIWL* seasonal service Paris–Basle–Milan (with portion for Berne and Interlaken), ran 1927–31.

Gotthard Pullman Express
A *CIWL* seasonal service Basle–Milan, ran 1927–31.

Gov/Government, The, (RS)(obs)
A parliamentary train (qv).

Go When Ready
Nickname for the GWR.

Goyle (RS)
Any train or loco considered to be ugly or unappealing. Applied in particular to BR class 31 diesel-electric locos. From gargoyle.

Gozunda/er (RS)
A rail-mounted device for inspecting the undersides of viaduct and tall bridge arches from track level, introduced 1974; 'goes-under'.

GP-TRAMM
Acronym for General Purpose Track Maintenance Machine, BR.

Grabber (USRS)
A conductor (*3*) or a ticket collector.

Grab iron (USRS)
The hand rail on a loco or other rail vehicles.

Grade (US)
Formation (*1*), also gradient and ground level.

Grade, crossing at
A crossing on the level.

Gradient measure/inclination
In Britain, South America, South Africa and Australasia this is usually quoted as a direct proportion: e.g. 1 in 50 = a rise of 1 ft in 50 ft of line. In mainland Europe it is normally given as per thousand (pro mille) and expressed as $^0/_{00}$. In North America and elsewhere gradients are expressed as percentages, 1 per cent equalling 1 in 100, 5 per cent 1 in 20 etc. Thus the British 1 in 10 is the same as

$100^0/_{00}$ or 10 per cent. Except in very dry tunnels rail vehicles need some special device to tackle gradients steeper than 1 in 10.

Gradient posts
Lineside signs indicating whether a gradient is up or down and its measure/inclination.

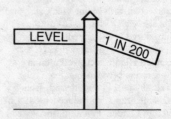

Grampian
A 3-hour express between Glasgow (Buchanan St.) and Aberdeen, introduced 1962.

Grampian Corridor Express
An Edinburgh–Glasgow–Aberdeen service of the CR (*1*), introduced 1905.

Grampus
TC for civil engineer's 20-ton dropside wagons.

Grand confort (Fr)
Luxury First class coaches introduced by the *SNCF* from 1969.

Grand Ducal
A Brussels–Luxembourg service, introduced 1973.

Grand Junction Line
Stechford–Bescot–Bushbury. From GJR (qv).

Grandes lignes (Fr)
Main lines, the principal trunk lines.

Grand union (obs)
A US term, adopted in UK, and mainly applied to tramways (*3*), signifying a right-angled intersection of two sets of double track with double track connections at *all four* corners.

Granite City
An express between Glasgow (Buchanan St.) and Aberdeen, introduced 1933, restored 1949.

Granite City Express
An Edinburgh–Glasgow–Aberdeen service, introduced 1906. Re-introduced 1933 for a Glasgow–Aberdeen service.

Grano
GWR TC for hopper wagon carrying grain.

Granville & Westgate-on-Sea Special Express
A LC&DR express between London (Victoria) and Ramsgate, introduced 1878. Title underwent various changes, name eventually dropped 1904. Reappeared as Granville Express 1921, name dropped 1927. Name derives from the Granville Hotel, St Lawrence-on-Sea, Ramsgate.

Granville Special Express
A SER First class 'Special Private Express' service between London and Ramsgate, introduced 1876 in connection with the Granville Hotel, St Lawrence-on-Sea, Ramsgate, which offered the SER a guarantee. Arguably Britain's first officially-named train. Title dropped 1880, revived at various periods with title in various forms between 1884 and 1904.

Graphiste (Fr)
A timetable compiler. From his use of train graphs (qv).

Grasshoppers
1. (RS) LB&SCR Billinton 4–4–0 locos. Also GWR 90XX 'Dukedog' 4–4–0s. From a tendency to wheel slip on starting. *See also* Hopper.
2. (USRS)(obs) A vertical-boilered loco. From its appearance when in motion.

Grass wagon (USRS)
A tourist coach.

Gravedigger (USRS)
A section hand.

Graveyard (USRS)
Sidings accommodating condemned locos or rolling stock.

Graveyard shift (USRS)
Midnight to 08.00.

Gravitation/Gravity sidings/yard
Sidings or a yard arranged on a gradient so that shunting and marshalling can be done by gravity, minimizing use of locos. *See also* Hump.

Grazing ticket (USRS)
A meal voucher.

Grease monkey (RS)
An employee designated to oil rolling stock or (USRS) to pack grease into axle boxes; a carman (qv).

Grease the pig, to (USRS)
To oil a loco.

Great Eastern
BR brand name for ex-GER (qv) lines, introduced 1958.

Greathead shield
A tunnelling shield invented by J.H. Greathead (1844–96). Extensively used in construction of deep level tube rlys.

Great North
Abbreviation for GNofSR (qv).

Great Northern
BR brand name for ex GNR (qv) lines, introduced 1958, also NSE (qv) brand name for London (Kings Cross)–Hertford/Stevenage–Cambridge/Huntingdon electric services.

Great Orme
A 3 ft 6 in/1,067 mm cable tramway at Llandudno, north Wales, opened 1902, connecting the town with the summit of Great Orme.

Great Scottish & Western Rly Company
Private charter operators using BR lines.

Great Uhuru Rly
Tanzam Rly (qv).
Great Way Round
Nickname for GWR.
Greek Line
A boat train between London
(Waterloo) and Southampton Docks in
connection with GL sailings, 1954–66.
Green Arrow (obs)
A system of registered consignment
fast freight transit, formerly available
on payment of a premium for a
package or train load. Introduced by
GWR in 1930 and subsequently by the
other British rly companies. Ceased
1939. Re-introduced 1953 to expedite
export consignments; fully restored
1957 but subsequently withdrawn.
Also L&NER V2 2–6–2 locomotives,
introduced 1936 and used on trains
carrying Green Arrow freight.
Greenball (USRS)
A train solely composed of fruit or
vegetable vans.
Greenbat
Greenwood & Batley Ltd, Leeds,
manufacturers of electric locos. Part of
Hunslet (qv) from 1981.
Green carrier (USRS)
The first section of a train which is
running in two parts.
Green caterpillars (RS)(obs)
The original L&SWR electric trains as
introduced in 1915.
Green eye (USRS)
A clear signal.
Green fire (RS)
A part of loco fire which is unburnt.
Greenhouses (RS)
GER 1300 (later L&NER F7) 2–4–2T
locos. From their disproportionately
large side-windowed cabs.
Green tanks (RS)
L&SWR Urie H16 4–6–2T locos.
Greyhounds (RS)
1. L&SWR small Drummond T9

4–4–0 locos of 1899–1901. From
their high speed on down
gradients.
2. CIG (qv) emu sets (Class 421/4)
upgraded for 100 m.p.h running on
the London (Waterloo)–Guildford–
Portsmouth line.
GRI
BR (SR) four-car emu corridor set
with griddle (qv) cars converted from
restaurant cars 1964, formation as
BUF (qv) with griddle car instead of
buffet car, 4-GRI.
Grice, a (RS)
A good cop (qv). Derived from gricer
(qv).
Grice, to (RS)
To exhibit the characteristics of a
gricer (qv), i.e. any or all of the
following: to travel enthusiastically
over a particular rly line for the first
time, or to ride with enthusiasm
behind a particular locomotive for the
first time, or to see or photograph it
for the first time etc.; to watch trains
obsessively; to enthuse fanatically over
a locomotive, item of rolling stock or
rly line; to go on a trip in pursuit of
rly interests.
Gricer (RS)
The most fanatical and extreme type
of rly enthusiast, intent on travelling
over all existing rly track, seeing all
existing locos etc. Often used in a
derogatory sense to denote the
scruffily-dressed, camera-, binocular-
and notebook-carrying rly voyeur and
collector of useless information. The
origins of the term are obscure and
beset with false trails, but it seems to
have emerged in northern England
during the 1940s, spreading into
general use in the late 1950s and
early '60s; it was not used in
the popular rly periodicals until
c. 1970.

Griddle car
A BR catering vehicle with bar and buffet saloons and central kitchen fitted with griddle plates, introduced 1961.

Gridiron (RS)(obs)
A marshalling yard, usually gravity-worked.

Gridirons (RS)
BR class 56 diesel locos.

Griever (USRS)
A trade union official at an investigation or inquiry.

Gril Express (Fr)
SNCF cafeteria cars (qv), introduced 1970.

Grind (USRS)
A Shay loco (qv).

Grip car
A tramcar equipped with a device to grip and release hold on moving cables beneath the track. Sometimes with passenger seating to supplement that in its trailer car.

Grip man
The driver of a grip car (qv).

Gronk, to (RS)
To travel over rlys normally difficult of public access. Also gronkage, such lines; and gronker, one who indulges in gronking. In use from *c.* 1980.

Ground disc
A small disc-shaped signal with banner indicator, placed on the ground to control movements in sidings or over crossovers.

Ground frame
A small mechanical frame set apart from a signal box, often in the open, to control signals in sidings. Unlocked electrically from the nearest signal box, or by a release key. *See also* Annett's Key.

Ground hog (USRS)
A brakeman or yardmaster.

Ground signal
Any type of signal placed at ground level to control movements in sidings or shunting, usually one with miniature semaphore arms and spectacles. *See also* Dummy (*3*).

Groupie (LTRS)
A group manager.

Grouping
The amalgamation of most British rly companies into four groups (LM&SR, L&NER, GWR and SR), which took place following the Railways Act, 1921, and was effective from 1 January 1923.

Group station tickets (obs)
Scheme tickets (qv).

Growlers (RS)
BR diesel locos generally. Specifically, class 37.

Grunt (USRS)
A loco driver.

GRWU
General Railway Workers' Union; formed 1890, amalgamated with ASRS (qv) and UP&SS (qv) to form NUR (qv) in 1913.

GS&WR
Great Southern & Western Rly (Ireland), inc 1844, Dublin to Cashel and later, Cork. Blackpool, just outside Cork, reached 1849, Cork (Glanmire) 1855. Many small lines absorbed and others built until it became the largest rly system in Ireland with 1,130 route miles in 1914, mainly in southern Ireland. Part of GSR from 1924.

GSR
Great Southern Rlys Co. (Ireland), formed 1924–5, to include GS&WR, CB&SCR, MGWR, D&SER and various smaller undertakings. 2,187 route miles in 1927. Part of CIE from 1945.

GSRPS
Great Southern Railways Preservation Society; preserved line Tralee–Fenit, on former GS&WR/GSR Fenit branch.

GTI (US)
Guilford Transportation Industries Inc;
includes B&M and Maine Central RR.
GTS
Guard's Trailer Second/Standard class;
a BR HST coach with guard's
compartment and parcels area.
GTW (US)
Grand Trunk Western RR Co.
Guard rail
see Check rail.
Guard's bedroom (RS)(obs)
A freight train brake van.
Guard truck
An additional low-bodied wagon
marshalled next to wagons containing
long items which overhang, or between
two flat wagons carrying a long load.
Guildford New Line
Surbiton–Effingham Junction–
Guildford. Still so called to distinguish
it from the original line to Guildford via
Woking, although it dates from 1885.
Gunboats
1. (RS) SER Mansell 0–4–4T locos.
2. (USRS) Steel hopper wagons.
Gustav Eiffel
An EC service between Paris and
Frankfurt, introduced 1989. Extended
to Leipzig 1991.
Gut (USRS)
The brake air hose.
GUV
General Utility Van, BR; no guard's
compartment, side and end doors,
non-gangwayed.
GVR
Gwendreath Valley Rly, inc 1866,
Kidwelly to Mynydd-y-garreg, opened
1871, worked by BP&GVR 1886–
1905. Part of GWR 1923.
GVT
Glyn Valley Tramway, Chirk to Glyn
Ceiriog, tramway (*4*), inc 1870,
opened with 2 ft 4¼ in/717.55 mm
gauge, 1873, 1874. Horse worked until

1886, passenger traffic then ceasing
until resumed in 1891. Gauge
converted to 2 ft 4½ in/723.9 mm for
start of steam working in 1887–8.
Closed passengers 1933, freight 1935.
GW&BR
Great Western & Brentford Rly, inc
1855, Southall to Brentford Dock,
opened 1859, 1860, leased to GWR,
part of GWR 1872.
GW&GCJC
Great Western & Great Central Rlys
Joint Committee formed 1899, to
manage Northolt Junc–Princes
Risborough–Aylesbury/Ashendon
Junc, opened 1906 (except for existing
High Wycombe–Princes Risborough–
Aylesbury line). GWR and L&NER
from 1923. Part of BR from 1948.
GW&TVJ
Great Western & Taff Vale Joint, inc
1867, Merthyr, Brandy Bridge Junc to
Mardy Junc, opened 1877, part of
GWR from 1922.
GW&UR
Great Western & Uxbridge Rly, inc
1846, West Drayton to Uxbridge,
opened 1856, part of GWR from 1847.
Gwili Rly
Preserved rly on former BR
Carmarthen–Aberystwyth line just
north of Carmarthen (Bronwydd
Arms–Llwyfan Cerrig). First section
opened 1978.
GWR
Great Western Rly, inc 1835, 1837,
London to Bristol, opened 1838, 1839,
1840, 1841. Many other lines
subsequently built and absorbed.
3,025 route miles in 1914. Re-formed
by inclusion of many smaller
companies 1922–3, bringing total route
miles to 3,820. Part of BR from 1948.
GWR Magazine
House journal of GWR, published
1888–1947.

H

H
Handbrake fitted vehicle (BR).

Hack (USRS)
A caboose (qv).

Hackney Gurkhas (RS)(obs)
Rlymen in Army rly units.

Hairspring, as tight as a (RS)
A mean or greedy individual.

HAL
1. SR two-car emu set with lavatory
   in one car only (hence HALf
   lavatory); Second/Standard class
   compartment brake motor car and
   side corridor driving trailer
   composite with lavatory, introduced
   1939 and 1948, 2-HAL.
2. Heathrow Airport Ltd [London
   Airport], a wholly-owned subsidiary
   of British Airports Authority,
   owners of the electric units used on
   the Paddington–Heathrow service,
   and partners with NSE in the
   Heathrow Express project.

Halesowen Joint
Inc 1865 as Halesowen and
Bromsgrove Rly, Halesowen Junc to
Northfield Junc, name changed to
Halesowen Rly 1876, opened 1883,
worked and maintained by GWR and
Midland Rly, vested in GWR and
Midland jointly from 1906, GWR and
LM&SR 1923–47.

Half dirties (RS)(obs)
Train crews employed on both steam
and electric traction in the period
when both existed on BR main line
services.

Half section
An upper or lower 'double berth' in a
US Pullman sleeping car.

Hall's Tramroad
A horse-worked tramroad built by
Benjamin Hall from Hall's Road,
Risca to Abercarn Ironworks and
Manmoel and branches, first section
opened 1809. Leased to GWR for
1,000 years from 1877 and opened as a
rly 1886 and 1912. GWR opened an
extension at Manmoel 1905, and
Cwmcarn branch 1911.

Halt (obs)
A minor stopping place without full
station facilities, usually unstaffed,
serving an area of light traffic,
platforms usually of timber and
amenities confined to a simple shelter
and lighting. The term came into
general usage in the 1900s with the
introduction of railmotors and auto-
trains. The GWR originally made a
special distinction between a halt and
a 'platform' (qv), the latter having
sufficient length to accommodate an
ordinary branch line or stopping train.

Halte
French and Belgian term for a minor
stopping place, briefly adopted in UK
by GWR and Metropolitan Rly from
1903 but very soon discarded for the
anglicized version.

Ham
1. (RS) Overtime; hence 'fatty ham',
   excessive overtime work. *See also*
   On the ham.

2. (USRS) A learner rly telegrapher.

Hamlet
EC Hamburg–Copenhagen, introduced 1991.

Hammersmith & City [Rly]
Inc 1861, opened 1864, Hammersmith–Green Lane Junc, Westbourne Park, and curve Latimer Road–Uxbridge Road WLR. Vested in GWR and Metropolitan Rly 1867. Worked by Metropolitan Rly. Electrified 1906. Joint GWR and LPTB 1933–47, BR and LT 1948–69, then wholly LT.

Hampstead/Hampstead Tube
see CCE&HR.

Hand Bomber/Grenader (USRS)
A steam loco not fitted with a mechanical stoker.

H&BR
Hull & Barnsley Rly, inc 1880 as Hull, Barnsley & West Riding Junction Rly & Dock Co., first line opened, with Alexandra Dock, Hull, 1885. Renamed H&BR 1905. 92 route miles by 1914, Hull to Cudworth and Wath. Absorbed by NER 1922.

H&C (obs)
Horse & carriage traffic (qv).

H&C[R]
Hammersmith & City [Rly] (qv).

H&HR
Hull & Holderness Rly, inc 1853, Withernsea to Hull, opened 1854, worked by NER 1860, part of NER 1862.

Handle (LTRS)
The master controller in the cab of an electric train. *See also* On the handle(s).

Handle winder (LTRS)
The motorman of an electric train.

H&MR
Hounslow & Metropolitan Rly, inc 1880. Hounslow Town to Mill Hill Park (now Acton Town) opened 1883.

Worked by MDR. Branch Osterley to Hounslow Barracks (now Hounslow West), 1884. Terminal at Hounslow Town closed 1886, reopened 1903, finally closed 1909. Part of MDR from 1903. Electrified 1905.

H&OJR
Halifax & Ovenden Junction Rly, inc 1864, opened Holmfield–Halifax 1874, passenger service 1879, jointly vested in GNR and L&YR 1870; LM&SR and L&NER 1923–47.

Hand-on (USRS)
A train order (qv) taken up by a member of the train crew on a moving train.

H&SYER
Hull & South Yorkshire Extension Rly, inc 1897 Wrangbrook Junc–Wath, opened 1902. Part of H&BR from 1898.

H&WNR
Hunstanton & West Norfolk Rly, an 1874 merger of Lynn & Hunstanton Rly and WNJR. Part of GER 1890.

Hanging buffers
Vertical wooden buffers on a wagon to permit coupling with wagons having buffers at lower levels.

HAP
BR (SR) two-car epb emu set with lavatory in only one of the cars (HAlf corridor electro-Pneumatic brakes); motor brake Second/Standard class and driving trailer composite with lavatory, introduced 1957–8, 1961–2; 2-HAP.

Harbour lights (RS)
'Arbour lights (qv).

Hard class
Term used on certain overseas rlys to describe the most inferior form of passenger accommodation, 'hard' being related to the quality of the seating. On the SZD (qv), the equivalent of Second class, with

leathercloth seating. *See also* Fourth
class; Soft class.

Hard hat man (RS)
An inspector. From his once
obligatory bowler hat.

Hard road (RS)
A lack of resilience in the track due to
frost in the ground.

Hard-up (RS)(obs)
A lack of steam in a loco.

Harlequin Line (obs)
A short-lived brand name and logo
adopted by BR in 1988 for Euston–
Watford dc electric services, said to be
a combination of Hatch End,
Harlesden and Queen's Park.
Superseded by North London Lines
(qv).

Harness (USRS)
The uniform of passenger train crews.

Harpic signals (LTRS)
Round The Benders (qv). From the
famous lavatory-cleaning product and
its advertising slogan.

Harrogate Pullman
An unofficial name for an all-Pullman
service between London (Kings
Cross), Leeds, Harrogate, Ripon,
Darlington and Newcastle, introduced
1923, extended to Edinburgh, 1925,
but still not officially named, though
known as Edinburgh Pullman or
Harrogate–Edinburgh Pullman.
Became Queen of Scots 1927 (qv).

Harrogate Sunday Pullman
An all-Pullman train between London
(Kings Cross) and Harrogate/Bradford
(Exchange), introduced 1927, restored
1950.

Harrovian
MDR London commuters' 'express',
South Harrow to Mansion House (non-
stop Hammersmith–Sloane Square),
introduced 1915, ceased 1932.

Harton Electric Rly
The Harton Coal Co. operated colliery

lines at South Shields connecting
Harton Low Staiths, Westoe Colliery
and Harton Colliery; these were
electrified in 1908 on the overhead
system at 550V dc. Harton was the
only British standard gauge surface
colliery rly with electric traction. Part
of NCB Rlys from 1947. Electric
traction replaced by diesels 1989. *See
also* SSM&WCR.

Hastings Car Train
A service operated with US-built
Pullman-type cars, rebuilt at Ashford
Works, and introduced by the SER in
1906 between London (Charing Cross
and Cannon St.) and Hastings.

Hat (USRS)
An incompetent rlyman (useless except
as a resting place for his hat).

Hat check (USRS)(obs)
A receipt issued in exchange for a
collected ticket.

Haughley Mail (RS)
East Anglian TPO (qv). So called
because the Norwich and
Peterborough trains originally joined/
divided at Haughley Junc.

Haulage basher (RS)
A gricer (qv) with an obsession to ride
behind as many different types of loco
as possible or every loco of a particular
class.

Haul dead, to
To haul an inoperative loco.

Hauptbahnhof (Ger)
The central/main station in a city or
large town.

Hauptlinie (Ger)
A main (or trunk) line.

Hawker Siddeley Group
Absorbed Brush (2) (qv) 1957,
Crompton Parkinson (qv) 1967,
Westinghouse (qv) 1979; Hawker
Siddeley Rail Projects then formed to
bring together the Group's related rly
activities.

Hawkeye (RS)
A messroom attendant.
Hawthorn, Leslie
R&W Hawthorn, Leslie & Co. Ltd,
loco builders, Newcastle upon
Tyne, established 1831 as R&W
Hawthorn. Amalgamated with Robert
Stephenson & Co. as Robert
Stephenson & Hawthorns, 1937. Part
of EE, 1955.
Hayburner (USRS)
1. An antiquated loco, little better
   than a horse.
2. A horse used for traction on a rly
   or tramway.
3. A handlamp.
Haycock fire (RS)
A steam loco fire built up by feeding
coal to centre of firebox and thus
forming a cone.
Haystacks (RS)
Steam locos with very high fireboxes.
Haytor Granite Tramroad
Haytor Rocks quarries to Stover canal
near Teigngrace, 4 ft 3 in/1,295 mm
gauge on granite block 'rails'. Opened
1820 with horse traction. Carried
stone used for the 1831 London
Bridge, the National Gallery (1832–8)
and other public buildings in London.
Disused from *c.* 1858. M&SDR
(opened 1866) used part of alignment
between Teigngrace and a point near
Brimley.
Hay wagon (USRS)
A caboose (qv). From (S) 'hit the hay'
= to go to bed.
HB (obs)
BR abbreviation for a horse box (qv).
H-Bahn (Ger)
Hochbahn; an elevated rly.
HCR&D
Humber Commercial Rly & Dock, inc
1901, 1904, Ulceby–Immingham
Docks, opened 1910 and leased by
GCR; completed 1912. In 1912 it
absorbed the Barton & Immingham
Light Rly (completed 1910–11), which
was also leased to GCR. Part of
L&NER 1923.
Head
The top or running surface of a rail.
Headcode
An arrangement of boards, discs,
or lights exhibited at the front of
a loco or train to indicate the nature of
the train and/or its route. In
more recent years stencils, roller blind
indicators and latterly dot
matrix displays have been used,
showing letters and/or numbers,
combinations of both, or the full
destination.

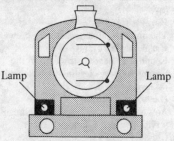

Express passenger headcode

Head end
That end of a train nearest the loco/
front cab.
Head end car (USRS)
The mail/baggage car, normally
coupled between loco and remainder
of train.
Head ender (USRS)
A head-on collision.
Head end revenue/traffic (USRS)
Mail, express, newspaper, luggage and
milk traffic (carried in the head end
car(s) (qv)).
Head in, to (USRS)
To take a loop road when meeting a
train coming in the opposite direction
on a single track.

Head lights
see Headcodes.

Head man (USRS)
The head end or front brakeman on a freight train.

Head shack (USRS)
A conductor (*3*). *See also* Shack.

Head shag/twit (LTRS)
The Headquarters Controller.

Head shrinker (RS)
A doctor paid to examine rly staff.

Heads of Valleys Line
Merthyr to Abergavenny; originally the Merthyr, Tredegar & Abergavenny Rly, inc 1859, first section opened 1862. Leased to L&NWR, part of L&NWR 1866.

Headshunt
A length of track allowing shunting movements to be made into a group of sidings without fouling the running lines, to which it may have a connection.

Headstock
The transverse end of vehicle frame, to which buffers, couplings etc. are attached.

Headway
1. The service interval (usually stated in minutes) between trains, trams or LRVs on the same line. Not to be confused with frequency (qv).
2. The clear height from the top of the rails to the underside of any fixed structures over the track.

Headway chart
A recorder used on London Underground, originally worked by headway clocks (qv), which marks against a time dial the passage of each individual train past certain points on the system throughout each 24-hour period.

Headway clock (obs)
A dial on the end of certain station platforms showing a driver the number of minutes since the preceding train left the station. Introduced on the London Underground in 1907.

Hearse (USRS)
A caboose (qv).

Heart of Midlothian
An express between London (Kings Cross) and Edinburgh (Waverley), so named 1950. Extended to Perth 1957. Name dropped 1968.

Heart of Wales Line
BR brand name for [Swansea–] Llanelli–Llandrindod–Craven Arms [–Shrewsbury] line.

Heater (RS)
A hot box (qv).

Heavy rly
A conventional rly; used only where necessary to distinguish such from a light rly (qv) or light rail transit (qv).

Heavy stop (LTRS)
A train brought to stand with hard braking, rapidly decelerating.

Hebden Bridge route
Healey Mills/Bradford–Hebden Bridge–Rochdale–Rose Grove.

Hebridean/Hebridean Heritage
A service between Inverness (through coach from Glasgow) and Kyle of Lochalsh in connection with Skye sailings, introduced 1933. Re-introduced 1966; renamed Hebridean Heritage and equipped with observation car, 1988.

Hedjaz **Rly**
A 1,050 mm gauge line from Damascus to Amman and Medina, with branches to Haifa, Nablus and Bofra, built primarily to carry Moslem pilgrims to Medina (for Mecca). Completed 1908, and severely damaged by Col. T.E. Lawrence's campaigns in the First World War, after which the section south of Ma'an (Jordan) was left derelict. The Damascus–Amman–Ma'an section

remains in use. Work in the 1960s to restore the link to Medina was suspended after considerable progress had been made. The line featured in the epic 1962 film *Lawrence of Arabia*.

Heel (USRS)
A wagon or coach left at end of a track with brakes on.

Heel [of points]/switch heel
The pivoted end of points at which the rails carrying a train on to the diverging line begin.

Heinrich Heine
TEE Frankfurt–Dortmund, introduced 1979. Ceased 1983. Re-introduced as Paris–Frankfurt EC service 1987.

Hellas Express
A Dortmund–Athens service 1963–88, combined in winter with a Munich–Istanbul service, the *Hellas–Istanbul Express*, in 1965–88.

Hellenic Rlys [Greece]
see CH.

Helvetia
A Zurich–Hamburg service introduced 1954, *TEE* 1957, lost *TEE* status 1979. EC 1987.

Hendre–Ddu Tramway
Hendre–Ddu Quarry–Gartheiniog–Aberangell [MR (*1*)] and branches, 1 ft 11 in/584 mm gauge, opened *c.* 1868; mostly closed *c.* 1940; last section lifted 1954. Worked by horses and gravity, and from *c.* 1920 by petrol tractor. Farmers, quarrymen and tourists were carried.

Henry Dunant
A Paris–Geneva *TGV*, introduced 1986.

HER
Hammersmith Extension Rly, inc 1873, Earl's Court–Hammersmith Broadway, opened and amalgamated with MDR 1874.

Herapath
Herapath's Railway Magazine, full title *Herapath's Railway Magazine, Commercial Journal and Scientific Review*, a renaming of *The Railway Magazine* in 1841. Further renamed *Herapath's Railway & Commercial Journal* in 1845 but usually called *Herapath's Railway Journal*, a shortened title officially adopted in 1894. Incorporated in *The Railway Times* in 1903. After the proprietor; John Herapath (1790–1868).

Herder (USRS)
A rlyman in shunting yard or terminal station who couples and uncouples locos.

Heritage fleet (US)
Amtrak passenger cars inherited from pre-1971 company fleets and mostly steam-heated.

Heritage Line
Brand name adopted 1990 for BR services between Bishop Auckland, Darlington and Saltburn.

Heritage stock
BR standard Mark 1 and early Mark 2 coaches and first generation BR dmus retained for special workings after the early 1990s fleet modernization.

Herringbone (rhyming S)
A telephone.

Hertford Loop
London (Bounds Green)–Enfield–Hertford North–Langley Junc (Stevenage). Also known as the 'Cuffley Loop'.

HHL&N&SJR
Halifax High Level & North & South Junction Rly, inc 1884, opened Holmfield–Pellon–Halifax (St Paul's) 1890, vested jointly in GNR and L&YR 1894, closed passengers 1917; LM&SR and L&NER 1923–47.

HHR
Hemel Hempstead Rly, Boxmoor L&NWR to Hemel Hempstead, inc 1863, extension to Harpenden

authorized 1866, opened 1877, worked
by Midland Rly. Part of Midland Rly
1886. Passenger service extended from
Hemel Hempstead (Mid) to Heath
Park Halt [Hemel Hempstead], 1905.

Hiawatha
Milwaukee RR steam-hauled
streamlined express between Chicago
and Minneapolis–St Paul, introduced
1935. Diesel-hauled from 1941. Now
an Amtrak service.

Hibernian
A service between London
(Paddington) and Fishguard Harbour,
connecting with Rosslare sailings,
introduced 1987.

High, to go (USRS)
see Decorate, to.

Highball, to (USRS)
To drive at high speed.

Highball, to give a (USRS)
To make a signal by raising a lamp,
indicating that a train should be
started: also any other 'proceed'
signalling indication. From an early
type of signal in which a ball was
hauled to the top of a mast to indicate
the line ahead was clear.

Highball artist (USRS)
A loco driver with a reputation for
skilful fast running over a clear road.

High Fliers/Flyers (RS)
1. L&NWR Singles.
2. L&YR Aspinall 4–4–2 locos, from
the high-pitched boiler.

High grass [line] (USRS)
A little-used rly line. From the tall
grasses that grow between and along
its tracks.

High Iron (USRS)
Through running lines, as distinct
from sidings and yard tracks.

Highland Chieftain
An HST between Inverness and
London (Kings Cross), introduced
1984.

Highland Line
Inverness–Perth.

Highlandman
A summer-only night express between
London (Kings Cross) and Inverness,
so named 1927.

High level passenger car
A double deck coach with seating and
dining facilities on upper deck, and
lavatories, vestibules and baggage
storage at lower level. First introduced
by AT&SFRR in 1957.

Highliner (USRS)
A fast passenger train.

Highwayman
A service operated at moderate speeds
between London (Finsbury Park),
Stockton and Newcastle carrying
passengers at cheap rates and designed
to compete with road coaches. Ran in
the summers of 1970 and 1971.

High wheeler (USRS)
A high speed loco designed for fast
passenger trains.

Hikari
see Shinkansen.

Hikers (RS)
1. GER 1500 class 4–6–0 (L&NER
B12) fitted (in 1927–32) with *ACFI*
(qv) feed-water heaters mounted on
top of the boiler and resembling a
hiker's back-pack.
2. Scottish name for Black Fives (qv).
They went everywhere.

Hiking (LTRS)
A train crew learning a depot (by
'hiking' around it).

His Master's Voice (RS)
A deputy foreman, usually an ex-
footplateman. Also applied to any
'crawler' or sycophant. From the
famous gramophone trade name.

Hispania
A Copenhagen–Basle–Port Bou service,
introduced 1963, later Hamburg–Port
Bou, then Basle–Port Bou.

Hit a stick, to (LTRS)
To overrun a signal at danger and be tripped.
Hitler salute (RS)(obs)
An upper quadrant semaphore in the 'off' position.
Hit the dirt, to (RS)
see Dirt, to hit the.
Hi Vi (LTRS)
A high visibility orange-coloured vest.
HJR
Hampstead Junction Rly, inc 1853, promoted by L&NWR, Camden Road–Hampstead–Willesden Junc– Acton Wells Junc. Opened 1860, worked by NLR. Part of L&NWR 1867. Managed by NLR 1867–72 and always carried NLR passenger services.
HL
High Level.
HLP (Fr RS)
Haut Le Pied; trotting; applied to light engine working.
HMRI
Her Majesty's Railway Inspectorate. Part of the Health & Safety Commission. *See also* RI (*1*).
HMRS
Historical Model Railway Society, founded 1950.
HofM&ST
Hundred of Manhood & Selsey Tramway. A light rly between Chichester and Selsey, opened 1897, 1898; name changed to West Sussex Rly 1924, closed 1935.
Hog (USRS)
A loco, hence yard hog etc.
Hogger (USRS)
A loco driver. *See* Hog.
Hoghead (USRS)
Alternative for Hogger (qv).
Hog law (USRS)
A federal regulation preventing train crews from working more than twelve

hours at a stretch. *See also* Bear law; Dog law; Monkey, caught by the.
Hog mauler (USRS)
A loco driver.
Hole, The
1. (RS) The Severn Tunnel.
2. (RS) Any steeply graded descent into a tunnel.
3. (USRS) A passing loop.
Hole, in the (USRS)
On a siding or loop, to allow other trains to pass.
Holland–Scandinavia Express
Hook of Holland–Copenhagen, introduced 1958, Schiphol Airport– Copenhagen from 1988.
Holland–Wien Express
An Amsterdam–Vienna service introduced 1960.
Holy City, the (RS)
St Albans.
Holytown route
Glasgow (Central)–Holytown–Midcald-er–Edinburgh(Waverley).
Home guard (USRS)
A rlyman who has long service with a particular company; opposite of a boomer (qv).
Homer
GWR TC for 30-ton 43 ft/13.1 metres bogie open wagon.
Home signal
The stop signal which controls entry to a block section; usually placed on the approach side of the associated signal box. Normally protects a station or junction. *See also* Inner home signal; Outer home signal.
Hondskop (Dutch RS)
A type of emu with a front end resembling a dog's head.
Hoo branch
Hoo Junc–Grain.
Hook (USRS)
A breakdown train. From the large crane hook.

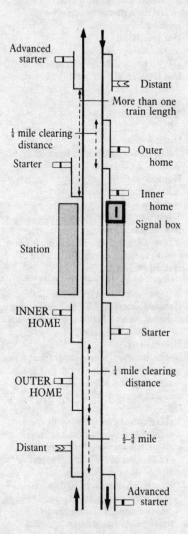

Advanced
starter

Distant

More than one
train length

¼ mile clearing
distance

Outer
home

Starter

Inner
home

Signal box

Station

INNER
HOME

OUTER
HOME

Starter

¼ mile clearing
distance

½–¾ mile

Distant

Advanced
starter

Home signals

Hook Continental
see Continental Express.
Hooker (RS)
A shunter.
Hook off, to
To uncouple vehicles.
Hook on/up, to
1. To couple up vehicles.
2. (USRS) To set regulator lever high
for fast running.
Hoovers (RS)
BR class 50 diesel electric locos. From
a characteristic noise, later modified.
Hope Valley Line
[Sheffield–]Dore–Hope–Chinley
[–Manchester].
Hoppers
1. (RS) L&SWR Drummond 4–4–0
locos (K10 class of 1901–2 were
'small hoppers'; the L11 class of
1903–7 'large hoppers'). From
grasshoppers.
2. Wagons with hinged base allowing
load to fall out quickly.
Hoptoad, to (USRS)
To derail.
Hornby (RS)
BR diesel locos class 08, from their
supposed resemblance to model train
set engines.
Hornby Trains
Clockwork and electric toy trains,
gauge 'O' and (later) 'OO', produced
from 1920 onwards by Frank
Hornby's factory at Binns Road,
Liverpool.
Hornet
GWR TC for a timber wagon.
Horse & carriage traffic (obs)
Conveyance by passenger train of
private horse-drawn carriages, with or
without horses, a horse box (qv) being
provided for the latter. Special loading
platforms were available at many
stations for this traffic, and 24 hours'
notice was required. Owners were

allowed to remain in their private carriages during the journey if they so wished. 'This traffic requires prompt attention to prevent delay to the passenger service' — Jenkinson, Lamb & Travis, in *The Passenger Station and Signalling*, 1914.

Horse & carriage workings (obs)
Trains carrying horse & carriage traffic (qv), and later, trains composed of miscellaneous vans and empty coaches etc.

Horse & cart (RS)
Train consisting only of a loco and brakevan.

Horse box (obs)
A van (usually four-wheeled) designed to carry horses, with passenger half-compartment (coupé) at one end for the person or persons accompanying the animals on the journey.

Horse over, to (USRS)
To reverse a loco.

Hose jumper (obs)
A very small steel bridge, with grooves, temporarily put down to enable street tramcars to avoid fire hoses laid across the tracks.

Hostile territory (RS)
Any area away from the speaker's own; another region of BR.

Hostler (US)(obs)
Term for employee who takes charge of a loco for cleaning, replacing fire, lighting the new fire etc. Adopted from horse transport usage.

Hot and cold (LTRS)
Hammersmith & City line LT. From the initials.

Hot box
Overheated axle journal or bearing caused by poor lubrication, admission of sand or grit etc., or overtight fit of axle ends.

Hotel trains
European sleeping car trains, introduced in the mid-1990s, incorporating hotel type on-board services.

Hot foot (USRS)
A conductor (*3*) engaged in shunting operations and always in a hurry.

Hot jewel (USRS)
A hot box (qv).

Hot loco (USRS)
A loco with steam up, ready to move off.

Hot pot (RS)(obs)
A loco blowing off steam from safety valve.

Hot rail (USRS)
A live rail (qv).

Hot shot (USRS)
A fast train (usually freight).

Hot worker (USRS)
A fitter who carries out adjustments or repairs on a hot loco (qv).

Hounslow Loop
Barnes–Hounslow–Feltham Junc/ Whitton Junc. L&SWR/SR/BR(S).

Houston Control (LTRS)(rhyming S)
Cobourg Street Control Centre. From its location near Euston.

Hoverspeed
Brand name for Seaspeed (qv) after its merger with Hoverlloyd Ltd in 1981. Hoverspeed was sold to its management in 1984.

HR
1. Harborne Rly, Harborne to Edgbaston (Monument Lane), Birmingham, inc 1866, opened 1874, worked by L&NWR, part of LM&SR from 1923.
2. Hayle Rly, Hayle to Redruth and Tresavean and branches, inc 1834, opened 1837, 1838, passenger traffic 1843 (passengers conveyed on an irregular basis in mineral wagons from 1841). Part of WCR from 1846.
3. Hayling Rly, inc 1860, Havant–

Hayling Island, opened 1865, 1867. Leased to LB&SCR 1872, part of SR 1923.

4. Hay Rly, inc 1811, 3 ft 6 in/ 1,067 mm gauge tramroad, Eardisley to the Brecknock & Abergavenny Canal at Brecon via Hay. Opened 1816, 1818. Purchased by Hereford, Hay & Brecon Rly 1860. Section south of Three Cocks became part of MWR and B&MJR.

5. Helston Rly, Gwinear Road (GWR) to Helston, inc 1880, opened 1887, worked by GWR, part of GWR from 1898.

6. Highland Rly, formed 1865, a merger of Inverness & Aberdeen Junction Rly (Inverness–Nairn–Keith) and Inverness & Perth Junction Rly (Forres–Dunkeld). Other lir es added subsequently. 432 route miles by 1914, all in northern Scotland. Part of LM&SR from 1923.

7. Holywell Rly, inc 1864 Holywell–Holywell Harbour, but not completed, the finished sections used for quarry traffic for some years. Purchased by L&NWR and opened throughout Holywell Town–Holywell Junc, 1912.

8. Horncastle Rly, inc 1854, Horncastle & Kirkstead Junction, opened 1855, worked by GNR. Part of L&NER 1923.

9. Hoylake Rly, inc 1863, opened 1866 Hoylake–Birkenhead (Bridge Rd), closed 1869. Purchased and re-opened 1872 by Hoylake & Birkenhead Rail & Tramway Co. (inc 1872). Hoylake–West Kirby extension opened 1878. In 1879 the H&BR&T's street tramway in Birkenhead was sold to the Birkenhead Tramways Co. and the

rly was renamed the Seacombe, Hoylake & Deeside Rly in 1881. Wallasey and New Brighton branch opened 1888. Part of the WR (qv) 1891.

HSH
Hëkurudhë Shqipërisë; Albanian State Rlys.

HST
High Speed Trains (BR); very successful fixed-formation train sets with integral diesel-electric locos at each end, one pulling, one pushing, later known as IC 125. Introduced 1976.

Hst (Ger)
Haltestelle; unstaffed halt; also a stopping place for tramway (3).

HSTRC
BR High Speed Track-Recording Coach.

Hudson (US)
A steam loco with 4–6–4 wheel arrangement, from the Hudson River Line of the New York Central RR, where they were first used.

Hudson Tubes
Hudson & Manhattan RR, electric lines connecting New York (Manhattan) to Jersey City and Newark by means of tube tunnels under the Hudson River, opened in 1908–10. Taken over by PATH (qv) 1962.

Hudswell, Clarke
Hudswell, Clarke & Co. Ltd, Railway Foundry, Leeds, loco builders from 1860. Acquired by Hunslet (qv), 1972.

Hull Executive
A renaming of the Hull Pullman, 1978.

Hull Pullman
An all-Pullman train between London (Kings Cross) and Hull, introduced 1967, renamed Hull Executive 1978.

Humber Lincs Executive
Name given to a through HST

between London (Kings Cross),
Grimsby and Cleethorpes, 1984.

Hump
An artificial mound in a marshalling
yard arranged so that uncoupled
wagons may run down by gravity from
its summit and be directed by points
movements to the appropriate sorting
siding, hence hump yard, hump
shunting. First used at Feltham Yard,
L&SWR in 1922.

Hump back run (USRS)
A local freight working.

Humpies (RS)
L&NWR 0–6–0ST. From their
appearance.

Humping the bricks/coal (RS)(obs)
Working a brick/coal/etc. train.

Humpties (RS)
GWR 0–6–0ST. From their
appearance.

Humpty-Dumpties (RS)
GER 2–4–0 express locos. From their
ungainly appearance after 1902–4
rebuilding.

Hunch-backs (RS)
S&DR 4–4–0ST. From their
appearance.

Hundred of Hoo Rly
Inc 1879, part of SER 1881, opened
1882, Hoo Junc (near Higham) to Port
Victoria. *See also* Hoo branch.

Hunslet
Hunslet Engine Co. Ltd, Leeds, loco
builders, founded 1864. Later Hunslet
(Holdings) plc, and Hunslet GMT.
Also Hunslet TPL, Hunslet
Transportation Projects Ltd,
Birmingham, founded 1989, suppliers
of passenger rail vehicles. *See also*
Barclay (Hunslet–Barclay). Hunslet
GMT, Hunslet TPL and Hunslet–
Barclay are all now part of the Telfos
Group. *See also* Ganz–Hunslet.

Huns, set of (RS)(obs)
Enginemen from another depot.

Hunting
The side-to-side movement of wheel
sets in vehicle trucks, usually apparent
at very high speeds.

Hurdy gurdy (RS)
A hand generator for working electric
point motors.

Hurst, Nelson
Hurst, Nelson & Co. Ltd, established
1880, public company 1909, works at
Motherwell, builders of railway rolling
stock and tramcars. Acquired by
Roberts (qv) 1958, ceased production
1959.

Hush-hush (RS)
L&NER 4–6–4 (strictly 4–6–2–2) four-
cylinder compound loco 1000, built
1929 with marine water tube boiler
generating steam at 450 lb per sq in.
A failure, it was rebuilt in 1937 as a
three-cylinder simple 4–6–2. From the
secrecy surrounding its construction.

Hush Puppies (RS)
Silencers on dmus. After the famous
shoe trade name.

Hustle alarm
An audible warning sounded on BR
sliding door trains that the doors are
about to close.

Hustler
An audible warning which
automatically sounds to warn staff and
passengers on a crowded platform (on
London Underground) that the train
has spent the appropriate interval in
the station and should be despatched.
See also Bruiteur.

Hut (USRS)
A caboose (qv), also a brakeman's
shelter built on to a loco tender.

HWst (Ger)
Hauptwerkstatt; a main overhaul
works.

Hydra
GWR TC for well-trucks for carrying
road vehicles.

Hymek
Name of a co. formed by Beyer, Peacock, J. Stone & Co. (Deptford) and Bristol–Siddeley Engines Ltd to act as designers and main contractor for diesel hydraulic and diesel electric locos. Hence the name for the 101 Type 3 B-B diesel–hydraulic locos supplied to BR (W) in 1961.

I

I&AJR

Inverness & Aberdeen Junction Rly,
inc 1856, Nairn to Keith, opened
1857, 1858. Absorbed Inverness &
Nairn Rly (opened 1855) in 1861 and
Findhorn Rly (opened 1860) in 1862.
Part of an amalgamation to form HR
(6), 1865.

I&RR

Inverness & Ross-shire Rly, inc 1860,
Inverness–Invergordon, opened 1862,
1863, part of I&AJR from 1862.
Extended from Invergordon to Bonar
Bridge 1864.

Iberia Express

A Paris–Irun service, with Madrid
connection, 1957–88, replacing the
Pyrénées–Côte d'Argent Express.
Through couchettes Paris–Madrid
from 1969.

IBJ

Insulated Block Joints.

IBS

Intermediate Block Signals, usually
electrically-controlled colour lights,
installed to replace an intermediate
box.

IC

1. InterCity, or Inter-City, term used
   by BR from 1966 to describe its
   fast trunk services connecting major
   population centres. Also, from
   1982, a 'business sector' of BR.
2. Internal inter-city services
   introduced by DB 1968, hourly
   from 1979. *See also* ICE (*1*) and
   IC-netz.

3. Internal inter-city services
   introduced by FS 1985.
4. (US) Illinois Central RR, merged
   1972 with Gulf, Mobile & Ohio RR
   to form IC Gulf RR. Name
   changed back to IC 1988.

ICC

Interstate Commerce Commission,
formed in 1887 to regulate rlys etc.
operating across state boundaries in
the US, controlling operating rights,
rates and charges, services, accounting
and valuation.

ICE

1. Inter-City Express; *DB* high speed
   (300 km/h) electric trains and lines.
2. Queensland Rlys Inter-City Electric
   express mu trains.

IC-netz

A term used from 1971 for lines
carrying *DB* high speed inter-city
services (IC (*2*)), some of them newly-
built rlys.

ICOBS

InterCity On Board Services, BR,
supplying train catering to IC (*1*).

IC-225

Trains of BR IC Mark IV coaches
and class 91 electric locos, introduced
on ECML in 1989 and London
(Kings Cross) to Edinburgh in
1991.

IC-250

BR 250 km/h electric trains planned
for introduction on WCML between
London (Euston)–Birmingham/
Manchester/Glasgow in 1995.

Idlers (USRS)
Unused flats (qv) positioned to accommodate overhang loads on adjacent wagons.

IE
Ianrod Eirrean (Irish Rail), Republic of Ireland Rlys, formed 1986.

IECC
Integrated Electronic Control Centre. A signalling control centre based on SSI (qv), and a computer programmed with the WTT (qv), which sets up non-conflicting routes, the first at Liverpool St., London, BR, in 1989. In IECC the panoramic SDS (qv) is replaced by vdus reproducing track layout and the description and location of trains in occupation. Operators oversee the computer's activity and set up routes for special trains and trains running out of normal course by the use of a tracker ball and push buttons.

Igloos (RS)
Platform shelters with transparent walls and barrel–shaped transparent roofs adopted by BR from *c*. 1985.

ILE
Institution of Locomotive Engineers, founded 1911.

Île de France
TEE Paris–Amsterdam, introduced 1957. EC from 1987.

Ilfracombe Goods
W.G. Beattie 0–6–0 locos of 1873–80, built by the L&SWR for the steeply-graded Ilfracombe branch and initially largely confined to it.

Immunization
Measures taken to protect signalling and telecommunications equipment from interference from electric traction currents.

Impedance bond
A device which makes electrical connections, permitting the free flow of traction current while impeding track circuit (qv) currents.

Imperial Indian Mail
A Bombay–Calcutta service introduced 1926 by the EIR and GIPR in connection with sailings of P&O ships to and from Britain.

Impériale, à l' (Fr)(obs)
Any double-deck rly or tramway car, or the top deck of one. Also applied to the railed-in luggage enclosure on the roofs of early rly coaches.

Improved Engine Green
A yellow livery adopted by the LB&SCR soon after William Stroudley became its Locomotive, Carriage & Marine Superintendent in 1870.

IMR
1. Isle of Man Rly: *see* IofMR.
2. Interlocking Machine Room.

IMV
Internal Movements Vehicles; unlicensed tractors etc. used within rly premises.

Incident
A term used by BR to describe any accident or dislocation of service from a coach door found open on a moving train to a major collision.

Indian country (RS)
'Foreign' (qv) rlys, particularly Eastern Region BR for any rlyman from another region.

Indian Pacific
A through trans-Australian (Sydney–Melbourne–Perth) standard gauge service with air-conditioned coaches, introduced 1970 with a 64 h 15 min schedule. Route changed to serve Adelaide from 1986.

Indian Rlys
Formed 1950–1 to integrate all main rly systems in India. Abbreviated to IR. Between 1951 and 1966 nine zonal units were established: Central; Eastern; North Eastern; North East

Frontier; Northern; South Central; South Eastern; Southern; and Western.

Indian Valley Railroad (USRS)

An imaginary rly, on which all is perfect.

Indicators

1. The route and destination information displays on the front of trains, tramcars and LRV; also sometimes on the sides of the last two.

2. The information displayed on rly platforms or on the concourses of large stations, showing destinations, intermediate stopping points, departure times etc. of the next trains.

3. Devices used to measure changes of pressure in loco cylinders.

Indicator shelter (obs)

A temporary wooden shelter placed on the front end of a steam loco to protect indicators (*3*) and other recording instruments, and the men attending them, when a loco was under test on the line. Later developments made it possible to provide indicator diagrams and other information remotely in a dynamometer (qv) car.

Indusi (Ger)

Induktive Zugsicherung; a form of ATP (qv).

Injector

A part of steam loco which employs a jet of steam to force water into the boiler.

Inner Circle

A shallow subway line around the edge of inner London, Paddington–Kings Cross–Liverpool St.–Charing Cross–Victoria–South Kensington–Notting Hill Gate–Paddington, completed 1884, partly MDR, partly Metropolitan Rly, partly jointly-owned by those companies. Jointly operated

by Metropolitan and MDR until 1933. Electrified 1905. LPTB etc. from 1933. Now known as the Circle or Circle Line.

Inner home signal

A designation used when an outer home signal is also installed. On the LM&SR/ BR (M) this signal is known as Home no. 2. *See also* Home signal; Outer home signal.

Inox

Stainless steel coach construction, normally under the Budd (qv) patents.

Insects (RS)

Occasional or seasonal rly enthusiasts, liable to 'swarm' at certain special events such as open days, or at certain periods of the year.

Inside tracks (US)

The central pair of tracks allocated for fast running in a four-track layout.

Insixfish

GWR TC for insulated fish van.

Instanter (obs)

A two-position, three-link coupling; a transitional stage design for coupling freight wagons which could be turned to a short position to bring the buffers of adjacent wagons closer together, reducing the snatching of loose couplings on an unfitted train. The use of instanters allowed connection of brake pipes in a partially-fitted train.

Institute, Rly

A social and educational centre for rly employees, usually with library, reading room, meeting hall, and games room. Such facilities were provided at London (Euston, Nine Elms, Kings Cross), Crewe, Derby, Eastleigh, Gateshead, Swindon, York and other rly centres.

Intelligentsia Brainbox (LTRS)

A facetious term for LT Headquarters staff.

Interavailability
An arrangement in which a ticket is honoured by an alternative route, especially another company's route.

Inter-City
A label for named trains in Canada and Australia as early as 1930. For BR and other modern usage *see* IC.

InterCity Executive
An express between Manchester and London (Euston), introduced 1983.

Inter-City [Express]
A service between London (Paddington) and Birmingham, so named 1950; to and from Chester 1962, name dropped 1965.

Intercontainer
International Company for Transport by Transcontainers. A centralized commercial agency representing the interests of major European rly systems in the international transport of containers, founded 1967. Owned by European rly undertakings and Interfrigo.

Interfrigo
International Society for the Carriage of Refrigerated Goods by Rail/*Société Ferroviaire Internationale de Transports Frigorifiques*. Founded 1949 to rationalize rail movement of commodities requiring temperature control in transit, and to make good wartime losses of wagons. It is grouped with Intercontainer and owns a large fleet of wagons which operate throughout Europe.

Interlaced track
see Gauntletted track/Gauntletting.

Interlocking
A mechanical and/or electrical means of ensuring that when a signal or point lever is moved to admit a train on to a section of line, all other signals and points which might allow conflicting movements are locked. Interlocking

also prevents signals from being cleared from the 'on' or danger indication until the points to which they apply are correctly set and facing points are locked.

Intermediate box
A signal box which is provided to break up a long block section and allow the operation of a more intensive train service. Such boxes, which are manned as required, usually only control distant and home signals for each line. In modern practice often replaced by IBS (qv).

International Express
A service between Bangkok (Thailand) and Butterworth (for Penang, Malaysia).

International Limited
A Grand Trunk RR, later CNR, express between Montreal, Toronto and Chicago, introduced 1900. 6 h 30 min schedule in 1935. Now an Amtrak service between Toronto and Chicago.

Inter-Rail
A railcard allowing unlimited travel for one month in twenty-four countries for persons under twenty-six. Introduced 1972 to mark the 50th anniversary of the UIC. The age limit was abolished in 1991 and a fifteen-day ticket available in twenty-one countries was introduced.

Inter Regio
see IR (*1*).

Interurban (US)
A form of electric rly linking cities and towns, or urban centres with distant suburbs and extra-urban communities, primarily passenger-carrying, running in the streets in inner urban areas and on private right of way or alongside the highway elsewhere. Rolling stock was heavier and much faster (65–75 m.p.h. maximum) than that of conventional tramways (*3*), while in

the US, ticketing and luggage arrangements followed those of ordinary rlys, and freight traffic was often interchanged with the latter. Most services were worked with single cars but trains of two, three, four or more cars were also found. Traction supply was almost universally by overhead wire and trolley pole or pantograph. A small number of lines of this type were also built in Canada, Europe and elsewhere. The US interurbans were mainly constructed between 1890 and 1908 and the largest mileage was in the state of Ohio (2,798). Reaching its zenith around 1916, the US interurban had almost entirely succumbed to road competition by the 1950s.

In the chair (RS)
see Chair, in the.

In the dirt (RS)
see Dirt, in the.

In the slough (RS)
see Slough, in the.

Invalid carriage (obs)
A special coach, fitted out with bed, armchairs, wheelchair etc., which could be chartered for the carriage of invalids.

Invert
The base section of a tunnel lining, its lowest visible surface, forming an arch that is concave upwards. Tunnels are sometimes built without inverts.

INWR
Irish North Western Rly, formed 1862 from Dundalk & Enniskillen Rly (inc 1845) and Londonderry & Enniskillen Rly (inc 1845). Part of GNR (I) 1876.

IofALR
Isle of Axholme Light Rly: *see* Axholme

IofMR
Isle of Man Rly, 3 ft/914 mm gauge system on the Isle of Man, connecting

the principal towns with Douglas, inc 1870. Opened 1873, 1874, 1879. Closed 1965. Reopened 1967–8 only. Douglas–Port Erin line reopened again 1969. Taken over by Manx Government and amalgamated with MER (qv) as Isle of Man Rlys, 1978.

IofWCR
Isle of Wight Central Rly, inc 1887, an amalgamation of Ryde & Newport (opened 1875), Cowes & Newport (opened 1862) and IofW (NJ) Rlys. Absorbed Newport, Godshill & St Lawrence Rly (opened 1897, extended to Ventnor West 1900) in 1913. Part of SR from 1923.

IofW (NJ) Rly
Isle of Wight (Newport Junction) Rly, inc 1868 Sandown–Merstone–Newport, opened 1875, 1879, became part of IofWCR (qv) when that was formed in 1887.

IofWR
Isle of Wight Rly, inc 1860 as Isle of Wight Eastern Section Rly, Ryde to Ventnor, opened 1864, 1866, renamed IofWR 1863, purchased Brading Harbour & Rly (Bembridge branch, opened 1882) in 1898. Part of SR from 1923.

IR
1. *Inter-Regio Netz* (Ger); Rail and bus feeder services to *IC-netz* (qv).
2. Irish Rail: *see IE*.
3. Indian Rlys (qv).
4. Israel Rlys.

IRCA
see AICCF.

IRCH
Irish Railway Clearing House, established 1848, inc 1860; role similar to that of RCH; dissolved 1974.

Iris
1. *TEE* Brussels–Zurich, introduced 1974, lost *TEE* status 1981.
2. EC Brussels–Chur, introduced 1987.

Irish Mail
Day and night services between
London (Euston) and Holyhead
connecting with sailings for Kingstown
(Dun Laoghaire) for Dublin, and
carrying the Post Office mail traffic as
well as passengers. So described from
1848 but name not officially adopted
until 1927. Winter day service
withdrawn 1947; now runs only
overnight, retaining its historic title.

Irishman
An express between Glasgow (St
Enoch) and Stranraer Harbour in
connection with sailings to Larne,
Northern Ireland, introduced 1933,
restored 1949. Name dropped 1967.

Iron (USRS)
Rly track, as in high iron (qv), single
iron (qv) etc.

Ironclads (RS)
1. GER Adams 4–4–0 locos of
   1876–7.
2. SER Ramsbottom 2–4–0 locos of
   1875.
3. L&SWR 4–4–0T of 1879.
4. L&SWR steel-panelled corridor
   coaches of 1921.
All from the naval vessels of this type,
introduced in the 1860s.

Iron horse, the (obs)
A popular metaphor for a steam loco
until *c.* 1950; also current in US.

Iron lungs (RS)
Austerity 2–8–0 locos of the Second
World War. Also used for Franco-
Crosti (qv) Class 9F BR locos of 1955,
whose exhaust was emitted from a
chimney halfway along the right hand
side of the boiler, polluting the
fireman's supply of air. From the
popular name for the artificial
respirators introduced for medical
treatment in the 1930s.

Iron man (RS)
An IBS (qv) post.

Iron road
An early name for a rly, which
outlived the nineteenth century despite
the fact that malleable iron rails were
replaced by steel from the 1850s.
Several European languages adopted
this as their word for rly, e.g. *strada
ferrata* (It), *chemin de fer* (Fr),
eisenbahn (Ger), *järnvag* (Swedish),
ianrod (Irish).

Iron work (LTRS)
The complicated parts of trackwork at
junctions.

Iron worm (LTRS)
A tube (qv) train.

IRRS
Irish Railway Record Society, formed
1946.

IRS
Industrial Railway Society, founded
1949.

IRSE
Institute of Railway Signalling
Engineers, founded 1910.

ISG (Ger)
CIWL (qv).

Island platform
A platform with two faces for through
lines, i.e. accommodating trains each
side, and only accessible by footbridge
or subway or by walking across the
tracks.

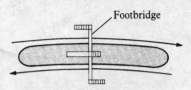
Footbridge

Isle of Wight Steam Rly
A preserved rly on the former BR
Ryde–Newport line between
Smallbrook Junc (near Ryde) and
Wooton. First section opened 1971;

connection with BR at Smallbrook, 1991.

Istanbul Express
A Munich–Istanbul service, introduced 1965; Frankfurt–Istanbul from 1977.

Italia Express
A Hamburg–Rome service, introduced 1960; Frankfurt–Rome from 1977.

IU
Internal Unit. BR rolling stock used only within certain closely defined premises.

Ivory Tower, The (LTRS)
Facetious term for LT headquarters, 55 Broadway, Westminster.

J

Jack (USRS)
A loco.

Jack-in-the-Box (RS)(obs)
A freight brake van with its guard in residence.

Jacko (RS)
A small shunting loco on GWR and BR (W).

Jack catches/Jack traps (RS)
Catch points.

Jack points (RS)
The third pair of points at the entrance to a yard from a hump (qv), the first and second being King and Queen points (qv).

Jacobite
A Friday-only service between Glasgow and Inverness, introduced 1984. Name dropped 1986.

Jaffa cake (RS)(obs)
An orange and brown livery adopted by BR(S) in the mid-1980s, after the popular orange-flavoured chocolate comestible.

Jam buster (USRS)
An assistant yardmaster.

Jam roller (LT rhyming S)
The Line controller.

Janney, to (USRS)
To couple up. From the Janney auto-coupler.

Janus (RS)
An electric or diesel loco with a central cab. From the Roman god with two heads, facing opposite ways.

Javanic (US)
A steam loco with 2–12–2 wheel arrangement.

Jawbone shack (USRS)
A pointsman's hut.

Jay rod (USRS)
A hook for breaking up clinker in a loco firebox. From its shape.

Jazzers (RS)
GNR/L&NER K3 2–6–0 locos. From their rough riding characteristic.

Jazz trains/service (obs)
A journalist's nickname for the GER 'intensive service' introduced in 1920 as a cheap alternative to electrification for the Liverpool St. West Side suburban services.

J-door
The door between driving cab and passenger accommodation on LT trains, normally kept locked. From the letter it is allocated to distinguish it from other doors in the car.

Jean Jacques Rousseau
A Paris–Geneva *TGV*, so named 1983.

Jeeps (RS)
NCC WT class 2–6–4T locos. Like the famous US Army vehicle, they were said to be 'usable for many sorts of task'.

Jellicoe Specials (obs)
Coal trains worked through from English and Welsh coalfields to Thurso in the First World War to bunker naval vessels moored in Scapa Flow. The term was also applied to special through trains between Thurso and London (Euston) operated for

naval personnel in the First World War. A similar service was operated for RN, Army and RAF personnel in the Second World War, when the name was resurrected. After Admiral of the Fleet Earl Jellicoe.

Jenners (RS)
GNR locos and men. From the initials GN.

Jenny Lind (RS)
A steam loco with 2–2–2 wheel arrangement.

JER
Jersey Eastern Rly, St Helier–Gorey Pier, inc 1872, opened 1873, 1891. Closed 1929.

Jerk a drink, to (USRS)
To take up water from water troughs at speed.

Jersey Central
Central RR of New Jersey (US).

Jersey Lilies (RS)
GCR 4–4–2 locos. After their graceful lines – 'Jersey Lily' was the nickname of a contemporary beauty, Lily Langtry, a favourite of Edward VII.

Jewett
Jewett Car Co., builders of electric interurban and tramcars at Jewett, Ohio, US, from 1894, and, from 1900, at Newark, Ohio. Ceased production 1917.

Jigger (USRS)
A fully-loaded train.

Jim Crow (RS)
A manual tool used for bending rails, hence also a platelayer.

Jim Crow car (USRS)
A coach set aside for the use of black people in those US states where they were obliged to travel separately from white people. From Jim Crow Regulations, defining racial segregation, and the 1828 'nigger minstrel' song of that name.

Jimmy
1. (RS)(obs) A piece of metal (sometimes a coupling drawbar) illicitly placed in blast pipe of a steam loco to increase draught, and thus obtain a brighter fire and better steaming.
2. (USRS) A four-wheeled ore wagon.

Jinties (RS)
LM&SR 3F 0–6–0T locos introduced 1924. Its origins are obscure but it dates from the 1930s, if not earlier and may derive from earlier usage to describe Midland Rly 0–4–0T. 'This beastliest of locomotive nicknames was certainly not coined by any railwayman and I have no doubt we have some misbegotten gricer to thank for it' — George Dow in the RM, 1973.

JNR
Japanese National Rlys. From 1987 JR (2) (qv).

Job (LTRS)
A generic term for the whole rly or the train service on a particular line (e.g. 'The job's up the wall' = the train service is badly disrupted).

Jock (RS)
Food, hence Jock tin.

Jockos (RS)
LM&SR 3F 0–6–0T locos, introduced 1924, otherwise known as Jinties (qv).

Johannes Keppler
An EC Frankfurt–Linz, introduced 1991.

Johann Strauss
A Vienna–Frankfurt service introduced 1968. Became EC Vienna–Cologne, 1987.

John o' Groat
The unofficial name for restaurant car train between Inverness and Wick between the wars, officially adopted by the LM&SR in 1939.

John Peel
A Carlisle–London (Euston) service, introduced 1988.
Johnson Bar (USRS)
The reversing lever of a steam loco.
Joint circular
see TC (2).
Join the birds, to
see Birds, to join the.
Joint line
A section of rly owned by two or more companies.
Joint Line, The (obs)
This could be applied to any joint line, but was most often heard to describe:
1. March–Lincoln–Doncaster (GER and GNR Joint) and
2. Northolt Junc–High Wycombe–Ashendon Junc (GWR and GCR Joint).

Joint men (RS)
Employees of a jointly-owned line or joint committee.
Joker (USRS)
Loco brakes as distinct from those in the train.
Jones Goods (RS)
Highland Rly 4–6–0s, introduced 1894; the first of this wheel arrangement in Britain. After their designer, David Jones, Locomotive Superintendent, HR.
Journal
That part of an axle inside the axle box.
Journal box (US)
Axle box.
JR
1. Jedburgh Rly, Roxburgh to J, inc 1855, opened 1856, worked by NBR, part of NBR 1860.
2. Japanese Rlys [Realisation Company], formed 1987; short title Japan Rail.

JR&T
Jersey Rlys and Tramways, St Helier–St Aubin–Corbìere, inc 1869, opened 1870/1884–5, 1899. Converted to 3 ft 6 in/1,067 mm gauge 1885. Winter services ceased after 1928, closed 1936.
Jubilee
A steam loco with 4–4–4 wheel arrangement.
Jubilee Line
A London tube rly between Baker St. and Charing Cross. It took over the Stanmore service of the Bakerloo Line when it was opened in 1979.
Originally designated the River Line, then the Fleet Line, it was planned to run beyond Charing Cross to Fenchurch St. and Thamesmead but the necessary capital could not be obtained. Named at the suggestion of a Conservative Greater London Council administration, after the Silver Jubilee of Elizabeth II (1977) but not ready until two years later. When asked what he thought of the renaming, Prince Philip is alleged to have replied: 'Does that mean the trains will run every twenty-five years?'. An extension to London Bridge, North Greenwich and Stratford is proposed.
Jubilees (RS)
1. L&SWR A12 0–4–2 locos. After the 1887 Golden Jubilee of Queen Victoria.
2. Metropolitan Rly Cravens coaches of 1887. After the 1887 Golden Jubilee of Queen Victoria.
3. GER passenger 0–6–0T and 2–4–2T locos. After the 1897 Diamond Jubilee of Queen Victoria.
4. LM&SR 6P 4–6–0 express passenger locos. After the 1935 Silver Jubilee of King George V.

Jubilee track
A form of light prefabricated track for portable rlys (qv).
Jubilee wagon
A small tipper wagon used on Jubilee track.
Juggler (USRS)
A freight handler.
Juggle the circle, to (USRS)
To fail to catch a train order when it is proffered from a hook or fork at the lineside to a crew member on a moving train.
Juice (RS)
Traction current.
Juice box (LTRS)
A current rail indicator box.
Juice bug/hog (USRS)
An electric loco.
Juice hogger (USRS)
The driver of a petrol, diesel or electric loco.
Juice rail (RS)
A conductor/live rail.
Juicers (RS)
Electric trains or locos.
Juice wagon (RS)
An electric loco.
Jules Verne
TEE Paris–Nantes, 1980–7. Now an un-named *TGV* service.
Jumbos (RS)
1. A generic term for L&NWR 2–4–0 locos. 'Big Jumbos' had 6 ft 9 in/ 2.06 metres diameter driving wheels; 'Little Jumbos' 6 ft 3 in/ 1.9 metre.
2. SE&CR B1 and F1 4–4–0 locos.
3. Caledonian Rly 0–6–0s.
4. L&SWR Beattie 4–4–0s.
5. NBR 4–4–2 locos.

In each case usage derives from a famous elephant so named, and accidentally killed in the US in 1882.
Jumper
1. (RS) A travelling ticket inspector.
2. A ticket inspector on tramways (*3*).
3. (LTRS) An overhead trolley lead for moving cars inside a depot.
Jumping point (LTRS)
Any undesirable job given to a newly-promoted employee while waiting for something better.
Junction Diagrams
An RCH (qv) publication, *Official Railway Junction Diagrams*, published at intervals from 1867, containing plans of all areas where two or more rly companies had physical connections, showing each company's lines, depots, stations and sidings in distinctive colours with the precise distances between stations and junctions. The running powers and working arrangements of each company were also listed, as were joint lines. Its primary purpose was to facilitate the calculation of mileage apportionments of traffic passing over the lines of two or more companies and to remove any basis for dispute over these.
Junior Scotsman
An express between London (Kings Cross) and Edinburgh, introduced 1928 as a second portion of The Flying Scotsman.
Junk pile (USRS)
A run-down and out-of-date loco.
JZ
Jugoslav State Rlys.

K

K&BR
Kilsyth & Bonnybridge Rly, extension of KVR to Bonnybridge and Bonnywater Junc, inc 1882, opened 1888, jointly vested in Caledonian Rly and NBR. Co. became part of L&NER 1923 but joint working with LM&SR continued until 1947.

K&DR
Kircaldy & District Rly, inc 1883 as Seafield Dock & Rly, Foulford Junc near Cowdenbeath to Invertiel Junc near Kirkcaldy, renamed K&DR 1888, part of NBR 1895, opened 1896.

K&ESR
Kent & East Sussex Rly, a light rly, LRO 1896 as Rother Valley Rly, Tenterden to Robertsbridge; extension Tenterden–Headcorn authorized by LRO 1902, name changed 1904. Opened 1900, 1903, 1905. Part of BR(SR) from 1948. Closed passengers 1954, freight 1961. Reopened in part under same name as a preserved line from 1974.

K&WVR
Keighley & Worth Valley Rly, Keighley to Oxenhope, inc 1862, opened 1867, worked by Midland Rly, leased by Midland Rly 1876, part of Midland Rly from 1881. Closed 1961 (passengers), 1962 (freight) but reopened to the public in 1968 by K&WVR Preservation Society, founded 1962.

Kangourou (Fr)
Kangaroo; *see* Piggy-back.

Kärnten Express
An Ostend–Klagenfurt summer service, 1956–8; Hamburg to Klagenfurt from 1958.

Karpaty
A Warsaw–Lvov–Bucharest service, introduced 1960. Diverted through Czechoslovakia 1988, avoiding USSR and the double change of gauge.

Katy
Nickname of MK&T (qv).

KCR
1. Kent Coast Rly, inc 1861, extension of the Margate Rly (whose name was changed to KCR) from Margate to Ramsgate. Opened Herne Bay–Margate–Ramsgate 1863, worked by LC&DR, part of LC&DR 1871.
2. Kowloon–Canton Rly, China.

KCS
Kansas City Southern Rly (US).

Keel the goods, to (RS)(obs)
To code freight for loading.

Kenny Belle
Nickname for peak hours only service between Clapham Junction and Kensington (Olympia) operated by NSE.

Kent Coast Express
A LC&DR service between Margate, Ramsgate and London, introduced 1882, ceased 1905; also SER service between same places, introduced 1888, ceased 1904.

Kentish Belle
A renaming of the summer-only

Thanet Belle, 1951, with through
Pullman cars to Canterbury, which
ran 1951 and 1952 only. Ceased 1958.

KER

Knott End Rly: *see* G&KER.

Kerosene Castle (RS)

A GWR gas turbine loco.

Kerr, Stuart

Kerr, Stuart & Co. Ltd, loco builders,
Stoke-on-Trent, 1893–1930. Goodwill
purchased by Hunslet.

Kestrel

A 4,000 hp prototype diesel electric
loco manufactured by Hawker
Siddeley Group, which worked on BR
1968–71 and was then sold to the
USSR (SZD).

Kettle (USRS)

Any steam loco, especially one that is
old and worn out.

Kettle-basher (RS)

One who indulges in kettle-bashing
(qv); anyone sentimental about steam
locos generally.

Kettle-bashing (RS)

Riding on special trains worked by
steam locos over BR lines, or on
steam-hauled trains in other countries.

Kettle on the boil (RS)

A loco in steam.

Key

1. A block of wood (usually pressed
oak) or a steel block driven in to
secure a rail into a chair (qv).

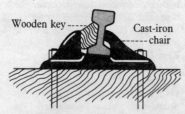

Wooden key ----- Cast-iron
------ chair

2. (USRS) A rly telegraph instrument.

Keyman (RS)

A maintenance man who inspects

track, driving in loose keys and
spikes, tightens loose bolts, replaces
broken fastenings etc.

Khyber Mail

A service between Karachi and
Peshawar.

Kicker (USRS)

A defective triple valve in an air brake
which locks the brake into the
emergency position when no air
application is made.

Killarney Express

A summer service between Dublin and
Killarney/Tralee 1953–6.

Killers (RS)

Diesel units. From the quietness of
their approach to anyone on the track.

King lever

A lever in a signal box which 'cuts
out' the box and allows its signals and
points to be worked remotely from
another box, or to function
automatically via track circuits.

King pin (USRS)

A freight train conductor.

King points (RS)

The first set of points at the entrance
to a marshalling yard from a hump
(qv). *See also* Jack points; Queen
points.

Kings

1. (RS) Drivers, especially on SR and
BR (S).

2. (USRS) A freight train conductor
   (*3*) or a yardmaster.

Kingston Roundabout

A service working London (Waterloo)–
Richmond–Kingston on Thames–
Wimbledon–London (Waterloo) and
vice versa.

Kip (obs)

An incline on which wagons are
assembled to be run off by gravity as
required, usually at a colliery to feed a
loading point. A similar arrangement was
also used in some places for brake vans.

Kipper trip (RS)(obs)
A special train for anglers.
Kitchen (USRS)
The cab of a steam loco.
Kitsons
Todd, Kitson & Laird, loco builders, Leeds, established 1837, later renamed Kitson, Thompson & Hewitson, then in 1899, Kitson & Co. Ltd. Also built steam tramway locos and cars 1878–1901. Ceased production 1938.
Kléber
TEE Paris–Strasbourg, 1971–87.
Kleinbahn (Ger)
A secondary or minor rly.
Klondyke
A name given by rlymen to rly installations or equipment broadly contemporary with the Klondyke (Canada) Gold Rush of 1898–1900, e.g. Klondyke Sidings, and the Klondykes (GNR 4–4–2 locos of 1898).
KLR
Kingsnorth Light Rly, Sharnal Street to Kingsnorth Pier, LRO 1926, 1929, applying to this existing section of the CNT (qv) after its disposal by the Admiralty. The powers included provision for carrying passenger traffic but this was never exercised. Closed 1940.
Knee Knockers (RS)(obs)
BR (S) 4-SUB emu. From the cramped nature of their compartments, in which the passengers' knees tended to touch those of others sitting opposite.
Kneeling cows (RS)
Any steam loco built for a steeply-graded track rly with the front portion designed to be lower than the rear in order to keep the water over the firebox. From their resemblance to the kneeling animal.
Knifeboard seat (obs)
Back to back bench seating running along a tramcar roof from one end to the other so that seated passengers faced the sides of the car, looking outwards. From its resemblance to the board used for cleaning knives in the kitchen.
Knobbing up (RS)
Operating points, hence knobber up, a shunter who operates points in a marshalling yard.
Knobsticked, to be (RS)
To be beaten.
Knocker-up (obs)
A lad sent out from a loco depot to arouse sleeping enginemen to prepare for duty, usually by knocking at their front doors.
Knotty
Nickname for the NSR. From the armorial Staffordshire Knot appearing in the company's monogram.
Knowledge box (USRS)
A yardmaster's office.
Knuckle (RS)
A slight raising of track to permit gravity shunting of wagons in a yard. *See also* Hump; Kip; Pimple.
Knucklehook (US)
A type of rotating coupling hook, closed by a catch or lock.
Kodama
see Shinkansen.
Komet
A sleeping car service between Hamburg and Basle, with through coaches to other Swiss destinations, introduced 1954.
KR
1. Kepwick Rly, 8 m north-east of Thirsk, opened 1833 to carry limestone from Kepwick quarry in the Hambleton Hills, west to kilns near Leake Church. Horse traction and a rope-worked incline. Disused from *c*. 1890.
2. Killin Rly, inc 1883 Killin Junc–Loch Tay, opened 1886, worked by Caledonian Rly, part of LM&SR from 1923.

3. Kington Rly, inc 1818, opened as 3 ft 6 in/1,067 mm gauge horse-worked tramroad, Eardisley–Kington, 1820. Extended to limeworks at Burlinjobb *c.* 1835. Virtually disused after opening of Leominster & Kington Rly in 1857. Purchased by Kington & Eardisley Rly 1862 and part of formation used for the construction of that standard gauge line (opened 1874).

4. Kinross-shire Rly, inc 1857, Kinross–Lumphinnans Junc (near Cowden-beath), opened 1860, part of Edinburgh, Perth & Dundee Rly 1861.

5. Kircudbright Rly, inc 1861, Castle Douglas to Kircudbright, opened 1864, worked by G&SWR, part of G&SWR 1865.

Kreisbahn (Ger)
A rly which is or was the responsibility of a *Kreis*, a local authority broadly equivalent to a district council.

Kremlin, The (RS)
BR headquarters.

Krugers (RS)
GWR 4–6–0/2–6–0 locos of 1899. After the Boer leader, the national enemy of the period; probably a reflection of their ugliness.

KSR
Sleeping car services on the *JZ* (qv).

KVR
Kelvin Valley Rly, inc 1873, Maryhill [Glasgow] to Kilsyth, opened 1879, worked by NBR, part of NBR 1885.

Kylchap
A multiple jet blast pipe for steam locos invented by the engineers Kylälä and Chapelon.

Kylporta
A multiple jet blast pipe for steam locos invented by the engineers Kylälä and Porta.

L

LA (LTRS)
Lengthy Absence. LA 1, 2, and 3, 3 being the most serious; also used for reprimands for lateness and/or absence.

L'aal Ratty
Alternative form of Ratty (qv).

LA&NQLR
Lampeter, Aberayron and New Quay Light Rly, LRO 1906, opened (to Aberayron only) 1911, worked by GWR, part of GWR from 1922.

Labour gain[s], one/two (RS)
Colour-light signal showing single/ double yellow aspect. From the phrase used at the time of parliamentary and local authority elections when the Labour Party wins a seat from another party.

Ladder
1. A layout of facing and trailing crossovers in which switches follow in sequence to allow movements across several parallel lines. This has replaced the more costly and complicated arrangement involving straight through connection with diamond crossings and double slips.
2. (US) The main track in a marshalling yard.

Lading (US)
The load in a freight car.

Lairage (obs)
Accommodation provided at a freight terminal for cattle and horses.

Lakes Express
A summer-only service between London (Euston) and Windermere/ Keswick and Workington, introduced 1927; later ran on weekdays throughout the year.

Lakeside
see L&HR.

LAMA
Locomotive & Allied Manufacturers' Association. A 1956 renaming of the LMA (qv). Again renamed RIA (qv), 1971.

Lambourn Valley
see LVR (1).

Lambton Waggonway/Rly
Opened *c.* 1770 to connect collieries owned by J.G.Lambton (later the first Earl of Durham) at Fencehouses to the River Wear. Amalgamated with the Newbottle waggonway (opened 1813) in 1819 after which the two lines were linked and extended. Some parts of the system remained in use as NCB rlys until 1986–7.

Lamping/to lamp (obs)
To place lighted oil lamps into the purpose-built holes in coach roofs as darkness approached.

Lancashire Pullman
A service between London (Euston) and Blackpool, introduced 1986.

Lancaster
Lancaster Railway Carriage & Wagon Co. Ltd, Lancaster, 1863–1902. Became part of MCW (qv).

Lancastrian
An express between London (Euston) and Manchester, introduced 1928, name restored 1957, dropped 1962.

L&A (LTRS)
Late & Absent staff return.

L&AR
Lanarkshire & Ayrshire Rly, inc as Barrmill & Killwinning Rly, 1883, name changed to L&AR 1884 and further lines authorized. Opened Barrmill– Ardrossan 1888, Kilbirnie branch 1889, Irvine branch 1890, Newton [Glasgow]–Cathcart–Lugton–Giffen 1903, 1904. Worked and maintained by Caledonian Rly. Part of LM&SR from 1923.

L&BER
1. Leeds & Bradford Extension Rly, inc 1845, Leeds (Leeds & Bradford Rly) to Keighley, Skipton and Colne Junc (ELR (1)). Leased to Midland Rly 1846, opened 1847, 1848, 1849. Part of Midland Rly 1851.
2. Letterkenny & Burtonport Extension Rly (Ireland), 3 ft/914 mm gauge, LRO 1898, opened 1903, worked by L&LSR (qv).

L&BR
1. Listowel & Ballybunion Rly (Ireland), a Lartigue (qv) monorail line, inc 1886, opened 1888, closed 1924.
2. London & Birmingham Rly, inc 1833, opened 1837, 1838, London (Euston)–Birmingham (Curzon St.). Part of L&NWR from 1846.
3. London & Blackwall Rly, inc 1839, opened 1840,1841. 5 ft/1,524 mm gauge, with cable haulage, London (Fenchurch St.) to Blackwall [Pier]. Converted to standard gauge and loco haulage 1849. Leased to GER 1866; part of L&NER from 1923.
4. London & Brighton Rly, inc 1837, opened 1840 and 1841, became LB&SCR 1846.
5. Lynton & Barnstaple Rly, 1 ft 11½ in/597 mm gauge, inc 1895, opened 1898, part of SR from 1923, closed 1935.

L&CBER
Llandudno & Colwyn Bay Electric Rly, interurban type operation between Old Colwyn and Llandudno West Shore, using ordinary single- and double-deck electric tramcars; 3 ft 6 in/1,067 mm gauge. LROs 1899, 1903, 1907, 1912. Originally promoted as L&CB Light Rly, name changed 1906 to L&CB Electric Traction Co., then L&District Electric Tramway Construction Co. Opened 1907, 1908, 1915. Name changed to L&CBER 1909. Closed 1956.

L&CR
London & Croydon Rly, inc 1835, opened 1839, part of LB&SCR, 1846.

Land crabs (RS)
Another form of crabs (qv).

Land cruise
A term coined in 1925 by a New York travel agency which commissioned the construction of an 'hotel train' for special tours. Accommodation included a recreation car with gymnasium and cinema facilities, barbers' shop, library, sleeping cars, lounge, dining, observation and baggage cars. In 1927 the GWR advertised so-called 'land cruises' or tours by special train and road coach for an inclusive charge, including ordinary hotel accommodation. The full US concept, involving an 'hotel train' was, however, adopted in 1933 by the L&NER – *see* Northern Belle. The term was devalued by BR to describe day circular tours by trains operated in North Wales each summer from 1950 until 1961. These started and finished at Rhyl, Llandudno or Pwllheli running via Denbigh, Corwen, Barmouth and Caernarvon in both directions. From 1955 some had

radio commentaries. Various names were used: North Wales Land Cruise; Festival Land Cruise (1951); Welsh Land Cruise; Coronation Land Cruise (1953); Cambrian Radio Cruise; Welsh Chieftain Land Cruise; North Wales Radio Land Cruise; and John Peel. 'Land cruises' of a similar nature, using dmus, were operated in the Lake District by BR for a few seasons from 1955. BR's Inter-City Land Cruises, introduced in 1987, are closer to the original concept.

L&DR
Lanarkshire & Dumbartonshire Rly, inc 1891, Stobcross (GCR (2))– Dumbarton–Balloch, and short lines at Partick and Maryhill. Dumbarton to Balloch jointly vested in Caledonian and NBR, worked by Caledonian. Opened 1894, 1896, 1897. Company became part of Caledonian Rly from 1909.

L&ECR
Louth & East Coast Rly, inc 1872, Louth to Mablethorpe, opened 1877, linked to the Sutton & Willoughby Rly (opened 1886) at Sutton-on-Sea in 1888. Worked by GNR, part of GNR 1908.

L&EofFR
Leven & East of Fife Rly: *see* EofFR and LR (4).

L&GR
London & Greenwich Rly, inc 1833, opened 1836, the first passenger rly in London. Leased to SER from 1845, part of SR 1923.

L&HCTAC
London & Home Counties Traffic Advisory Committee. Set up under Transport Act, 1919 and London Traffic Act, 1924. Issued reports of enquiries into transport in north-east, east and south-east London, 1925–6.

L&HR
Lakeside & Haverthwaite Rly. Part of former BR Ulverston–Lakeside branch (closed to passengers 1965, to freight 1967), northern section reopened as a preserved rly, 1973.

L&LSR
Londonderry & Lough Swilly Rly, Londonderry–Letterkenny–Gweedore–Burtonport, with branch to Buncrana and Carndonagh, inc 1853, first section opened 1863. Buncrana–Londonderry altered from 5 ft 3 in/1,600 mm to 3 ft/914 mm gauge 1885, all other lines built to that gauge. Last section closed 1953.

L&MMR
Llanelly & Mynydd Mawr Rly, Llanelli–Cynheidre–Cross Hands, inc 1875, opened 1883, part of GWR from 1923.

L&MR
Liverpool & Manchester Rly, inc 1826, opened 1830; first public rly to be operated entirely by locos, first rly to operate passenger trains to a timetable and first to work all traffic itself, with its own locos and rolling stock. Part of GJR 1845.

L&MVLR
Leek & Manifold Valley Light Rly, Waterhouses–Hulme End, 2 ft 6 in/ 762 mm gauge, LRO 1899, opened 1904, worked and maintained by NSR, part of LM&SR from 1923, closed 1934.

L&NER
London & North Eastern Rly, formed 1923, a grouping of GCR, GER, GNofSR, GNR, NBR, NER, and various minor companies and joint lines. Part of BR 1948.

L&NWR
London & North Western Rly, formed 1846; a merger of the GJR, L&BR (2) and the Manchester & Birmingham

Rly. Many extensions and other lines absorbed subsequently; 2,063 route miles by 1914, covering area between London and Carlisle, much of Wales and central England. Absorbed the L&YR in 1922. Part of LM&SR 1923.

Land of Plenty (RS)
Overtime.

L&OR
Llynvi & Ogmore Rly, inc 1866, an amalgamation of LVR (*2*) and the OVR. C&OVR absorbed 1876. Worked by GWR from 1876. Pencoed branch (Tondu to Bryncethin Junc) opened 1877. Extension Nantyffyllon to Cymmer and Abergwynfi opened 1878 (Cymmer), 1880 (passengers), 1886 (Nantyffyllon). Part of GWR 1883.

L&SDR
Launceston & South Devon Rly, Launceston to Tavistock, inc 1862, opened 1865, worked by SDR, part of SDR 1869.

L&SR
1. Leicester & Swannington Rly, inc 1830, opened 1832 and 1833, acquired by the Midland Rly 1847.
2. London & Southampton Rly, inc 1834, opened 1838, 1839 and 1840, renamed L&SWR 1839.

Land surveyor (RS)
Second man (qv).

L&SWR
London & South Western Rly, inc 1839; a renaming of the L&SR, which had obtained powers to extend to Portsmouth. Many other lines subsequently built and absorbed; 1,037 route miles by 1914. Part of SR from 1923.

L&TVJR
Llantrisant & Taff Vale Junction Rly, inc 1861, 1866, Treforest to Llantrisant and Common Junc, opened 1863 (passengers 1865); and Waterhall

Junc (Cardiff, Ely) to Common Branch Junc (near Cross Inn), opened 1886. Leased to TVR from 1875, part of TVR from 1889.

L&WLR
Leadhills & Wanlockhead Light Rly, Elvanfoot–Wanlockhead, highest standard gauge line in Great Britain, 1,498 ft/456.6 metres above sea level. LRO 1898, opened 1901, 1902 as part of Caledonian Rly. LM&SR 1923, closed 1938.

L&YR
Lancashire & Yorkshire Rly, formed 1847, a merger of Ashton, Stalybridge & Liverpool Junction Rly, Huddersfield & Sheffield Junc Rly, Liverpool & Bury Rly, Manchester, Bolton & Bury Canal Navigation & Rly, Manchester & Leeds Rly, Wakefield, Pontefract & Goole Rly and West Riding Rlys. Subsequently there were further extensions and other lines were absorbed including the ELR (*1*) in 1859. 600 route miles by 1914, mainly in south Lancashire and south Yorkshire. Part of L&NWR 1922.

Lane, The (RS)(obs)
Stewarts Lane [London] loco depot, SR, BR (S).

Languish[er] & Yawn[er]
Nickname for L&YR.

Lanky, The (RS)
L&YR, its locos and trains, or its employees.

Lanky Claughtons (RS)
L&YR/LM&SR Hughes 4–6–0 locos of 1921 and 1923.

Lanky Yorky
Nickname for L&YR.

Lartigue [system]
A species of monorail, patented by Charles F.M. Lartigue in 1883, in which the single rail is carried on angle-iron trestles about 3 ft/1 metre

high. A light guide or stabilizing rail is placed either side of the trestles about 1 ft 6 in/457 mm below the carrying rail. The locos and vehicles must therefore straddle the track like the panniers placed over a pack-animal. The L&BR (Ireland) was constructed on this principle in 1888 as were a handful of short lines in North Africa, France, Russia and South America.

Lartigue signals (obs)
Semaphore signals designed by Charles F.M. Lartigue and used in France.

Lasers (RS)
BR class 87 electric locos. From the brilliance of their headlights.

Last vehicle indicator (obs)
A small board attached to the last vehicle of a train when lamps not in use, to indicate to signalmen and others that the train is complete.

Late [and] Never Early
Nickname for the L&NER.

Late fee box
A letter box at a rly station in which, for an extra charge over normal postage rates, items could be posted up to a short time before the departure of a TPO, to be carried and sorted on the TPO.

Launching pad
1. (RS)(obs) A steam loco turntable.
2. (RS) A wc seat.

LAV
SR emu sets of 1932 and 1940 for semi-fast services, comprising three Third Class compartment cars and one composite trailer with side corridor and LAVatory accommodation, 4-LAV.

Lavender Line
A short section of the former BR (S) Lewes–Uckfield line at Isfield, operated as a preserved rly.

Lawn, The (RS)
1. Fast lines.
2. The passenger concourse (formerly parcels and mails area and originally the site of the track ends and turnplates area) of Paddington Station, London, possibly after a grass slope that existed here when the station was first opened.

Lay-out, to (USRS)
To side-track or delay a train.

Layover
The time a train and its crew spend at a terminus or terminating point before leaving again in the opposite direction. Also an interval between duties.

LB&SCR
London, Brighton & South Coast Rly, formed 1846, a combination of the L&BR and L&CR. Subsequently many lines built and absorbed. 456 route miles by 1914. A great favourite with railwayacs (qv), who admired its handsome and smartly kept locos. Part of SR from 1923.

LC
Level Crossing.

LC&DR
London, Chatham & Dover Rly, inc 1853 as East Kent Rly (qv), first section opened 1858. Renamed LC&DR 1859. Other lines subsequently built and absorbed until total reached 187 miles, almost all in Kent. Fiercely competitive with the SER until 1899, from which year both lines were worked under a managing Committee as the SE&CR (qv).

LCGB
Locomotive Club of Great Britain, founded 1949.

LCL (US)
Less than Carload Lot; sundries or 'smalls' traffic.

LD&ECR
Lancashire, Derbyshire & East Coast

Rly, inc 1891 to build a line from Warrington to Chesterfield, Lincoln and docks at Sutton-on-Sea, with branches to Manchester and Sheffield, but opened only from Chesterfield to Lincoln, with a branch to Beighton Junction near Sheffield, in 1897 and 1898. Taken over by the GCR 1907.

LD Line
Chesterfield to Lincoln (LD&ECR (qv)).

Lead [of a track crossing]
The distance from the nose of a crossing to the heel of the points, measured along the straight.

Lead (LT)
The feeder cable from an overhead trolley wire, used for moving cars in depots.

Leader
1. The L&NWR term for a passenger brake van or other non-passenger vehicle placed between the loco and the rest of a train to steady riding and minimize the nuisance created by any overflow when the loco was taking up water from water troughs.
2. (obs) Another word for a control trailer (qv).
3. A controversial and experimental 0-6-6-0T loco design for the SR by O.V.S. Bulleid. The project was abandoned by BR after unsuccessful trial runs in 1949 and 1950.

Leadhills
see L&WLR.

Leak down, to
To allow air to escape from the brake system until the brakes become inoperative.

Leamside Line
Ferryhill–Washington–Pelaw.

Leave a train over, to (LTRS)
To hold a train, usually at a reversing

point so that it omits a round trip in order to restore it to correct timing.

Lecky (RS)
Electric train. Also (in Liverpool) a tramcar.

Leeds Executive
An express between London (Kings Cross) and Leeds, introduced 1973. Name dropped 1986.

Leeds Forge
Leeds Forge Co. Ltd, Leeds, rly rolling stock builders, 1869–1923. Became part of Cammell–Laird (qv).

Leeds Northern Line
Leeds–Harrogate–Northallerton.

Lee Moor
Lee Moor Tramway, a 4 ft 6 in/ 1,372 mm gauge horse-worked tramroad built for the carriage of china clay between Lee Moor [Cholwichtown] and Plymouth, incorporating two rope-worked inclines, opened 1858. Steam working on upper section introduced *c.* 1899. Mostly disused by 1947 and completely closed in 1960.

Leen Valley Line
Bulwell Common–Annesley North Junc (the former GCR line).

Left hand running
The normal method of operation over double tracks in the British Isles. Also in Algeria, Argentina, Australia, Austria (some lines), Belgium, Brazil (most lines), Burma, Chile, China (some lines), Egypt, France (most lines), Ghana, India, Indonesia, Italy, Japan, Kenya, Malaysia, Nigeria, Pakistan, Portugal, South Africa, Spain (some lines), Sri Lanka, Sweden, Switzerland, Tanzania, Turkey, Uganda, and Zimbabwe.

Légers, trains (Fr)(obs)
Rail motors or railcars.

Lemano
TEE Geneva–Milan, introduced 1958,

lost *TEE* status 1982. Name used for
Paris–Lausanne *TGV* 1984 and also
for its Geneva–Milan EC connection,
1987.

Lemonade turn (RS)
The midday (14.00–22.00) shift, so
called because there is little or no
chance of obtaining alcoholic
refreshment after duty.

Lemon time (RS)
An officially-sanctioned refreshment/
recreation break for men engaged in
shunting work. From the practice of
sucking lemons at halftime during
football matches.

Lempor
A multiple jet blast pipe for steam
locos invented by the engineers
Lemâitre and Porta.

Length (obs)
A stretch of line allocated to a
particular crew of track maintenance
workers.

Lengthmen (obs)
The track maintenance staff allocated
to a particular length (qv) which they
normally patrolled every day. Now
known as trackmen/ track maintenance
teams.

Leningrad Express
A Berlin–Leningrad service,
introduced 1972, extended in summer
to Paris, Cologne or Hanover.

Leonardo da Vinci
An EC service between Milan and
Munich via Brenner Pass, introduced
1987.

LER
London Electric Rly, formed 1910, a
merger of BS&WR, GNP&BR and
CCE&HR. Part of LPTB from 1933.

Let Me Sleep
Nickname for (LMS) LM&SR.

LEV (obs)
Leyland Experimental Vehicle, later
interpreted as Light Economy Vehicle;

a prototype for a new generation of
BR light railcars, 1978–81.

Lever collar/clip
A device placed on the handle of a
signal lever as a reminder that the line
controlled by that lever is already
occupied by a train. The action of
collar/clip engages the catch-spring,
preventing the signal being moved to
the 'off' position.

Lever jerker (USRS)
A signalman.

Leverman (US)
Signalman.

Lewisman
Service between Kyle of Lochalsh and
Dingwall, with through Glasgow
coach, introduced 1933.

Lézard Rouge
Red Lizard; a tourist train operated
between Tabeditt and Metlaoui,
Tunisia.

LFK (obs)
BR Lounge Corridor First class coach,
converted in 1967 from Mark 1 FK
vehicles to incorporate a ten-seat
lounge area.

LHB (Ger)
Linke-Hoffman-Busch GmbH; a
rolling stock manufacturer.

Library
1. (RS) A messroom.
2. (USRS) A cupola (qv).

Lickey route
Birmingham–Bromsgrove–Gloucester.

LIFT
London International Freight
Terminal, Stratford E., opened 1967.

Lift (RS)
A train; e.g. 'a lift of three wagons
and two vans'.

Lift [tickets], to (USRS)
To collect tickets from passengers,
usually in exchange for a 'hat check'
(qv). Sometimes expressed as to
'uplift'.

Lifting bar
see Clearance/depression bar.

Lifting barrier
A pivoted boom lowered across a roadway at level crossings when a train is due.

Light engine
A loco moving along the line on its own, or with a brake van.

Lightning slinger (USRS)
A rly telegrapher.

Light rail/light rail rapid transit/light rail transit
Versions of a generic term in use from the early 1970s for a public transport facility using electric tramcars or light emu sets (LRV (qv)) on street tracks, segregated street or roadside alignments, shallow subways, elevated structures or surface private right of way, or conventional rly tracks and alignments, singly or in combination, to provide a flexible and environmentally-friendly low-cost urban/suburban passenger transport facility constructed and operated on light rly principles. In essence an updated form of tramway (*3*).

Light rly
A rly purposely built more simply and below the engineering standards of normal rlys, to reduce the cost of construction and attain economy in working. Gradients may accordingly be steeper and curves sharper than those normally provided. Tracks may be unfenced and placed alongside or in the centre of public roads and there may be intermingling with tramways (*3*). A narrower gauge than standard may be chosen to facilitate and cheapen construction. The constraints mentioned may result in lower average speeds than normal and signalling and safety systems may therefore be much less elaborate than on a conventional

rly. In Britain the majority of such lines have been constructed under the provisions of the Light Railways Act, 1896 but the term is also applied to similar lines built before that legislation existed and to others authorized subsequently by private legislation. For convenience, some tramways (*3*) were authorized under the 1896 Act and were therefore formally entitled light rlys although wholly or mainly laid along streets and in every other respect no different from tramways (*3*). *See also* Light rail/light rail rapid transit/light rail transit.

Light Railway & Tramway Journal
see LR&TJ.

Light rapid transit
A generic term embracing light rail transit (qv) and also unconventional rail and non-rail modes fulfilling a similar role at similar cost.

Ligne Impériale, la (Fr)
The rly between Paris and Marseille (the former *PLM* (qv) main line), since it led to the port serving the French overseas empire.

Ligure, le
TEE Marseilles–Milan, introduced 1957. Extended to Avignon 1969–82. Lost *TEE* status 1982.

Lijn, de
Brand name of the *VVM* (qv).

Limited
A train on which all seats must be pre-booked and to which passengers who have no seat reservation are denied access.

Limited, The (RS)
Cornish Riviera Express (qv).

Limits of deviation
The extreme outer boundaries within which new rlys authorized by parliament must be built.

Line-basher (RS)
Track-basher (qv).

Line blocked
The normal indication of a signalling block instrument, the others being 'Train on line' and 'Line clear'.

Line capacity
The maximum number of trains which can be passed over any particular line in a given period. Constrained by the signalling system, the physical characteristics of the line (less important with electric traction), train speeds, speed restrictions and the required pattern of service.

Line-haul railroad (US)
Term for a rly performing main trunk line common carrier functions.

Line occupation
1. Use of a line in terms of trains.
2. Obstruction of a section of line by a train; or by engineers' plant and vehicles during maintenance and reconstruction work ('engineer's occupation').

Liner (USRS)
A luxury passenger train.

Liner train
Freightliner (qv).

Linesider (RS)
One who enjoys watching and photographing steam-hauled special trains from bridges or the lineside but tends not to ride on them or give them other financial support.

Linesiding (RS)
The activities of a linesider (qv).

Link
A combination of duties providing a sequenced pattern of work over a given period of time for a group of personnel qualified to undertake them. The 'top' or 'first' link (obs since *c.* 1960) were those engine crews enjoying the highest rates of pay and monopolizing the principal passenger express workings. *See also* Fluffy link; Long link.

Link and pin (USRS)
The traditional type of freight wagon coupler until the 1970s, hence by association, any old-fashioned rlyman or practice.

Link span
A form of lifting bridge between a train ferry (qv) and the tracks on shore.

LIRR (US)
Long Island Railroad, formerly a subsidiary of the Pennsy (qv), it now operates its suburban services between Long Island and New York under contract to the MTA (qv).

Lisboa Express
A day service between Madrid and Lisbon, introduced 1967. Replaced by *Luis de Camoes* (qv) in 1989.

Littleboy (LTRS)
A surveying tool, placed next to a rail to check alignment of track. After its designer.

Little Eds/Edwards (RS)
BR electro-diesel locos, class 73. From Electro-Diesel.

Little Egberts (RS)
L&YR 0–8–2T. From a troupe of performing elephants to which they were compared by crews impressed by their versatile abilities.

Little North Western
The NWR (qv).

Little Ratty
Ratty (qv).

Little Sharps/Sharpies (RS)
GNR 2–2–2 locos of 1874–9, built by Sharp, Stewart and converted to tank engines in 1852.

Little Sir Echo (RS)
His Master's Voice (qv).

Littl'un (RS)
A dwarf shunting signal.

Live engine
A loco with steam up, ready to move.

Liver & Bacon (RS)
Nickname for the LB&SCR in the
period when its locos were lettered
'L&B'.

Liverpool Executive
A service between London (Euston)
and Liverpool, introduced 1984. Name
dropped 1985. *See also* Merseyside
Pullman.

Liverpool Pullman
A service between London (Euston)
and Liverpool (Lime St.), introduced
1966 with new Pullman cars. Ceased
1975.

Livery
The manner in which locos and rolling
stock are painted, including lettering
and symbols.

Lizard scorcher (USRS)
The Chief Steward of the restaurant
service on a train.

Lizzies (RS)
LM&SR 8P 4-6-2 locomotives,
introduced 1933. After 'Princess
Elizabeth', the second to appear.

LJR
Lowestoft Junction Rly, inc 1897,
Lowestoft Line Junc near Yarmouth
(Beach) to Gorleston (North)
[N&SJR], opened 1903 as part of
M&GNR.

LL
Low Level.

Llanberis Lake
Llanberis Lake Rly, 1 ft 11½ in/597 mm
gauge tourist line over part of the
former Padarn Rly near Llanberis.

Lloyd Express
A *CIWL* service between Hamburg
and Genoa, introduced 1907. Restored
after the First World War. Connection
made with the sailings of
Norddeutscher Lloyd liners between
Genoa and the USA.

LLR
1. Lauder Light Rly, known locally as

'Auld La'der Licht', Fountainhall
to Lauder, LRO 1898, opened
1901, worked by NBR. Part of
L&NER 1923. Closed to passengers
1932, entirely 1958.
2. Llanberis Lake Rly (qv).

LMA
Locomotive Manufacturers'
Association, formed 1875. Renamed
LAMA (qv), 1956.

LM&SR
London, Midland & Scottish Rly,
formed 1923, a grouping of L&NWR,
Midland Rly, NSR, FR (*2*), CR (*1*),
G&SWR, HR (*6*) and various minor
and joint lines. Part of BR 1948.

LMR
Longmoor Military Rly, Bordon–
Woolmer–Liss, built and operated by
the Royal Engineers and Army rly
units; first sections opened 1906, 1907.
Originally titled Woolmer
Instructional Military Rly (WIMR).
Renamed LMR 1935; latterly operated
by RCT (qv) as their training ground
for rly operation. Closed 1969,
training transferred to 79th Rly
Squadron in Germany.

LMS
see LM&SR.

LNR
Leeds Northern Rly, a renaming of
the Leeds & Thirsk Rly (which was
extending to Stockton) in 1851.
Absorbed into York, Newcastle &
Berwick Rly and then the NER in
1854.

Load factor
The average use made of a train or
service capacity. Usually calculated by
dividing passenger miles (qv) by seat
miles (qv).

Loading gauge
1. The absolute size limits for rail
    vehicles proceeding over a given
    stretch of line or group of lines,

measured both laterally, in relation to position of the platform edges, tunnel walls etc., and vertically in relation to the height of bridges and tunnels. It can vary considerably for the same track gauge (qv gauge) e.g. the British loading gauge is more restricted than that applying on the mainland of Europe and much more so than that applying in North America. *See also* Berne gauge.

2. A metal frame suspended over a track to indicate the limits to which an open freight wagon may be safely loaded.

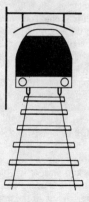

Local rly
Term used (mostly on the mainland of Europe) to describe any rly serving a limited area. Such lines are normally no more than about 20 to 30 m long and are usually of light rly (qv) type.

Local traffic (obs)
Traffic arising on a specific rly system, as distinct from that originating on 'foreign' (qv) rlys.

Lock and block
A signalling system, incorporating mechanical or electrical safety and locking devices which are interconnected with the block instruments and signal levers positively to ensure that only one train at a time occupies a block section. Invented by W.R. Sykes and introduced from 1875. *See also* Release key.

Locked up (RS)
Prevented from moving signal or points levers by the action of the interlocking mechanism or locking bar.

Locking bar
A bar placed on the inside of the rails which is depressed by wheel flanges and prevents points being changed while a vehicle is passing over them.

Locking frame
see Interlocking.

Loco
Locomotive or (RS), locomotive shed or MPD (qv), e.g. 'Kings Cross Loco'.

Locomotiva (It)
A steam loco.

Locomotore (It)
An electric or diesel loco, as distinct from *locomotiva* (qv).

Loco spotter (RS)
Train spotter (qv).

Lodging turn (obs)
A duty which required enginemen and guards to spend a night away from home in a rly staff hostel or lodgings.

Lok (Ger)
Abbreviation for *lokomotiv/e* (loco/s).

Lokalbahn
Austrian word for local rly (qv).

Lokey (NZ RS)
A loco.

Lollipop (RS)
A tool used by lengthmen for testing condition of sleepers. From its shape.

Lombardy Express
A service between Paris and Milan, introduced 1962.

London and South East Sector
A BR business sector formed 1982 to cover passenger facilities (other than InterCity) in London and SE England, reconstructed as NSE (qv) 1986.

London Area
The LPTB area (qv). *See also* Extended London Area.

London Commuter Area
Extended London Area (qv).

London–Merseyside Express
A service between London (Euston) and Liverpool (Lime St.), introduced 1927, renamed Merseyside Express (qv), 1928.

London Necropolis Co.
Inc as the LN & National Mausoleum Co. in 1852, it operated funeral trains, including its own hearse vans, from a private station at Waterloo (resited and rebuilt in Westminster Bridge Road in 1902), using the L&SWR (later the SR) between Waterloo and Brookwood. At the latter, the funeral trains moved on to a line with two private stations inside the company's cemetery. This operation lasted from 1854 to 1941. Some Necropolis specials may have been worked from Waterloo (SR) to Brookwood after 1941, but the tracks in the Brookwood cemetery were removed *c.* 1947.

London Smash 'em and Turn 'em over
Nickname for the LC&DR.

London Traffic Combine
A term used (mainly by politicians and journalists) for the UERL (qv).

London Travel Centre
see Travel centres.

Londres Vichy Pullman
A *CIWL* all-Pullman First Class train (connecting with Folkestone–Boulogne sailings) 1927–30.

Lone wolf (USRS)
An employee who does not belong to a trade union (brotherhood).

Long and Narrow, The
Nickname for the L&NWR; from its initials and geographical shape.

Long Charleys (RS)
GWR eight-wheeled coaches with fixed wheelbase but some lateral play available to the wheels.

Long Drag, The (RS)
The Settle to Carlisle line.

Long link (RS)(obs)
Crews available only for normal duties. *See also* Fluffy link; Link.

Long Toms (RS)
1. (obs) Yorkshire coal.
2. GNR 0–8–0 coal traffic locos of 1901 (L&NER classes Q1,2,& 3). From their sound, said to resemble that of the 'Long Tom' field gun used in the South African War, 1899–1902.
3. (obs) A tall tail lamp used on GWR slip coaches.

LonSLR
Lee on the Solent Light Rly, Fort Brockhurst to Lee on the Solent, inc 1893, opened 1894, worked by L&SWR from 1909. Part of SR 1923.

Look-out
An employee equipped with red and green flags and horn or whistle, and given the task of warning others working on or close to the track of the approach of a train.

Loop/loop siding
A track with connection to main running lines at each end, allowing shunting and overtaking.

Loop, The (RS)
The March–St Ives–Cambridge line.

Loop, to (RS)
To put a train into a loop to allow a more important service to overtake it, hence 'to be looped', to be put into a loop.

Loose-coupled [freight/train] (obs)
A train of wagons and vans connected

only by three-link couplings or instanter couplers (qv) in the extended position, i.e. without continuous braking, relying solely on the loco brakes and guard's handbrake. However on steep gradients some manual brakes on the wagons would be pinned down (qv).

Loose gang
A group of track maintenance staff not attached to a length (qv), but available for attending accidents, relaying work etc.

Loose shunting
Shunting by propelling vehicles into a siding without coupling them up to the loco. *See also* Flying shunt.

LOR
Liverpool Overhead Rly, inc 1888, opened 1893, 1894, 1896 as a mainly elevated electric rly serving the docks area; closed 1956.

Lord of The Isles
A service between Edinburgh and Mallaig/Oban, so named 1989.

Lord's My Shepherd
Nickname for (LMS) LM&SR.

Lord Willoughby's Rly
Built by Lord Willoughby de Eresby to connect his Grimesthorpe Castle, near Edenham with the GNR main line at Little Bytham, opened in 1856. Passenger and freight traffic was carried but the former (begun in 1857) was occasionally suspended owing to poor maintenance of track and locos. Horse traction was resorted to in the line's last days and the line closed *c*. 1882. Part of the formation was used by the Bourne–Castle Bytham section of the M&GNR.

Lorelei
An express between Hook of Holland and Basle/Lucerne 1953–74; Hook/Amsterdam–Basle 1975–86; Hook–Basle 1987; Hook–Cologne 1988, renamed *Colonia Express* 1989.

Loreley
A Blackpool–Sheffield–Harwich diesel car service in connection with Continental sailings, ran only in 1988. Name used for Birmingham/Liverpool–Harwich service, 1989. *See also* Britannia.

Loriot
GWR TC for well wagons carrying agricultural and other machinery (eighteen types).

Lose 'em, Mix 'em and Smash 'em
Nickname for (LMS) LM&SR.

Lose its feet, to (RS)
Used of a loco suffering from wheel-slip ('She's lost her feet' etc.).

Lot, to give it/her the (LTRS)
To make an emergency brake application.

Lothian Coast Express
A summer service between Glasgow and North Berwick/Gullane/Dunbar, introduced 1914, restored 1922 to North Berwick and Gullane only, to North Berwick only from 1933, withdrawn at end of 1933 season. Possibly the first British train to carry its name on a loco headboard.

Louse cage (USRS)
A caboose (qv).

Low Iron (USRS)
Sidings and yard lines, as distinct from High Iron (qv).

Low Level Line, The
Ditton Junc–Warrington–Arpley–Timperley.

Lower quadrant
A semaphore signal whose arm, normally horizontal, falls to about 45 degrees below horizontal when pulled 'off'. See illustration overleaf.

LPTB
London Passenger Transport Board, formed 1933. It included the rlys formerly operated by the UERL (qv) and the Metropolitan Rly and was

replaced by LTE (*1*) 1948. Popularly known as 'London Transport' or 'LT'.

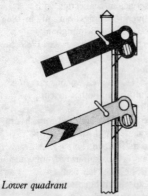

Lower quadrant

LPTB or London Passenger Transport Area

The area controlled by the LPTB after 1933. This extended from Wendover, Tring, Luton and Bishops Stortford in the north to Guildford, Horsham and Edenbridge in the south; and from Amersham, Slough and Chertsey in the west to Brentwood, Grays and Sevenoaks in the east, covering a total of 1,986 square miles. This territory was also assigned to the LPTB's immediate successors (i.e. until 1970).

LR

1. Lanark Rly, opened 1854 as private line, freight only, Cleghorn Junc–Lanark, worked by Caledonian Rly, passenger traffic 1855. Inc 1860 as part of CR.

2. Leslie Rly, inc 1857, Markinch–Leslie, opened 1861, worked by Edinburgh, Perth & Dundee Rly, part of NBR from 1872.

3. Lesmahagow Rly, Motherwell (Lesmahagow Junc)–Lesmahagow [Brocketsbrae]–Coalburn–Galawhistle Pit/Spireslack, first section opened 1856, worked by

Caledonian, passenger service to Lesmahagow 1858. Part of Caledonian Rly from 1881.

4. Leven Rly, inc 1853, Thornton to Leven, opened 1854. Worked by Edinburgh, Perth & Dundee Rly. Amalgamated with EofFR as L&EofFR 1861, extended to Anstruther 1863, part of NBR 1877.

5. Londonderry Rly, or Marquis of Londonderry's Rly, rope-worked line from Penshaw Collieries to Seaham Harbour opened *c*. 1831. Extended from Seaham to Sunderland, as Londonderry, Seaham & Sunderland Rly, opened 1854, passenger service worked over NER into Sunderland station, 1855. Part of NER 1900.

6. Lydd Rly, inc 1881, Appledore–Lydd–Dungeness, opened 1881, 1883, extended to New Romney 1884. Part of SER 1895.

7. Lymington Rly, inc 1856, Brockenhurst–Lymington, opened 1858, worked by L&SWR, part of L&SWR 1879, extended to Lymington Pier 1884.

LR&D

Llanelly Rly & Dock, Llanelly–Llandilo; Pantyffynnon–Brynamman/Gwaun cae Gurwen; Tirydail–Cross Hands, inc 1828 as Llanelli Rail-road & Dock Co. (dock & colliery tramroad). Llanelly Rly & Dock Co. 1835, opened 1833 (Dafen branch), 1839, 1840, 1841, 1857. Extended to Llandovery by leasing Vale of Towy Rly 1858. Llandilo Junc–Carmarthen opened 1865, Pontardulais to Swansea and Penclawdd branch 1867. These last two lines inc 1871 as Swansea & Carmarthen Rly, worked by L&NWR and name changed 1877 to Central Wales & Carmarthen Rly. Absorbed by L&NWR 1891. Rest of LR&D absorbed by GWR from 1889.

LR&H
Lowestoft Rly & Harbour, rly inc 1845, Reedham to Lowestoft, opened 1847, leased by NR 1846, part of ECR 1848.

LR&TJ
Light Railway & Tramway Journal, founded 1899, renamed *Electric Railway & Tramway Journal* 1914, *Electric Railway, Bus & Tramway Journal* 1932, *Passenger Transport Journal* 1938, later shortened to *Passenger Transport*. Amalgamated with *Buses Illustrated* as *Buses*, 1968.

LRC
1. Light Railway Commmission, established under the Light Railways Act, 1896 and empowered to make orders authorizing construction of light rlys, the orders to be submitted to the BoT (qv) for confirmation (until this was received, they were known as provisional orders). Confirmation gave the order the same status as an act of parliament. The LRC was wound up in 1922 when powers to make orders passed to the MoT (qv).
2. Light, Rapid & Comfortable diesel push-pull, tilt-body high speed trains developed by a consortium of Canadian companies from 1967 onwards. First train delivered to Amtrak, 1980.

LRO
Light Rly Order: *see* LRC (*1*).

LRPC
London Regional Passengers' Committee. *See also* CTCC.

LRPHJC
Lots Road Power House Joint Committee, (London). Inc 1911 with representatives of MDR and LER, to acquire the Lots Road power station from the UERL and lease it to these statutory companies. Ceased to exist with formation of LPTB in 1933.

LRRS
London Railway Road Services, a BRB organization which formerly provided all cartage services (qv) within the London area for the London-based regions of BR.

LRT
1. Light rail transit (qv) or light rapid transit (qv).
2. London Regional Transport, formed 1984, under the London Regional Transport Act, 1984, to take the place of LTE (*2*) and remove control from the Greater London Council to the Secretary of State for Transport. Like its predecessors, it was soon popularly known as 'London Transport' and this subsequently became accepted officially. *See also* LUL.

LRTA
Light Rail Transit Association, founded as the Light Railway Transport League, 1938, name changed 1979. Devoted to the advocacy and study of light rail transit and tramways (*3*). Publishes MT (*2*) (qv).

LRV
Light Rail Vehicle, as operated on light rail transit systems (qv), normally electrically-propelled, usually wider than conventional tramcars of tramways (*3*) and often incorporating special features such as variable height platform access.

LStH&SLR
Liverpool, St Helens & South Lancashire Rly, inc 1885 as St Helens & Wigan Junction Rly, renamed LStH&SLR 1889, opened 1895, Lowton St Mary's to St Helens, to

passengers 1900. Worked by MS&LR. Part of GCR from 1906.

LT

London Transport. The popular abbreviated title for the various public transport authorities restless politicians have devised for London since 1933, i.e. LPTB, LTE (*1*), LTB, LTE (*2*) and LRT (and no doubt more to come).

LT&SR

London, Tilbury & Southend Rly, inc 1852, eventually extending from London (Gas Factory Junc with GER, in Bow)–Southend–Shoeburyness via Tilbury and via Upminster; branches Upminster to Romford, Upminster to Grays and Stanford le Hope–Thames Haven. Promoted jointly by L&BR (*3*) and ECR. First sections opened 1854, 1855, 1856, stock provided by ECR. Leased to contractors, Peto, Brassey & Betts, 1854. Partial independence achieved 1862 but GER and L&BR appointed two-thirds of the board of directors. Operated with GER stock from 1875, own rolling stock and locos introduced 1877–80. A fully independent company from 1882. Became part of Midland Rly from 1912 when there were 79¼ route miles of line.

LTB

London Transport Board, formed 1963 on the dissolution of the BTC, as an independent statutory undertaking reporting directly to the Minister of Transport. It was succeeded by LTE (*2*) (qv) at the beginning of 1970.

LTE

London Transport Executive. There were two bodies so named, the first, LTE (*1*), which existed from 1948–62, was a subsidiary of the BTC and was replaced by the LTB (qv); the second, LTE (*2*), whose life extended from

1970–84, as formed under the Transport (London) Act, 1969, which transferred the overall policy and financial control of London Transport to the Greater London Council; it was succeeded by LRT (qv). Both bodies were popularly known as 'London Transport' or 'LT'.

LTIS

An organization originally set up by LT in 1968 as the LT Consultancy Service, to provide advice on underground rly planning, construction, operation etc. to overseas clients. Became LTIS, London Transport International Services Ltd, a wholly-owned subsidiary of LTE (*2*), in 1976.

LTPC

London Transport Passengers Committee, formed 1948. Became LRPC (qv).

Lufthansa Express

A special service for air passengers operated between Frankfurt Airport station and Düsseldorf since 1982.

Luftseilbahn (Ger)

An aerial cableway (also known as a *Seilschewebebahn*).

Luigis (AusRS)

Australian rly track maintenance workers. From their predominantly Italian origin.

Luis de Camoes

A *TALGO* day express between Lisbon and Madrid, introduced 1989.

LUL

London Underground Ltd, formed 1985 as a subsidiary trading company of LRT, as required by London Regional Transport Act, 1984. Popularly known as 'the Underground' or (less correctly) as 'the Tube' (qv).

Lunar lights

A form of route indicator used in combination with colour-light signals at junctions, in which a series of white lights are aligned at 45, 90 or 135 degrees to left or right, according to the direction of divergence, to inform the driver which route has been set up by the signalman for his train. From their whiteness.

Lung (USRS)

1. A drawbar.

2. The main line air hose.

Lung doctor/jerker/specialist (USRS)

A heavy-handed loco driver apt to strain or even pull out drawbars.

LUR

Lancashire Union Rlys inc 1864, opened 1868, St Helens–Haigh Junc–White Bear [Adlington]/Wigan and Chorley-Cherry Tree [near Blackburn]. Passengers 1869. Part of L&NWR from 1883 but Boar's Head–White Bear and Chorley–Cherry Tree were joint L&NWR and L&YR from opening in 1868 (under an Act of 1865) until 1921.

Lurry (obs)

A manually-propelled wagon used by platelayers to carry materials etc.

LURS

London Underground Railway Society, founded 1961 for those interested in the history and operations of the LT rlys. Publishes UN (qv).

Lusitania Express

A night service between Madrid and Lisbon, introduced 1943.

Lusso, treno (It)(obs)

A luxury fast train with double supplementary fare.

Lutetia

An express between Geneva and Milan, introduced 1981. Name used for Paris–Lausanne (connections at Geneva for Milan) *TGV* 1984.

Luxe, trains de (Fr) (obs)

Important fast trains with superior accommodation, usually *CIWL*

restaurant/sleeping/Pullman cars, and normally restricted to First class passengers.

Luxor Express

A *CIWL* train between Cairo and Luxor, introduced 1898.

LV

1. The Last Vehicle of a train. *See also* Last vehicle indicator.

2. A Luggage Van.

LVR

1. Lambourn Valley Rly, Newbury –Lambourn, inc 1883, opened 1898. Part of GWR 1905.

2. Llynvi Valley Rly, Nantyffyllon–Bridgend/Porthcawl, inc 1846. Acquired Duffryn, Llynvi & Porthcawl Rly (a 4 ft 7 in/ 1,397 mm gauge tramroad opened 1829) and Bridgend Rly (a 4 ft 7in/ 1,397 mm gauge tramroad opened 1834, Bridgend to the former near Tondu). Re-inc 1855 with powers to operate as an ordinary steam rly. Opened as conventional steam rly (7 ft/2,134 mm gauge) 1861 (Tondu–Porthcawl was mixed broad and standard gauge, the latter used by OVR trains); passengers 1865. Amalgamated with OVR 1866 to form L&OR (qv) and by 1868 mixed gauge track had been laid throughout on the former LVR.

3. (US) Lehigh Valley RR.

LWR/LWT

Long Welded Rails/Track, in which unit lengths, usually 60 ft/18.28 metres, are welded together in lengths of up to half a mile/0.8 km. *See also* CWR.

Lyntog

Lightning Trains. Diesel-electric expresses introduced by the Danish State Rlys in the mid-1930s.

Lyonnais, le

TEE Paris–Lyon, introduced 1969

with 3 h 47 min schedule. Lost *TEE* status 1976.

LZB (Ger)
Linienzugbeinflussung; an ATP (qv) system used on *DB* lines authorized for high speed running.

L-Zug (Ger)(obs)
Luxuszug; a First class only luxury train on *DR*.

M

M
Motor car in a mu train set.

Macarthur (US)
Term for a steam loco with 2–8–2
wheel arrangement, used in the
Second World War (and named after
the famous US general in preference
to the Japanese term *Mikado* (qv)).

Macaw
GWR TC for various kinds of bolster
truck for carrying rails, timber etc.

Machine-tender (Fr)
Tank loco.

Madhouse (USRS)
The loco foreman's office.

Magistral
Polish and USSR term for a high
capacity main line, especially when
newly-built or newly-upgraded.

Maglev
Magnetic levitation transit system. In
use between Birmingham Airport and
BR's Birmingham International
station.

Mahogany, on the (RS)
On the cushions (qv).

Maidens & Dunure
see M&DLR.

Mail Rail
Line name for PO Rly (qv).

Main, the (RS)
The principal through passenger line
between any two points.

Main iron (USRS)
see Main line.

Main line
To a rlyman this term means any

tracks on which trains run between
given points, as distinct from sidings,
yards etc. In a wider sense, it signifies
the principal lines between major cities
and towns, on which the fastest trains
run, as distinct from the branch and
suburban lines.

Main line company/rlys
A rly company/system handling all
types of business, passenger and
freight, on a significant scale over say
more than 100 route miles, e.g. the
four 'grouped' companies of 1923–47
LM&SR, L&NER, GWR, SR.

Main pin (USRS)
A high ranking rly official.

Main stem (USRS)
A principal trunk line, a main line.

Main tracker (USRS)
A long distance service, calling only at
principal stations.

Mak (Ger)
Maschinenbau Kiel; a Krupp company
manufacturing rly locos.

Make a joint, to (USRS)
To couple wagons or coaches.

Make a road, to
Setting up points and signals over a
certain route for a train approaching a
signal box or signal control area.

Malle des Indes
Indian Mail; the popular and
unofficial name for service from Calais
(connecting with Dover sailings) to
Marseilles and later to Brindisi
(connecting with P&O Line sailings at
both the latter ports). Operated from

1852, passengers carried from 1880. Replaced by Peninsular Express (qv) 1890.

Mallet

A steam loco with a single boiler but two sets of coupled driving wheels, the rear set rigidly mounted to the main frame, the other jointed to the main frame. At first Mallets were usually compounds (qv) with low pressure cylinders in the front unit. The design was patented in 1884 by Anatole Mallet (1837–1919) and was highly-developed in the US, culminating in the 540-ton Union Pacific 'Big Boy' 4-8-8-4 type, of 1941–4, the world's largest and heaviest steam locomotives.

MAN (Ger)

Maschinenfabrik–Augsburg–Nürnberg AG; loco builders since 1840.

Manchester Pullman

Express between London (Euston) and Manchester (Piccadilly) introduced 1966 with new purpose-built Pullman cars. By 1978 it was the last traditional Pullman service in Britain. Ceased 1985, but the cars were retained for charter service. The Pullman name thereafter was applied by BR to 'Executive' trains using standard First class stock.

Manchurian Express

see Trans-Manchurian Express.

Mancunian

Express between London (Euston) and Manchester, introduced 1927, restored 1949. Name dropped 1966.

M&BR

Manchester & Birmingham Rly, inc 1837, opened Manchester–Stockport–Crewe, 1840, 1842. part of L&NWR 1846.

M&CR

Maryport & Carlisle Rly, inc 1837, first section opened 1840, completed 1845; part of LM&SR from 1923.

M&DLR

Maidens & Dunure Light Rly, Alloway Junction (near Ayr)–Dunure–Girvan, LRO 1899, G&SWR, opened 1906, last section closed 1968.

M&DRJC

Metropolitan & District Rlys Joint Committee, managing joint section Mansion House to Aldgate/St Mary's, 1879–1932.

M&EE

Mechanical & Electrical Engineers' [Department].

M&ER

Midland & Eastern Rly, inc 1866, an amalgamation of the Spalding & Bourn and Lynn & Sutton Bridge Rlys. Leased Norwich & Spalding Rly, which it absorbed in 1877. Part of E&MR 1883.

M&G

Mountain & Gibson Ltd, Bury, manufacturers of tramcar trucks in the Elton Fold Works which had been set up in 1902 by McGuire Manufacturing Co. of Chicago, exploiting the McGuire designs. Also built complete works cars. Ceased production *c.* 1908, but Mountain & Gibson Truck & Engineering Co. Ltd continued to supply truck parts until *c.* 1915.

M&GNJC

Midland & Great Northern Joint Committee, inc 1893, to take over existing E&MR (qv). Bourne–Kings Lynn–Yarmouth; Peterborough–Sutton Bridge; branches to Norwich and Cromer from Melton Constable. Joint Midland and GNR 1893–1922, LM&SR & L&NER 1923–47, Worked by L&NER from 1936. BR (E) from 1948. *See also* N&SJRC.

M&MR

Manchester & Milford Rly. This company, inc 1860, aimed to complete a direct rail link between Manchester and the port of Milford Haven by constructing a line between Llanidloes and Pencader, north of Carmarthen. An Aberystwyth branch was authorized in 1865 and the line between Aberystwyth and Pencader was opened in 1866 and 1867; this was leased to the GWR in 1906 and vested in the GWR in 1911. The remaining section of the 'main line', between Llanidloes and Strata Florida, completed only between the Mid-Wales line and Llangurig, was never used for public traffic.

M&SDR
Moretonhampstead & South Devon Rly, Moretonhampstead to Newton Abbot, inc 1862, worked by SDR, opened 1866. Part of GWR 1872.

M&SMR
Madras & Southern Mahratta Rly, India, formed 1852, taken over by Government 1907.

M&StJWR
Metropolitan & Saint John's Wood Rly, inc 1864, Baker St. to Finchley Road, branch Swiss Cottage to Hampstead authorized 1865 but never built. Opened 1868 and worked by Metropolitan Rly. Vested in Metropolitan Rly, 1882.

M&SWJR
1. Midland & South Western Junction Rly, Cricklewood to Acton Wells Junction, London; inc 1864 as Finchley, Willesden & Acton Rly (M&SW Junction), opened 1868, freight only, Cricklewood–Acton section only. Absorbed by Midland Rly 1874. Sometimes known as the 'old' M&SWJR, to avoid confusion with M&SWJR (2).
2. Midland & South Western Junction Rly, Andoversford–Cirencester–Swindon–Marlborough–Andover,

inc 1884, first section opened (as Swindon, Marlborough & Andover Rly) 1881, part of GWR from 1923.

Mangle (RS)
A manual drilling machine.

Mankillers (RS)
GWR 47XX 2–8–0 locos.

Mania, The
see Railway Mania.

Manifest
List of vehicles in a train, also (USRS) a redball (qv).

Manifold Valley
see L&MVLR.

Manned conditional
A development of Q services (qv) in which locos and crews are booked for trains which run, as required by traffic, to one or more possible alternative destinations as shown in the working timetable.

Manning Wardle
Manning, Wardle & Co. Ltd, Boyne Engine Works, Hunslet, Leeds, loco builders from 1858. Became part of Kitsons (qv), 1927.

Man of Kent
Express between London (Charing Cross) and Folkestone, Dover, Deal, Sandwich, and Margate, introduced 1953, ceased on electrification of the route, 1961.

Mansell wheel
A wheel consisting of a wooden disc or segments forced inside a heated iron or steel tyre by hydraulic pressure, patented 1848, 1862 and 1866 by R.C. Mansell, Carriage & Wagon Superintendent SER. Widely used in Britain, where it delayed the introduction of track-circuiting. Also loosely used for any type of solid, spokeless wheel.

Mansfield Rly
Kirkby (junction with GCR main line

London to Sheffield) via Mansfield to Clipstone, junction with former LD&ECR Chesterfield–Lincoln line. Opened 1913–17, worked by GCR, part of L&NER from 1923.

Man trap (RS)
Catch points (qv).

Manxman
Summer-only express between London (Euston) and Liverpool, in connection with sailings to and from Isle of Man, introduced 1927, restored 1951. Name dropped 1966.

Manzoni
EC service between Zurich and Milan via Gotthard route, introduced 1989.

Maple Leaf
Montreal–Chicago service of CNR, introduced 1927, ceased 1971. Name now used for Amtrak Toronto–Chicago service.

MARC (US)
Maryland Rail Corporation.

Marches Line
BR brand name for Shrewsbury–Hereford–Newport services.

Marco Polo
Rome–Venice–Trieste–Udine service, introduced 1977.

Mare Nostrum
Day service between Port Bou and Valencia/Alicante, introduced 1966.

Margin
Time allowance required for a slower train to precede a faster one on the same track to avoid impairing the running of the fast train.

Markers (USRS)
Lamps or flags attached to the front (head) and the last vehicle of a train. White head end markers denote an extra train, green head end markers indicate that the train has been split and a second section is following.

Märklin
The pioneer commercial

manufacturers of model rly equipment (from 1890). Based since 1900 at Göppingen, Germany.

Marmara Express
Belgrade–Istanbul service, 1967–77, carrying through cars between Paris and Istanbul off the Direct Orient Express (qv) also through cars Munich–Istanbul off the Tauern Orient Express (qv).

Maroc Express
Paris–Algeciras–Casablanca rail/ship service, 1948–52.

Marquis of Londonderry's Rly
see LR (5).

Marshalling
The breaking up of freight train formations and the subsequent sorting of wagons into train loads for final destination, carried out in a marshalling or sorting yard.

Marshalling yard
A complex of sidings in which marshalling (qv) takes place. Usually divided into arrival sidings, main yard and departure sidings. The first was built at Edge Hill, Liverpool by the L&NWR, 1875–82. Later yards incorporated refinements such as humps (qv), control towers and wagon retarders/accelerators (qv).

Mars light (USRS)
An oscillating head end or tail end light.

Marys (RS)
Class 405 emus, originally known as 4-SUBs (qv). From the liner *Queen Mary*.

MAS
Multiple-Aspect Signalling [scheme]. Area scheme for colour-light signalling, usually connected to one control centre. *See also* Multi-aspect signal.

Mass transit (US)
Rapid transit (qv).

Master/Master of the Cars (USRS)
A conductor *(3)*.

Master Cutler
Express between London
(Marylebone) and Sheffield (Victoria),
so named 1947, operated as an all-
Pullman service from Kings Cross to
Sheffield (Victoria) from 1958.
Pullman service ceased 1968 and
London terminus changed to St
Pancras. Renamed Master Cutler
Pullman, 1987.

Master Maniac (USRS)
A master mechanic.

Master Room
Accommodation on US long distance
trains from *c.* 1940, comprising an
apartment with four movable
armchairs for day use and two
beds, one longitudinal, one transverse,
also an en suite lavatory/wc and
shower.

Mastodon
Originally a US term for steam locos
with 4–8–0 wheel arrangement but
later applied to those with 4–10–0
wheel arrangement.

Matchboxes (RS)
GWR 57XX 0–6–0 pannier tanks.
From their appearance.

Match dials, to (USRS)
To compare or synchronize watches.

Match truck
1. A wagon with a dual set of buffers
   at each end which can be placed to
   run between two others having
   buffers and draw gear at varying
   heights.
2. Any wagon placed beneath an
   overhanging freight load or crane
   on an adjoining vehicle.

Mate (obs)
Another word for ganger.

Matterhorn
EC service Frankfurt–Brigue,
introduced 1989.

Maul [her], to (USRS)
To work a steam loco at full stroke
and full throttle.

Maurice Ravel
EC service Paris–Munich, introduced
1989.

MAV
Magyar Allamvasutak; Hungarian State
Rlys.

Maximum traction truck
A type of tramcar truck which has one
motored axle with large wheels and an
unmotored pony axle with smaller
wheels. A variation is the 'reversed
maximum traction truck' with the
smaller wheels facing towards each
end of the car.

Mayflower
Express between London (Paddington)
and Plymouth, introduced 1957.
Name dropped 1965, revived 1970.
Name dropped 1971, revived 1984,
dropped 1985.

Mayfly
GWR TC for well truck used to
transport large electrical transformers.

Maze, the (RS)
Clapham Junction.

M-bahn (Ger)
A version of Maglev (qv).

MB&MR
Macclesfield, Bollington & Marple
Rly, inc 1864, opened 1869, 1870,
1871, 1873, vested jointly in MS&LR
and NSR 1871, GCR & NSR 1897,
L&NER and LM&SR 1923–47.

MBC
BR Motor Brake Composite coach.

MBCL
As MBC (qv) but with Lavatory.

MBM&MJR
Manchester, Buxton, Matlock &
Midland Junction Rly, inc 1846,
opened Rowsley to Ambergate 1849.
Leased jointly by L&NWR and
Midland 1852. Rowsley–Buxton

completed by Midland 1863. Part of Midland Rly 1871.

MBS
BR Motor Brake Second class.

MBSL
As MBS (qv) but with Lavatory.

MBSO
BR Motor Brake Second/Standard class Open coach.

MBTA
Massachusetts Bay Transportation Authority, controlling the rly passenger system in the Boston area (USA).

MC
BR Motor Composite (First and Second/Standard class) coach.

MCB
1. (US) Master Car Builders' Association, later the Mechanical Division of the AAR (qv).
2. (LT) A Miniature Circuit Breaker.
3. (US) A form of automatic coupler approved as a US standard by (1).
4. (US) A form of truck recommended by (1) for passenger stock. Known in Europe as the Pennsylvania bogie/truck.

McGuire
McGuire Manufacturing Co., Chicago, producers of car trucks/bogies from 1888, later builders of rly, tramway (3) and interurban cars and other rolling stock. Name changed subsequently to McGuire–Cummings Manufacturing Co., then Cummings Car & Coach Co. Vehicle production ceased 1930, parts business continued until 1943. *See also* M&G.

McKenzie & Holland
A Worcester firm manufacturing signalling equipment from the 1860s, absorbed J.F. Pease & Co.'s signalling interests in 1901, amalgamated with Westinghouse Brake Co. *c.* 1907 to form McKenzie, Holland &

Westinghouse Power Signalling Co. *See also* Consolidated Signal Co.

MCL
As MC (qv) but with Lavatory.

MCO
Mutual Change Over; a mutually agreed exchange of duties (LT).

MCR
Midland Counties Rly, inc 1836, Nottingham to Derby, and Nottingham to Leicester and Rugby, opened 1839, 1840. Part of Midland Rly from 1844.

MCT
Maritime Container Terminal.

MCTA
Metropolitan Commuter Transportation Authority [for the New York Area], formed 1967 to take over the Long Island RR and assume control of NYCTA (qv), the Manhattan & Bronx Surface Transit Operating Authority, the Triborough Bridge & Tunnel Authority and Staten Island Rapid Transit. Now known as MTA (qv).

MCW
Metropolitan Carriage & Wagon Co., Saltley, Birmingham, originally established in 1835 by Joseph Wright, later known as Joseph Wright & Sons. MCW established 1862, renamed Metropolitan Amalgamated Railway Carriage & Wagon Co. 1902, after merger with Ashbury (qv), Brown, Marshalls (qv), Lancaster (qv) and Oldbury (qv). Renamed Metropolitan Carriage, Wagon & Finance Co. 1912. Wholly-owned subsidiary of Vickers Ltd, 1919. Became Metro–Cammell (qv) in 1929. Builders of rly coaches, wagons and tramcars. *See also* MV.

MD&HB
Mersey Docks & Harbour Board; operated docks lines at Liverpool and Birkenhead which were also used by

L&NWR and GCR (LM&SR and
L&NER from 1923, BR from 1948).
Last lines closed 1973.

MDET

Metropolitan District Electric Traction
Co. Formed 1901 to erect and equip
Lots Road Power Station, London,
and supply funds for the electrification
of the MDR. Largely US-financed;
taken over by UERL (qv), 1902.

MDR

Metropolitan District Rly, inc 1864,
first section South Kensington to
Westminster Bridge, opened 1868.
Extended to serve Hammersmith,
Ealing, Putney, Hounslow and other
western suburbs and owned
Whitechapel & Bow Rly jointly with
LTSR, which gave it access to Barking
and Upminster. 28 route miles by
1914. Part of LPTB from 1933.

Meat run (USRS)

An express perishable freight train.

Mediolanum

TEE Milan–Munich, via Brenner
Pass, introduced 1957. Lost *TEE*
status 1984. Replaced by Leonardo da
Vinci (qv), 1987.

Medloc

Mediterranean Line of
Communication; British Army rail
service across France between Toulon
and Dieppe, set up after the Second
World War to carry British servicemen
returning home from the
Mediterranean area and the Middle
East. Trains were composed mainly of
ex-*DR* and *FS* third class stock, but
some L&NER coaches were also used.

Medway Valley Line

BR brand name for Strood–
Maidstone–Paddock Wood.

Meet/meet order (US)

A planned crossing of two trains at a
loop on a long section of single line
and the train order specifying this.

Mega-wedged (RS)

An extremely overcrowded train.

Melon

GWR TC for bogie or six-wheel brake
van with Third class seating (six
types).

Memling

TEE Paris–Brussels, 1974–84. Name
used for EC service between Ostend
and Frankfurt, 1987.

Mentor

Mobile electrical network testing,
observation and recording [coach], BR
(M), 1972. Used to inspect overhead
line equipment under operating
conditions and to monitor performance
of electric circuits in locos and emus.

Meon Valley

The former L&SWR line from Alton
to Fareham.

MER

1. Manx Electric Rly, Douglas to
   Ramsey, inc 1893 as Douglas &
   Laxey Coast Electric Tramway Ltd,
   3 ft/914 mm gauge, opened 1893,
   1894, 1898 and 1899. Renamed Isle
   of Man Tramways & Electric
   Power Co. Ltd 1894. MER (inc
   1902), took over the undertaking
   from the IMTEP liquidator.
   System includes the Snaefell
   Mountain Rly (SMR), Laxey to
   Snaefell Summit, electrically-
   worked, 3 ft 6 in/1,067 mm gauge,
   with Fell (qv) centre rail, opened
   1895. Purchased by Manx
   Government, 1957.

2. Millwall Extension Rly, authorized
   1865, Millwall Junction (L&BR) to
   North Greenwich, opened 1871,
   1872. Some sections were owned by
   the Blackwall Rly, the remainder
   by dock companies. Passenger
   services ceased 1926. In 1929 the
   new lock entrance from Blackwall
   Reach severed the line. The

southern part is now used by the DLR (qv).

Merchandise peddler [pedlar] (USRS) Way freight train (qv).

Merchants Limited
Express between New York and Boston, introduced 1903 on 5 h schedule. 4 h 15 min in 1940. Coach class included from 1949. Now an Amtrak day train Boston–New York–Washington DC.

Merchants' Rly
Otherwise known as the Portland Rly, inc 1825, 4 ft 6 in gauge, Portland (Dorset) (Castletown Pier)–Priory Corner, built to convey stone from the quarries to ships, opened 1826, with horse traction and cable-worked incline. Closed 1939.

Merchant Venturer
Express between London (Paddington), Bath, Bristol and Weston-super-Mare, so named 1951. Name dropped 1965, revived 1984. Name dropped 1986.

Merkur
TEE Stuttgart–Copenhagen, introduced 1974. Lost *TEE* status 1978, became IC Copenhagen–Karlsruhe; diverted to Frankfurt 1985, EC from 1987.

Mermaid
TC for 14-ton tipping ballast wagon.

Merry-go-round
1. MGR (qv).
2. (USRS) A loco turntable.
3. (USRS) A telegraph circuit.

Merrymakers (obs)
BR (M) brand name for excursions, introduced 1971.

Mersey Loop and Link
Terminal loop opened 1977 beneath the centre of Liverpool, James St.–Moorfields–Lime St.–Central–James St. for the Mersey/Wirral lines together with a new underground link between Central and Moorfields for the Southport/Ormskirk/Kirkby–Garston–Hunts Cross electric services, with interchange at Central.

Merseyrail
Brand name introduced in 1971 for the local passenger services operated by BR for the Merseyside Passenger Transport Executive in the Liverpool/Wirral area (Merseyside County).

Merseyside Express
Service between London (Euston) and Liverpool (Lime St.), introduced 1928, a renaming of the 1927 London–Merseyside Express. Restored 1949. Name dropped 1966.

Merseyside Pullman
Partly Pullman service between London (Euston) and Liverpool, introduced 1985, replacing Liverpool Executive (qv).

Met, The
Abbreviation semi-officially adopted by the Metropolitan Rly [London] about 1914, but see also Metro (*2*). Since 1933, the popular abbreviation for the Metropolitan Line of London Transport. Also an abbreviation for the Metropolitan Electric Tramways (London, 1902–33).

Metadyne
A complicated system of traction motor control for electric trains, in which a rotary converter is arranged to supply current exactly equivalent to the effort required. Tested by the LPTB on ex-Metropolitan stock running on the Inner Circle in 1934–5, it was claimed to eliminate resistances and thus save wasted current. Deceleration was mainly effected by enabling the motors to return current to the line, thus saving brake wear. Fifty-eight two-car and nineteen six-car metadyne-fitted trains were placed in service on the Metropolitan

and Hammersmith & City lines in 1937–8 but in the postwar period maintenance of this stock became very expensive and difficult due to shortage of skilled staff and from 1955 the cars were converted to PCM control (qv).

Metals
Rails/track.

Met&GC Joint
Harrow to Chesham, Aylesbury and Verney Junction. This section of the Metropolitan Rly was leased to the Metropolitan & GCR Joint Committee 1906–32. LPTB & L&NER Joint 1933–47, became part of LTE 1948–50. Amersham to Aylesbury passed to BR from 1961–2.

Met&L&NER Joint
Watford branch, opened 1925, L&NER passenger trains withdrawn 1926. Became part of LTE 1948–50.

Meterspur (Ger)
1,000 mm gauge.

Met gang (RS)(obs)
The regular Metropolitan Link at Kings Cross depot, responsible for working suburban services.

Methley Joint
Joint Committee of GNR, L&YR and NER set up in 1864 to work a line between Lofthouse GNR and Methley L&YR, opened 1865, passengers 1869. Worked by GNR. GNR, NER and L&NWR 1922. LM&SR and L&NER 1923–47, BR 1948.

Metra
The operator of commuter rail services in the Chicago region.

Métrazur
Métro Côte d'Azur, a regular interval service between Cannes, Nice, Monaco and Menton, introduced 1970.

Metro
1. In recent years this term (an abbreviation of 'metropolitan rly') has come to be accepted almost as *lingua franca*, for urban rail systems, normally 'heavy', as distinct from light rail, usually including substantial underground sections and operating over a small number of self-contained, elaborately-signalled lines, carrying the heaviest traffic and using rly-type rolling stock, although normally independent of conventional main line rail systems. Absolute ticket control at entry and/or exit is another distinguishing feature. Examples include London Underground, the Paris Métro, and the Moscow Metro. *See also U-bahn.*
2. An abbreviation officially adopted by the Metropolitan Rly [London] in 1920.
3. An abbreviation for Metro Trains (qv).

Metro–Cammell
Name used after the 1929 merger of MCW (qv) and Cammell–Laird car building activities as the Metropolitan–Cammell Carriage, Wagon & Finance Co. Ltd. Full title altered to Metropolitan–Cammell Carriage & Wagon Co. Ltd, 1934, Metropolitan–Cammell Ltd from 1965, with car building concentrated at Washwood Heath, Birmingham. Absorbed Cravens (qv) 1965. Part of GEC–Alsthom, 1989.

Metro gnome (LTRS)
Driver on LT Metropolitan Line.

Metro-land
A term officially adopted by the Metropolitan Rly from 1915 to describe the residential and country areas it served. Popular use lingered after the formation of the LPTB (qv) in 1933.

Metroliner
Fast emu service between New York and Washington DC, introduced 1969.

Metrolink
Light rapid transit system in
Manchester, first section Altrincham–
Piccadilly–Victoria–Bury, partly in
streets, but mostly over former BR
lines, opened 1992.

Métrolor
Local electric service Nancy–Metz–
Thionville, introduced 1970. The
pioneer *TER (1)* (qv) service.

Metro–North
Passenger rail operator in the Hudson,
Harlem and Connecticut areas around
New York, under contract to MTA
(qv).

Metropolitan
1. Metropolitan Rly [London], inc
   1853 as North Metropolitan Rly,
   name changed 1854. First section
   opened 1863, Paddington–
   Farringdon, the world's first urban
   underground rly. Extended to
   South Kensington and Aldgate,
   operating the Inner Circle with the
   MDR, and also to Harrow/
   Uxbridge, Chesham, Amersham,
   Aylesbury and Verney Junction, 66
   route miles by 1914. Operated
   freight and parcels traffic and
   claimed to be a main line company.
   Part of LPTB from 1933.
2. Metropolitan Railway Carriage &
   Wagon Co. Ltd: *see* MCW.

Metropolitan [City] Widened Lines
see City Widened Lines.

Metro tanks (RS)
GWR 2–4–0T, originally introduced
1869. Fitted with condensing
gear to enable them to be run over
the Metropolitan (*1*), hence the
name.

MetroTrains
BR services operated for West
Yorkshire PTA.

Metrovick
see MV.

Mets (RS)(obs)
Freight and parcels trains working to
and from main lines over the City
Widened Lines between Kings Cross/
St Pancras and Farringdon (London).

Mex
GWR TC for cattle wagon.

Mez (Ger)
Mittel Europäische Zeit; Middle
European Time.

MGR
Merry-go-round. A system of
operating continuously-moving
permanently-coupled block trains
(qv) between collieries and electric
power stations, ports, steel
works etc. using bottom door
discharge hopper wagons loaded
and emptied automatically as the
train slowly passes through the
installation. Introduced by BR
1965–70. Conceived and named by
Gerard Fiennes, general manager BR
(WR) and developed by R.T. Munns
and others.

MGWR
Midland Great Western Rly
(Ireland), inc 1845, Dublin to
Mullingar and Longford, first section
opened 1847. Subsequently extended
to Athlone, Westport and Achill,
Galway and Clifden, Sligo, Cavan
etc.; 538 route miles by 1914, all in
central Ireland. Part of GSR from
1925.

MH&R
Morecambe Harbour & Rly, inc 1846,
harbour at Morecambe and rly to
Lancaster, opened to Lancaster (Green
Ayre) 1848. Part of NWR (qv) 1846.

MHE&R
Muswell Hill Estate & Rlys, Muswell
Hill to Alexandra Palace, promoted by
the Muswell Hill Estate Co., inc 1866
and 1871, opened 1873, worked by
GNR as part of its branch from

Highgate. Renamed Muswell Hill &
Palace Rly 1886, closed at various
times since its fate was linked with the
fluctuating fortunes of Alexandra
Palace. Part of GNR from 1911.

MHR
see Mid-Hants.

Mica
GWR TC for various types of meat
van, some refrigerated.

Michelangelo
Day service between Munich and
Rome, introduced 1988.

Micheline
Rubber-tyred petrol-engined railbus
introduced in France 1930. So called
after Michelin tyre firm, sponsors of
the prototype.

Mickey Mouse or Mickey (RS)
Term applied severally to LM&SR
Class 2 2–6–2T, Class 2 Ivatt 2–6–0,
class 5 4–6–0 and BR Standard
2–6–4T locos.

Micro-buffet
BR term for an open saloon coach
with a small counter from which an
attendant serves refreshments carried
on a standard catering trolley which
has been loaded on to the train.
Introduced 1979.

Midday Scot
Express between London (Euston) and
Glasgow (Central)/Edinburgh (Princes
St.), name offically introduced 1927
for a train which had run since 1889
(The Corridor, (qv)). Restored 1949,
Euston–Glasgow (Central) only. Name
dropped 1966.

Middlebere Plateway
Norden to Middlebere Wharf on Poole
Harbour, 3 ft 9 in gauge, built
by Benjamin Fayle for the transport
of excavated ball clay, opened with
horse traction 1806 and 1807.
Abandoned *c.* 1867 after the
construction of another line fron

Norden to Goathorn Pier (Fayle's
Tramway, (qv)).

Middle Circle (obs)
London train service worked 1872–
1905 by the GWR from Moorgate,
later Aldgate, via Baker St.,
Kensington (Addison Road) [now
Olympia], and Victoria to Mansion
House; Earls Court–Moorgate only
from 1900; Kensington (AR)–
Moorgate only from 1905; Kensington
(AR)–Edgware Road only from 1906
until 1940.

Middle man (USRS)
The second or middle brakeman on a
freight train.

Middle road(s)
Line(s) at a station, between the
platform roads, used for through
running, or for shunting, or for engine
run-round movements.

Middleton
Middleton Rly, Hunslet, Leeds, to
collieries at Middleton, a horse-worked
wagonway, the first rly to be
sanctioned by an act of parliament
(1758). 4 ft 1 in/1,245 mm gauge
steam locos used from 1812 until
1835, then horse worked again. Steam
locos re-introduced 1866. Converted to
standard gauge 1881 and connections
made to Midland and GNR. By 1958
only Parkside GNR to Middleton
Colliery remained. Hunslet Moor to
Middleton Park taken over
by Middleton Railway Preservation
Society, 1960, to become the
first standard gauge preserved
line.

Mid-Hants
Inc as Alton, Alresford & Winchester
Rly 1861, name changed to MH Rly
1864. Opened 1865, worked by
L&SWR and leased by that company
from 1880. Part of L&SWR 1884.
Alton to Alresford now operated as a

preserved line, the Mid-Hants Rly, first section opened 1983.

Midi
Chemin de fer du Midi (France), jointly managed with *P–O* (qv) from 1934.

Mid-Kent
Lewisham (London) to Beckenham, inc 1855 as the Mid-Kent & North Kent Junction Rly, opened 1857, extended to Addiscombe Road 1864, part of SER from 1866. The seemingly misleading title arose because the promoters envisaged extension through the area later occupied by the LC&DR main line. Also Mid-Kent (Bromley & St Mary Cray) Rly, inc 1856, to extend from the WEL&CPR (qv) at the present Shortlands station to St Mary Cray. Opened Shortlands to Bickley 1858, leased and worked by SER as an extension of its Mid-Kent Line (qv). Linked at eastern end to LC&DR main line 1860, leased and worked by LC&DR 1863. Part of SR 1923.

Mid-Kent Line
London (Charing Cross/Cannon St.) to Elmers End and Hayes/Addiscombe/ Sanderstead. For origins of the name *see* Mid-Kent.

Midland
1. Midland Rly, inc 1844 by amalgamation of the North Midland, Midland Counties and Birmingham & Derby Junction Rlys. Subsequent extensions and absorptions brought the Midland to London, Birmingham, Bristol and Bath, Lincoln, Leeds, Bradford and Carlisle, 2,169 route miles by 1914. Part of LM&SR from 1923.
2. Midland Railway Carriage & Wagon Co. Ltd, originally the Midland Waggon Co., rly wagon builders from 1853, renamed 1877. Main works at Shrewsbury, also at

Birmingham (Washwood Heath) until 1912. Part of Cammell–Laird (qv) from 1919. Name continued as the wagon-hire subsidiary of MCW (qv).

Midlander
Express between London (Euston), Birmingham and Wolverhampton, introduced 1950, name dropped 1966.

Midland Metro
A light rail transit scheme for the Birmingham–Wolverhampton conurbation; first line Birmingham (Snow Hill)–Wednesbury– Wolverhampton 1994.

Midland Pullman
BR diesel-electric mu, all-First class air-conditioned six-car all-Pullman trains, painted blue, introduced 1960 between London (St Pancras) and Manchester/Leicester, also St Pancras– Nottingham from 1961. Withdrawn 1966.

Midland Railway Centre/Trust
Preserved line between Ironville and Hammersmith, Derbyshire, first section opened 1982.

Midland Scot
Express between Birmingham, Glasgow and Edinburgh, introduced 1970, name dropped 1975.

Midline
Brand name of passenger services operated by BR for West Midlands Passenger Transport Authority (Centro). Not used after 1991; *see* Centro.

Mid-Notts
Mid-Nottinghamshire Joint, LM&SR/ L&NER line from Checker House near Retford to junction with former GCR line at Hucknall, north of Nottingham, inc 1926, opened 1931, but only from Ollerton to Farnsfield. Part of BR (M) 1948.

Mid-Suffolk
Mid-Suffolk Light Rly, Haughley to

Laxfield and Cratfield, LRO 1901,
opened 1904–6, passenger services
1908, sections closed 1912 and 1915,
part of L&NER from 1924, BR from
1948, completely closed 1952.

Mid-Sussex & Midhurst Junc
see MS&MJR.

Mid-Sussex Line
[Dorking/Three Bridges]–Horsham–
Arundel–Ford. *See also* MSR.

Mid-Wales
see MWR.

Mid-Wales Line
Shrewsbury–Newtown–Aberystwyth.

Mindbender (RS)
An instructor.

Mikado (US)
Term for steam loco with 2–8–2 wheel
arrangement, used also in UK.
Derived from the destination of the
first ones built (Japan). *See also*
Macarthur.

Mike
1. (RS) Any loco employed in a
   shunting yard or for moving other
   locos around in a depot (a
   shedturner's Mike).
2. (USRS) *Mikado* (qv).

Mikes (RS)
GER Holden 0–6–0T.

Milan–Ancona Pullman Express
CIWL service operated 1927–9.

**Milan–Genoa–Livorno–Montecatini
Express**
CIWL all-Pullman summer service
operated 1926–9.

**Milan–San Remo–Nice[–Cannes]
Express**
The first all-Pullman train operated by
the *CIWL*, ran 1925–35.

Milan–Venice Express
CIWL all-Pullman service, ran
summer only, 1926, 1927 and 1929.

Mileage (obs)
1. Portion of fares or freight rates
   divided between rly companies

according to the distance travelled
over each and computed by the
RCH.
2. Sum received from a 'foreign'
   company for use of a vehicle on
   that company's lines.

Mileage boy/hog (USRS)
A loco driver who uses his seniority to
get the best-paid duties when these are
paid on a mileage basis.

Mileage traffic (obs)
The GWR term for station-to-station
truckload freight traffic such as coal,
bricks or stone, carried at rates
exclusive of collection or delivery.

Mileage yard (obs)
GWR term for any siding/yard with
facilities for loading and unloading to
and from customers' own vehicles, i.e.
for mileage traffic (qv).

Milk dock (obs)
A platform at a station set aside for
loading or unloading milk in churns,
or later, milk tankers.

Milk float (RS)
A derogatory description for emus.

Milking the tubes (LTRS)(obs)
A form of fraud practised by
some booking clerks in which
preprinted tickets were sold to
passengers, out of numerical order,
and taken from the middle of the
'tubes' or cylinders holding them,
instead of in sequence from the base.
The fares paid were pocketed by the
clerk and the missing tickets remained
undetected until all those below them
were sold.

Milk van (RS)
An LB&SCR electric motor coach
with driving compartment.

Mill (USRS)
A loco.

Milnes
George F. Milnes & Co. Ltd, works at
Birkenhead (closed 1902) and Hadley

(Shropshire) (1900–4), tramcar builders, 1886–1904.

Milnes–Voss
G.C. Milnes, Voss & Co., established 1902 (public company 1906), builders of tramcars and electric rly cars, suppliers of tramcar equipment. Ceased production 1913.

Milta
GWR TC for milk tank wagon.

Milwaukee (US)
Chicago, Milwaukee, St Paul & Pacific RR. *See also* St Paul.

Mineral traffic (obs)
Low value goods other than coal and coke, not necessarily minerals, passing in bulk, and charged on the basis of what transport cost the commodity could bear.

Miners' Friends (RS)
LM&SR 'Royal Scot' 4–6–0 locos. From their heavy appetite for coal.

Minfits
Vacuum-fitted mineral wagons.

Mini[ature] buffet
BR term for purpose-built coach with small saloon areas at each end and counter section in centre for the serving of refreshments and hot drinks, but not hot food. Introduced 1958.

Miniature lever frame
An interlocking frame with very small levers, controlling power signalling.

Miniature rly
A passenger-carrying line of any gauge between 7¼ in/184 mm and 2 ft/ 609 mm, operated with locos which are models of real or imaginary full size types from one-eighth full size upwards. Mostly built primarily for pleasure purposes but some operate a public service and some have been sanctioned as light rlys (qv).

Mink
GWR TC for various types of covered freight wagon.

Mins (RS)(obs)
Mineral wagons.

Minx
GWR TC for standard freight box van.

Misery Pacific (USRS)
Nickname of Missouri Pacific RR.

Missouri
Missouri Pacific RR.

Mister Punch's Rly
Nickname for WLR (*I*), much lampooned in *Punch* soon after its opening.

Misti, treno (It)
A mixed train (qv).

Mistletoe men (RS)
Employees not belonging to a trade union, i.e. parasites.

Mistral
Express between Paris, Lyon and Marseilles, introduced 1950, extended to Nice, 1952. Fastest day train between Paris and Nice until 1982. *TEE* 1965. Became a two-class train, losing *TEE* status, 1981. Replaced by *TGV*, 1982

Mite
GWR TC for twin timber wagon.

Mitropa
Mitteleuropäische Schlafwagen und Speisewagen Aktiengesellschaft; Middle European Sleeping & Dining Car Company. Formed 1917, taking over all restaurant and sleeping car services in Germany and extending its workings to Austria, Czechoslovakia, Denmark, Hungary, Netherlands, Poland, and Switzerland. Its cars ran through to Istanbul, Turkey until the end of the Second World War.

Mixed traffic loco
Any loco usable for both passenger and freight train haulage.

Mixed traffic train
A train containing both freight and passenger vehicles.

MJR
Methley Joint Committee, GNR
(originally WYR), NER and L&YR,
opened 1865, Lofthouse–Methley.
L&NER and LM&SR 1923–47.

MK&T
Missouri, Kansas & Texas RR.

ML
Main Line.

MLR
Marland Light Rly, owned by North
Devon Clay Co. and opened 1880, 3 ft
gauge, Torrington to Peters Marland.
Torrington to Dunsbear abandoned
when ND&CJLR opened in 1925.
Last section closed 1982.

MLV
Motor Luggage Van, non-gangwayed,
introduced 1959–61 for BR (S) boat
trains. Worked from batteries or third
rail as required, driving cab at each
end. *See also* GLV.

MMM
Moore's Monthly Magazine (qv).

MMR
Melbourne Military Rly. LM&SR line
between Chellaston Junction and
Ashby-de-la-Zouch, taken over in 1939
as a Royal Engineers' Railway
Training Centre and bridging school
to supplement the LMR. Handed back
to LM&SR 1945.

MNM&HJR
Marple, New Mills & Hayfield
Junction Rly, inc 1860, opened
Marple to New Mills 1865, leased and
worked by MS&LR, part of S&M
Joint (qv) 1869.

MNR
Manx Northern Rly, first section
Douglas–St Johns opened 1879, 3 ft/
914 mm gauge. Part of IofMR (qv)
from 1905.

MOB
Montreux–Oberland–Bernois Rly,
Switzerland.

Mogo
GWR TC for end-door van used for
carrying motor cars.

Mogul (US)
Term for steam loco with 2–6–0 wheel
arrangement; also used in UK.

Mogul Forney (US)
A steam loco with 2–4–4 wheel
arrangement.

Mohawk (US)
1. A steam loco with 4–8–2 wheel
   arrangement.
2. Chicago–Detroit service of Grand
   Trunk Western RR, ceased 1971.
   Name revived by Amtrak for New
   York–Syracuse service.

Molière
Renaming of Paris–Ruhr (qv), 1973
(Paris–Düsseldorf). Paris–Cologne from
1975. Lost *TEE* status 1979 and became
IC. EC Paris–Dortmund, 1987.

Monday (RS)
A heavy hammer usable only by
strong, fit men.

Money box (RS)
Mail train carrying registered packets
etc. containing money.

Money Sunk & Lost
Nickname for MS&LR.

Mongolipers (RS)
SR N class 2–6–0.

Monitor roof
A car roof with raised central section
running longitudinally from end to
end and incorporating ventilators in its
sides, i.e. a form of clerestory.

Monkey (USRS)
A brakeman.

Monkey, caught by the (USRS)
To be still at work after twelve hours'
continuous duty. *See also* Bear law;
Dog law; Hog law (qv).

Monkey money (USRS)
A staff pass affording free travel.

Monkey motion (USRS)
Walschaert or Baker loco valve gear.

Monkey Special (RS)
A train chartered for school outing; also trains to Clifton Down, for Bristol Zoo.

Monkey tail (RS)
A door handle on mineral wagon.

Monmouthshire Rly & Canal
Monmouthshire Canal Company (inc 1792); narrow gauge tramroads dating from 1798 were converted to rlys by the Monmouthshire Rly & Canal Co., inc 1845. First rly opened, Newport to Pontypool, 1852; all were converted by 1855. By 1879 owned Newport–Blaenavon/Abersychan; Newport–Crumlin–Ebbw Vale/Nantyglo; Risca–Nine Mile Point. Worked by GWR from 1875, part of GWR from 1880.

Monster
GWR TC for bogie 50-ft theatrical scenery van.

Montaigne
Express between Paris and Bordeaux (4 h 5 min) introduced 1980. replaced by TGV 1990.

Mont Blanc
IC Hamburg–Geneva, introduced 1982, EC from 1987.

Mont Cenis
Express between Lyons. Turin and Milan. *TEE* from 1957. Lost *TEE* status 1972.

Moonlight merchant (USRS)
The night foreman at a loco depot.

Moore's Monthly Magazine
First published 1896, and concerned primarily with loco matters. Renamed *The Locomotive Magazine* 1897, *The Locomotive Railway Carriage & Wagon Review*, 1916. Ceased publication 1959, merging with TI (qv).

Moorgate protection
Safety measures adopted by LT after the 1975 Moorgate accident to automatically slow down and stop trains entering a terminal road.

Mopac (US)
Missouri Pacific RR.

Morel
GWR TC for three types of wagon designed to carry ships' propellers.

Morning Talisman
Express between London (Kings Cross) and Edinburgh, introduced 1957. Renamed Fair Maid (qv) in that year.

Morpeth boards
Advance lineside warning of speed restrictions, introduced following an accident at Morpeth in 1969.

MoT
Ministry of Transport, formed 1919, inheriting the rly responsibilities of the BoT (qv). Renamed Ministry of War Transport 1941, MoT again 1946. Part of the Department of the Environment 1970, reconstituted as DTp (qv) 1976.

Mother Hubbard (USRS)
A camel loco (qv).

Motion [of a loco]
The pistons, connecting rods and valve gear.

Motorman
The driver of an electric multiple unit train, electric railcar or tramcar.

Motorail
A brand name introduced by BR in 1966 for special services (car carriers, car sleepers) operated since 1955 to carry motorists, their passengers and their cars in the same train.

Motor Rail
Motor Rail [& Tram Car] Co. Ltd, Bedford, builders of 'Simplex' locos and railcars.

Motor train
see Auto-train (qv).

Mountain
US and, later, European term for steam loco with 4–8–2 wheel arrangement.

Mountaineer
Vancouver–Chicago service,
introduced 1920, ceased 1958.
Mountain pay (USRS)
Overtime payments.
Mountains of Mourne (RS)(obs)
Piles of ashes and clinker at loco
depots.
Mourners (RS)
L&NWR Webb 0–6–2T locos. Painted
in unrelieved black livery.
Movable crossing
Track crossing with moving nose,
providing a continuous running rail
and thus allowing higher speeds at
turnouts.
Moving block
An electronic system designed to
overcome the inflexibility of the block
system (qv), with its fixed length
sections and consequent constraints on
frequency of service, by providing a
block system with variable section
lengths according to circumstances,
the exact position of each train being
known to the central computer.
Moving spirit (USRS)
A train dispatcher. *See also* Train
order.
Mozart
A day train between Paris and
Salzburg, introduced 1954, extended
to Vienna 1964, EC 1987.
MPD
Motive Power Depot. In the UK this
term began to replace the older usage
'engine shed/loco shed/loco depot' in
the 1930s, led by the example of the
LM&SR.
MR
1. Maenclochog Rly, or Narberth
   Road & Maenclochog Rly,
   authorized 1872, opened 1876,
   Clynderwen to Rosebush slate
   quarries, closed 1882, vested in
   NP&FR (qv) 1881.

2. Malmesbury Rly, Dauntsey
   Junction to Malmesbury, inc
   1872, opened 1877, worked by
   GWR, part of GWR from 1880.
3. Mansfield Rly: *see* Mansfield Rly.
4. Margate Rly, inc 1859, Herne Bay
   to Margate, a renaming of the
   Herne Bay & Whitstable Rly;
   extension to Ramsgate authorized
   1861 and name changed to KCR
   (qv) [opened Herne Bay–Ramsgate
   1863].
5. Marlborough Rly, Savernake
   (Low Level) to Marlborough
   (High Level), inc 1861, opened
   1864, worked by GWR, part of
   GWR from 1896.
6. Mawddwy Rly, Cemmaes Road to
   Dinas Mawddwy, inc 1865,
   opened 1867, closed 1901 to
   passengers, to freight 1908. LRO
   1910, reopened 1911 after
   rebuilding as light rly, worked by
   Cambrian Rlys. Part of GWR
   from 1923.
7. Mersey Rly, inc 1866, as Mersey
   Pneumatic Rly, but steam locos
   used when opened 1886,
   Liverpool to Birkenhead.
   Electrified 1903, LM&SR Wirral
   electric services ran over the MR
   from 1938. Part of BR from 1948.
8. Metropolitan Rly: *see* Metropolitan.
9. Middleton Rly: *see* Middleton.
10. Midland Rly: *see* Midland.
11. Milford Rly, Johnston Junction to
    Milford Haven, inc 1856, opened
    1863, worked by GWR. Part of
    GWR from 1896.
12. Minehead Rly, Watchet WSR to
    Minehead, inc 1871, opened 1874,
    leased to and worked by B&ER and
    then by GWR. Part of GWR 1897.
13. *Modern Railways*; a 1962
    renaming of TI (qv).

14. Moffat Rly, Beattock to Moffat, inc 1881, opened 1883, leased and worked by Caledonian Rly, part of CR 1889.

15. Mold Rly, Saltney Ferry to Mold, inc 1847, opened 1849, worked by Chester & Holyhead Rly and part of that rly 1849. [C&HR taken over by L&NWR 1858.]

16. Monmouth Rly,inc 1810, Howler Slade [Forest of Dean] to Coleford and May Hill, Monmouth, opened *c.* 1817 as a 3 ft 6 in gauge horse tramroad. Part of its course used by Coleford, Monmouth, Usk & Pontypool Rly, completed 1857, and the section from Wyesham to Coleford by the Coleford Rly, opened 1883.

17. Morayshire Rly, inc 1846, opened 1852 Elgin to Lossiemouth; Orton to Rothes and Dandaleith 1858, Elgin to Rothes 1862, Dandaleith to Craigellachie 1863. Worked by GNofSR from 1866, part of GNofSR 1880.

18. Mumbles Rly: *see* Mumbles.

MR&CC

see Monmouthshire Rly & Canal.

MR&FoDJR

Mitcheldean Road & Forest of Dean Junction Rly, Bilson to Drybrook and Speedwell, inc 1871, part of GWR 1880, opened 1885 to Speedwell, 1907 to Drybrook.

MRC

Model Railway Club, founded 1910.

MRCE

Metropolitan Railway Country Estates Ltd, an associate company of the Metropolitan Rly [London], formed in 1919 to develop middle class housing estates in the rly's catchment area, using surplus rly-owned land and purchasing new sites. On the formation of the LPTB in 1933, this company was not taken over, becoming an independent organization dealing with all kinds of property development in all areas; it subsequently became the Metropolitan Estates & Property Corporation Ltd.

MS

BR Motor car Second/Standard class.

MS&LR

Manchester, Sheffield & Lincolnshire Rly, formed 1847 by amalgamation of the Sheffield, Ashton-under-Lyne & Manchester Rly, Sheffield & Lincolnshire Rly, the Sheffield & Lincolnshire Extension Rly, the Great Grimsby & Sheffield Junction Rly and the Great Grimsby Docks undertaking. Various absorptions and extensions followed, including a line to London, opened 1899. Renamed GCR (qv) 1897.

MS&MJR

Mid-Sussex & Midhurst Junction Rly, Petworth to Midhurst, inc 1859, opened 1866, worked by LB&SCR, part of LB&SCR 1874.

MSCR

Manchester Ship Canal Co. Rlys, inc 1885, opened 1894. Used its own locos and rolling stock. Provided connections between the canal docks, warehouses etc. and main line rlys at Ellesmere Port, Runcorn, Warrington, Partington, Irlam, Barton, Manchester Docks etc. Closed *c.* 1978.

MSDR

Manchester South District Rly, inc 1873, Manchester to Alderley and branches, part of Midland Rly 1876, opened 1880 from Heaton Mersey Junction (Stockport) to Chorlton-cum-Hardy and Throstle Nest Junc near Cornbrook, [CLC]. Section north of Chorlton Junc [Chorlton-cum-Hardy] became part of CLC 1891.

MSJ&A
Manchester, South Junction &
Altrincham Rly, inc 1845, opened
1849, Altrincham to Manchester
(London Rd). Jointly controlled by
MS&LR & L&NWR, owned its own
rolling stock but local trains were at
first worked by MS&LR locos, also by
L&NWR locos from 1899. After 1923
the LM&SR and L&NER as joint
owners, took over full responsibility
for alternate five-year periods.
Electrified 1931.

MSL
As MS (qv) but with Lavatory.

MSLR
see Mid-Suffolk.

MSR
Mid-Sussex Rly, inc 1857, Horsham
to Pulborough and Petworth
[Coultershaw], opened 1859. Leased
and worked by LB&SCR, part of
LB&SCR 1864.

MSW Line
Manchester–Penistone–Sheffield/
Barnsley–Wath.

MT
1. *Modern Transport*, a weekly
   newspaper, founded 1919; acquired
   by Ian Allan Ltd 1963. Monthly
   publication from 1966, subsequently
   ceased publication; revived as a
   quarterly 1978, then ceased again.
2. *Modern Tramway & Light Rail
   Transit*, monthly organ of LRTA,
   founded as *Modern Tramway* in
   1938.

MTA
Metropolitan Transportation Authority
(New York).

MT&AR
see Head of Valleys Line.

MTR
Mass Transit Rly, heavy rapid transit
system on Hong Kong Island and
Kowloon, first section opened 1979.

Mtys (USRS)
Empty wagons.

MU
Multiple Unit (qv).

Mucho, to do a (LTRS)
To agree an MCO (qv).

Muck/Mud, Sludge & Lightning
Nickname for MS&LR.

Mucker (USRS)
A labourer engaged in excavation work

Mud chicken (USRS)
A surveyor.

Mud digger (RS)
A loco with a tendency to derail.

Muddle, Goes/and Go Nowhere
Nickname for M&GNJR.

Mud hen (USRS)
A loco without a superheater.

Mud hop (USRS)
A clerk employed in a yard.

Mud, Slush & Lumber
Nickname for MS&LR.

Mud sucker (USRS)
A choked injector on a steam loco.

Mule (USRS)
A brakeman.

Müller's Lights
Small windows in the partitions
between rly compartments, introduced
by several rly companies following the
murder (the first on a British train) by
Franz Müller of a clerk named Briggs
in a NLR compartment in July 1864.

Multi-aspect signal
A form of colour-light signal with
separate lamps and lenses for each
aspect, normally mounted one above
the other, with red at the lowest
(driver's eye) level.

Multiple Unit/MU
An electric (emu) or diesel-powered
(dmu or demu) train in which the
motive power is distributed over a
number of car axles instead of being
concentrated in a loco or driving car.
All motors can be controlled by the

driver at the front of the train through a master controller connected to all equipments, irrespective of their location. Since the number of motored units can be varied and placed in any desired position in a train and trains can be driven from either end without reversal, mu formations are very flexible in use. The emu system was invented by the American Frank J. Sprague in 1897.

Multiple working

Electric or diesel-electric locos coupled together to enable the driver of the leading one to have complete control of power and braking in all of them. *See also* Tandem working.

Mumbles

Mumbles Rly, Swansea to Mumbles Pier, inc 1804, as Oystermouth Railway or Tramroad, Oystermouth to Swansea, opened 1806, about 4 ft gauge, passengers carried (horse traction) from 25 March 1807, the earliest known date for regular carriage of passengers by rail. Closed to passengers *c.* 1827, passenger traffic resumed 1860. Steam traction introduced 1877. Extended to Mumbles Pier 1898. Leased to Swansea Tramways Co. (later South Wales Transport Co.) from 1899, electrified 1929, using large double deck tramcar type vehicles. Closed 1960.

Music master (USRS)

A paymaster.

Mutual, to do a (LTRS)

To arrange an MCO (qv).

Muzzle loading hog/muzzle loader (USRS)

A steam loco which has to be fired by hand.

MV

1. Metropolitan Vickers Electrical Co. Ltd, Trafford Park, Manchester, successors to Westinghouse (qv), formed 1919 and controlled by Vickers Ltd and MCW (qv). Vickers sold out their interest to the International General Electric Co. (US) in 1928. Became part of AEI, 1959.

2. (Fr)(obs) *Marchandises et Voyageurs*; a mixed train (qv).

MW&SJR

Much Wenlock & Severn Junction Rly, Much Wenlock to Buildwas Junc, SVR, inc 1859, opened 1862, worked by WMR and GWR, part of GWR 1896.

MWR

Mid-Wales Rly, Talyllyn Junc–Rhayader–Llanidloes, inc 1859. Tallyllyn Junc to Three Cocks section acquired from Hereford, Hay & Brecon Rly. Opened 1864, worked by Cambrian from 1888, amalgamated with Cambrian from 1904.

MZA

Madrid, Zaragoza & Alicante Rly, absorbed by *RENFE* in 1941.

N

Nags (RS)
BR 350 hp diesel shunters with three coupled axles.

Nahverkehr (Ger)
Local transport.

Nahverkehrzug (Ger)
Local train.

Namer (RS)
Train spotters' term for any loco with a name on a nameplate.

N&BJR
Northampton & Banbury Junction Rly, inc 1863, opened Blisworth–Towcester 1866; to Cockley Brake Junc (L&NWR), 1872. Renamed Midland & South Wales Rly 1866, reverting to N&BJR 1870. Part of S&MJR, 1910.

N&BR
Neath & Brecon Rly, inc 1863, opened 1864, 1867. Part of GWR from 1922. *See also* DVMR.

N&ER
Northern & Eastern Rly, inc 1836, Stratford [London] to Bishop's Stortford, opened, 5 ft gauge, 1840, 1841, 1842, 1843 with running powers over ECR into London (Shoreditch). Converted to standard gauge, 1844. Leased to ECR 1844, vested in GER 1902.

N&R Joint
Nantybwch & Rhymney Joint, L&NWR and Rhymney Rly from 1867, LM&SR & GWR from 1923–47.

N&SJRC
Norfolk & Suffolk Joint Rly

Committee, inc 1898, M&GNJC and GER: North Walsham–Mundesley–Cromer, opened 1898, 1906, and Yarmouth–Lowestoft via Gorleston, opened 1903. LM&SR & L&NER 1923–47, BR(ER) 1948. *See also* M&GNJC.

N&SWJR
North and South Western Junction Rly, Willesden L&NWR to Old Kew Junction (with L&SWR) and branch South Acton to Hammersmith & Chiswick, London, inc 1851, opened 1853 and 1857, and worked by the L&NWR and L&SWR, passenger service provided by NLR from 1853; jointly leased by L&NWR, Midland and NLR 1871–1922. LM&SR from 1923.

N&W (US)
Norfolk & Western RR. From 1959 included Virginian RR; from 1964 also included Nickel Plate, Wabash & Pittsburgh, and West Virginian Rly. Acquired Erie RR 1968.

Napoli Express
Paris–Naples service introduced 1979.

Narrow gauge
Any track gauge narrower than the standard 4 ft 8½ in/1,435 mm.
During the period when it had broad gauge (qv) lines, the GWR always referred to standard gauge track as 'narrow gauge'.

Nasmyth, Wilson
Nasmyth, Wilson & Co. Ltd, Patricroft, loco builders, 1838–1939.

National Sunday League/NSL Excursions

The NSL, founded in 1855 to support Sunday opening of museums and parks, extended its activities to the organization of rly excursions between London and the south coast resorts, particularly over the LB&SCR. It chartered complete trains, printed its own handbills and issued its own tickets. NSL excursions continued over the SR but ceased in 1939.

Navette (Fr)

A shuttle service (qv).

Navetteur (Fr)

A commuter.

Navigator

A navvy (qv).

Navvies' wedding cake (RS)

Bread and margarine.

Navvy

1. An abbreviation of 'navigator' which has become a word in its own right; a manual labourer, employed originally on canal and navigable waterway (inland navigation) construction (hence the name), and later on rly building and other maintenance and construction projects.

2. (US)(obs) A steam shovel.

Navvy King, The

Popular term for Thomas Brassey (1805–70), rly contractor, who employed up to 80,000 navvies (qv).

Navvy Mail (RS)(obs)

A train operated to transport rly and dock construction gangs.

NBL

North British Locomotive Co. Ltd (qv).

NBR

North British Rly, inc 1844, first section, Edinburgh to Berwick and Haddington, opened 1846. By 1914 it operated over 1,375 route miles,

mainly in central and eastern Scotland. Part of L&NER 1923.

NCB

National Coal Board.

NCC

Northern Counties Committee, formed 1903 to manage the B&NCR (Ireland) when it was acquired by the Midland Rly [of England]. Part of LM&SR from 1923, purchased by UTA from BTC 1949.

NCIT

National Council on Inland Transport, founded 1962.

NCL

National Carriers Ltd. Former Sundries Division of BR, established as a subsidiary of NFC under Transport Act, 1968.

NCR

1. North Cornwall Rly, inc 1882, first section, Halwill Junc–Launceston opened 1886, completed to Wadebridge 1895. Worked by L&SWR, part of SR 1923.

2. Northumberland Central Rly, inc 1863, Scotsgap to Rothbury, opened 1870. Part of NBR from 1872.

NCU

Non-Common User; a rly vehicle confined to the system which owns it.

ND&CJLR

North Devon & Cornwall Junction Light Rly, LRO 1914: a reconstruction to standard gauge of the 3 ft gauge Torrington & Marland with a new line thence to Halwill Junction. Opened 1925, worked by SR, BR from 1948, closed 1965.

NDM

Non-Driving Motor car in a mu set, i.e. a car with motors and control gear but no cab.

NDR

North Devon Rly, inc 1851, opened

1854 Crediton to Barnstaple, leased to L&SWR 1863, converted from 7 ft to standard gauge 1863, absorbed by L&SWR 1865.

NE
Abbreviation used by the L&NER on freight wagons, and from 1942–6, on locos. *See also* NER.

Nearside car
A US design (1911) of tramcar in which passengers boarded and left by a large doorway at the front end. The conductor was stationed behind the driver to take the fares of passengers boarding and control the doors. Later many nearside cars were given a central exit. The name derives from the practice on some tramway (*3*) systems of locating stops on the near side of intersecting streets.

Nebenbahn (Ger)
A local rly (qv) of standard gauge.

NEFR
North East Frontier Rly [of India], formed 1958.

Neggy (LTRS)
The negative conductor rail.

Neilson
Kerr, Mitchell & Neilson, loco builders, Glasgow, from 1843; Neilson & Mitchell 1845; Neilson & Co. 1855; Neilson, Reid & Co. 1898. Amalgamated with Sharp (qv) and Dübs (qv) to form North British (qv), 1903.

Nelson (RS)
Jim Crow (qv).

Nelsons (RS)
SR emu corridor stock introduced for the 1937 Portsmouth Direct electrification. Derived from the 'one-eyed' appearance of the front ends, with driver's window at one side of the corridor connection and route indicator at the other. *See also* COR and RES.

Nene Valley
Peterborough–Wansford–Yarwell Junction; a preserved rly using part of former BR Peterborough–Market Harborough line. First section opened 1977.

NER
1. North Eastern Rly, inc 1854, an amalgamation of York, Newcastle & Berwick Rly, Y&NMR, Malton & Driffield Rly and Leeds Northern Rly. Newcastle & Carlisle Rly absorbed 1862, S&DR (qv) absorbed 1863. 1,249 route miles by 1914, mainly in Yorkshire, Durham and Northumberland, part of L&NER from 1923.
2. North Eastern Region, BR; merged with ER from 1 January 1967.
3. North Eastern Rly [of India], formed 1958.

Nerve Centre, The (RS)
Control Office; or, even more facetiously, the yard foreman's cabin.

Networkers
NSE dc emus classes 465, 466 and 471.

Network NorthWest
BR brand name, introduced 1989, for local passenger services in Greater Manchester, Lancashire (except Merseyrail (qv)), north-west Cheshire and between Manchester and Macclesfield and Buxton.

Network SouthEast
see NSE.

Neubaustrecken
Inter-city lines of *DB* built for fast running, and constructed from 1974 onwards.

Neutralisée, ligne (Fr)
A rly which is completely closed between two stations (exclusive in each case), thus severing through operation, but on which freight services still operate over the sections at each end.

Neverstop Railway
A transport system invented by Adkins and Lewis, in which the motive power is provided by a circular shaft laid beneath the track and fitted with a spiral metal band with which a mechanism on each car engages. The shaft is rotated at a uniform speed but the speed of the car is controlled by the pitch of the spiral band so that when passing through stations, the cars slow to 1–1.5 m.p.h./1.6–2.4 km/h to allow passengers to board and alight. With the widening of the spiral, cars accelerate to 20 m.p.h./32 km/h or more on leaving stations. The system, which obviates the need for signalling, since there is no possibility of collisions, enables cars to be spaced along the line so that there is always one in each station. After a demonstration in the grounds of the Kursaal at Southend-on-Sea in 1923, a line was provided for the 1924–5 British Empire Exhibition at Wembley, London. There have been no subsequent installations.

Newcastle Executive
Service between London (Kings Cross) and Newcastle, so named 1973. Name dropped 1986.

Newcastle hook (RS)(obs)
A shunting pole.

Newcastle Pullman
BR Newcastle–London (Kings Cross) service introduced 1991.

New Haven
see NH.

New Line
1. see Guildford New Line.
2. Roade–Northampton–Rugby.

News butcher (USRS)
A vendor of newspapers, confectionery, fruit etc. on trains, Usually an employee of the Union News Company.

NFC
National Freight Corporation; set up under the Transport Act, 1968, to exercise powers, in conjunction with BRB, to provide, secure or promote properly-integrated services for carriage of freight by road and rail and secure that in the provision of such services, freight should be carried by rail whenever that was efficient and economic. The NFC was given power to operate road freight services and enter into arrangements with BRB for rail transport. Its business comprised the road freight and shipping facilities of the former THC, the sundries and medium weight business of BR handled by NCL, and 51 per cent of the business of Freightliners Ltd. In 1982, under the first Thatcher Conservative administration, the NFC was sold off to the management and staff.

NGR
Narrow Gauge Rlys Ltd, registered 1911, directors Robert Proctor Mitchell amd W.J. Bassett-Lowke. NGR installed and operated 15 in gauge miniature rlys at Southport and Rhyl and opened the R&ER and the Fairbourne Rly as 15 in gauge passenger lines in 1915–16.

NGRS
Narrow Gauge Railway Society, founded 1951.

NH
New York, New Haven & Hartford RR. Later known as the New Haven Co.

Niagara (US)
A loco with 4–8–4 wheel arrangement, also known as Northern or Pocono.

Nibble
Nickname of S&MJR.

Nickel Plate (US)
Nickname for New York, Chicago &

St Louis RR. From the saying of Jay
Gould, who entered a low bid for the
purchase of this company but when
challenged to raise it, replied he would
not do so, even if the lines were
nickel-plated.

Nidd Valley
see NVLR.

Nigger Chiefs (RS)
Nickname for L&YR 4–4–2 locos,
'Big, black and powerful'.

Niggerhead (USRS)
Steam dome or turret on a loco.

Nigger heaven (USRS)
The roofs of freight cars when used
for illicit free rides.

Nigger track (USRS)
A little-used line.

Night Aberdonian
Service between London (Kings Cross)
and Aberdeen, so named 1971.
London terminal moved to Euston
1987.

Night Caledonian
Service between London (Euston) and
Glasgow (Central), introduced 1970,
ceased 1976. Name revived 1986.

Night Capitals
Sleeping car train between London
(Kings Cross) and Edinburgh, so
named in 1971, name dropped 1979.

Night Ferry
London (Victoria) to Paris and
Brussels, with through *CIWL* sleeping
cars carried on purpose-built train
ferries Dover–Dunkerque, introduced
1936, suspended 1939–47, ceased
1980.

Night Limited
Service between London (Euston) and
Glasgow (Central), introduced 1964,
with Pullman lounge bar. Ceased
1988.

Nightrider
London (Kings Cross)–Edinburgh/
Glasgow–Aberdeen service with First

class air-conditioned stock (dimmed
lighting), all-night buffet and
continental breakfast service.
Introduced, with reduced fares, to
meet road coach competition, 1982.
London (Euston)–Glasgow (Central)
service added 1983, all services ran via
WCML from 1988. Discontinued
1990.

Night Riviera
Sleeping car train London
(Paddington)–Plymouth–Penzance. So
named, with new cars, 1984.

Night Scot
Sleeping car service between London
(Euston) and Glasgow/ Edinburgh, so
named officially 1927. Name dropped
1939.

Night Scotsman
Sleeping car service between London
(Kings Cross) and Edinburgh/
Glasgow/Perth/Aberdeen, so named
officially 1927. Edinburgh only 1939.
Name dropped 1968, revived 1971.
London terminal moved to Euston,
1987.

Niles (US)
Niles Car Co., Niles, Ohio, car
builders, notably of interurban cars,
inc 1901. Ceased car production,
1917.

Nineteen Order (USRS)
Train order requiring no signature
which could be handed over on a hoop
or delivery fork without stopping the
train. From the form number.

Nipper
1. (RS) The junior member of any
   gang, obliged to run errands, make
   tea etc.
2. (USRS) A brakeman.

NIR
Northern Ireland Rlys Ltd, formed
1967 to take over the running of the
remaining rlys in NI after the
dissolution of the UTA/UTR (qv).

NITHC
Northern Ireland Transport Holding
Co.; owns and manages the
immovable property required by NIR
to operate its rail services.

Nith Valley Line
Dumfries to Kilmarnock.

NJT
New Jersey Transit, operating
passenger rail services in and around
Newark and Hoboken, NJ, US.

NLLR
North Lindsey Light Rly, inc 1900,
Scunthorpe to Winterton and Thealby.
Opened 1906, worked by GCR,
extended to Winteringham 1907, to
Whitton 1910. Part of L&NER from
1923.

NLR
North London Rly, inc 1846 as
E&WID&BJR (qv), first sections
opened 1850,1851, renamed NLR
1853. Largely under the control and
ownership of the L&NWR but existed
until 1922 as a nominally independent
concern with its own locomotives and
rolling stock; senior management posts
taken over by the corresponding
officers of the L&NWR from 1909.
Became a part of the L&NWR from
1922.

NMBS
Initials of the Flemish name for the
SNCB (qv).

NMR
1. North Midland Rly, inc 1836,
 Derby to Leeds, opened 1840,
 became part of new Midland Rly,
 1844.
2. North Metropolitan Rly; *see*
 Metropolitan.

NMVB
Initials of the Flemish name for the
SNCV (qv).

NNR
North Norfolk Railway; a preserved

rly using the former BR line between
Sheringham and Holt. First services
began 1975.

No-Bill (USRS)
An employee not belonging to the
trade union (brotherhood).

NOL
SR emu compartment stock two-car
sets with NO Lavatories, converted
from L&SWR corridor stock in
1934–6, 2-NOL.

NOMO
No-Man Operation; a proposed LT
fully-automatic system of train
operation.

Non stop
Strictly a train proceeding between
two points without any intermediate
stops for passenger purposes. The
London Underground rlys, however,
for many years used both noun and
verb in a misleading fashion to denote
trains merely omitting only one or
some intermediate stops.

Non-token lock and block
A method of single line working
devised by the Sykes' Interlocking
Signal Co. and first used in 1905. The
instruments are arranged so that no
signal for a train to enter a single line
section can be put to clear ('off')
without the sanction of the signalman
at the other end, and after that signal
has allowed a train to enter, it is
automatically restored to danger
without the consent of the signalman
in advance and cannot be altered until
the train has left the single line
section, this action releasing the
instruments. The system met all
contingencies except that of a train
becoming divided while on the single
line section, leaving to the human
element (i.e. the signalman in advance)
the task of checking that every train
leaving the section was complete.

Nord
Chemin de fer du Nord; Northern Rly of France. Part of *SNCF* (qv), 1938.

Nord Express
CIWL service Paris/Ostend–Berlin–St Petersburg, introduced 1896. Suspended in the First World War, curtailed at Riga, 1921; Hamburg and Copenhagen portion 1929. Also from 1920s, portions for USSR frontier, with connection thence to Moscow, and for Bucharest via Breslau. Suspended in the Second World War, re-instated 1946 as Paris/Ostend–Hamburg–Copenhagen–Stockholm. Became Paris–Copenhagen sleeping car service 1975. From 1986 Ostend–Aachen–Copenhagen only (Paris–Scandinavia traffic was then transferred to new Viking Express (qv)).

Nord-Sud
A section of the Paris Métro formerly operated by an independent company, *Chemin de fer Électrique Souterrain de Nord-Sud*. Became part of *CMP* (qv) in 1930.

Nord-Sud (Brenner) Express
CIWL service Berlin–Munich–Rome–Naples via Brenner, introduced 1897. Cannes portion 1901.

Norfolk Coast Express
Service between London (Liverpool St.) and Cromer, with portions for Sheringham and Mundesley, Trimingham and Overstrand, introduced 1907, replacing Cromer Express. Withdrawn 1914.

Norfolkman
Express between London (Liverpool St.), Norwich, Cromer and Sheringham (the latter two in summer only), introduced 1948, name dropped 1962.

Normal Clear system
A signalling system in which the main running signals display a clear aspect at all times when it is safe for them to do so.

Normal Danger system
Signalling system in which all signals are kept at danger and indicate clear only as required for the passage of a train.

Normal position
The position in which signalling equipment lies when not set for the passage of a train.

Normandy Express
Boat train London (Waterloo)–Southampton Docks for Channel Islands and St Malo/Le Havre sailings, introduced 1952. Ceased 1964.

Norseman
Summer-only express between London (Kings Cross) and Newcastle (Tyne Commission Quay for Scandinavian sailings), introduced 1931, restored 1950. Name dropped 1965.

Norte
Northern Rly of Spain, absorbed by *RENFE* (qv), 1941.

North & West Line
Newport (Mon)–Abergavenny–Hereford–Shrewsbury–Crewe.

North Atlantic Express
Belfast–Portrush service, introduced by NCC in 1934.

Northbound
see Eastbound.

North British
North British Locomotive Co. Ltd, Glasgow, loco builders. Formed 1903 as an amalgamation of Sharp (qv), Dübs (qv) and Neilson (qv). Ceased production 1962.

North Briton
Express between Leeds (City) and Glasgow (Queen St.), so named 1949, terminated at Edinburgh from 1965. Name dropped 1968, restored 1972 as Leeds–Edinburgh service. Name dropped 1975.

North Country Continental
Unofficial name for the GER
Harwich–York/Liverpool service,
introduced 1885 and latterly Harwich–
Manchester. Replaced 1983 by the
European (qv).

North Devon
see NDR.

North Downs Line
NSE brand name for Tonbridge/
Gatwick–Redhill–Guildford–Reading
services from 1989.

North East Corridor
Boston–New York–Washington.

North Eastern
Express between London (Kings
Cross), Darlington and
Middlesborough, so named 1964,
name dropped 1968. *See also*
Newcastle Executive.

Northern (US)
A steam loco with 4–8–4 wheel
arrangement.

Northern Belle
A land cruise (qv) train for sixty
passengers, introduced by L&NER
1933, including sleeping cars, lounge/
writing room car, dining car, shower
and hairdressing facilities. This train
toured scenic lines, offering road and
water side trips, mainly in Northern
England and Scotland, over seven
days, for an inclusive charge of £20. It
ran each year in June until 1939
inclusive.

Northern City/Line
Name for the Finsbury Park to
Moorgate service, when operated by
LT.

Northerner
Auckland to Wellington overnight
service, introduced 1974.

Northern Heights, The
GNR publicity term for the residential
zone served by its lines to Edgware,
High Barnet and Alexandra Palace.

Northern Irishman
Boat train between London (Euston)
and Stranraer Harbour (for Larne
sailings), so named 1952, ran via Castle
Douglas until 1965 then via Mauchline
and Ayr. Name dropped 1966.

Northern Line
Name adopted 1937 for LT tube
service Mill Hill East/High Barnet to
Morden via London Bridge and via
Charing Cross.

North Kent Line
London (Charing Cross and Cannon
St.)–Deptford (North Kent East Junc)
–Blackheath–Woolwich–Dartford
[–Strood].

North Lindsey
see NLLR.

North London Line (obs)
London (Broad St.)–Gospel Oak–
Willesden(HL)–Kew Bridge/Richmond.

North London Lines
BR brand name, introduced 1989, for
the Euston/ Liverpool St.–Watford and
the North Woolwich–Willesden
Junction– Richmond electric services.

Northumbrian
Express between London (Kings
Cross) and Newcastle, introduced
1949. Name dropped 1964. Revived
1988 for service between Poole and
Newcastle via Birmingham. Name
dropped 1990. *See also* Dorset Scot.

North Wales Land Cruise
see Land cruise.

North Warwick[shire] Line
Birmingham (Tyseley)–Henley in
Arden–Bearley. *See also* BNW&SR.

North-West Dane
Blackpool–Manchester–Harwich
service connecting with sailings for
Esjberg and connection for
Copenhagen, so named 1987. Name
dropped 1988. *See also* Loreley.

North Yorkshire Moors
see NYMR.

North Western

1. L&NWR (qv).

2. (US) Chicago & Northwestern RR.

North-West Express

Hook of Holland–Copenhagen service, extended to Stockholm in summer. Introduced 1952.

Norwest (RS)(obs)

The L&NWR, its locos, or its men.

Nose [of a crossing]

The point at which the outer rail of diverging line crosses inner rail of the line it is leaving.

Nose [of a loco] (USRS)

The head or front end.

Nosebag (RS)

Food carried to work and eaten while on duty.

Nosing (USRS)

An unpleasant and alarming oscillation sometimes appearing when railcars and interurban cars are driven at very high speeds.

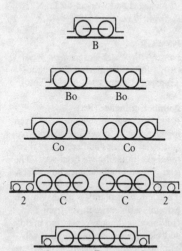

Notation (electric and diesel locos)

Notation [of electric and diesel locos]

The most usual form is that in which a single motored axle is denoted by 'A', two coupled motored axles by 'B', three by 'C' and so on. Carrying wheels in front and behind motored axles are shown by a numeral denoting the number of axles. Axles individually-driven are similarly lettered but suffixed 'o'. Thus 1D1 = one pair of carrying wheels in front, four coupled motored axles and one pair of carrying wheels behind, Bo Bo = four axles, each individually driven.

Notation [of steam locomotives]

see Continental notation; Whyte's notation.

Notch, to give it/her a, (LTRS)

To apply power at first notch briefly, with brakes on, to call the guard's attention or to shake the train in the hope of dislodging a sticking air-door.

Notch up, to (RS)

To reduce the period in which steam enters the cylinders of a loco, or to increase power on electric trains and tramcars.

Notre Métier

The *SNCF* magazine, founded 1938. Since 1952 known as *La Vie du Rail* (qv).

Nottingham Pullman

Service between London (St Pancras) and Nottingham, introduced 1990.

Notworker (RS)

Facetious term for BR Network SouthEast class 442 Wessex electric emus. From their initial unreliability and late delivery.

Nought nought (RS)(obs)

Standard 95 lb bullhead rail.

NP (US)

Northern Pacific RR.

NP&FR

North Pembrokeshire & Fishguard

Rly. Inc 1878 as Rosebush &
Fishguard Rly, name changed to
NP&FR 1884. Absorbed Narberth
Road & Maenclochog Rly 1881,
opened Clynderwen to Letterston 1895
(Clynderwen–Rosebush section
reopened) and Letterston to Fishguard
& Goodwick 1899, part of GWR from
1898.

NR
1. Norfolk Rly, inc as Yarmouth &
   Norwich Rly 1842, opened 1844,
   amalgamated with Norwich &
   Brandon Rly and adopted title of
   NR 1845, leased by ECR, 1848,
   purchase completed 1850.
2. Northern Rly [of India], formed
   1952.

NRDC (obs)
Non Repairs Domestic Coal; a
branding on old wooden coal wagons
used by BR in the 1950s to augment
coal stocks.

NRHS
National Railway Historical Society
Inc, founded 1935, incorporated in US
1937. Over 15,000 members in 1990.

NRM
National Railway Museum (York). An
outstation of the Science Museum,
established under Transport Act,
1968, opened 1975 and the inheritor of
the former BTC and rly company
collections.

NRPC
see Amtrak.

NRZ
National Rlys of Zimbabwe, formed
1980. *See also* RR (6).

NS
1. *Nederlandse Spoorwegen NV*; Dutch
   State Rlys, formed 1938.
2. Newcomen Society for the study of
   the history of engineering and
   technology, founded 1920, inc
   1961.

3. Norfolk Southern [Corporation]; a
   merger of N&W and SR (5) in
   1982.

NSB
Norges Statsbaner; Norwegian State
Rlys.

NSE
Network SouthEast; a BR business
sector covering all passenger services
in London and south-east England not
worked by InterCity. Established June
1986 to succeed L&SE sector (qv).

NSL
National Sunday League (qv).

NSR
1. North Staffordshire Rly, inc 1847,
   first section opened 1848 Stoke–
   Crewe, 220 route miles by 1914,
   centred around Stoke-on-Trent.
   Part of LM&SR from 1923.
2. North Sunderland Rly, inc 1892,
   opened 1898, Chathill (NER) to
   North Sunderland and Seahouses;
   managed and worked by L&NER
   from 1939, and by BR 1948, closed
   1951.

NSWGR
New South Wales Government Rlys
(Aus); from 1972 part of the Public
Transport Commission of New South
Wales.

Number cruncher (RS)
A fanatical type of rly enthusiast given
to collecting or 'observing' locomotives
and other vehicles and recording their
numbers until all have been seen. The
gear carried often includes binoculars,
personal tape recorder and camera.
The somewhat pointless obsession is in
extreme cases carried over from
childhood and adolescence into middle
and old age and is almost exclusively
confined to males. *See also* ABCs;
Cop, to; Gricer; Ref; Train spotter.

Number grabber
Number cruncher (qv).

Number snatcher (RS)
A freight wagon checker; also another word for number cruncher (qv).

Number takers (obs)
Outdoor employees of the RCH, stationed at junctions between different companies' systems to record and report the movement of all vehicles and wagon tarpaulins between one company and another. These men were the rock on which the whole clearing system was established: 'It is to them in great measure that the efficiency of the Clearing House is due' —*The Times* 26 January 1892. Before 1847, men had been employed by individual companies on the same task – they were also known as 'wagon tellers' at that time.

NUR
1. North Union Rly, inc 1834 as an amalgamation of the Preston & Wigan Rly and the Wigan Branch Rly (opened 1832). Wigan to Preston opened 1838. Amalgamated with Bolton & Preston Rly (completed 1843) in 1844. Joint L&NWR and L&YR 1846–1921. Part of L&NWR 1922.
2. National Union of Railwaymen, founded 1913 by amalgamation of ASRS, GRWU and UP&SS (qv). Initial membership 267,611. Became RMT (qv), 1990

Nutcrackers (RS)(obs)
The original L&SWR electric mu motor cars, after the characteristic clicking of their cab-mounted electrical contactors.

NVBS
Nederlandsche Vereeniging van Belangstellenden in het Spoor-en Tramwegen; the senior Dutch society catering for those interested in rlys and tramways.

NVLR
Nidd Valley Light Rly, Pateley Bridge to Lofthouse and Angram Dam, built by Bradford Corporation. LRO 1901, opened 1907, public passenger service to Lofthouse ceased 1929, line closed 1936.

NVR
see Nene Valley.

NWMR
North Wales Mineral Rly, inc 1844, opened Ruabon–Saltney 1846, amalgamated with Shrewsbury, Oswestry & Chester Junction Rly 1846 to form Shrewsbury & Chester Rly.

NWNGR
North Wales Narrow Gauge Rly, 1 ft 11½ in gauge, Dinas Junction (L&NWR) to South Snowdon (Rhydd-ddu) and branch to Bryngwyn, inc 1872, opened 1877, 1878, 1881. Part of WHR from 1922.

NWR
1. North Western Rly, inc 1846, opened Lancaster to Morecambe 1848, Skipton to Ingleton 1849, Clapham to Lancaster 1850. Worked by Midland Rly from 1852, vested in Midland 1871. Known colloquially as 'The Little North Western' to distinguish it from the L&NWR.
2. North Western Rly [of India]. After the partition of India it became the NW Rly of Pakistan (NW or NWR).

NWSR
North Western State Rlys [India], formed 1886. Later NWR (2).

NY&CR
North Yorkshire & Cleveland Rly, inc 1854, Picton–Grosmont, opened 1857, 1858, 1861, 1865; part of NER 1859.

NYC (US)
New York Central RR.

NYCTA
New York City Transit Authority, formed 1953 to operate and manage the bus, tramway (3) and local passenger rly systems in the NY City area. Part of MCTA (qv) 1957.

NYMR
North Yorkshire Moors Rly, preserved rly operating over the former BR line between Grosmont and Pickering since 1973.

NZGR
New Zealand Government Rlys, formed 1876.

O

OA&GB
Oldham, Ashton-under-Lyne & Guide Bridge Junction Joint, MS&LR and L&NWR 1862, LM&SR & L&NER, 1923–47, BR (M) 1948.

O&AT
Oxford & Aylesbury Tramroad, inc 1888; leased and worked WT (qv) 1894–1900, but did not build its proposed line from Brill to Oxford.

O&I
Otley & Ilkley Joint Midland & NER 1865, LM&SR & L&NER 1923–47.

O&K
Orenstein & Koppel AG, established 1876, loco works at Potsdam, this becoming *VEB Locomotivbau Karl Marx* from 1948.

Oban bogies (RS)
Caledonian Rly 4–4–0 locos of 1882.

OBB
Österreichische Bundesbahnen; Austrian Federal Rlys.

Oberland Express
Paris–Interlaken, introduced 1895. Calais–Interlaken winter sports train 1920–39. Through coaches for this route attached to other trains from 1946, but name dropped.

Observation car
A coach specially constructed with large windows, and end windows or open balcony, normally running as the last vehicle in a train, to provide passengers with the best possible views. Often furnished with special seating to facilitate enjoyment of the passing scenery. *See also* Vistadome.

Occupation crossing/level crossing
A facility for crossing a rly provided for the owner/user of land severed by its construction. Not necessarily a public right of way.

Ocean Liner Express
A generic title used on roofboards of London (Waterloo)–Southampton boat trains.

Ocean Specials (obs)
Boat trains with restaurant cars and luxury saloons operated by GWR and BR(W) between Plymouth Docks and London (Paddington) in connection with ocean liners, usually in the 'Up' direction only.

Ocean terminal
Facilities for interchange of traffic between ocean liners and boat trains to and from London (Waterloo) opened at Southampton Docks, 1950, including two reception halls, a VIP lounge, customs examination halls etc. The 1950 building was demolished in 1963 but later terminal facilities remain in use.

OCS
On Company's Service; indicating that an item so marked travelled free.

OCTI
Office Central des Transports Internationaux par Chemins de Fer; Central Office for International Rly Transport, the chief executive body controlling application of the

international conventions concerning carriage of freight, parcels and passengers by rail (CIM and CIV), mediating and conciliating in disputes related to these conventions.

OES
One Engine in Steam (qv).

OEZ
Ost Europäische Zeit; East European Time.

Off
The signal indication signifying that the line is clear and it is safe to proceed.

Officer (RS)
A signalman. This term derives from the early use of policemen as signalmen.

Official Guide
The Official Guide of the Railways and Steam Navigation Lines of the United States, Porto Rico, Canada, Mexico and Cuba. The North American equivalent of 'Bradshaw', first published 1867. It contains timetables and other particulars of all rlys in US and Canada, and is issued monthly. In modern times air line timetables have also been admitted.

Off sheet (LTRS)
An error in train register made by a signalman.

Off the book (LTRS)
Train service running out of timetable order.

Off the front(s) (LTRS)
Employee demoted from motorman to guard after committing a disciplinary offence.

Off the pipes/road (RS)
Derailed.

OFQ
Organization For Quality. BR reorganization of 1990–2 abolishing regions and establishing 'profit centres' etc.

Ohio
TC for 'Send on with all speed to . . .'.

OHL
Overhead Line (carrying traction current).

Oil can (USRS)
A tank wagon for petroleum or other oil products.

Oiseau Bleu
TEE Paris–Brussels introduced 1957. Ceased 1984.

Oiseau Bleu Pullman
CIWL service Paris–Antwerp, introduced 1929, extended to Amsterdam 1936, ceased 1939, restored (Paris–Brussels) 1947–57 with *SNCF* stock, then replaced by a *TEE* – *Oiseau Bleu* (qv).

Oldbury
Oldbury Railway Carriage & Wagon Co. Ltd, Oldbury, Birmingham, 1863–1902. Became part of MCW (qv).

Old Line, The
Roade–Weedon–Rugby.

Old Reliable, The (US)
The slogan of the Louisville & Nashville RR.

Old Road, The
Chesterfield (Tapton Junc)–Killamarsh–Rotherham.

Old Worse & Worse, The
Nickname of the OW&WR (qv).

OMC
Operating & Maintenance Centre (DLR).

Omnibus, train (Fr)/ ***omnibus, treno*** (It) (both obs)
Train stopping at most but not necessarily all the stations on its route. *See also* Tramway, train.

OMO (obs)
One Man Operation. Now replaced by the 'non-sexist' OPO (qv).

On
The signal indication which requires a train to stop.

One arm bandit
1. (RS) AWS equipment.
2. (LTRS) Stock with a combined traction and brake controller handle.

One back, to go (LTRS)
Reversing the motors of an electric train, especially for an emergency stop. From the movement of the controller handle.

One Engine in Steam (obs)
A method of working single lines (usually dead end single line branches) which restricted operation to one train on the line at any given time. A wooden staff for A to B or B to A was carried to authorize each journey and normal block working (qv) was dispensed with. Any points at intermediate locations or at the branch terminus were worked from a ground frame unlocked by a key incorporated in the train staff. Now called 'One Train on Line'/OTL. *See also* Annett's Key; Train staff/tablet/token and ticket.

One on (RS)
A shouted warning of a train approaching.

One rounder (LTRS)
Duty with only one round trip to be worked.

One under (LTRS)
A person fallen under a train (normally at a station and normally a suicide attempt).

On juice (LTRS)
A train picking up traction current.

Only Way, The
Slogan of the Chicago & Alton RR, 'The only way between Chicago and St Louis'. From the title of a dramatization of Dickens' *The Tale of Two Cities*, performed in Chicago in 1899.

On the Advertised (USRS)
On time, i.e. a train running precisely according to the advertised timetable.

On the back (LTRS)
Working as a guard.

On the bells (RS)(obs)
A freight train under permissive working (qv).

On the block (RS)
Held at a stop signal, line congested.

On the blood (RS)(obs)
At full steam pressure. From the red mark on the pressure dial in the cab.

On the board (LTRS)
The appearance of a train on the train describer/ indicator board.

On the cars (US)
On the train.

On the cushions (RS)
Footplatemen and other uniformed employees travelling in public passenger accommodation while on duty. Also on the mahogany (RS).

On the deck/floor/ground (RS)
Derailed.

On the front(s) (LTRS)
Driving an electric train (usually used by guard/motormen).

On the ham (RS)
Working overtime.

On the handle(s) (RS)(obs)
Driving an electric or diesel train as distinct from steam loco driving.

On the juice (RS)
Running over electrified lines.

On the Panel (LTRS)
1. Off sick. Panel (obs)(S) = the pre-NHS appointed panel of National Insurance doctors.
2. On the trainers' panel, qualified to train other staff in the same grade.

On the pitch (LTRS)
A senior uniformed employee undertaking duty on station platform.

On the shovel (RS)(obs)
Firing a steam loco.
On the stops (RS)
Next to the buffer stops.
Op (USRS)
A telegraph operator.
Open
GWR TC for various types of open
wagon.
Open coach
A passenger coach with a centre
gangway and seats either side and no
compartments.
Opening out
The removal of dirty track ballast.
Open line
A section of line in which signals are
normally left in the 'off' position.
Open station
A station without ticket inspection and
collection at the exit and entry to
platforms.
Open the gate, to (USRS)
To switch a train into or out of a
siding.
Open up, to
1. (LTRS) To open train doors.
2. (RS) To accelerate a train.
OPO
One Person Operation; a train
controlled entirely by its driver, i.e.
without any guard or conductor.
Opposing trains
Trains moving towards one another
over a single track.
OR
1. (obs) Owner's Risk parcel traffic
   handled at cheap rate.
2. Okehampton Rly, inc 1862, 1863,
   1864, leased to L&SWR 1863, first
   section, Yeoford to North Tawton
   opened 1865. Name changed to
   D&CR 1865.
3. Oldbury Rly, inc 1873, as Dudley
   & Oldbury Junction Rly, Langley
   Green Junc to Oldbury, name

changed to OR 1881, opened 1884,
   1885, worked by GWR, part of
   GWR 1894.
4. Oxford Rly, inc 1843, Didcot–
   Oxford, opened 1844, part of GWR
   1844.
5. Oystermouth Rly: *see* Mumbles.
Orange Peel (RS)
The high visibility warning jackets
worn by persons going on to the
tracks.
ORC
*1. Organisme Repartiteur Centrale
   Voitures-Lits*; European sleeping car
   pool.
2. (US) Order of Railroad
   Conductors; hence, a conductor.
Orcadian
A restaurant car service between
Inverness and Wick/Thurso, so named
1936. Name revived 1962 but soon
dropped, perhaps because connections
with the Orkney sailings were not
good. Name revived 1983, and now
used for a BR 'Land Cruise' train.
Ords (RS)(obs)
Term for local services, usage mainly
confined to GCR and L&NER.
Presumably from 'ordinary'.
ORE
Office des Recherches et des Essais;
Research and Trials Office. A *UIC*
(qv) organization which pools the
means and the results of research and
trials carried out by member rly
administrations, and studies the
costing and rationalization of
innovations.
Orient Express
CIWL pioneer 'hotel train' service
between Paris and Constantinople
(Istanbul) via Munich, Vienna and
Bucharest, composed of sleeping and
dining cars, introduced 1883, with
some sections by sea and river
transport. Through rail coaches Paris–

Istanbul from 1889 (then 67 h 35 min) reduced to 61 h (via Belgrade) by 1902, suspended 1914. Re-introduced 1919 as Paris–Vienna–Warsaw service. From 1921 this service provided through sleeping cars Paris to Bucharest and Istanbul, also a through sleeper Calais–Bucharest, in connection with sailings from Britain. Through sleeping cars between Ostend and Istanbul and Amsterdam and Bucharest were attached/detached at Linz. After the Second World War, the OE divided at Stuttgart, one portion running to Prague and Warsaw. The Paris–Bucharest through service was fully resumed in 1955. Discontinued east of Vienna, and beyond Prague 1961, extended to Budapest in summer 1964 and again to Bucharest 1965. Ceased 1987 and replaced by daily Vienna–Bucharest through sleeping car and one through ordinary coach between Paris and Bucharest. *See also Arlberg–Orient Express*; Direct Orient Express; Simplon–Orient Express; VSOE.

ORT
Oil Rail Terminal; a BR facility providing reception, storage and distribution facilities for trainloads of petroleum products for more than one oil company.

OS
1. (USRS) On the sheet, a record made by a signalman or dispatcher of the passing time of trains; hence 'O'sing', recording the passing times.
2. (USRS) On schedule, i.e. on time.

Osgood Bradley
Osgood Bradley Car Co., Worcester, Mass, US, established 1833, rly, tramway and interurban car builders. Absorbed by Pullman Standard (qv), 1930.

OsSShD
Organisation für die Zusammenarbeit der Eisenbahnen; Organization for Railway Collaboration, operating in Eastern Europe and Asiatic communist countries since 1957.

Ostend–Cologne Pullman
CIWL service 1929–39 in connection with sailings to and from Britain. In its period, it provided the fastest surface link between Britain and Germany.

Ostend–Karlsbad Express
Introduced 1895, ceased 1914, restored after the First World War, ceased finally in 1939.

Ostend–Vienna Express
CIWL service (via Brussels) introduced 1894 in connection with sailings to and from Britain. Revived after the First World War and again in 1950 (name restored 1951).

Ost–West Express
Through sleeping car train between Paris and Moscow, introduced 1960.

OTL/OTOL
One Train on Line; modern term for One Engine in Steam (qv).

Ottley
A Bibliography of British Railway History by George Ottley, first published 1966, a definitive work. Second edition 1983 and also *Supplement*, 1989, covering publications 1964–80.

Otto Lilienthal
EC Berlin–Zurich, introduced 1991.

Ouest
Chemin de fer de L'Ouest; Western Rly of France. Part of *État* (State Rlys) from 1909.

Outer Circle (obs)
A London train service worked by the L&NWR, 1872–1909:
Broad St.–Hampstead Heath–
Willesden Junction High Level–

Kensington (Addison Road)–Earls Court–Mansion House. A Willesden Junc–Earls Court remnant lasted until 1940.

Outer home signal

A home signal (qv) about ¼ m on the approach side of what is then called the inner home signal. Provides additional overlap at busy points. On the LM&SR and BR (M) known as 'Home 1'. *See also* Home signal; Inner home signal.

Outfit car (US)

A coach fitted out for the feeding and accommodation of construction and maintenance men working on the rly.

Out of gauge load

A very wide load which exceeds the loading gauge of its intended route and possibly fouls adjacent tracks, but is still capable of being handled under special working arrangements.

Outrider (RS)

An employee not belonging to the appropriate trade union.

Outside porter

Badge porter (qv).

Outside swingers (RS)

Locos with outside frames and outside cranks to the coupling rods.

Outward half

Half an Edmondson ticket applying to the outward journey. The other section is known as the 'return half'.

Overbridge

Any bridge over a rly, also known as an overline bridge.

Overhead

Generic term for traction current and supporting cables over an electric rly or tramway (3).

Overland (US)

A steam loco with 4–10–2 wheel arrangement.

Overland road

Light track laid over the surface of the ground by contractors during rly construction, used for removal of spoil etc.

Overland Route, The (US)

Slogan of the Union Pacific RR.

Overlap

In signalling, the distance in advance of a stop signal which must be free from obstruction before a movement is allowed to approach that signal. The standard British overlap beyond a home signal is 440 yd/402.3 metres although this is modified in special circumstances.

Overlap track circuit

A short safety margin in advance of a signal operated by track circuits (qv).

Over the Alps (RS)

see Alps/over the Alps.

Overthrow

The extra overhang at the centre and ends of a vehicle on curved and canted track which must be taken into account when assessing lateral clearances; it is dependent on the radius of the curve and the length of the wheelbase of the vehicle.

Over time

Delayed.

OVR

Ogmore Valley Rly, inc 1863, opened Tondu–Nantymoel 1865, amalgamated with LVR and L&OR, 1866.

OW&WR

Oxford, Worcester & Wolverhampton Rly, inc 1845, opened 1850, 1852, 1853, 1854, 1855, 1858, 1859, amalgamated 1860 with Newport,

Abergavenny & Hereford and
Worcester and Hereford Rlys to
become WMR (qv).

Owl (USRS)
A late-night train, or a night
operator.

Owl car (US)
An all-night service tramcar.

Owl service (US)
An all-night rly or tramway (*3*) service.

Oxford Pullman
All-Pullman service introduced 1967
between London (Paddington) and
Oxford, ceased 1969.

Oyster
TC for the civil engineer's ballast
brake van.

P

PA
Public Address [system].
Pablo Casals
EC *TALGO* sleeping car service
between Barcelona and Berne,
introduced 1989, extended to Milan
1989; Zurich portion added 1990.
Pacers
BR four-wheeled diesel railcars with
bus type bodies introduced 1983
onwards (classes 140, 141, 142, 143
and 144).
Pacific
US and, later, also British term for
steam loco with 4–6–2 wheel
arrangement. From the rly first
ordering this type – the Missouri
Pacific RR.
Packers (RS)
Platelayers, track maintenance men.
From packing (qv).
Packing
Forcing ballast under and around
sleepers to strengthen the trackbed
and on curves to raise the outer rail.
Hence packers (qv).
Paco
GWR TC for various types of horse
box.
PACT
BR acronym for Paved Concrete Track.
PAD
see PA panels.
Padarn
4 ft/1,219 mm gauge rly built to carry
slate from quarries around Llyn
Padarn (near Llanberis) to Port

Dinorwic. Opened 1843. Main line
closed 1961, completely closed 1969.
Part of route along Llyn Padarn
reopened 1971, 1972 as Rheilffordd
Llyn Lanberis (Llanberis Lake Rly).
Padded cells (obs)
Popular name for the original C&SLR
cars which had no windows apart from
narrow toplights and were upholstered
up to that level.
Paddle
1. (RS) A wooden tool which can be
inserted between the collector shoe
of an electric train and the live rail
to isolate traction current in an
emergency.
2. (USRS) A semaphore signal arm.
Paddle boxes/boats (RS)
L&SWR Drummond T14 4–6–0 locos
of 1911–12. From the shape and width
of their driving wheel splashers, which
resembled this feature of a paddle
steamer.
Paddle wheel (USRS)
A narrow gauge loco with an outside
frame. From the resemblance to a
paddle steamer's wheels.
Paddy (RS)
1. A train which removes coal from a
pithead.
2. The Irishman express.
3. Any train to and from Stranraer or
other ports for Ireland.
Paddy Mail (RS)(obs)
Any train specially provided to carry
navvies or colliers to and from their
workplace.

Pair, to do a (LTRS)
To adjust the disposition of crews on
two trains.

Pair of wheels (RS)(obs)
The traditional type of two-wheeled
hand barrow for use by platform staff.

Palace (USRS)
A caboose (qv).

Palatine
Express between London (St Pancras)
and Manchester (Central), so named
1938, ceased 1939, name restored
1957, dropped 1966.

Palatino
Overnight express between Paris and
Rome, introduced 1969.

Palwag/van
TC for pallet-carrying vehicle.

PAN
SR six-car emu corridor set including
one PANtry car, for fast services,
1935, 6-PAN.

Pan
Abbreviation for pantograph.

Panama Limited
Illinois Central RR express between
Chicago and New Orleans, formerly
the Chicago & New Orleans Limited.
Renamed Panama Limited in 1911 on
completion of the Panama Canal.
Schedule of 21 h in 1926, 18 h in
1942. Now operated by Amtrak as
City of New Orleans.

Pan catcher (RS)
A device which prevents pantograph-
equipped locos and cars
from proceeding beyond the end
of overhead traction current
wires with their pantographs still
raised.

P&D
Preparation and Disposal; a term in
use in motive power depots.

P&LJ
Preston & Longridge Joint, LNWR
and L&YR, 1867–1921.

P&N (US)
Piedmont & Northern Rly.

P&O Express
see Peninsular or P&O [Overland]
Express.

P&O Punjab Express
An express between Bombay, Delhi
and Peshawar, in connection with
P&O liner sailings, introduced 1927.

Pandrol® clip
The trade name for a widely-used fb
rail-fastening spring steel clip which is
hammered into position and extracted
by mechanized devices (Pandriver® and
Pandrex®). Adopted by BR from 1959.

Baseplate   Steel clip

P&WJ
Preston & Wyre Joint, L&NWR and
L&YR, 1849–1921.

P&WJR
Portpatrick & Wigtownshire Joint
Rlys, Portpatrick–Newton Stewart–
Castle Douglas formed 1885 from
PR (*1*) and WR (*6*). Purchased jointly
by CR (*1*), G&SWR, L&NWR and
Midland Rly and operated as joint line
1885–1922. Then LM&SR.

Panhandle, The
St Louis, Cincinnati and Pittsburgh
line of the Pennsylvania RR. From
the slender (pan handle-shaped)
northern part of West Virginia it
traversed.

Panhandle line/service
A circular line or service (the pan)
starting or finishing at different points,
on lines diverging from the circle (the
handles).

Pannier tank
A steam loco with its water tanks placed high up on the sides of the boiler, not resting on the frame plates. From the resemblance to the panniers on a pack horse.

Pannonia Express
Berlin–Budapest–Bucharest service, introduced 1958.

Panto
Abbreviation for pantograph.

Panzer link (RS)
Link (qv) allocated to tasks performed under instructions of Control (qv).

PA panels
Pre-assembled lengths of track, thus PAD = PA Depots.

Paper car (USRS)
A van carrying newspapers.

Paper weight (USRS)
A clerk.

Paraffin burners (RS)
Diesel cars and locos.

Parallel rail (obs)
An early form of rail in which the upper and lower flanges were of equal size, intended to give a double life by turning. This proved unsatisfactory in practice and the bullhead rail (qv) was developed from it.

Parallel working
A four-track layout in which the two 'Up' lines are on one side and the two 'Down' lines on the other, so that a train may run from the main/fast line to the relief/local/slow line without fouling the path of traffic in the opposite direction.

Parcel
GWR TC for parcels van.

Parcels Group
A BR business sector with its own board from 1991. Divided into Red Star (qv), Trainload and Track 29 (qv).

Parcels traffic
Any freight conveyed by passenger or parcels trains in small consignments not requiring the provision of special rail vehicles.

Paris–Côte Belge–Pullman Express
CIWL Pullman service between Paris and Knokke, ran in summer 1928 only.

Paris–Côte d'Azur
Paris–Ventimiglia couchette service, so named 1957.

Parisienne
London (Waterloo)–Southampton service connecting with overnight sailings for le Havre and train to Paris, introduced 1981, subsequently altered to operate via Portsmouth Harbour. Name and through rail bookings ceased 1983 but connections remained available.

Paris–Madrid TALGO
Sleeping car service introduced 1981.

Paris–Ruhr
Service between Paris and Cologne (later Dortmund), introduced 1954, *TEE* from 1957, terminated at Düsseldorf 1971, renamed Molière (qv) 1973.

Paris–Scandinavia Express
Paris–Stockholm service introduced 1955. Name dropped 1975.

Parkway
A term coined by BR to describe a main line station equipped with a very large car park and within reasonable driving distance or taxi/bus ride of a large city or town or otherwise serving an important catchment area. Some such stations are sited near motorways. The first was Bristol Parkway, opened in 1972.

Parliamentary fares/trains
Gladstone's 1844 Regulation of Railways Act required all passenger rly companies to run at least one train daily each way on all lines, calling at all stations, at a fare not exceeding one

old penny (1d) a mile, the minimum overall speed to be 12 m.p.h., the accommodation to be protected from the weather. Receipts from such trains were not liable to passenger duty (qv). Although the Parliamentary fare distinction virtually disappeared after the passing of the Cheap Trains Act in 1883 (after which all Third class fares came down to 1d a mile) most lines retained 'Parliamentary', all-stations services daily until the early years of the BR era.

Parlor (USRS)
A caboose (qv).

Parlor car (US)(obs)
A Pullman (qv) type passenger vehicle designed for daytime use.

Parlor maid/man (USRS)
Rear brakeman or flagman riding in the parlor (qv).

Parlor shack (USRS)
Rear end brakeman riding in the parlor (qv).

Parl(e)y (RS)(obs)
Parliamentary train (qv) but loosely used for any main line stopping train until the 1970s.

Parmalee Transfer (US)
A pre-arranged and prepaid transfer by limousine between two Chicago terminal stations, primarily for the benefit of travellers between the East and West Coast centres, e.g. from New York to Los Angeles.

Parsifal
TEE Paris–Dortmund, introduced 1957, extended to Hamburg 1960. Became IC 1979, EC Paris–Cologne 1987.

Parsons & Prawns Line
London & Southampton, described in 1834 as likely only to carry 'parsons and prawns – the one from Winchester, the other from Southampton.'

Parspex
TC for an unadvertised party special train.

Parthenon
Summer service Paris–Brindisi with ferry connection to Greece, so named 1978.

Partially-fitted (obs)
A train in which only some wagons are fitted with continuous brakes (qv).

Parto
GWR TC for covered van with internal partitions.

Passed fireman (obs)
A fireman qualified to drive a steam loco but not yet employed as a driver.

Passenger Duty
A central government tax on passengers carried by rail, imposed from 1832 and collected by the British rly companies for the Inland Revenue. Introduced to compensate for the alleged loss of revenue caused by rly abstraction of road coach traffic, which had been taxed for many years. Removed from all fares up to and including 1d a mile by the Cheap Trains Act, 1883, effectively exempting most Third class fares. Removed from all fares by Finance Act, 1929.

Passenger mile
A measurement of traffic, the equivalent of one passenger travelling for one mile.

Passimeter (obs)
A free-standing kiosk in a ticket hall of a station, designed to combine the facilities for issuing tickets on entry and checking them on exit and equipped with turnstiles operated by the booking clerk. First used in the US; introduced on the London Underground in 1921 and widely adopted by that undertaking between the wars. Also introduced by the

Metropolitan Rly and the L&NER at suburban stations in the 1920s and 1930s. All Underground installations withdrawn as part of the UTS (qv).

Passing loop
Crossing loop (qv).

Patentee (obs)
A steam loco with 2–2–0 wheel arrangement.

Pates (RS)
LM&SR Patriot class 4–6–0 locos.

PATH
Port Authority Trans-Hudson; operated underground rlys beneath the Hudson River between New York and Jersey City and Newark (Hudson Tubes (qv)) from 1962. Now part of the MTA.

Path
Planned routing and timing of a train over specific lines relative to others using the same lines, i.e. a space for its unimpaired working without its interfering with other trains running ahead and behind it.

PAYE
Pay As You Enter; system and vehicle design for tramways (3) and other road services, in which passengers pay their fare or show their ticket on entry. Originated in Montreal, Canada *c.* 1906.

Payload
Proportion of the total hauled weight of a train which is earning revenue.

PAYP
Pay As You Pass; system and vehicle design for tramways (3) in which passengers pay their fare or show their ticket as they pass the desk of a seated conductor. Originated in Peter Witt (qv) cars.

Pay-trains
BR term for local or branch line services in which tickets are issued/ checked on the train by conductors. Introduced 1967.

PBA
Port of Bristol Authority.

PB&SSR
Portmadoc, Beddgelert & South Snowdon Rly, 1 ft 11½ in/597 mm gauge, inc 1901, partly built 1906–10, never officially opened. Acquired by WHR (qv) 1922.

PC
Penn Central (qv).

PCC car
Presidents' Conference Committee [tram]car. Tramcar design for tramways (3), aiming to provide smooth acceleration, quiet running, good riding qualities and high traffic speeds, produced by a committee organized in 1929 by the presidents of the leading USA city transport undertakings. The first completed car was built by Pullman Standard and the first production orders were delivered in 1936. PCC cars were widely used in the US from that time and were also adopted in Canada, Europe and elsewhere.

PCM
Pneumatic Camshaft [Control] Mechanism. An improved light and compact type of electric train control gear incorporating cam-operated contactors with camshaft driven by an air-operated, oil-damped engine. Modified from a US design of *c.* 1928, it was introduced by LT on 1938 Tube and later Underground stock.

PD&SWJR
Plymouth, Devonport & South Western Junction Rly, inc 1883, opened from Lydford to Devonport via Tavistock 1890, leased to and worked by L&SWR. Branch from Bere Alston to Gunnislake (ECMR) opened 1908. Part of SR from 1923.

PDWCL/PDS
Powell Duffryn Wagon Co. Ltd,
absorbed Gloucester (qv) 1986 and
Standard Wagon Co. Ltd 1989,
becoming PDS – Powell Duffryn
Standard,1989.

PE/PER
Pakistan Eastern Rly, formerly the
Eastern Bengal Rly.

Peak, the
Busiest periods of the traffic day, thus
morning/evening peak, peak hours.
See also Peak hour.

Peaked end, the (USRS)
The front or head end of a train.

Peak Express, The
Service between London (St Pancras)
and Manchester (Central), so named
1938.

Peak Forest Line,
Ambergate–Millers Dale–Chinley.

Peak Forest Tramroad
Inc 1794 in association with Peak
Forest Canal, from Dove Holes
quarries to the canal at Bugsworth
(now Buxworth), in use from 1796. By
subsequent legislation, the canal and
tramroad eventually passed to the
MS&LR and were vested completely
in that rly in 1883. Operated by horses
and gravity on flanged rails of 4 ft
2½ in/1,283 mm gauge, laid on stone
block sleepers. Closed *c.* 1925.

Peak hour
The period in which the maximum
number of passengers join or alight
from trains at a city terminus or all
termini, or use a metro/underground
rly system.

Peak Rail
Peak Railway Society, Peak Rail
Operations Ltd; a preservation project
using the former BR line between
Buxton and Matlock.

Peaks
BR Class 44/45 diesel locos (RS).

From the names originally carried by
class 44.

Peanut roaster (USRS)
Any small loco.

Peck (USRS)
A twenty-minute meal break.

Peckett
Originally Fox, Walker & Co., loco
builders, Atlas Works, Bristol, from
1864; became Peckett & Sons Ltd,
1880. Loco production ceased 1968.

Peckham
Peckham Motor, Truck & Wheel Co.,
New York, manufacturers of tramcar
motors, wheels and trucks.

Peddle (USRS)
A local freight train.

Peddle, to (USRS)
To set out freight wagons.

Pedestal frame
The framework holding the shelf of
block instruments in a signal box.

Peg (RS)
A semaphore signal, hence 'pegged'
meaning a signal is in the off position.
From to peg-up (qv).

Peg-up, to (RS)
To move a block instrument from
'Line Blocked' to the 'Line Clear' or
'Train on Line' position, the
preliminary to pulling-off signals.

Pelican pond, the (RS)(obs)
The concentration of ooze and slime
on the ground in a steam loco yard
arising from the blowing out of
boilers.

Pembroke Coast Express
Service between London (Paddington)
and Pembroke Dock, introduced 1953,
ceased 1963. Name revived (as
Pembroke Coast Holiday Express) in
summer only, 1985.

Pendelzug (Ger)
A push and pull train.

Pendolino
A tilt body train developed by Fiat.

The first emu design entered public service in 1976.

Pendulaires (Fr)
Swiss term for commuters.

Pendular suspension
A system which allows coach bodies to tilt on curves.

Peninsular or P&O [Overland] Express
The popular and unofficial name for the service between Calais (connecting with sailings from Dover) and Brindisi via Turin and Bologna, introduced 1890 for passengers on the P&O line sailings to India and the Far East. In 1898 when the P&O liners started to call at Marseilles, an additional service, known as the P&O Overland Express ran between there and Calais. Between the wars, the two trains were known as P&O Marseille and P&O Brindisi, but the latter was withdrawn in the 1930s, after which the survivor became known as the P&O Express, with a 22 h timing between Calais and Marseille. This service was not re-introduced after the Second World War. The Indian and Far East mails were carried by the same routes in separate non-passenger trains until transferred to air.

Penn-Central
Penn Central Transportation Co., formed 1968, a merger of the Pennsylvania RR and NYC. The co. absorbed the NH in 1969.

Pennsy (obs)
Nickname of Pennsylvania RR (US) and also the Pennsylvania terminal station in New York City, erected in 1910 and demolished in 1963–4.

Pennsylvania
1. (US) A steam loco with 6–4–4–6 wheel arrangement.
2. (USRS) Coal.

Pennsylvania bogie/truck
see MCB (*4*).

Pennsylvania Limited
An overnight express between New York and Chicago, introduced 1881 as the New York and Chicago Limited, renamed PL 1891. Replaced by Broadway Limited in 1902 (qv).

Penrhyn
Penrhyn Rly, built to carry slate from Penrhyn quarries near Bethesda to Port Penrhyn, opened 1801, 1 ft 11 ⅝in/585 mm gauge; re-routed and adapted for steam traction on 1 ft 11 in/584 mm gauge, 1875–6. Main line closed 1962, completely closed 1965.

PEP
BR (S) prototype high density emu set of 1971–2 with automatic sliding doors (the first appearance of this feature on BR (S)). Originally designated PER (Prototype Electro-Rheostatically braked) but recoded for presentational reasons.

Percentage cut-off
see Cut-off (*1*).

Periodical ticket (obs)
Another term for season ticket (qv).

Peripheral station
BR term for an outer suburban station designated for main line stops, to save passengers travelling to and from a city terminus, e.g. Watford, Wilmslow.

Perishable
Nickname for 12.15 Penzance–Glasgow van train.

Permanent way
Rly track; rails, sleepers, fastenings and ballast; so called to distinguish it from the temporary way laid during rly construction.

Permissive block
A system of signalling, usually with special block instruments, allowing more than one train to be in a block section at any one time; used only on freight lines, or for freight trains on

passenger lines, or where platform lines in a block section are required to accommodate two or more trains at the same time.

Permissive signal (LT)
Original name for a draw-up signal.

Permissive working
A system in use on certain freight-only lines whereby trains are allowed to follow one another, within sight of each other, at low speeds. *See also* Permissive block.

Persecuted minority (RS)
Employees over age sixty-five and still at work.

Personal Rapid Transit
see PRT.

Personenzug (Ger)(obs)
A stopping train.

Persuader (USRS)
A blower on a steam loco.

Perth (General) Station Committee
Committee of representatives of CR (*1*), NBR and HR (*6*), formed 1863 to administer this jointly-owned station. LM&SR & L&NER 1923–47.

Peter Witt
A front-entrance, centre-exit tramcar designed in 1917 by Peter Witt, a Cleveland St. Rly Commissioner. Widely adopted in US and Canada and also in Milan, Italy. The conductor was positioned in the centre of the car by two side doors ('front centre' and 'rear centre'), the entire front section forming an internal platform for passengers waiting to pass him and pay their fare. Passengers had the choice of dropping their fare in a box and walking to the rear, leaving by the 'rear centre' door, or paying as they left by the 'front centre' door. There was a modification in which passengers could also enter by one of the centre doors, paying as they passed the conductor.

Petticoat (USRS)
A shield which guides steam into the throat of a loco chimney.

Physical
Physical needs relief; allowance in working timetables to allow train crews to use lavatories.

Physical connection
A connection between the tracks of two separately-worked lines, or two different companies' lines, enabling through running, as distinct from a 'walk-over' connection, in which passengers have to detrain and cross to another platform or, on a tramway (*3*) or interurban, walk from one vehicle to another.

Picc/Piccy (LTRS)
Piccadilly Line (qv).

Piccadilly/Piccadilly Line
The LT tube line from Cockfosters via Piccadilly Circus to Heathrow and Rayners Lane, originally GNP&BR (qv).

Picking-up (LTRS)
1. Train skidding on braking or acceleration, usually due to wet rails.
2. Train crew taking over a train.
3. Track circuit re-energizing after passage of a train.
4. Giving a signalman emergency release.

Picking the wheels up (RS)
Skidding.

Pick-up goods (obs)
A freight train calling at each goods yard along a stretch of line to leave and collect wagons.

Pick-up services (obs)
Freight routes radiating from a primary marshalling yard.

Picture, going to see the
(RS)(obs)(GWR)
A disciplinary interview held in the company boardroom. The offender

faced a full-length portrait of Charles Russell, chairman of the co., 1839–55.

Pie card (USRS)
A ticket entitling the holder to a meal.

Pig (USRS)
A loco.

Pig iron (USRS)
A loco.

Piggery (RS)
Staff canteen or messroom.

Piggy-back
A freight system in which loaded heavy road trucks and road trailers (usually the latter) are carried by rail on specially-adapted low-loader flat wagons. Developed from 1937, but principally in the 1950s, in the US. *See also* TOFC.

Pig mauler (USRS)
A loco driver.

Pig pen (USRS)
A loco depot.

Pigs (RS)
Clodhoppers (qv).

Pig's ear (RS)
A small side light in a colour-light signal which enables a driver drawn right up to it to see a change in aspect.

Pigtail (LTRS)
The braided copper lead on a dc electric loco or motor car which connects the collector shoe to the power cable.

Pike (USRS)
Any particular rly line or system.

Pike's Tramway
see Furzebrook Tramway.

Pilchard
TC for civil engineer's flat wagon.

Pilot
1. (US) Term for the front end of a loco.
2. Pilotman (qv).
3. (obs) Early term for train staff (qv).

Pilot engine
1. (obs) A loco carrying the pilotman (qv), designated to haul every train in either direction over a single line section.
2. (obs) A light engine which until c. 1914 ran ahead of royal or other very important trains to ensure the line was clear.
3. A loco allocated to standby, shunting, banking assistance or other special duties at particular locations or to work between two specific points, e.g. station pilot, bank pilot.
4. Any loco assisting the train engine. This usage is condemned by purists who prefer 'assisting engine'.

Pilotman
1. An employee wearing a distinctive cap or armband and allocated to a section of single line, or, more usually, double track temporarily under single line working, who accompanies a train on the single line section, no train being allowed to proceed over it without him on board, or without his authority. Formerly he travelled on the pilot engine (qv).
2. A driver familiar with the route who joins a train or engine crew to give guidance and warnings.

Pilot plow (US)
Cowcatcher (qv).

Pimple (RS)
Hump (qv).

Pimps (RS)
Material used for lighting a loco fire. From eighteenth-century colloquial usage – faggots used to 'introduce the fire to the coals'.

Pin (USRS)
Coupler.

Pin, to (USRS)
1. To couple cars together.
2. To complete a day's work.

Pinch bar
Long wooden bar with metal end;
with the rail as a fulcrum, it was used
to move vehicles in yards etc. when no
loco or horse was available.

Pinch point (LTRS)
Heavily congested location on LT
Rlys.

Pin down, to (obs)
To operate the hand brakes on
individual wagons, e.g. before a loose
coupled train descended a gradient.

Pines Express
Service between Manchester (London
Rd)/Liverpool (Lime St.) and
Bournemouth via Bath and S&DJR.
So named 1927, restored 1949,
diverted via Oxford 1962, ceased 1967.

Pinhead (USRS)
A brakeman (qv). From his handling
of pins (qv).

Pink City Express
Service between Delhi and Jaipur.

Pin lifter (USRS)
A pointsman or yard brakeman. From
pin (qv).

Pin puller (USRS)
A shunter. From his handling of pins
(qv).

Pioneer Zephyr
The first US streamlined lightweight
diesel-electric three-car set, worked
between Chicago and Denver from
1934, originally called the Burlington
Zephyr (qv). Withdrawn 1960.

Pipe (LTRS)
A tube (qv) tunnel.

Piped wagon/piped only (obs)
An unfitted (i.e. loose-coupled) wagon
or other vehicle equipped with
through pipes which allowed
continuous train brakes to be applied
elsewhere on the train.

Pipe-fitted (RS)
Train or vehicle fitted with continuous
air or vacuum brakes. Also, from this,

the traditional rlymen's question to a
new father: 'Is it pipe-fitted [male] or
common user [female] ?'

Pips (RS)
BR diesel locos class 31.

PIRATES
Passenger Information, Reservations,
Accounting & Ticketing Computer
System for Europe.

Pitch-in (LTRS)
Collision between trains.

PKP
Polski Koleje Państwowe; Polish State
Rlys.

PLA
1. (obs) Passengers' Luggage in
   Advance. A system started in the
   1900s in which, for a low inclusive
   charge, a passenger's luggage was
   collected, carried to destination and
   delivered to hotel or other holiday
   accommodation or residence to
   await arrival; similar arrangements
   were made for its return journey.
2. Port of London Authority. *See also*
   PLA Rlys.

Plaisir, train de (Fr)(obs)
An excursion train: 'their cheapness is
more than counterbalanced by their
discomfort' — Baedeker.

Planet
A steam loco with 2–2–0 wheel
arrangement.

Plank (obs)
The size of an open wagon was
formerly designated by the number of
planks of wood in its sides, e.g. 'a
three-plank wagon'.

Plant, The (RS)(obs)
Doncaster Works, GNR/L&NER/
BREL.

PLA Rlys
Port of London Authority dockside
rlys; the PLA operated rlys with its
own fleet of locos, and connected to
the main system, at its London and

Tilbury dock complexes. The London system closed in 1970 and PLA operations at Tilbury ceased a few years later.

Plasser (RS)
A track tamping machine. From the name of a firm manufacturing this equipment.

Plastic pigs (RS)
BR Wessex Electric emu sets class 442. Suggested by the cab design.

Platelayer (obs)
Surfaceman or track maintenance worker, inspecting and laying permanent way. From the laying of cast iron angle plate rails on plateways.

Plateway (obs)
A tramroad (*1*) with flanged plate cast or wrought iron rails.

Platform
Apart from the normal meaning, the GWR used this term to denote a station, usually staffed, of sufficient length to accommodate a short train, i.e. an intermediate category between a halt (qv) and a standard fully-appointed passenger station.

Platform hustler
see Hustler.

Platform lines/roads
Tracks serving a passenger platform.

Pliers (USRS)
A ticket punch used by a passenger train conductor.

PLM
Compagnie de chemins de fer de Paris à Lyon et à la Méditerranée. Part of the *SNCF* from 1938.

Plonker (RS)
An extremely dirty loco requiring heavy work in removing encrusted filth before cleaning. Probably from plonk (S), meaning mud.

Plough
Shoe and mounting fitted to tramcars

to pick up traction current from conduit track (qv).

Plug (USRS)
Throttle of a loco.

Plug puller (USRS)
A steam loco driver. From plug (qv).

Plug run (USRS)
A local train.

Plush/Plush haul/Plush run (USRS)
A passenger train/working.

Plym Valley
Marsh Mills–Yelverton; preservation project on former GWR/BR (W) Launceston branch.

PMV
A parcels and miscellaneous van, BR; fitted with side and end doors, and not gangwayed.

PNB/PNR
see Physical.

Pneumatic railway
Atmospheric railway (qv).

Pneumonia Junction (RS)
Any station where waiting for trains is rendered uncomfortable by lack of adequate shelter.

PO
1. Pullman Open, BR First class IC 125 Mark 3 coach.
2. Private owner wagon (qv).

P–O
Compagnie de chemins de fer de Paris–Orléans, jointly managed with *Midi* (qv) as *PO-Midi* from 1934. Part of *SNCF* from 1938.

Poached eggs (LTRS)
1. External door indicator lights on trains. From their colour.
2. (RS) Gold braid on uniforms. From its appearance.

Pocatello Yardmaster (USRS)
A fraud or a liar. From the false claims made by boomers of having experience as yardmasters at Pocatello, or wherever.

Pocono (US)
A steam loco with 4–8–4 wheel arrangement.

Poggy (RS)(obs)
Another version of Puggy (qv).

Point (USRS)
The front or head end of a train. *See also* Peaked end, the.

Pointe du matin/Pointe du soir (Fr)
Morning/evening peak hour (qv).

Point detector
A device for proving that points are correctly set, allowing a clear signal to be given for a train to pass over them.

Point heater
An electric or Calorgas heater to melt snow or ice that might otherwise impede correct operation of points.

Point lock
A bolt fitted to facing points in passenger lines, operated by a locking lever in the signal box, ensuring that the point blades are securely held in the correct position. The associated signals cannot be cleared until the bolt is fully home.

Point machine
Apparatus which changes the position of points by use of compressed air or electric power.

Points
The moving parts of a turnout (qv) which control the route to be followed, consisting of a pair of switch or tongue rails each tapered to fit a stock or side rail. A right hand set of points will turn a train to the right of a person facing the points, a left hand set to the left. Points are described as facing or trailing according to whether the train passes over them from toe (qv) to heel (qv) of a switch or heel to toe respectively. *See also* Catch points; Switches; Turnout.

Pointsman (obs)
An early term for a signalman.

Point to point ticket
A ticket allowing no break of journey.

Point wedges
Wedges, worked from a signalbox, which hold facing points in position to reduce the risk of an accident.

POIS
Passenger Operating Information System; a BR computer system.

Pole, to (USRS)
1. To run light engine (qv).
2. To move a wagon on a parallel track by using a pole against the buffer beam of the loco.

Pole pin (USRS)
A telegraph superintendent.

Pole shunting (obs)
Use of a pole mounted on a loco to move wagons on an adjacent track, particularly on the NER. *See also* Pole, to.

Police (obs)
1. Signalmen. Rly signalling was originally entrusted to sworn constables (rly police); the use of this term and police type uniform continued for some time after the introduction of specialized signalmen and mechanical signalling. *See also* Bobby; Officer.
2. A loosely-used term for other traffic staff carrying out purely rly duties formerly performed by sworn constables. These included 'booking constables' (booking clerks) and ticket collectors.

Policeman (LTRS)
1. A blind train stop not associated with a signal.
2. A signal halfway down a platform, especially a 'creeper' (qv).
3. (RS)(obs) An employee of the rly carrying out duties formerly the responsibility of sworn constables.

See also Police (*1*) and (*2*).

Pollen
GWR TC for various types of girder-carrying truck. Pollen 'E' was also used as a gun-carrier.

Polmont route, The
Edinburgh (Waverley)–Falkirk(High)–Glasgow (Queen St.).

Polonez
A Moscow–Warsaw service, introduced 1973.

Polonia
A Warsaw–Budapest–Sofia service, introduced 1963.

Pom-Poms (RS)
GCR 0–6–0 locos of 1901 (9J/J11). From the sharp sound of their exhaust beat, supposed to resemble that of the quick-firing 'Pom-Pom' guns used in the South African War, 1899–1902.

Ponderosa (RS)(obs)
A word used by steam loco crews to describe a line inadequately provided with water columns, particularly London (Kentish Town) to Barking. A reference to a fictional ranch in the 1950s' TV series *Bonanza*.

Pony truck
A single axle truck placed before or behind the driving wheels of a steam loco.

Pop, to (USRS)
To release a loco safety valve and reduce boiler pressure.

Po phone (LTRS)
The external, as distinct from the rly, telephone. From Post Office (now British Telecom) telephone service.

Pop safety valve
Manufactured by R.L. Ross & Co., Ltd, Stockport, and designed to release a large volume of steam from the moment it lifts, the blowing-off starting very suddenly (with a 'pop') and ending equally suddenly. These valves release steam at the exact pressure to which they are set.

Pop-up (LTRS)
A signal which lights up as a train approaches.

PO Railway
Post Office [Tube] Rly, London, 2 ft/609 mm gauge, authorized 1913, opened 1927 between Paddington rly station, Paddington District Office (now Paddington Letter Office) and Eastern District Office (now North East Letter Office), Whitechapel Road, via Mount Pleasant and Liverpool St. station.

Porridge box (RS)(obs)
Royal Scot express (qv).

Portable railways
The lightest possible form of rly, in use since 1870s for construction projects, industrial, military, and agricultural purposes, employing prefabricated track which is easily dismantled and re-used. Manual, animal, steam, electric battery or petrol/diesel engine traction may be used in combination with light tip wagons etc. *See also* Decauville track; *Feldbahn*; Jubilee track.

Porter (obs)
A person employed on general manual duties at passenger and freight stations, cleaning, closing train doors, assisting passengers, loading and unloading trains, handling luggage, parcels, freight etc. Now known on BR as a railman/railwoman.

PORTIS
Portable Ticket Issuing System (BR); used by conductors on rural and local services. *See also* SPORTIS.

Port Road, The (RS)
Carlisle–Dumfries–Stranraer.

Portrush Flyer
A Belfast–Portrush service introduced 1934.

Portsmouth Direct [Line]
Woking–Guildford–Havant.

Ports to Ports Express
The unofficial name for a Newcastle–
Sheffield–Banbury–Cheltenham–
Cardiff–Barry service, introduced by
the GWR and GCR in 1906. Ceased
1915. Restored 1920 and extended to
Swansea. Ceased 1939.

POS
Post Office Sorting van, BR.

Possession
Period in which a section of line is
taken over by the civil engineer for
maintenance, renewal or alteration;
can be 'partial' or 'absolute'. *See also*
White period.

Possum belly (USRS)
Toolbox slung beneath the frame of a
caboose.

Possy (pronounced *pozzy*) (RS)
Positive rail on an electrified track.

Poste (Fr)
A signal box.

POT
Post Office Tender, BR; an open van
for the stowage of mailbags.

Pot (RS)
An insulator holding a conductor rail
(qv).

Potato Cans (RS)
L&SWR 2–2–0T of 1906, later
converted to C14 0–4–0T locos.

Pot sleepers
Circular iron supports like large
inverted saucers used in some
countries, without much success, as an
alternative to transverse sleepers, to
give track stability in sandy soil or to
prevent destruction by termites.

Potter (RS)(obs)
An employee who walked along the
coach roofs towards dusk, dropping lit
oil lamps into the lamp recesses to
illuminate the interiors.

Potts, The
Nickname for PS&NWR, also carried
over to S&MLR.

Pourrie (RS)
An oil can with an elongated spout.

POW
Private Owner Wagon (qv).

Power box
A signal box in which all signal
and point movements are controlled
by, and routes set by, electrical
power. Miniature levers, thumb
switches or push buttons are used in
combination with electrical
interlocking.

Power frame
The interlocking signal frame in a
power box (qv).

Power signalling
The operation of signals and points by
compressed air, hydraulic power or
electricity.

PP (LTRS)
Penalty Payment; extra pay, e.g. for
working a rest day.

PR
1. Portpatrick Rly, inc 1857, Castle
   Douglas–Stranraer–Portpatrick,
   opened 1861,1862, worked by
   Caledonian Rly 1864, amalgamated
   with WR (6) 1885 to form P&WJR
   (qv).
2. Peebles Rly, inc 1853,
   Hardengreen (near Dalkeith)–
   Leadburn–Peebles, opened 1855,
   worked by NBR; leased by NBR
   1861, part of NBR 1876.
3. Pentewan Rly, 2 ft 6 in/762 mm
   gauge, St Austell–Pentewan,
   opened 1829, worked by gravity
   and horses. Converted to rly using
   steam locos, 1874–5, closed 1918.
4. Portsmouth Rly, or Direct
   Portsmouth Rly, inc 1853,
   Godalming–Havant (LB&SCR),
   opened 1859, leased by L&SWR,
   amalgamated with L&SWR 1859.
5. Palestine Rlys; operated under the
   British mandate, 1920–48.

Prairie (US)
A steam loco with 2–6–2 wheel arrangement.

Prawn
TC for S&T 30-ton wagon.

Precaution signal
A fishtailed semaphore signal, usually with ring on centre of arm which, when at danger, indicates that a platform line is already partly occupied and stopping short will be necessary.

Pre-métro
A Belgian term (1966) for an electric tramway using shallow subways, which could easily be converted to a full 'heavy' metro (qv). The term *semi-métro* was used in the same sense earlier.

Premier Line, The
Self-styled title of the L&NWR.

Preserved line/rly
Term used to describe sections of BR or other abandoned rlys which have been restored and reopened by enthusiasts, who operate train services with restored steam and diesel locos and rolling stock. Services are usually seasonal, and oriented towards tourist/ pleasure riding rather than providing a useful year-round, full day public transport facility. There is a heavy dependence on volunteer labour. Many such lines have associated static museum exhibits and other 'sideshow' features.

Presflo
A sealed BR hopper wagon with a compressed air discharge system, used for carrying powders in bulk, e.g. cement or fly-ash.

Priam
A steam loco with 2–2–0 wheel arrangement.

Primary yard (obs)
BR term for a marshalling yard in which the originating traffic received its initial marshalling to form up trains for other yards and which served a local area of collection and distribution.

Priming
Term used to describe the situation in which water from an over-full boiler passes with the steam into the cylinders of a loco.

Primrose Line
Brand name for Dart Valley Rly (qv), 1990.

Prince of Wales (RS)(obs)
Loco steam blowing off through safety valve. From the resemblance to Prince of Wales feathers.

Prinz Eugen
TEE Bremen–Vienna (10 h 29 min), introduced 1971; ran Hanover–Vienna from 1976, lost *TEE* status 1978, became EC service 1987.

Priv (RS)
A privilege ticket (qv).

Private car
1. A rly car luxuriously fitted out for the exclusive use of one wealthy individual and guests, or of the company's president or owner, or senior officials. Such cars, which were usually attached to scheduled trains, included kitchens, lounge, dining and sleeping accommodation, bathrooms, lavatories etc. Some were made available for private charter use. There were similar private interurban cars and less elaborate private cars were operated on some tramways (*3*).
2. (US) A private owner wagon (qv).

Private owner wagon
A freight wagon or van provided for or by a particular customer of the rly, at the customer's expense, to be used exclusively for their traffic and labelled with the user's name.

Private right of way/track
Sections of tramway (*3*) or interurban away from public roads.

Private siding
A siding provided for the exclusive use of a particular customer of the rly, at the customer's expense, on the customer's property, connected to but normally gated-off from the running lines.

Private varnish (USRS)
A private car (*1*) (qv).

Privilege cab
A cab licensed to ply for hire on rly premises.

Privilege ticket
A ticket issued at a heavily-discounted fare to rly and RCH employees and their families.

Prize length
A length (qv) for which the responsible track gang has been awarded a prize in recognition of their high standards of maintenance.

PRO
Public Record Office. *See also* BTHR.

Procar 80
A high capacity motor car transporter wagon introduced by Procor in 1979.

Procor
Procor Engineering (UK) Ltd, established 1970 in Wakefield. Designers, builders, repairers and hirers of freight rolling stock. Acquired the Standard Railway Wagon Co. fleet of wagons, 1971, BRT (*1*) (qv), 1974 and Roberts (qv), 1974. Part of Bombardier Inc (Canada), 1990 and renamed Bombardier Prorail Ltd.

Programme machine
A signalling system introduced by LT in 1958, in which the appropriate routeing through interlocking machines is remotely-controlled by machines activated by a roll of punched plastic tape on which the train service for the day is stored. The operation of the machines is monitored from a Central Regulating Room, whose staff can take over operation of the signalling if required.

Progress
Berlin–Prague midday service, introduced 1974.

Propel a train, to
To push a train from the rear.

Propping (RS)(obs)
Pole shunting (qv).

Provincial/Provincial Rlys
A BR business sector established in 1982 covering all passenger services other than NSE, InterCity and those provided for PTAs. Renamed Regional Rlys, 1990.

PRT
Personal[ized] Rapid Transit; a rapid transit system (qv) with very low capacity vehicles running at close headways, capable of being summoned to a designated point to pick up, and of running to a designated point to set down, computer-controlled and generally designed to offer a close approximation to taxi-type service.

PRW
Private Right of Way (qv).

PS
Private Siding (qv).

PS&NWR
Potteries, Shrewsbury & North Wales Rly, inc 1865, opened Shrewsbury–Llanymynech 1866 with branches to Breidden (Criggion) and to Llanyblodwel. Closed 1866, reopened 1868, closed again 1880. Llanyblodwel branch reopened 1886 and worked by Cambrian Rlys. Taken over by Shropshire Rlys 1888, acquired by S&MR (qv) 1909.

PSB
Power Signal Box.

PSO
Public Sector Obligation; a central
government block grant made to BR
from January 1975, under the
Railways Act, 1974, to compensate for
losses arising from meeting general
obligations in respect of passenger
services which are imposed by the
government.

PT
1. Privilege Ticket (qv).
2. Pannier Tank (qv).

PTA/PTE
Passenger Transport Authorities/
Executives. Originally set up under
the Transport Act, 1968. The PTEs
are responsible for implementing the
local transport policies made by the
PTAs, which are, in England, the
corresponding Metropolitan County
Councils, and in Scotland, Strathclyde
Regional Council. There are seven
PTA/PTEs in all: Greater Manchester
(formerly south-east Lancs and north-
east Cheshire), Merseyside, South
Yorkshire, Strathclyde (formerly
Glasgow & Clydeside), Tyne & Wear
(formerly Tyneside), West Midlands
and West Yorkshire.

PTR&D
Port Talbot Rly & Docks, inc 1894,
opened 1897, 1898, Port Talbot–
Maesteg–Pont y Rhyll; Port Talbot–
Pyle/Cefn Junc; and Port Talbot–
Whitworth/Blaenavon. Part of GWR
1922.

PUD (US)
Pick Up and Delivery service.

Puddle Jumper (USRS)
A shunting loco.

Puerta del Sol
A through overnight sleeping car
service between Paris and Madrid,
introduced 1969.

Puffler (RS)
A foreman, ganger (ex-miners' S).

Puggies (RS)(Scots)(obs)
Any small shunting loco.

Puggy (RS)
GCR or GCR employee or train.

Pugs (RS)
L&YR 0–4–0ST dock locos;
also a general term for contractors'
locos and for small shunting locos of
any type in Scotland. *See also* Puggies.

PUL
SR six-car corridor emu set including
one PULlman car for fast services,
1933 (6-PUL and later, 4-PUL).

Pull and push train
see Push and pull train/unit.

Pull-down, to (LTRS)
To stop a train by using the
passenger-operated emergency brake
valve; hence a pull-down, to be
pulled-down.

Pullman
1. In Britain this term was normally
used for the specially-appointed
parlor (obs) or lounge cars,
originally of US design, in which
passengers were served at their
armchair seats with drinks, light
refreshments and full meals and
given other attendance by the
Pullman Co.'s staff in return for
payment of a supplementary fare
and gratuities. The first P cars ran
on the Midland Rly in 1874 and on
the GNR in 1879, and the first all-
Pullman train (Pullman Limited
Express (qv)) on the LB&SCR in
1881. Between 1875–1908 some
British rlys also operated US-built
P sleeping cars. After 1908, all
P cars operated in Britain were
built in the UK by or on behalf of
the Pullman Car Co. Ltd (qv),
which also staffed and operated the
service. BR continued to operate
P services after the Pullman Car
Co. became a wholly-owned

subsidiary in 1963 but its own catering staff eventually replaced the former P employees. From 1985 BR applied the brand name 'Pullman' to a facility offering high quality service of meals and drinks at seats in its normal First class Inter-City coaches, some of which were given names, in the P tradition. P cars were also operated in North America by Pullman USA (qv) and by the *CIWL* (qv) in mainland Europe (until 1971) and Egypt. The word derives from George Mortimer Pullman (1831–97), the US inventor of this concept of luxury rail travel and designer (in 1859–68) of the original P sleeping, dining and 'parlor' cars.

2. (RS)(obs) Shunting truck, GWR, BR (W).

Pullman Car Co. Ltd
Established in Britain 1882 as the Pullman Co. Ltd, purchased by Davison Dalziel in 1907, re-formed in 1915 as the PC Co., taken over by BR, partly in 1954, and wholly in 1963.

Pullman Co./Pullman Inc. (USA)
Formed as Pullman's Palace Car Co. 1867, name changed to P Co. 1899. The company built and operated most sleeping and dining cars in North America and Mexico for many years. Tramcars were also built from 1891. At the height of its operation in the 1920s, it boasted itself as 'The World's Grandest Hotel' with some 100,000 guests sleeping nightly in its cars. Manufacturing facilities (Pullman Standard Car Manufacturing Co. since 1934) remained under the Pullman parent corporation along with the car services until 1947 when ownership of the latter was transferred to a group of US rly companies. The existing independent services organization was, however, retained. From the beginning of 1969 all North American rlys cancelled their Pullman operating contracts and began to operate their own services. Production of rail vehicles by Pullman in Chicago ceased in 1979.

Pullman Limited Express
All-Pullman service between London (Victoria) and Brighton, introduced 1881, the first such in the UK.

Pullman Pup (RS)(obs)
Six-wheeled battery vans for providing lighting power in some British Pullman Co. cars.

Pull off, to (RS)
To place a signal in the 'Off' position.

Pull the air, to (RS)
To apply brakes from a valve on the train.

Pull the back one, to (RS)
To set the distant signal in the 'Off' position.

Pull the handle, to (LTRS)
To use the passengers' emergency brake handle.

Pull the pin, to (USRS)
To resign.

Pull the plug, to (USRS)
To drive a loco.

Pull the string(s), to (RS)
To release vacuum or air brake valves manually.

Pump (LTRS)
The air compressor on a train.

Pump up, to (LTRS)
To recharge the air reservoirs in a train.

Punching turn (LTRS)
A duty restricted to supervision of entry barriers, not involving imposition of excess fares.

Punch up, to (LTRS)
1. To operate a lift manually in event of failure.

2. To transmit a train's description by depressing the button on the train describer.

Punctuality Parkes
Charles Henry Parkes, appointed chairman of the GER 1875.

Punjab Limited
An exclusively First class boat train between Bombay and Peshawar, introduced 1927 for the sole use of passengers to and from Europe.

Pups (USRS)
Small four-wheel shunting locos.

Purlin/purline
The longitudinal roof members extending over carlines (qv), and with them, forming an anchor for the roof.

Push and pull train/unit
A train capable of being driven from either end. When a steam loco was used, the usual arrangement was to have controls connecting with the driver's brake valve and the regulator in the driving compartment at the end opposite to the loco (or in the two driving compartments if the loco was in the centre of the train). There was also some form of audible warning operable from the remote driving compartments and some means of communication with the fireman on the footplate.

Push back, to (LTRS)
To propel a train, or the act of so doing.

Push down, to (RS)
To close gaps between wagons in sidings.

Push-in trains (LTRS)
Additional trains injected into the rush hour services at suitable intermediate points to provide extra capacity.

Push out, to (LTRS)
To give assistance to a defective train by pushing it with another train in rear.

Put back, to (LTRS)
To return a signal to danger, usually by putting lever in normal position.

Put [it] away, to (RS)
To stable a train.

Put [it/him] inside, to (RS)
To by-pass a train by sending it into a loop or siding.

PW
Permanent Way (qv).

P Way
Permanent Way (qv).

PWD
Permanent Way Department.

PWF
Private Wagon Federation.

PWI
The Permanent Way Institution, founded 1884, inc 1908.

PWR
1. Permanent Way Repairs/Restriction; a speed restriction imposed during or immediately after track repairs or replacement or after damage to the formation by subsidence, earth fall etc.
2. Pakistan Western Rly, formerly the North Western Rly [of India].

PWS
Permanent Way Slack: *see* PWR (*1*) (qv).

Pyrénées–Côte d'Argent Express
A *CIWL* service between Paris and Hendaye/Pau, introduced 1911, restored after the First World War as a night train Paris–Irun–Tarbes. Replaced by Iberia Express (qv), 1957.

Python
GWR TC for van used for private horse carriages or motor cars.

Q

Q, The (US)
Chicago, Burlington & Quincy RR.

Q-paths/services
Trains for which paths (qv) are allocated but which only run as required by traffic or operational needs. Locos and crews are not specifically allocated but are found as required by Control from reserve capacity or cancelled booked services. *See also* Manned conditional.

Q Train
A special train manned by British Transport Police officers and supported by other police in radio contact travelling in road vehicles in the vicinity of the train. The train can be stopped at any time, at the direction of the officer in charge, to enable the police to deal with any incidents of vandalism, trespass or other crimes encountered on the journey. Introduced *c.* 1983.

Quad-arts
Articulated suburban stock of 1914–24 designed by Nigel Gresley for the GNR and L&NER, consisting of sets of four compartment coaches mounted on five four-wheel trucks/bogies, two four-coach sets being coupled to make an eight-car train, in which the two sets (each with a different arrangement of accommodation) were close-coupled with short buffers at the inner ends. Similar sets were also built for the L&NER from 1924. Withdrawn 1966.

Quads (RS)(obs)
Bolster wagons (qv) with four bolsters, designed to carry long steel girders, steel bars etc.

Quarry Line
LB&SCR line opened 1899–1900 between Coulsdon and Earlswood to by-pass congestion at Redhill and over the original SER and LB&SCR joint line between Coulsdon and Redhill.

Quarter lights
Fixed windows in passenger coaches, originally those either side of the doors of passenger compartments.

Queen Mary (RS)(obs)
Vacuum-braked, long wheel base freight guard's van, larger than older types. From the RMS *Queen Mary* (1936).

Queen of Scots
Pullman train between London (Kings Cross), Edinburgh and Glasgow, so named 1927. Restored 1948, name dropped when partly replaced by White Rose Pullman (qv) 1964.

Queen of Shebas (RS)(obs)
SR four-car suburban emu sets with six-aside seating, first introduced 1941; SUB (qv). 'She came to Jerusalem with a very great train' — I *Kings* x, 2.

Queen points (RS)
The second pair of points in the sequence leading from the hump (qv) of a marshalling yard to the sorting sidings. *See also* Jack points; King points.

Queenslander
An air-conditioned express between
Brisbane and Cairns, introduced 1986.
Queen Street route, The
Edinburgh (Waverley)–Falkirk (High)
–Glasgow (Queen St.).
Quike (LTRS)
A four-wheel rail-mounted cycle used
for track inspection in tube tunnels. A
combination of QUeer and bIKE.
Quill (USRS)
A loco whistle.
Quilling
1. (RS)(obs) The process of picking
out wealthy-looking passengers, and
offering to handle their luggage
(usually performed by an off-duty
employee). Also a verb – to
quill. From earlier (S) usage of
same word meaning to curry
favour.
2. (USRS) Manipulation of loco
whistle to play tunes or make other
distinctive sounds. From quill (qv).
Quint-arts
Similar to quad-arts (qv) but in five-
coach sets which could run coupled
together or separately. They were
allocated to former GER suburban
services by the L&NER when
provided from 1924 onwards.
Quintishill
Britain's worst rail disaster, 1915, in
which 226 died.
Quints (RS)(obs)
Bolster wagon (qv) with five bolsters,
designed to carry very long steel
girders or bars etc.

R

RA
Route Availability, followed by a number (BR); no loco may work on a route of lower numbered RA than that of its RA classification.

Rabbit (USRS)
Catch points (qv).

Rabbits (RS)
Short distance passengers, also fare dodgers with an 'alibi' ticket.

Race track (USRS)
Section of line safe for high speed running and used for such.

Race trains
Special trains run to stations at or near horse race courses on race days.

Rack railway
Line using a mechanical system (Abt, Riggenbach, Strub or Locher) which features arrangements of steel teeth set continuously along the track to engage pinion wheels or cogs in the specially-equipped locos or motor coaches.

Wheel housing   Axlebox journal

Brake drums

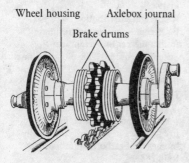

Rack railway (Abt system)

Such systems enable trains to climb very steep gradients up to 1 in 2.

Radial axle
An axle and wheel set which is able to move within a fixed radius.

Radials (RS)
LB&SCR E4 0–6–2T locos.

Radial tank (obs)
Tank loco in which the carrying wheels move in radial guides to enable it to negotiate sharp curves. Applied in particular to L&SWR Adams 4–4–2T, built from 1882.

Radial truck (obs)
A four-wheel truck (usually on tramcars) in which the axles can move freely relative to the truck frame to adjust more closely to track curvature.

Radio train
A special train for tourists in which a commentary on passing scenery or points of interest is given through radio loudspeakers in each coach. The first was operated by CIE in 1950. BR adopted the concept in 1953. *See also* Land cruise.

Raffaello
An EC service between Basle and Rome, introduced 1989.

Raft (RS)
Two or more wagons coupled together, usually during shunting.

Rafter (RS)
A fully-loaded train.

Ragtimes/Ragtimers (RS)
GNR '630' 2–6–0 locos (L&NER class K2) – from the appearance of their

outside Walschaerts motion, which was associated with the movements of a contemporary dance craze. 'We believe this slang description is applied to the "1000" class, it is neither dignified nor appropriate, and is certainly not worthy of perpetuation' — *The Railway Magazine*, January, 1922.

Rag waver (USRS)
Flagman.

RAI
Iran Islamic Republic Rlys.

Rail
1. A nineteenth-century alternative for 'railway'.
2. (USRS) A rly employee.

Rail a train, to (LTRS)
To move a train, using overhead trolley lead, from the unelectrified depot tracks to the electrified line outside.

Rail bender (RS)
A driver who thrashes his loco.

Rail bond
A device to maintain electrical connection between one rail and another across a rail joint, ensuring conductivity for track circuits.

Rail buff (US)
Term for any person interested in rlys. This expression has gained some currency in the UK in recent years but is mainly used by journalists and others lacking such interest.

Railbus
A lightweight low-capacity diesel or petrol railcar with bus or bus type body, usually on four wheels, used for passenger services on branch and other lightly-trafficked lines.

Railcar
A passenger-carrying car, running singly or with others, propelled by an integral light steam engine, a petrol or diesel engine, or by electric traction.

Railcard
An identification card sold by BR to enable particular categories of passenger (e.g. senior citizens, young persons) to obtain discounted fares, introduced 1975.

Rail creep
The tendency of rails to move very slowly out of position longitudinally, in the direction of traffic, as a result of braking action by trains.

Rail Drive
A self-drive car hire service for BR passengers, introduced 1969.

Railed road
see Rail road/railroad (qv).

Rail Europ Junior
Discounted fares applying to international journeys within Europe and available for persons under twenty-one, introduced 1970. British and Irish rlys included from 1973.

Railex
see RLS.

Railfan (US)
Term for a person interested in rlys.

Railfreight
A BR business sector devoted to freight movement, formed 1982, but the term was in fact in use before that time to describe BR's freight activities. Became Railfreight Distribution (qv) in 1988.

Railfreight Distribution
BR freight organization, resulting from a merger of Freightliner (qv) and Speedlink (qv) in 1988. Bulk business separated off as Trainload freight (qv) in 1990.

Rail grinder
A vehicle equipped with the means of smoothing out imperfections and irregularities in rail surfaces, usually by means of carborundum blocks.

Railhead
1. The nearest rly facilities to any

given location. In military usage, this term denotes the nearest point to the combat zone to which troops, equipment and ammunition may be brought by rail.

2. The top part of a rail, including the running surface.

Rail motor [car] (obs)
A combination of a steam engine and coach. *See also* Railcar.

Railnews
BR newspaper for staff, established 1963. Separate regional editions published until 1971.

Railophone (obs)
A system for telephoning to and from trains in motion introduced in 1911.

Railpax (obs)
National Railway Passenger Corporation (US). A federally-subsidized rail passenger system, introduced 1971. Superseded by Amtrak (qv).

Rail road/railroad
1. (obs) Term used to describe tramroads (*1*) and tramways (*1*) from the early eighteenth century until those words came into common use.
2. Originally an alternative term for 'railway' in UK and other English-speaking countries but by the late nineteenth century this usage became largely confined to North America, though 'railway' is also current there, especially in company titles, the two forms proving useful for making legal distinctions.

Railroad bull (USRS)
A policeman or detective employed by a rly company.

Railroad Magazine
see RM (*3*).

Railroadman's Bible (USRS)
The rly company's rule book.

Railroad roof
see RR roof.

'Railroad that went to sea, The'
see Flagler's Folly (qv).

Rails (obs)
Rly company stocks (e.g. Home Rails).

Rail tractive effort
Net tractive effort at the rail of a loco power plant after taking account of all internal losses but excluding resistance forces met by the train. *See also* Tractive effort.

Rail Way (obs)
Same as Rail road/railroad (*1*) (qv).

Railwayac (obs)
A term current from *c.* 1890 to *c.* 1925 to denote a person interested in rlys.

Railway Acts [of Parliament]
These fall into four groups:-
1. *General Acts*, laying down general conditions for rly operation (e.g. the Railways Clauses Consolidation Acts, 1845 and 1863).
2. *Private Acts*, authorizing private rly companies to construct new works (including new rly lines), extensions of time for new works previously authorized and sanctioning other specific powers. Such Acts incorporate the relevant provisions of (*1*).
3. *Transport Acts* (qv).
4. *British Railways Acts*, essentially the same as (*2*) but applying to the nationalized rly system. There is usually one each year.

Railway & Canal Commission
This was established in 1873 (reconstituted 1888), to regulate rlys and canals, giving judgement on disputes arising between companies and to arbitrate between companies.

Railway & Travel Monthly
see R&TM.

Railway Club
see RC (*1*).
Railway Directory & Year Book
see RYB.
Railway Dog (obs)
see Dog Collector.
Railway Engineer
see RE (*2*).
Railway Executive (RE)
Established as a corporate body under
the policy-making BTC (qv) in 1947 to
undertake detailed management and,
through its regional organization,
operation of the newly-nationalized
rlys (BR). In 1953 a Conservative
Government abolished the RE and the
rlys were then directly managed by the
BTC and the BR regions. Not to be
confused with the Railway Executive
Committee (REC (qv)).
Railway Fly Sheet
see RFS.
Railway Gazette
see RG (*1*).
Railway Herald
see RH.
Railwayist (obs)
Another version of railwayac (qv) and
contemporary with it. Preferred by the
RM (*2*) (qv) and used by it as late as
1934.
Railway King, The
George Hudson (1800–71). Involved,
not always honestly, in promotion and
financing of numerous rly schemes
and amalgamations, mostly in the
north and midlands; founder of the
RCH (qv).
Railway Letter [Service]
see RLS.
Railway Magazine
see RM (*1*) and (*2*).
Railway Mania
A period (1844–7) in which large
numbers of rly proposals, many of
them ill-founded and unwise

speculations, were submitted for
parliamentary approval.
Railway News
see RN.
Railway Observer
see RO (*2*).
Railway Official Gazette
see RFS.
Railway observer
1. Genteel term for one who notes
   down locomotive and rolling
   stock numbers, locations and
   movements.
2. Title of the monthly magazine of
   the RCTS (qv).
Railway of Death
A Japanese project to connect Burma
and Thailand by rail in the Second
World War, on which British and
other prisoners of war were employed
in appalling conditions. Completed in
October 1943, but the section north of
Nam Tok was abandoned soon after
the Second World War.
Railway Pictorial
see RP.
Railway rambling
Walking along the alignments of
abandoned rlys. A term coined
c. 1975.
Railway Record
see RR (*1*).
Railways
Popular illustrated monthly for rly
amateurs, founded 1939, renamed
Railway World 1952.
Railways Illustrated
see RI (*2*).
Railways South East
see RSE.
Railway Times
see RT.
Railway World
see Railways; T&RW.
Railway Year Book
see RYB.

Rajdani Express
Name used for fast trains between
Bombay, Calcutta and New Delhi.

Rake
A set of coaches, normally kept
together and usually semi-permanently
coupled.

Ram (USRS)
The injector on a steam loco.

**Ram a shot of air under the wheels,
to** (USRS)
To brake a train or loco.

R&CHS
Railway & Canal Historical Society;
founded 1954 to raise the standard of
original historical research and to
foster and maintain historical
investigation and research, also to
indicate and record where information
may be found. Publishes a *Journal*
three times a year.

R&CT
Rye & Camber Tramways Co. Ltd,
operating a 3 ft gauge light rly opened
1895, Rye to Rye Golf Course; extended
to Camber Sands, 1908. Public service
ceased 1939, dismantled 1948.

R&ER
Ravenglass & Eskdale Rly, Ravenglass
to Boot, 3 ft/914 mm gauge, inc 1873,
opened freight 1875, passengers 1876.
Closed 1908, reopened 1909, closed
1910, reopened 1911, closed again
1913. Converted to 1 ft 3 in/381 mm
gauge miniature rly by NGRL (qv)
and reopened 1915.

R&KFR
Rowrah & Kelton Fell Rly, inc 1874,
opened 1877. Disused by late 1920s,
track removed 1934.

R&LHS
Railway & Locomotive Historical
Society Inc. (USA), founded 1921, inc
1926.

R&L&NWR Jt
Rhymney & L&NWR Joint line,

Rhymney to Nantybwch, inc 1867,
opened 1871; LM&SR & GWR Joint
1923–47.

R&SBR
Rhondda & Swansea Bay Rly, inc
1882, Treherbert–Aberavon–Swansea
etc., first section opened 1885,
worked and managed by GWR 1906;
part of GWR 1922.

R&TM
Railway & Travel Monthly, founded
1910, renamed T&TM (qv), 1920.

Ransomes
Ransomes & Rapier Ltd, Ipswich,
founded 1868, manufacturers of rly
cranes, hydraulic buffer stops,
signalling equipment etc. Production
ceased 1987. (Not to be confused with
Ransomes, Sims & Jeffries, also of
Ipswich, manufacturers of agricultural
machinery, steam and electric road
vehicles and trucks.)

Rapid (LTRS)
Rapidprinter ticket issuing machine,
or the ticket it produces.

Rapide, train (Fr) (obs)
The fastest category of train, some of
them First class only, often carrying
mail.

Rapidi, treni (It)
Supplementary fare expresses, with
restaurant cars; in the period when
three passenger classes existed they
were confined to First and Second
class only.

Rapid transit (US)
Term, in use since *c.* 1885, to
describe an urban public passenger
transport system operating over
segregated routes, normally an
electric underground, elevated or
surface rly, or a mix of these. Not
always living up to its name,
hence the quip 'Transit it is, rapid
it isn't'. *See also* Light rapid
transit.

Rap the track, to (USRS)
To run a loco at high speed.

RAR
Royal Arsenal Rlys; an internal system in the Royal Arsenal, Woolwich, London, 1 ft 6 in/457 mm and standard gauge, opened 1870–6. Closed 1965.

RAS
Railway Air Services; formed by the four grouped British rly companies in 1934, in an attempt to control the development of competition from internal air services. Ownership transferred to British European Airways Corporation in 1947.

RAT
Rail Adhesion Train, LT; trains of converted passenger cars used to distribute Sandite (a compound of sand and stainless steel particles) on the surface of rails to improve adhesion and electrical contact when these are impaired by the slime generated from falling leaves.

Rat (USRS)
A freight wagon.

RATP
Régie Autonome des Transports Parisiens; Paris Transport Authority, controlling public passenger transport systems in the Paris region, established 1948.

Rats (RS)
BR diesel locos class 25. From their frontal appearance.

Rattle her hocks, to (USRS)
To drive a loco (i.e. an 'iron horse') very fast.

Rattler (USRS)
A freight train.

Ratty
Nickname for R&ER (qv).

Raves
A GWR term for the slightly projecting shaped steel plates at the top sides of a tender which help to retain piled-up coal.

Rawhider (USRS)
A disciplinarian, any supervisor who drives his men hard.

Razor gang (RS)
Audit staff, or any visiting staff from headquarters looking for economies.

RB
BR buffet car with kitchen and twenty-three seats at tables.

RBI
Railway Benevolent Institution, founded 1858.

RBR
BR buffet car which has been refurbished.

RC
1. The Railway Club, founded 1899. The oldest-established club catering for those interested in rlys, professional and amateur. It has a central London clubroom and an extensive library.
2. A misleading abbreviation formerly used in British rly timetables to signify *any* form of on-board refreshment service.

RCA (obs)
1. Railway Companies' Association, formed 1869.
2. Railway Clerks' Association. The original body of this name was formed in 1865 but proved to be a failure. A new association was founded in 1897 and survives today under the name adopted after nationalization – the Transport Salaried Staffs Association (TSSA).

RCAF (obs)
Restaurant/cafeteria car, BR.

RCH
Railway Clearing House; an organization established in 1842 (and inc in 1850 and 1897) to deal with questions relating to through traffic

passing over the lines of different rly companies, apportionment of receipts etc. The RCH also laid down standards and organized most other matters of mutual concern and interest, offering neutral ground for discussion and negotiation by the participating companies. Its statutory existence ceased in 1954 together with its separate identity and independence, but the name and a residual organization continued under the BTC until it was finally disbanded in 1963. 'The RCH' also came to mean the RCH headquarters offices in Seymour (now Eversholt) St., Euston, London NW. *See also* Number takers.

RCL
Railway Conversion League; founded 1957 by Brig. T.I. Lloyd to advocate total conversion of rlys into segregated motor roads, an idea mooted as early as 1928. Latterly known as Railway Conversion Campaign.

RCT
Royal Corps of Transport; a corps of the British Army formed in 1965 to take over the transport functions of the RASC and the rly and port operating and movement control responsibilities of the RE (*1*) (qv).

RCTS
Railway Correspondence & Travel Society, founded 1928. One of the largest British organizations for rly enthusiasts, primarily catering for those obsessed by the fine detail of day-to-day operations, particularly by the locos, trains and rolling stock, their movements and their numbering. Now has about five thousand members. Publishes the monthly *Railway Observer* and very detailed and well-regarded locomotive histories. Affectionately known as 'The Royal Corps of Train Spotters'.

RDA
Railway Development Association; founded in 1951 to advocate retention, modernization and extension of rly facilities in Britain. Amalgamated with the Railway Invigoration Society to form the RDS (qv), 1978.

RDC
1. (LTRS) Rest Day Cover.
2. Rail Diesel Car; a diesel railcar, carrying passengers, mail, baggage etc.

RDS
Railway Development Society; formed 1978 from the RDA (qv) and the Railway Invigoration Society.

RE
1. Corps of Royal Engineers; the part of the British Army which until 1965 was responsible for rly operating and workshops as well as rly construction and maintenance. Since 1965 it has been concerned only with rly and port construction and maintenance. *See also* RCT; REME.
2. *The Railway Engineer*; a periodical devoted to rly construction and engineering, founded 1880. The first modern rly technical journal. Came under the control of RG (*1*) (qv) in 1919; separate publication ceased and merged into RG (*1*), 1935.
3. The Railway Executive (qv).

REA
Railway Express Agency (US) formed in 1928 to handle nationwide express (qv) business.

Reading (US)
1. A steam loco with 4-4-4 wheel arrangement. The first being supplied to that company.
2. Philadelphia & Reading RR, eventually officially known as the Reading Co.

Real estate (USRS)
A facetious term for poor coal.

Rear, in the
In the context of signalling, this term denotes anything on the approach side of a given point when facing the direction of travel. Anything beyond that point is decribed as 'in advance' of it.

REC
1. Railway Executive Committee; formed 1912 of the managers of eleven leading rly companies under the nominal chairmanship of the President of the BoT (qv), to control and manage the rlys as a unit in the event of a national emergency. This control was operated throughout the First World War under the direction of professional rly officers. The REC was disbanded at the end of 1919 but was re-appointed by the MoT (qv) in 1938 with representatives of the four main line companies and the LPTB. It acted as the Minister's agent and as a channel of communication between the Government and the rlys during the period of Government Control in the Second World War, when it again facilitated the management and operation of the company-owned networks as a unified system throughout the period. Disbanded in 1947. (Not to be confused with the Railway Executive (qv).)
2. Railway Enthusiasts' Club, founded 1953.

Receiving office (obs)
Premises operated by a rly company, usually in the commercial centres of large cities, at which parcels and goods were received for transmission by rail, rly passenger tickets were issued and information about rly services dispensed. In London several were on the sites of historic coaching inns. The term became obsolete in the period between the wars when the rly companies rationalized their in-town enquiry and ticket offices.

Reception road/siding/track
Track(s) accommodating wagons awaiting sorting/marshalling or setting into position preparatory to loading or unloading.

Recovery margin/time
Extra time built into the working timetable timings of a train over unrestricted sections of line, providing a margin above its standard point to point running time, usually approaching the end of its journey. This allows drivers to recover punctuality after passing over those parts of the route liable to engender minor delays because they are congested, subject to speed restrictions etc. Introduced generally in Britain in the 1940s and 1950s.

Red Arrow *[Krasnaya Strela]*
A fast night service between Moscow and Leningrad, introduced 1938.

Redball (USRS)
A fast freight train.

Red board (USRS)
A stop signal.

Red Caps (obs)
Officially-used term for baggage porters at major US and Canadian stations. From their headwear.

Red cards, red carding
The procedure of placing a red card into the card holder on a wagon, van or coach to denote that it is faulty and must not be used.

Red Devils (RS)
Midland Rly compound 4–4–0 locos.

Red Dragon
An express between London (Paddington) and Carmarthen, so

named 1950, name dropped 1965.
Name revived for Swansea–London
service, 1984, became the Red Dragon
Executive in 1986 and, in 1988, the
Red Dragon Pullman.

Red engine (also blue/yellow) (obs)
GWR colour code which denoted the
axle load of a loco. Used on signs etc.,
e.g. 'Red engines must not pass this
board'.

Red eye (USRS)
A stop signal.

Red-eyed Devil/Monster (LTRS)
The Line Controller. From the red
light which shines on telephone
switchboards when the LC is calling.

Red onion (USRS)
A rly refreshment room.

Redpath Frauds
The fraudulent creation of GNR stock by
one of its employees, Leopold Redpath,
who was sentenced to transportation for
life in 1877. The company lost about
£244,000 at 1877 values.

Red Rose
An express between London (Euston)
and Liverpool (Lime St.), so named
1951. Name dropped 1966.

Red Star
The BR express 'to be called for'
registered parcels service, introduced
1963, designed to secure certainty and
speed in transit, using the first and
fastest trains available to provide a
same day or overnight service. In 1991
it became a profit centre of the Parcels
Group (qv).

Reefer (USRS)
A refrigerated wagon.

Ref (RS)
A list of loco numbers, usually
separated into types or classes and
drawn up by the owning train spotter
(qv). From reference book.

Refuge
An alcove in a tunnel, viaduct or
retaining walls to allow track workers
to shelter safely from passing trains.

Refuge siding
A siding, entered through a trailing
connection, which provides temporary
accommodation for slow non-passenger
trains out of the way of fast traffic.

Regelspur (Ger)
Standard gauge (qv).

Regency Belle
A privately-chartered Pullman car
train between London (Victoria) and
Brighton, available to the public; ran
only Saturdays and Sundays in March
and April 1964.

Regenerative braking
An arrangement which enables an
electric loco or train to reduce its
energy consumption by feeding back
into the traction supply power
generated by the motion of the train
when it is descending a gradient. In
effect while this is happening the
traction motors are temporarily
converted into dynamos. Where the
substation equipment is not designed
to receive regenerated power, the
controlled electric braking is similarly
arranged but the generated energy is
dissipated as heat in the starting
resistances instead of being returned to
the traction supply. This alternative is
known as *rheostatic braking*.

Regional Railways
A 1990 renaming of BR Provincial
Sector/Rlys (qv).

Régional, train (Fr)
see Train Régional.

Regulation [of passenger traffic]
A system (first introduced in 1918–19
by the L&YR, for peak traffic periods
in and out of Blackpool and
Southport), in which passengers were
required to book in advance for the
outward journey and were then given
tickets to travel by a specific

numbered train, thus allowing the operators to plan a regulated service of appropriate capacity, in punctual, evenly-loaded trains, while assuring the passenger a seat. On arrival at the destination, the passengers were given another special ticket bearing the number of a specific train on their chosen day of return. The special tickets used were known as Regulation tickets and no extra charge was made for the facility. An analogous system, introduced in 1904 by the GWR, and still used by BR at busy periods, is that of requiring all passengers on specified ('controlled' or 'limited') trains to have a numbered reserved seat ticket or 'boarding card', obtained in advance.

Regulator [handle]

The valve which allows the driver to control the quantity of steam admitted to the steam chest from the boiler; when the regulator is in the position known as 'fully open', the maximum amount of the steam available is being used.

REHAP

BR (S) emu sets, rebuilt from NOL sets (qv).

Relayer (RS)

A section of line which has been, or is about to be relaid, and which requires a reduction of speed.

Release key

A key provided to enable a signalman to release the plunger lock on a lock and block (qv) system, thus overriding the mechanical and electrical safety devices built into the system. The key is necessary for use if a fault develops in the train-actuated treadle release or when a train is offered forward and then cancelled. It should only be used when there is no train in the relevant block section. Misuse of

this key has been the cause of several serious accidents.

Relief

Staff allocated to replace others whose duty hours have expired but are not in position to sign off; also staff replacing others due for meal breaks etc.

Relief siding

Refuge siding (qv).

Relief train

A train not shown in the public timetable but operated in a suitable path (qv) to carry passengers who cannot be accommodated on the scheduled train.

Rembrandt

TEE Amsterdam–Munich introduced 1967. Amsterdam–Stuttgart 1980. Lost *TEE* status 1983. IC Amsterdam–Frankfurt, 1983–4, Amsterdam–Chur, 1984, became EC 1987.

REME

Royal Electrical & Mechanical Engineers; that part of the British Army which took over the RE (qv) rly workshop responsibilities in 1965.

'Remember Abermule'

see Abermule.

Remorque (Fr)

A trailer (qv).

Remus

A Vienna–Rome service, introduced 1977.

RENFE

Red Nacional de los Ferrocarriles Españoles; Spanish National Rlys, formed 1941.

REP

BR (S) emu corridor unit with Restaurant/buffet car and Electro-Pneumatic brakes, for Bournemouth electrification. Two motor cars Second/Standard class, one trailer brake First, one buffet car. Capable of working as a tractor unit with one or two TC (qv) sets, 4-REP.

Repeater
An electrically-worked indicator in a signal box which shows the position of a semaphore signal, usually one not visible from the box.

Repeater [signal]
Signal arms co-acting with the main arm and placed at a lower point on a signal post. Adopted in situations where the main signal cannot be clearly seen in sufficient time (e.g. when starting). *See also* Banner repeater.

REPTA
Railway Employees' Privilege Ticket Association.

Reptile (USRS)
A yard brakeman.

RER (Fr)
Réseau Express Régional; Regional Express Railway Network. Underground and surface electric rlys, financed by the state and local authorities, running through the centre of Paris and into the suburbs either side, linked with existing rlys, and providing communication between all zones of the city region via the central area. First section opened 1969.

RES
SR four-car corridor emu set with kitchen and REStaurant cars for Portsmouth Direct electrification, 1937, 4-RES.

Resarail
International rly seat reservation system.

RESCO
Railway Engineering & Supply Co., Woolwich.

Reserved track
A section of tramway (*3*) laid off public roads, or in the centre or at the sides of public roads in a 'reserved' alignment, not available to other traffic. When away from roads altogether, sometimes also known as 'private tracks'.

Reshaping/Reshaping Report
see Beeching.

Residential expresses/traffic (obs)
A late Victorian and Edwardian term for medium to long distance commuter traffic and services.

Resi (obs)
Abbreviation for residential traffic (qv).

Resilient wheel
A wheel containing a rubber section sandwiched between tyre and centre plate and used to reduce running noise in tramcars.

Restall's tours/trips
Frederick J. Restall was a pioneer organizer of half-day rail trips from Cambridge (in 1885) and (beginning in 1894) from London, largely at first for the benefit of shop staffs on early closing days. First using the LB&SCR from London, his activities soon spread to other companies and, by 1913, over 400 trips a year were being organized. The last of these trips ran in 1939. 'Rest-all and be thankful' — G.R. Sims.

Restroke, to (LTRS)
To put back, and then immediately pull off a signal lever.

Retarders, wagon
Rail-mounted brake to slow down and stop wagons moving by gravity into sorting sidings from a marshalling yard hump (qv). Remotely-operated from the control tower or manually-worked. A refinement also accelerated wagons moving too slowly (wagon accelerator/retarder). First used at Whitemoor, March, L&NER, 1929.

RETB
Radio Electronic Token Block; a system which combines a microprocessor and a mobile radio,

designed to work lightly-used single lines, replacing staffs, tablets, tickets and tokens. It provides direct radio communication between the driver and the signalman. First adopted on BR on Dingwall–Kyle of Lochalsh line 1984–5.

Return half
The right-hand half of an Edmondson ticket which the passenger retains for the return journey.

Reverse(d) curve
Track curving in contrasting directions in succession, i.e. in an 'S' conformation.

Reversible working
A section of track signalled for working in either direction according to traffic requirements.

Reversing station
A location on rlys constructed to ascend very steep gradients by using a zig-zag alignment at which trains are reversed. *See also* Switchback.

Reversing triangle
see Triangle.

Revue Générale (Fr)
La Revue Générale des Chemins de Fer; rly engineering journal founded in 1878.

RF
BR Restaurant car, First class, with kitchen and twenty-four seats at tables.

RfD
Railfreight Distribution (qv).

RFFSA
Rêde Ferroviaria Federal SA; Federal Rlys of Brazil, formed 1957.

RFM
BR Restaurant [car] First [class] Modular.

RFO (obs)
BR Restaurant car, First class, with loose chairs.

RFS
Railway Fly Sheet founded 1870,

renamed *Railway Official Gazette* 1882, merged with RN 1914.

RFS Industries
An engineering firm formed 1987 to take over Doncaster rly works from BREL (qv).

RG
1. *Railway Gazette*, founded 1892 as *Transport*, renamed *Transport & Railway Gazette* 1904, RG 1905, published monthly from October 1970 as *Railway Gazette International*.
2. BR griddle car with kitchen, bar and buffet counters and seating at tables.

RG&RR
Reigate, Guildford & Reading Rly, inc 1846, 1847, first section opened 1849, worked by SER, purchased by SER 1852.

RGP (Fr)
Rame de Grand Parcours; express diesel railcar units introduced by the *SNCF* in 1955.

RGS&SS
Railway Guards', Signalmen's and Switchmen's Society of the United Kingdom, formed 1866, lasting only one year.

RH
Railway Herald, a weekly paper for rly employees which also contained articles of general rly interest; its circulation was boosted by insuring subscribers against injury or death while at work. Ceased publication 1903.

RH&DR
Romney, Hythe & Dymchurch Rly, 1 ft 3 in/381 mm gauge miniature pleasure and public service line from Hythe to Dungeness, LRO 1927. First section opened 1927.

Rheingold
A Pullman-style Mitropa day train

between Hook of Holland (connecting with Harwich sailings), Amsterdam and Basle, so named 1928. Ceased 1939. Revived 1951; new rolling stock 1962, including vistadome cars which were withdrawn in 1976. *TEE* 1965, Amsterdam–Geneva/Amsterdam–Chur/Hook of Holland–Milan. Hook of Holland coaches ran only to Geneva, 1973 and Hook portion ceased in 1979. In 1980–2 the train ran Amsterdam–Berne/Zurich; in 1982–3 Amsterdam–Basle only; in 1983–6 Amsterdam–Basle/Salzburg. Ceased 1986. In 1987 the southbound working was replaced by the Rembrandt (qv), the northbound by the Erasmus (qv).

Rhein–Main
Diesel railcar set between Frankfurt and Basle, introduced 1949. *TEE* Amsterdam–Frankfurt, introduced 1957. Renamed Van Beethoven 1972 (qv).

Rheinpfeil
Rhine Arrow; express Amsterdam–Basle 1951–3. Name revived 1958 for Dortmund–Munich service, exchanging coaches at Duisberg with the Rheingold. *TEE* 1965–71. IC 1971. EC Hanover–Chur, 1987.

Rheostatic braking
see Regenerative braking.

Rhinelander
Service between Manchester and Harwich (Parkeston Quay) in connection with sailings to Hook of Holland, introduced 1987 in replacement of the European (qv), replaced 1988 by the Loreley (qv).

Rhodanien
TEE Paris–Marseille, so named 1971, lost *TEE* status 1978. *TEE* from 1981, name then dropped.

Rhodesia Express
A service between Capetown (connecting with Union Castle Line sailings) and Bulawayo (connections to Congo etc.). In 1932 it covered 1,354 m in 48 h 20 min on 3 ft 6 in/1,067 mm gauge.

RHP
Rail Horsepower.

RHT
Railway Heritage Trust; an independent trust, formed 1985 with the objective of preserving and enhancing Britain's rly buildings and structures of architectural and/or historical importance (both those in use and those no longer required for BR purposes). Also encourages public enjoyment of this heritage.

Rhymney
Rhymney Rly, inc 1854, Cardiff–Caerphilly–Hengoed–Rhymney. First section opened 1858. By means of joint lines with GWR and L&NWR, eventually also reaching Dowlais, Merthyr and Nantybwch, 62 route miles including joint lines. Part of GWR from 1922. *See also* R&L&NWR Jt.

RI
1. The Railway Inspectorate, established 1840. At first part of the BoT, then MoT, DTp. Until recent years all were officers of the RE (1) (qv). Their duties include inspection of new rlys and tramways, also reporting on accidents and safety etc. The Inspectorate was transferred to the Health & Safety Commission in 1990 and became HMRI (qv) in 1991.
2. *Railways Illustrated*, founded 1908, merged with RN 1908.

RIA
Railway Industry Association of Great Britain. A 1971 renaming of LAMA (qv).

Rialto
An express between Paris and Venice, introduced 1990.
Ribbons (USRS)
Tracks.
RIC
Regolamento Internazionale Carrozze; International Carriage & Van Union, regulates dimensions and operating requirements of vehicles used on international services. Founded 1921.
Ride high, to (USRS)
To travel on the roofs of box cars.
Rider (RS)
An engineman accompanying a loco being hauled by another.
Ride shotgun, to (RS)
To act as second man (qv).
Ride the bars, to (S)
To travel on a moving train by clinging to external handles, usually for the length of a station platform, a juvenile/adolescent amusement originating in London *c*. 1988.
Ride the point, to (USRS)
To ride on the loco. *See also* Point, the.
Ride the rods, to (USRS)
The hobo practice of travelling on the truss rods of wagons and vans.
Riff (USRS)
A refrigerated wagon.
Riggenbach
A form of rack rly (qv) after its inventor, Niklaus R., (1817–99).
Right hand side, on the (USRS)
The US rly driver's position in the cab, hence his status, thus 'Herb's now on the right hand side'.
Rijeka Express
A summer service between Ostend and Rijeka, so named 1969, and replacing the Dalmatia Express. Cut back to Villach and name dropped, 1975.
Ringer (RS)
A crowbar.

Ringmaster (USRS)
Foreman or yardmaster.
Rio Grande Zephyr
A service with vistadome cars between Denver and Salt Lake City (with bus link to Ogden), introduced 1971. Replaced by California Zephyr (qv), 1983.
Rio Tinto
British-owned rly between the Rio Tinto copper mines in southern Spain and the port of Huelva.
RIP (US)
Repair, Inspect and Paint; letters seen on wagon or car in need of attention.
Riprap
An embankment of large stones to protect a formation against erosion by water action.
Rip track (USRS)
Track on which damaged or faulty vehicles are parked to await repair or scrapping; it may include a repair facility. From RIP (qv).
RIV
Regolamento Internazionale Veicoli; International Wagon Union, regulates dimensions and operating requirements of wagons used on international services.
Riverside branch/loop, The
Newcastle–Walker–Carville–Percy Main.
Riviera Express
CIWL service Hamburg/Amsterdam/ Berlin–Nice, introduced 1900; re-introduced 1934 as Amsterdam/Berlin– Ventimiglia with Cologne portion. Ceased 1939. Re-introduced 1957 Cologne–Ventimiglia.
RK
BR Kitchen car, with kitchen only.
RKB
BR Kitchen/Buffet car, no seats.
RLO
BR Restaurant open lounge car.

RLS

Railway Letter Service; a facility introduced in 1891 by which for postage and a supplementary charge, letters could be handed in at rly stations for conveyance by the next train and any necessary onward connections to the station nearest the destination, where they could be called for, or alternatively posted from the station. Express facilities (called Railex from 1934) were also available in which letters were taken to the departure rly station by Post Office messenger and immediately delivered on arrival at the destination station. This service was discontinued in 1984, except for special occasions.

RM

1. *Railway Magazine and Annals of Science*, founded 1835, renamed *RM & Commercial Journal* 1839, then *Herapath's* from 1841 (qv).
2. *Railway Magazine*, founded 1897, the first periodical wholly catering for the amateur/popular interest in rlys, published monthly, no connection with (*1*).
3. *Railroad Magazine*, popular US rly, tramway and interurban journal, including fiction with a rly background. Founded 1906. Ceased separate publication 1975 when it combined with *Railfan* as *Railfan & Railroad*.

RMB

BR Miniature Buffet (qv) car Second/Standard class with a small kitchen and forty-four to forty-eight seats.

RMT

National Union of Rail, Maritime and Transport Workers. Formed 1990, an amalgamation of the NUR (qv) and the National Union of Seamen.

RN

Railway News, founded 1864, merged with RG 1918.

RO

1. An open merchandise wagon.
2. *Railway Observer*, the organ of the RCTS (qv), founded 1928 as *Railway News*, renamed RO 1929.

ROA (LT)

Railway Operating Apprentice; later used to denote any junior trainee.

Road

Term for a specific rly track (i.e. one set of rails), thus 'No. 2 Road', 'Through Road'; also for a specific rly route, thus 'learning the road' etc. On LT, the official meaning is any track other than a running line but staff use it of all lines. In the US the term is synonymous with railroad.

Road bed

Material supporting and draining the railway track, mainly the ballast (qv).

Road box/truck/van/wagon

see Station truck (*2*).

Road engine (US)

A loco available for through/long distance workings as distinct from shunting or local trips.

Road/roadside station

Any small intermediate station.

Roarers (RS)

BR class 81 electric locos.

Roaring rails

Another term for corrugation (qv).

Roberts

Charles Roberts & Co. Ltd, Horbury Junc, Wakefield, rly carriage and wagon builders, also manufacturers of tramcars and hirers of wagons. Established 1856. Acquired Hurst, Nelson (qv), 1958. Became part of Procor (qv) 1974.

Robert Stoltz

An EC service between Munich and Graz, introduced 1989.

Robin Hood

An express between London (St Pancras) and Nottingham (Midland), so named 1959. Name subsequently dropped. Re-introduced 1990 for London (St Pancras)–Leicester–Nottingham Pullman service.

Rock and Roll (USRS)
Excessive lateral movement of locos and rolling stock associated with low speeds and poorly-maintained jointed track.

Rock and Rollers (RS)
BR (S) Hastings line diesel electric mu sets. From their somewhat wild riding qualities at speed.

Rockets (RS)
L&SWR 2–2–0T of 1906 and later conversions to C14 0–4–0T. A facetious reference to their feeble power.

Rocking chair (USRS)
Retirement with pension.

Rocking horse (RS)(obs)
A freight guards' van offering a bumpy ride.

Rock Island (US)
Chicago, Rock Island & Pacific RR.

ROD (obs)
Railway Operating Division; a division of the British Army Royal Engineers, largely recruited from staffs of British rly companies, which controlled and operated standard and narrow gauge rlys and repaired and overhauled locomotives behind British fronts in France, Belgium, Greece, Egypt and Russia during the First World War. Formed in 1915. The total number of men in the ROD had reached twenty-four thousand by 1918.

RODs (RS)
GCR Robinson 2–8–0 locos, as used by the ROD.

Roland
A Bremen–Basle service, introduced 1957. *TEE* Bremen–Milan, introduced 1969, included Milan portion of *Rheingold* south of Basle. Withdrawn 1980. Name used for *TEE* Bremen–Stuttgart, 1980.

Roland the Rat (LTRS)
The LT RAT (qv). After the TV character.

Rollerman (RS)(obs)
A criminal who travels on trains to break open and rob unguarded luggage.

Rolling stock
Generic term for all types of rly vehicle other than locos, which are usually referred to separately.

Roma–Milano Express
An all-sleeping car *CIWL* service introduced 1924. Still runs, but now un-named.

Roma–Napoli–Palermo Express
An all-sleeping car *CIWL* service, introduced 1925.

Roma–Napoli Pullman Express
A *CIWL* Pullman service, ran only in 1929.

Roma–Turino Express
An all-sleeping car *CIWL* service introduced 1925.

Roma–Venezia/Trieste Express
An all-sleeping car *CIWL* service introduced 1925.

Rome Express
A *CIWL* service between Calais (connecting with UK sailings), Paris and Rome, introduced 1890, running in winter only. Ran from Paris only from 1902, by 1913 ran all year round, Paris–Rome 26 h 20 min. Re-instated after the First World War, as all year round working, with through coaches to and from Boulogne (connection for London (Victoria)) from 1924. By 1935 Paris–Rome timing was reduced to 22 h 35 min. Re-introduced 1951 Paris–Rome, but no longer exclusively a *CIWL* service. Extended to Naples 1979 and renamed *Napoli Express*.

Romulus
An express between Vienna and
Rome, introduced 1969.
Roof garden (USRS)
The assisting loco on a mountainous
section of line.
Roomette (US)
Term for cabins or compartments on
long distance train, entirely enclosed
each side of central gangway, each
forming a small day room, at night
convertible for sleeping with a
longitudinal bed lowered from the
wall. A private lavatory is provided.
Windows are necessarily on the outer
side only. This term is also now used
in Australia to describe a similar
facility on long distance services.
Rooters (RS)
LB&SCR Stroudley A1 0-6-0T of
1872.
Rope runner (obs)
A man whose duty it was to hitch
wagons on to the rope used to haul
them up steep inclines worked by rope
and stationary steam engine.
Rosenkavalier
An express between Munich and
Vienna, introduced 1969.
Roses Line, The
[Leeds/Bradford/Halifax-] Burnley-
Blackburn [-Preston-Blackpool]. The
name dates only from 1984. Also
known over part of the distance as the
Copypit Line (qv).
Rossiya
[Russia]; a service between Moscow
and Vladivostok.
Rosslare Express
A Cork-Rosslare boat train, ceased
1967.
Roster
Notices to show individual employees
which diagrams (qv) they are to
work and what duties they are to
perform.

Rotank
GWR TC for a flat wagon used to
carry road milk tankers.
Rotary coupler
A coupler designed to allow wagons to
be turned upside down for unloading
without uncoupling.
Rotary snow plough
A snow plough with a rotating fan
designed to disperse deep or
compressed snow.
Rough (RS)
Unsorted wagons.
Roughnecks (USRS)
Specifically applied in the rly context
to freight train brakemen – a tough
breed.
Rough turn (LTRS)
A period of duty with a high propor-
tion of train working.
Rounder (LTRS)
A round trip.
Roundhouse
A building, usually circular in plan, in
which locos are accommodated on
tracks radiating from a central
turntable. In the US the term is
synonymous with loco shed or depot.
Round the benders (LTRS)
Additional automatic signals installed
on curves in tube tunnels after the
1953 Stratford (Central Line) accident,
ensuring that the driver always has a
signal in sight.
Roustabout (USRS)
A duty for loco crews which involves a
number of short trips.
Route bells
Electric bells in signal boxes on which
signalmen in adjacent boxes describe
the class and destination of an
approaching train by means of an
audible code. *See also* Train describer/
indicator.
Route indicator
1. A device on a signal at a junction

exhibiting a stencil letter or number code corresponding to the designation of the route to be taken by an approaching train.
2. Information displayed on the front of a loco or train which informs signalmen and others of its route, destination etc. *See also* Train describer/indicator.

Route miles
A measurement of rly mileage disregarding the number of parallel tracks, i.e. the geographical distance covered by the line or lines.

Route relay interlocking
Route control of electrically-interlocked points and signals by use of thumb switches.

Route-setting signalling
A system of power signalling which automatically sets the points and signals over a section of a route selected by a signalman, following movement of a single lever at a control panel.

Royal clerestory
A design in which the clerestory (qv) is sloped down to merge with the roofline at each end of the coach.

Royal Duchy
An express between London (Paddington) and Penzance, so named 1957, name dropped 1965. Revived 1987 with 4 h 46 min timing.

Royal Highlander
A sleeping car express between London (Euston) and Aberdeen/Inverness, introduced 1927. Later to and from Inverness only. Ceased 1939, name restored 1957. Has at various times enjoyed the dubious distinctions of being the most unpunctual train on BR and one of the longest trains in the UK.

Royal Road
Nickname for the L&SWR.

Royal Scot
An express between London (Euston) and Glasgow (Central)/ Edinburgh (Princes St.), introduced 1927 as name for a day train that had run since 1848. Name dropped 1939, restored 1948. Timing 7 h 30 min in 1936, 7h in 1938, reduced to 4 h 52 min with electric traction by 1989.

Royal trains
Trains made up of special stock, provided as required for journeys made by the Royal Family and their Household staff. Now financed directly from the Exchequer. Stringent safety and operating instructions apply to the working of these trains and the crews are specially selected experienced staff. However, in recent years, unlike some Ministers of the Crown, the Royal Family also travel in specially-reserved coaches attached to normal public services.

Royal Wessex
A service between London (Waterloo) and Swanage/Weymouth, so named 1951. Ceased 1967.

RP
Railway Pictorial, founded 1946, renamed *RP & Locomotive Review*, 1949, ceased publication in 1950, when it was incorporated in *Railways* (qv).

RPAC
Railway Passengers' Assurance Co., founded 1849. By payment of a nominal sum at the ticket office at the time of booking, a passenger could obtain a RPAC policy in the form of a ticket, providing accident cover relating to that particular journey, over and beyond any legal liability of the rly undertaking to pay compensation.

RPS
Railway Photographic Society, founded 1922.

RPSI
Railway Preservation Society of Ireland.

RR
1. *Railway Record*, founded 1844, merged with RN 1901.
2. (US) Abbreviation for railroad.
3. Redditch Rly, Barnt Green–Redditch, inc 1858, opened 1859, worked by Midland Rly, part of Midland Rly 1874.
4. Ramsey Rly, inc 1861, Holme to Ramsey, opened 1863, worked by GNR, part of GER, 1875, leased to GNR 1875, part of L&NER 1923.
5. Richmond Rly, from what is now Clapham Junc–Richmond, inc 1845, opened 1846, part of L&SWR 1846.
6. Rhodesia Rlys, formed 1899. Beira Rly, Mashonaland Rly & Rhodesian Rlys amalgamated as RR 1927, purchased by Rhodesia Government 1947. Lines north of Victoria Falls became Zambia Rlys, 1967. Renamed NRZ (qv) 1980.

RR roof
Railroad roof, the US term for clerestory (qv).

RRT
Railway Rates Tribunal. *See also* TT.

RSA
Railway Study Association; founded 1909 as the Railway Students' Association of the London School of Economics & Political Science (University of London), for the purpose of furthering the study of rly transport. Receives the official support of the BRB and LRT.

RSB
BR Second/Standard class Buffet coach.

RSC
Railway Signal Co. Ltd; formed 1880, works at Fazakerley, Liverpool.

Became part of Westinghouse Brake & Signal Co. after the Second World War, works closed 1974.

RSE
Railways South East, illustrated magazine devoted to historical and current rly matters in London and south-east England, first published 1987.

RSI
Rolling Stock Inspector.

RSL
1. Railway Sites Ltd, formed by the BTC in 1962 to exploit commercially all sites not wanted for rly purposes. *See also* BRPB.
2. Rolling Stock Library.

RSNT
Rail[way] Staff's National Tribunal.

RSO
BR Restaurant car, Second/Standard class, Open; no kitchen.

RSUASS
Railway Signalmen's United Aid Sick Society, founded 1865. Subsumed by UP&SS (qv).

RT
Railway Times, founded 1837, merged with RG (qv) 1914.

RTA (US)
Regional Transportation Authority.

RTC
Railway Technical Centre, BR, Derby.

RTD
Returned To Duty.

RTG (Fr)(obs)
Rame de Turbine à Gaz; the first type of *SNCF* gas turbine train.

RTO
Railway Transport Officer; a British Army officer (colonel, major or captain) specifically designated to supervise and organize the movement of troops, horses and military equipment by rail in conjunction with

rly officials, and to report these movements appropriately. RTOs wear the uniform of their regiment, but are distinguished by a white armband bearing these initials and worn on the left arm.

RTR

Ramsgate Tunnel Rly; an electric rly, 2 ft/609 mm gauge, from Dumpton Park to Ramsgate Harbour, mainly using the former LC&DR tunnel leading to Ramsgate Harbour station. Opened 1936, closed during the Second World War, reopened 1946, closed 1965.

RU

BR Restaurant car, Unclassified, open with kitchen.

RUB

BR Restaurant/Buffet car, Unclassified, with kitchen.

Rubber (USRS)

Recovery time (qv). *See also* Take the rubber out of them, to.

Rubberneck car (USRS)

An observation car (qv). From US (S) rubberneck = tourist.

Rubens

TEE Paris–Brussels, introduced 1974, lost *TEE* status 1984. Name used by an EC in 1987 Ostend–Frankfurt.

RUG

Railfreight Users' Group, formed 1990.

Rugby bedstead, The (RS)(obs)

An unusually large and elaborate signal gantry erected on the London side of Rugby station in 1895. All signal arms were repeated, the higher ones being intended for long distance sighting.

RUK

BR Restaurant car, Unclassed, with Kitchen.

Rule 55

If a train is held at a signal more than two minutes (three before 1950) after giving audible indication of its presence, this rule requires a member of the train crew to go to the signal box to remind the signalman of the presence of the train in his block section. Once there, he signs the train register book (qv) and does not leave until the signalman gives the train a clear signal or until he has seen lever collars (qv) placed in position to protect his train. The rule is usually waived where lines are track-circuited or there is some means of communicating with the signalman from the lineside. Nowadays, with modern signalling installations operated remotely from widely-dispersed signal control centres, large areas of track-circuiting, and virtually all signals equipped with telephones, the rule is a much less important factor in rail safety than formerly.

Rule G (US)

Forbids possession or consumption of alcohol or narcotics when on rly duty.

Rule One car (USRS)

A freight car running on the rly to which it belongs.

Ruling gradient

The steepest gradient of significant length on a given stretch of line, which determines the load a given loco can haul at a given speed over that route.

Rumney

Rumney Railroad or Tramroad; horse-drawn tramroad built for carriage of iron from the Rhymney Ironworks to Newport, inc 1825, opened 1836, reconstituted as a rly company 1861, purchased by B&MR (qv) 1863, opened as a rly 1865, 1866.

Run a board, to (USRS)

To ignore a signal, accidentally or deliberately. *See also* SPAD (qv).

Run & Shove Behind
Nickname for R&SBR.

Runaway
A train, loco or vehicles moving along a running line out of control.

Runaway points/siding
see Catch points.

Run-in (USRS)
A collision.

Runner
1. *see* Guard truck (qv).
2. (RS) A platform inspector.
3. (USRS) A loco driver.

Running gear
Wheels, axles, axleboxes, springs and vehicle frame.

Running light
Light engine (qv).

Running line
Tracks for through train movements as distinct from sidings, bays, docks and yards.

Running powers
A formal arrangement by which one or more 'foreign' companies could exercise a right to operate trains over the owning company's lines in return for a rental payment.

Running round [a train]
The process of releasing a loco from the front of a train at the completion of a journey and moving it to the other end of the train ready for the return run. Hence a run-round layout.

Running shed (obs)
A small depot to house the locos in daily use on a particular stretch of line, possessing only minimal maintenance and repair facilities.

Running signals
Signals protecting movements on running lines.

Runt (USRS)
A dwarf signal. From runt, meaning an undersized or inferior person.

Rust (USRS)
Rly tracks.

Rustle/rustle the bums, to (USRS)
To search along a train for hobos taking illicit free rides.

Rusty rail (USRS)
A rlyman with very long service.

RV&HJR
Rhondda Valley & Hirwain Junction Rly: inc 1867, a colliery line at Blaenrhondda, opened 1878 (never completed to Hirwain [now Hirwaun]). Leased by TVR, part of TVR 1889.

RVO
BR Restaurant car, unclassed, open, no kitchen.

RVR
Rother Valley Rly: *see* K&ESR.

RW
Railway World: *see* Railways; T&RW.

RYB
Railway Yearbook, first published 1898, now known as *Railway Directory & Year Book*.

S

S
1. Station.
2. (obs) BR Second/Standard class non-gangwayed compartment coach.

SACM (Fr)
Société Alsacienne de Constructions Mécaniques; Belfort and Graffenstaden. Manufacturers of locos etc.

Sacred ox (USRS)
A very powerful loco.

Saddlebacks (RS)
L&SWR 0–6–0ST of 1876–7.

Saddle tank
A tank loco with water tank curved over the top of the boiler in the manner of a saddle on a horse. In Whyte's notation, abbreviation ST follows wheel arrangement, e.g. 0–6–0ST.

SAFB
Société Anglo-Franco-Belge; loco carriage and wagon builders.

Safety points
Catch points (qv).

Saint David/Executive/Pullman
A HST between London (Paddington), Cardiff and Swansea, so named 1984. 'Executive' added 1986, 'Pullman' added 1989.

St Louis
St Louis Car Co., St Louis (US), inc 1887. Builders of rly, interurban and tramcars; the only US builders of the last two to survive the Second World War.

St Louis–San Francisco (US)
St Louis–San Francisco Rly System.

Saint Mungo
Express between Glasgow (Buchanan St.) and Aberdeen, introduced 1937, restored 1949.

Saint Paul (US)
1. A steam loco with 4–6–2 wheel arrangement. From an order by Chicago, Milwaukee & St Paul RR.
2. Chicago, Milwaukee & St Paul RR.

Saint Petersburg–Nice–Cannes Express
A *CIWL* service introduced 1899.

Sairseal
A Limerick–Dublin service, introduced 1969. Name dropped 1975.

SAL (US)
Seaboard Airline Rly Co.

Salmon
TC for civil engineer's 50-ton bogie flat wagon.

Salmon tins (LTRS)(obs)
1920 MDR all-steel cars.

Saloon
A coach (or section of coach) with all its seats in one open area. Also used for coaches adapted for special purposes (e.g. royal saloon, inspection saloon).

Salts, give the Old Girl a dose of, to (USRS)
Dust her out, to (qv).

SANAL
Société Anonyme de Navigation Angleterre–Lorraine-Alsace. A company which operated the cross-Channel service between Newhaven and Dieppe and in which BR formerly held a financial interest.

S&BR
Shrewsbury & Birmingham Rly, inc
1846, opened 1849, 1854 (section
between Wolverhampton and
Birmingham not built). Shrewsbury to
Wellington was joint GWR &
L&NWR /LM&SR, remainder part of
GWR from 1854.

S&C
Switches and Crossings.

S&CER
Swindon & Cheltenham Extension
Rly, inc 1881, opened 1883, 1891,
amalgamated with SM&AR as
M&SWJR 1884.

S&CLER
Southport & Cheshire Lines Extension
Rly, inc 1881, 1882, Aintree–
Birkdale–Southport, opened 1884,
worked by CLC, part of BR 1948.

S&CR
1. Shrewsbury & Chester Rly, inc
   1846. Main section opened 1848.
   Part of GWR from 1854.
2. Sutherland & Caithness Rly, inc
   1871, Thurso–Wick; Helmsdale–
   Georgemas Junction, opened 1874,
   part of HR (6) 1884.

S&DJR
1. Somerset & Dorset Joint Rly, Bath
   to Wimborne with branches from
   Evercreech Junction to Burnham-
   on-Sea and from Glastonbury to
   Wells. Formed 1862 by
   amalgamation of SCR and DCR;
   leased jointly by Midland Rly and
   L&SWR 1876, vested in LM&SR
   and SR 1923, to BR (S) 1948.
2. Salisbury & Dorset Junction
   Rly, inc 1861, Adderbury Junction
   to West Moors, opened 1866,
   worked by L&SWR, part of
   L&SWR 1883.

S&DR
Stockton & Darlington Rly, first
section opened 1825, part of NER

from 1863. First public rly to open
with steam locos.

Sand drag
A container of sand built up to cover
the rails, designed to slow and stop a
train derailed at catch points (qv) or
approaching buffer stops.

S&H Joint
Shrewsbury & Hereford Rly inc 1846,
opened 1852, 1853, leased to
L&NWR, GWR and WMR 1862,
jointly vested in GWR & L&NWR
from 1870, LM&SR & GWR from
1923, to BR (W) 1948.

Sand Hutton
see SHLR.

San Diegan
A diesel-electric streamline train set
running between Los Angeles and San
Diego, introduced 1938, schedule 2 h
30 min. Name revived by Amtrak over
same route.

Sandies (RS)
L&NER B17 4–6–0 locos;
abbreviation of the class name
(Sandringhams).

S&K Joint
Swinton & Knottingley Joint, Midland
Rly and NER from 1879, LM&SR &
L&NER from 1923.

S&K Line
Swinton–Moorthorpe–Knottingley
(Ferrybridge).

S&MJL
Sheffield & Midland Joint Lines
Committee, Hyde to New Mills; New
Mills–Hayfield, (opened 1865), inc
1869, MS&LR and Midland Rly,
GCR and Midland Rly, L&NER &
LM&SR from 1923–47.

S&MJR
Stratford-upon-Avon & Midland
Junction Rly, formed 1908, an
amalgamation of the E&WJR,
ER&SJR and Stratford-upon-Avon,
Towcester & Midland Junction Rly.

N&BJR purchased 1910. Part of LM&SR 1923.

S&MLR

Shropshire & Montgomershire Light Rly, Shrewsbury to Llanymynech and branch to Criggion. A refurbishment and reopening in 1911–12 of PS&NWR (qv). Passenger service ceased 1933, requisitioned by the Army 1941: some passenger services worked during and immediately after the Second World War. Under dual military and BR administration (BR ownership) from 1948, main section closed 1960.

S&MR

1. Stratford & Moreton Rly; Moreton-in-Marsh to Stratford-upon-Avon and Shipston-on-Stour, inc 1821, 1825, opened 1826, 1836 as 4 ft gauge horse tramroad. Leased to OW&WR 1845 and partly relaid 1853. Moreton–Shipston converted to conventional rly and worked by GWR with locos from 1889. Closed to passengers 1929, to freight 1960. Shipston–Stratford section finally lifted 1918, although the northern section was disused from some time before then.
2. Swansea & Mumbles Rly: *see* Mumbles.

S&SJR

Surrey & Sussex Junction Rly, inc 1865, Croydon–Oxted–Groombridge, part of LB&SCR 1869, construction started but works abandoned. Eventually built by LB&SCR and SER, jointly owned between Selsdon Road, Oxted and Crowhurst Junction, LB&SCR owned Crowhurst Junc–East Grinstead and Hurst Green Junction–Groombridge. The joint section was administered by the Croydon, Oxted and East Grinstead Railways Joint Committee, formed 1884. Opened

1884, 1888. Part of SR, 1923.

S&ST&LR

Schull & Skibbereen Tramway & Light Rly, 3 ft gauge, inc 1883 as West Carbery Tramways & Light Rlys Co. (S&S branch), opened 1886, name changed to S&ST&LR 1886, part of GSR 1925, closed April 1944, reopened December 1945, finally closed at end of 1946.

S&T

Signals & Telegraphs/Telecommunications [department/engineers].

S&WR

Shrewsbury & Welshpool Rly, inc 1856, opened 1862, purchased by L&NWR 1864, vested jointly in GWR and L&NWR (LM&SR from 1923) from 1865.

S&WR&C/S&W Joint Rly

Severn & Wye Rly and Canal, inc 1809 as Lydney and Lidbrook Rly; re-inc as S&WR&C, 1810, opened as 3 ft 8 in gauge horse-worked plateway 1813, converted to 7 ft gauge rly from 1868 (first section Wimberry–Lydney). Amalgamated with SBR 1879. Purchased jointly by Midland & GWR (S&W Joint Rly), 1894. LM&SR and GWR from 1923–47. Lydney to Parkend now a preserved line: *see* Dean Forest Rly.

Sandy

see Sandies.

San Francisco Overland Limited

All-Pullman 'hotel train' service between Chicago and San Francisco, including, in the 1920s, a library car, observation car, showers, ladies' dressing room and maid service, gentlemen's valet and barber service, a club car, lounge cars, dining and sleeping cars.

San Francisco Zephyr

Amtrak daily each way service

between Chicago and San Francisco (Oakland), 2,390 m in 48 h, with double-deck observation coaches, introduced 1971, renamed California Zephyr 1983.

San Marco
A summer weekend service Vienna–Venice, introduced 1963.

Santa Fe (US)
1. Atchison, Topeka & Santa Fe RR, later amalgamated with Gulf, Colorado & Santa Fe RR and the Panhandle & Santa Fe Rly Co. as Santa Fe Lines.
2. A steam loco with 2–10–2 wheel arrangement. The first one was used on the AT&SF RR.

Santa Fe Chief
AT&SFRR service Chicago–Los Angeles, introduced 1926. renamed Super Chief (qv), 1936.

SAP
1. BR (S) HAP (qv) emu downgraded to Second/Standard class status for suburban service in 1976. Second class And electro-Pneumatic brakes, 2-SAP.
2. (USRS) A brake club (qv).

Saphir
An express between Ostend, Brussels, Cologne and Dortmund, introduced 1954. *TEE* from 1957, extended to Frankfurt 1958. Brussel to Frankfurt from 1966. Lost *TEE* status 1979. IC 1979. Re-extended to Ostend 1981. Replaced by Memling (qv), 1987.

Sap up binders, to (USRS)
To set the handbrakes on a freight train. *See also* Binders; SAP (2).

SAR
1. South Australian Government Rlys. *See also* ANR.
2. St Andrews Rly, inc 1851, Milton Junction, Leuchars, to St Andrews opened 1852. Part of NBR 1877.

SAR&H
South African [Government] Railways & Harbours Administration. Formed 1910 from the Central South African Rlys [Transvaal and Orange Free State], Cape Government Rlys and Natal Government Rlys. Rlys in South West Africa included from 1922. 'Privatized' 1990. *See also* SATS and Transnet.

Sassnitz Express
A Stockholm–Berlin–Munich service. Stockholm–Berlin only from 1973.

SATS
South African Transport Services; the holding company for the SAR&H (qv), South African Airways etc., denationalized 1990 and operated by Transnet (qv).

Saut de mouton (Fr)
A flyover (literally 'sheep's leap').

Saxby & Farmer
Saxby & Farmer Ltd, manufacturers of signalling equipment at Kilburn, London from 1863. Acquired by Consolidated Signal Co. (qv) 1901–2. The name continued in use from the new owners' Chippenham Works.

Saw-by (USRS)
A shunting operation at a siding on single track to allow one train to pass another when the siding is too short to allow a single movement.

SBAFB
Société Belgo–Anglaise des Ferry Boats. Co. in which BR has a financial interest, which operates the train ferry port installation at Zeebrugge (Belgium) and owns rail ferry vans.

S-bahn (Ger)
Schnellbahn; stopping services along main line rly routes , serving a conurbation or suburban areas.

SB&CR
Surrey Border & Camberley Rly, 10¼ in/260.4 mm gauge passenger

line (originally called Farnborough Miniature Rly). Opened 1934, eventually extended from Farnborough Green (near Frimley SR) to Camberley. Closed 1939.

SBB
Schweizerische Bundesbahnen; Swiss Federal Rlys. *See also CFF*; *SFF*.

SBR
Severn Bridge Rly, inc 1872 to bridge the Severn Estuary at Sharpness, opened 1879, part of S&WJR 1879.

SC
A self-cleaning smokebox which blows most of the fire ash up through the chimney.

Scalpers (USRS)
Agencies selling rly tickets at less than regulation rates.

Scandinavian
A summer-season express between London (Liverpool St.) and Harwich (Parkeston Quay) in connection with sailings to Esbjerg and rail connections beyond. Originally named the Esbjerg Continental. Introduced 1930, restored 1945, name dropped 1975.

Scandinavian–Swiss Express
CIWL service Stockholm–Chur, introduced 1948, renamed Scandinavia–Italy Express, 1949, through cars Stockholm/Copenhagen–Rome, renamed *Schweiz Express*, 1960.

Scarborough Flier/Flyer
Summer-only express between London (Kings Cross), York and Scarborough, so named 1927, Whitby portion included from 1934, 3 h 55 min London to Scarborough in 1935. Restored 1950. Ceased 1963.

Scarf (RS)
A foreman – 'always on the necks of his men'.

SCD
Short-Circuiting Device.

SCETA
Société de Contrôle et d'Exploitation des Transports Auxiliares; an *SNCF* (qv) subsidiary responsible for various auxiliary activities.

Scharfenberg coupler
An auto-coupler with a central buffer, designed to permit complete simultaneous coupling and uncoupling of air pipe, mechanical and electrical connections and all connections from the driver's cab. A patented design of LHB (qv).

Schedule
A list of the passing and stopping times of a particular train on one journey. In the US, a timetable.

Scheme ticket (obs)
A system in which the ticket issued to the passenger covers travel to any one of a group of stations to which the same fare applies; a list of the furthest stations to which the ticket is valid is printed on the ticket. Adopted by the London Underground in 1911.

Schmalspurbahn (Ger)
A narrow gauge rly.

Schnellzug (Ger)
A fast train.

School, The (LTRS)
White City Railway Training Centre.

Schumann
A Luxembourg–Brussels service, introduced 1973.

Schwebebahn (Ger)
A rly in which the train is suspended from an overhead running rail, as at Wuppertal.

Scissor bill (USRS)
Yard brakeman.

Scissors crossover
Connections between two parallel tracks in both directions, the two connections crossing each other diagonally at their centres. In plan it

resembles an open pair of scissors, hence the name.

SCL (US)
Seaboard Coast Line RR Co.; a 1967 merger of SAL and ACL. P&N absorbed in 1969. L&N wholly owned from 1972.

Scoff (RS)
Food.

Scoop
1. (USRS) A fireman's shovel.
2. (obs) The means of taking up water into a loco tender from water troughs (qv).

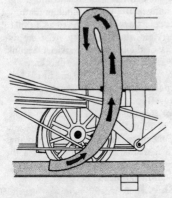

Scoot (USRS)
A shuttle (qv) working.

Scorpion
GWR TC for open truck used for carrying road carriages by passenger train (five types).

Scotch Arthurs (RS)
SR King Arthur 4–6–0 locos built by North British Locomotive Co. in 1925.

Scotch blocks
Wood blocks, fixed in frames and pivoted at one end, the other end when in use, projecting across a rail to prevent vehicles running down an incline, or on to another track. Sometimes worked from signal box and interlocked with signals. A substitute for catch points (qv).

Scotches
Triangular wooden blocks placed in front of wheels to stop movement when stabled. Also used in unmechanized yards to bring wagons to a stand by skidding.

Scotchmen (RS)
LC&DR 0–4–2T of 1866, named after Scottish rivers and islands; also LB&SCR B4 4–4–0s, made in Scotland by Sharp, Stewart.

Scotrail
BR brand name for Scottish Region services, introduced 1984. Became a division of Regional Rlys (qv) upon the dissolution of the Scottish Region in 1991.

Scottish Pullman
BR Pullman service Edinburgh/ Glasgow–London(Kings Cross), introduced 1991.

SCR
1. Somerset Central Rly, inc 1852, Highbridge–Glastonbury, opened 1854, 1858, 1859, 7 ft gauge, worked by B&ER. Part of S&DR 1862.
2. Scottish Central Rly, inc 1845, opened Perth–Castlecary 1848, part of CR (*1*) 1865.
3. South Central Rly [of India], formed 1966 from parts of CR (*6*) and SR (*6*).

Scrambled eggs (LTRS)
1. Gold braid on hats of senior uniformed staff; and the wearers.
2. Poached eggs (qv).

Screw coupling
see Coupling screw.

Screw down (LTRS)
To secure a train by applying handbrakes, especially when stabling (qv).

Screw jack
A device for lifting locos and rolling stock vertically (and often also moving them horizontally) in event of derailment. Usually carried on locos and in brake vans.

Scud (RS)
A travelling ticket inspector. From (S) scud = a fast mover.

SCV (obs)
Special Cattle Van.

SD&LUR
South Durham & Lancashire Union Rly, inc 1857, Spring Gardens Junc (West Auckland) to Tebay, first section opened 1861, part of S&DR 1862.

SD&TR
South Devon & Tavistock Rly, inc 1854, opened 1859, Plymouth–Tavistock, worked by SDR (*1*). Part of SDR (*1*) 1865.

SDR
1. South Devon Rly, Exeter to Plymouth, Newton Abbot to Torquay, inc 1844, 1846, first section opened 1846, Exeter to Teignmouth. Worked by GWR 1876, part of GWR from 1878.
2. South Devon Rly, name adopted 1990 for preserved rly on part of former GWR Totnes–Ashburton branch, formerly known as the Dart Valley Line (qv).
3. Sheffield District Rly, inc 1896, Treeton Junc–Tinsley–Brightside, opened 1900, 1903; worked by GCR, part of L&NER from 1923.
4. Snailbeach District Rly, Pontesbury–Snailbeach, gauge 2 ft

3¾ in/2 ft 4 in (704.8 mm/711.2 mm), inc 1873, opened 1877. After a period of closure reopened 1923. Finally closed 1963.

SDS
Signalling Display System. A panoramic display in a signal box showing the whole of the track layout controlled with all the trains occupying it. Equipped with buttons and switches for setting up routes, also train description apertures.

SDT
A Self-Discharging Train, carrying aggregates, solid fuels etc.

Seaboard
see SAL; SCL.

Sealink
Brand name, introduced 1970 for BR Shipping and International Services Division with its shipping services linking Britain with Ireland and continental Europe, including joint operations with French cross-Channel services, also BR harbours and the rly-operated lake steamer services. Sealink became an independent subsidiary company of BR in 1979 and in 1984, in conformance with the Conservative government's policy, was sold by BR for £66m to British Ferries Ltd, a wholly-owned subsidiary of Sea Containers. The non-shipping activities then became BR International while the French assets remained state-owned until the formation of *SNAT* (qv).

SE&CR
South Eastern & Chatham Rly. A managing committee formed by the SER (qv) and LC&DR (qv) 1899 to operate the rlys of both companies as a single entity. 637 route miles in 1914. Part of SR from 1923.

Seandun
Cork–Dublin service, introduced 1969, name dropped 1975.

Seapigs (RS)
LM&SR Fowler 2–6–4T; a reference to their ugliness.

Searchlight signal
A form of colour light signal with a single lamp and lens behind which a sliding spectacle plate with appropriately-coloured glasses moves to give the aspect.

Seashore (USRS)
Sand in a loco sand dome.

Season ticket
A ticket providing unlimited travel between two given points over a week, month, quarter, or a year and sold at a discount.

Seaspeed
Brand name given to BRH (qv) services from 1968. Became Hoverspeed after merger with Hoverlloyd Ltd in 1981. Sold off to the management in 1984.

Seat miles
A measure of capacity provided, the equivalent of one passenger seat moving over one mile.

Seat regulation
see Regulation [of passenger traffic] (qv).

Secondaire, chemin de fer (Fr)
A secondary rly (qv).

Secondary rly
Any rly not of major importance in the rly system of a country, whether or not built to main line standards.

Secondary sorting sidings (obs)
Additional sidings in a marshalling yard which were allocated to local distribution.

Secondary track (US)
A track on which train movements may be made without conforming to the timetable or train order (qv) and which is not controlled by signals.

Secondary yard (obs)
A yard which received traffic for second and subsequent marshalling into trains for other yards, fulfilling a staging function.

Second class
Originally the intermediate class between First and Third, provided on most rlys, beginning with the Liverpool & Manchester Rly on its opening in 1830. Abolished in Britain between 1875 and 1925 except on boat trains and the L&NER's former GNR and GER London suburban services. Withdrawn on London suburban services in 1938 ahead of electrification. This old Second class totally disappeared in Europe (except in Spain and Portugal) in 1956 with a general renaming of Third class as Second at that time (Spain converted 1965–73, Portugal in 1963). BR renamed its Third class as Second class in 1956 and this in turn became Standard class in 1987.

Second man
A qualified driver who travels in the cab with the driver of the fastest trains, assisting him in the observance of signalling and ready to act in an emergency.

Second mess room (LTRS)
A public house or bar room.

Sectionmen
Track maintenance workers.

Section 12 station (LTRS)
Any station below ground level. The reference is to Section 12 of the Fire Preventions Act, 1971, under which the Fire Precautions (Sub-Surface Rlys) Regulations, 1989 were made.

Sector table
A form of turntable not describing a full circle and used to give access to a part-roundhouse.

See Mum Immediately (LTRS)
SMI (qv) or a summons to see the SM (qv).

Seilbahn (Ger)
Any type of cable rly.
Seilschweibebahn (Ger)
A suspension or aerial cableway,
synonymous with *luftseilbahn*.

Sekon
Pseudonym of George Augustus Nokes
(1867–1948), rly author and journalist,
first editor of the RM (qv) (1897–
1910), editor of the R&TM (qv) (1910–
22) and pioneer of popular rly and
transport journalism.

Selby Diversion
A 14-mile double track, high speed
diversion of the ECML between
Temple Hirst, south of Selby, and
Colton, north of Ulleskelf, avoiding
Selby. Constructed to allow the NCB
to exploit coal seams under the old
line. Opened in October 1983.

Self-acting incline
An incline worked by ropes or cables,
on which the weight of descending
vehicles provides the power to haul up
others on adjoining track.

Self-trimming tender
A tender in which the coal slides down
towards the cab on a sloping surface,
maintaining an even level.

SELNEC
South-East Lancashire and North-East
Cheshire Passenger Transport
Authority/Executive. Became Greater
Manchester PTA/PTE in 1974.

SELTRAC
A moving block (qv) system developed
by Standard Electrik Lorenz AG (SEL).

Semaphore signal
An obsolescent form of signal,
normally operated mechanically by
wires from levers in a signalbox,
which gives an indication by the angle
of its arm or board to the vertical. At
night the position of the arm allows a
lamp on the post to shine through the
appropriately-coloured spectacle plate
(red, yellow or green). *See also* Lower
quadrant; Somersault; Upper
quadrant.

Semi/semi-automatic
A semi-automatic signal, i.e. one
normally worked by track circuits (qv)
but which can be controlled by a
signalman as necessary.

Semi-métro
see Pre-métro.

Semis (RS)
LM&SR Duchess class 4–6–2 locos
with streamlined casing removed or
built in non-streamlined form.

Sentinel
Alley & McLellan Ltd, marine engine
builders, produced steam road vehicles
at Glasgow from 1904, going on to
build a new works at Shrewsbury in
1915 and using the product name
Sentinel. This works became the
Sentinel Waggon Works (1920) Ltd,
also manufacturing locos and railcars.
Now part of Rolls Royce Ltd.

SEPTA (US)
Southern Pennsylvania Transportation
Authority, operating rail passenger
services in and around Philadelphia.

SER
1. South Eastern Rly, inc 1836, first
   section opened 1842, London
   Bridge to Tonbridge via L&CR.
   Expanded greatly through East
   Sussex and Kent, often in fierce
   competition with LC&DR. 430
   route miles by 1898. Working
   union with LC&DR 1899. *See also*
   SE&CR.
2. South Eastern Rly [of India],
   formed 1955 from part of ER (5).

Serene & Delightful
Nickname for S&DJR.

Serpent
GWR TC for goods truck designed to
carry furniture removal vans and other
large road vehicles.

Service
A rail service can be expressed either as a *frequency* (e.g. 5 t.p.h.) or as a *headway* (e.g. every 12 min).

Service application/rate
A gradual slowing of speed caused by use of air brakes throughout the train at a rate slower than an emergency application (qv).

Service slack
A reduction in speed permanently imposed on sharp curves, in congested areas, etc.

Service Time Book (obs)
Working timetable (qv).

Sesselbahn (Ger)
A chairlift.

Set, a (RS)
The crew of a loco – driver and fireman, or driver and second man (qv).

Set back, to
1. To reverse a train into a bay or side platform.
2. To reverse a train which has overshot a platform.
3. To make a shunting movement back towards the shunter.
4. To move a loco backwards on to a train. *See also* Back down, to.
5. To make the very short reversing movement necessary before a steam loco can move forward after stopping at dead centre (qv).

Set down, to
To unload passengers; thus a timetabled stop may be designated 'to set down only'.

Set number (LT)
The train running number.

Set of Huns (RS)
see Huns.

Settebello
A luxury emu service between Milan and Rome, introduced 1953 (5 h 55 min). Name adopted officially

1958. *TEE* 1974–84. Became Colosseum (qv).

Settle & Carlisle, The
Hellifield–Appleby–Carlisle.

Severn–Tyne
A service between Weston-super-Mare and Newcastle, introduced 1970, running that year only.

Severn Valley
Severn Valley Rly, Shrewsbury to Hartlebury, inc 1853, opened 1862, 1878. Leased to WMR 1860, part of GWR from 1870. Bridgnorth to Bewdley and Kidderminster reopened from 1970 onwards as a preserved line, using this name.

Sewer (LTRS)
LT Northern Line tube. Unloved by staff for its long section of tunnel running.

Sewer rat (RS)
A London Underground Rlys train driver.

SF
Santa Fe Lines: *see* AT&SF; Santa Fe (*1*).

SFF
Strade Ferrate Federali; the title of Swiss Federal Rlys in Italian-speaking area of Switzerland. *See also* CFF; SBB.

SGE
Siemens & General Electric Railway Signal Co. Ltd, with works at Wembley, Woolwich and Lewisham, London. Now part of GEC (qv).

SGR
Sudan Goverment Rlys.

SGRO
Saudi Government Railroad Organization.

Shack (USRS)
Brakeman, as in 'head shack', 'swing shack', 'rear shack'.

Shackle
1. The link of a chain coupling placed over the drawbar hook of the adjoining vehicle.

2. The link which connects signal wires to the chain of the signal box manual levers, or the crank at base of a semaphore signal post.

Shakespeare Express
A summer service between London (Paddington) and Stratford-upon-Avon, introduced 1928, ceased 1931.

Shakespeare Route,The
Brand name adopted by the S&MJR.

Shamrock
An express between London (Euston) and Liverpool (Lime St.), connecting with sailings to Belfast and Dublin, introduced 1954. Ceased 1966.

SH&DR
see WR (*1*).

Shanty
1. (RS) A staff mess room.
2. (USRS) A caboose (qv).

Shark
1. TC for civil engineer's ballast train brake van, usually fitted with a plough to level off tipped ballast.
2. (RS) A ticket inspector. From (S) shark = a swindler, a pilferer, a person who snaps up whatever comes up, like a shark.

Sharks (RS)(obs)
A link (qv) of men willing to take any kind of job that comes along. From (S) shark – *see* Shark (*2*).

Sharp
Sharp, Roberts, loco builders, Manchester, from 1833; became Sharp Brothers, 1843 and Sharp, Stewart, 1852. Moved works to Glasgow, 1888, taking over Clyde Locomotive Co. Ltd and becoming Sharp, Stewart & Co. Ltd. Amalgamated with Neilson (qv), and Dübs (qv) in 1903 to form North British (qv).

Sharpies (RS)
Locos built by Sharp (qv).

Shay
Steam loco with two or three sets of

wheels all driven by bevel-toothed gearing from a shaft along one side, powered by a vertical engine alongside the boiler. The shaft is in sections, jointed to allow each section to move independently.

She
In colloquial usage locos (especially steam locos) and trains, like ships, have traditionally been awarded the feminine gender, thus 'Here she comes', 'She's running late'. Also applies in the US, as in 'She'll be comin' round the mountain when she comes'.

Shed, to
To return a loco to its home depot or to denote mpd allocation of a loco (e.g. 'No. 3456 is shedded at X').

Shed bash (RS)
A visit (usually unofficial) to a loco depot for the purpose of noting/spotting/gricing/copping the numbers of the locos seen there, a process normally accomplished at great speed. Hence shedbasher.

Sheffield and Manchester Pullman
An all-Pullman train from London (Kings Cross) to Sheffield (2 h 57 min) and Manchester (Central) (4 h 7 min), introduced in summer 1925. It failed to attract traffic, and was diverted in September 1925 to become West Riding Pullman (qv).

Sheffield Pullman
An all-Pullman train between London (Kings Cross), Nottingham and Sheffield, introduced 1924 (3 h 15 min). It did not attract sufficient custom and became Sheffield & Manchester Pullman in 1925. Re-introduced 1958, running via Retford. Ceased 1968.

Sheppey
Sheppey Light Rly, Queenborough to Leysdown, LRO 1899, opened 1901,

worked by SE&CR, SR and BR (S), closed 1950.

Shin
Fishplates (qv).

Shiner (USRS)
A rlyman's lamp.

Shining time (USRS)
The departure time; time for use of the shiner (qv).

Shinkansen
Direct high speed standard gauge passenger rlys and trains of Japanese National Rlys. The first line (*Tokaido*) was opened between Osaka and Tokyo in 1964. Colloquially known in the west as 'Bullet trains' from their shape. Two types of service are provided; fast limited-stop trains (*Hikari* = Lightning) and fast stopping trains (*Kodama* = Echo).

Shirt button (RS)(obs)
The GWR logo/monogram introduced 1934 in which the company's initials were shaped to be enclosed in a circle.

SHLR
1. Sand Hutton Light Rly; opened 1910 as 15 in gauge miniature line in grounds of Sutton Hall near York, LRO 1920, converted to 18 in gauge light rly, serving estate farms etc. and providing a passenger service. Closed 1932.
2. Surrey Heights Light Rly; Orpington to Sanderstead, proposed 1925; widely publicized, but never built.

Shocvan
GWR TC for van fitted with shock-absorbing body.

Shoofly (USRS)
A temporary track around an obstruction.

Shooting galleries (RS)
NER Raven 4–6–2 locos. From the length of their boilers. Also known as skittle alleys for the same reason.

Shore (RS)
Any part of the rly other than a moving train. From naval usage.

Shore rlymen (RS)
Staff employed at stations etc., as distinct from those who work on trains. *See also* Shore.

Short flag, to (USRS)
To use flags or lamps at the rear of a stopped train in an endeavour to protect it but at a point which does not allow an approaching train on the same track an adequate distance in which to stop.

Shorting bar
A wood and metal tool used to cause a short circuit and so remove traction current from conductor rails in an emergency.

Short line (US)
A small rly undertaking, often one connecting a small town to a main line. Normally under 100 m long and handling only freight traffic.

Short of puff (RS)
A loco which is steaming badly.

Shorts (RS)(obs)
Wagons destined for local stations which were shunted out of freight trains at marshalling yards.

Short tail (USRS)
A rail worker who does not belong to a trade union (brotherhood).

Shoulder
Ballast heaped up against ends of sleepers to check lateral distortion of the track.

Showing the white feather (RS)
A steam loco emitting a wisp of steam from its safety valve.

Shrimp (RS)
A track tamping machine.

Shuffle, to (USRS)
To shunt.

Shunt ahead signal
A subsidiary signal fixed below the

signal controlling the entrance to a block section. When 'off' it authorizes a driver to proceed for shunting purposes only.

Shunting

1. The process of moving rolling stock from one line to another for the purpose of arranging vehicles in a certain order, or to place certain vehicles in a desired position in a train, or to place them at the point of discharge or loading. Hence shunter, shunting yard, shunting locomotive. Sometimes also called marshalling or sorting.
2. The withdrawal of a train from the main line into a siding or loop to allow another to overtake it.

Shunting neck/spur
see Headshunt (qv).

Shunting pole (obs)
A pole fitted a special hook which was used for manual coupling/uncoupling of loose-coupled vehicles from the lineside.

Shuttle/shuttle service
A service which simply operates between two points, usually not far apart.

SI (obs)
BR invalid saloon.

Siberia Express
A *CIWL* service between Moscow and Irkutsk, introduced 1899. *See also* Trans-Siberian Express.

Sick (RS)
Used of a wagon or coach in need of repair.

Sick and Tired (RS)
S&T Department.

Sick, Lame and Lazy (LTRS)
The paper work required for staff taking time off.

Side bay caboose (US)
A caboose (qv) with bay windows on each side instead of a cupola (qv), to allow observation of the train.

Side chains (obs)
Additional couplings formerly used between passenger vehicles to prevent severance should screw couplings fail; they were placed one on each side of the drawbar, between it and the buffers, and when connected, hung loose to allow for play on curves.

Side door Pullman (USRS)
A box car used by tramps (hobos) to steal free rides (qv).

Side lamps (obs)
Lamps placed on each side of a freight brake van when this was attached to an unfitted (loose-coupled) freight train.

Side swipe (LTRS)
A sideways-on collision.

Side tank
The conventional water tank arrangement for a tank loco, rectangular in shape and resting on the frames either side of the boiler.

Side track (US)
Any siding not used for passing trains on a single line.

Side winder

1. (RS) A diesel railcar or dmu set with starter button at side of body.
2. (USRS) A Shay (qv) loco.

Siding
Any track which is not a running line (qv), and on which vehicles may be loaded, unloaded, stabled, shunted or marshalled. In the US, a passing loop on a single line (any other siding in the US is a side track).

Siding traffic
Freight traffic which is normally loaded or unloaded by the customer's own staff and despatched from or received at private sidings (qv).

Siemens
Siemens Bros & Co., established at Woolwich in 1864, suppliers of electrical machinery, including

equipment for rlys and tramways (*3*). The electrical machinery side of the business was taken over by Siemens Bros Dynamo Works Ltd, operating from a new works at Stafford, in 1903. Acquired by DK (qv), 1918. *See also* SGE.

SIFA (Ger)
Sicherheits-Fahreinrichtung; a vigilance control system.

Sighting distance
The distance from which a signal is visible to the driver of an approaching train.

Signal warning boards
see Warning boards.

Silent death (RS)
An electric train. From its fast and comparatively noiseless approach to anyone on the tracks.

Silent partner (RS)
Second man (qv).

Silk hats (USRS)
Rly officers, senior officials.

Sillon (Fr)
A path (qv).

Silver Arrow
A combined road, rail and air service between London and Paris, cheaper than direct air flights, introduced 1956 via Lydd (Ferryfield) and le Touquet airports. In 1959 this facility was reorganized as London (Victoria)–Margate (rail), Manston airport–Le Touquet airport (air) and Etaples–Paris (rail), the complete journey taking about 6 h each way. The air journey was altered to Gatwick–Le Touquet in 1962. With a rail branch into the latter airport opened in 1963 and express *SNCF* railcars, the overall time was eventually reduced to 4 h. The introduction of hovercraft services and faster rail services in France resulted in the discontinuation of the service in 1981.

Silver bullets (LTRS)(obs)
Unpainted aluminium tube cars, especially when they were a new feature in the late 1950s and early 1960s.

Silver Fern
A day train between Auckland and Wellington, NZ.

Silver Jubilee
A supplementary fare express between London (Kings Cross), Darlington and Newcastle (4 h), introduced 1935 (the silver jubilee year of King George V). Britain's first streamlined train, it was given specially-designed 4–6–2 locos and articulated coaches. Ceased 1939. Name revived for a London (Kings Cross)–Edinburgh train 1977, discontinued 1978.

Silver Meteor
A Seaboard Coast Line streamlined diesel train between New York and Miami, introduced 1939 (25 h in 1940). Still operated as an Amtrak service.

Silver Princess
A prototype stainless steel coach produced by Budd; built in the US in 1947 and operated on BR. Scrapped in 1966.

Silver Standard
A BR InterCity package for full fare Standard Class passengers aimed at 'middle-management' businessmen and women, and introduced 1988.

SIMBIDS
Acronym for Simplified Bi-Directional Signalling, in which only selected locations, such as level crossings and crossovers, are signalled, to allow a limited train service while the other line of a double track is being repaired or renewed.

Simple engine
A loco in which the steam passes through the cylinders only once, in contrast to a compound (qv).

Simplon Express
A *CIWL* service between Paris and
Venice/Trieste, introduced 1906,
became Simplon–Orient Express (qv)
after the First World War. Name
revived 1962 for a Paris–Zagreb
service, altered to run Paris–Belgrade,
1969.

Simplon–Orient Express
A *CIWL* service introduced 1919,
Paris–Lausanne–Milan–Venice–
Zagreb–Belgrade–Sofia–Istanbul/
Athens. Through sleeping cars Calais–
Trieste–Istanbul and Paris–Bucharest–
Athens/Istanbul, giving a 76 h
London–Istanbul timing in 1927.
Paris–Cairo connection provided 1928
(Tripoli–Haifa covered by road
coaches). Revived 1949, Paris–Istanbul
only. Athens portion from 1951.
Renamed Simplon Express 1962 and
withdrawn east of Zagreb.

Single
A steam loco with one pair of driving
wheels, usually of large diameter.

Single driver
see Single.

Single iron (USRS)
Single track.

Single lead junction
A single track link between two
sections of double track or between
double track and a single line, to
reduce the complication and cost of
pointwork. Adopted by BR as an
economy measure from the 1960s.

Single line/track
One track, used for movements in
both directions. Crossing places or
loops are provided when such lines are
of more than two or three miles in
length and their spacing is related to
the frequency of the service.

Single line working
Movement of trains in either direction
over a single track. Controlled by one

of the following systems: (a) one
engine in steam (qv); (b) pilotman
(qv); (c) train staff/tablet and token
and ticket systems (qv); (d) tokenless
block (qv); (e) train order (qv); (f)
non-token lock and block instruments
(qv); (g) RETB (qv). *See also* Wrong
line working.

Single phase
A system of electrification using high
voltage alternating current (ac) at
industrial frequency (usually 50 Hz).
First satisfactorily used for rly traction
in Hungary in 1923. Since *c.* 1950
superseded by the use of industrial
frequency, 25 kV, 50 Hz ac, rectified
on the locos or emus for supply to
their direct current traction motors.

Single slip
A connection between two tracks when
one crosses the other at an angle.

Single stick (USRS)
A single camshaft on a diesel-electric
loco.

Siphons
1. GWR TC for milk/poultry/fish vans
   used in passenger trains (nine
   types).
2. (RS) BR diesel locos class 37.

SIR
1. Surrey Iron Rly, inc 1801, opened
   with horse traction 1803 from
   Wandsworth Basin to Croydon,
   closed 1846. *See also* CM&GR.
2. South Indian Rly, formed 1890,
   taken over by Government 1891.
   Part of SR (6), 1951.

Sirhowy
Sirhowy Rly, Sirhowy and Tredegar to
Nine Mile Point, inc as Sirhowy
Tramroad 1802, opened about 1805,
gauge 4 ft 2 in, name changed to
Sirhowy Rly 1860, converted to
standard gauge rly by 1863, opened to
passenger traffic 1865. Leased and
worked by L&NWR from 1876.

SISD (obs)
Shipping & International Services Division of BR, formed by merging the Continental Departments of BR (S) and BR (E). Became Sealink (qv).

Six Bells
Signalmen's block telegraph code for 'obstruction danger'.

Six-foot [way] (RS)
Space between any two adjacent parallel rly tracks, measured between the outsides of the adjacent rails, in fact usually about 6 ft 6 in/1,981 mm.

SJ
Svenska Statens Järnvägar; Swedish State Rlys.

SJR
Solway Junction Rly, inc 1864, 1867, Kirtlebridge–Annan–Bowness–Brayton (running powers over NBR Silloth line). Opened 1869, 1873. Vested in Caledonian Rly by acts of 1873 & 1895. Traffic over Solway viaduct ceased 1921. Part of LM&SR 1923.

SK
BR corridor Second/Standard class compartment coach.

Skateboard (LTRS)
A trolley (not rail-mounted) which is used for removing baskets of rubble from tube tunnels during maintenance work.

Skater (LTRS, rhyming S)
Escalator.

Skin (RS)
Driver's report form. *See also* Blister.

Skinheads (RS)
BR diesel locos class 31/0. From their appearance – the lack of indicator boxes resulting in a bare look.

Skipper (USRS)
A conductor (*3*). From (S) skipper = master, boss, captain.

Skittle Alleys (RS)
NER Raven Pacific locos. A reference

to the length of the boiler. Also known as shooting galleries for the same reason.

Skye line
Dingwall–Kyle of Lochalsh.

Skye Rly
Dingwall & Skye Rly, Dingwall–Kyle of Localsh, first section opened 1870, completed 1897. Part of HR (*6*) from 1880.

Skyliner (RS)(obs)
A steam loco in which the boiler fittings are enclosed in an aerodynamic casing.

Sky Rockets (USRS)
Red hot cinders ejected through a loco chimney.

Sky Train
Name of a monorail system opened in Vancouver 1986.

SL
1. *Storstockholms Lokaltraffik AB*; the Greater Stockholm Transport Co.
2. Thus written in Japanese text to denote a steam loco.

Slab track
Rails set into a concrete or asphalt base without sleepers or ballast.

Slack
A speed restriction.

Slacker
A device for damping down dust in coal wagons, using a water spray.

Slainte
A service between Dublin and Cork, so named 1960. Name dropped 1975.

SL&NCR
Sligo, Leitrim & Northern Counties Rly, (Ireland), Enniskillen to Collooney thence over M&GWR to Sligo Quay, inc 1875, opened 1879, 1880, 1881, 1882. Closed 1957, when it was the last privately-owned rly service in Ireland.

SLC
BR Sleeping Car First and Second/

Standard class, the latter with double berths.

SLE
BR Mark III sleeping car, either class.

Sleeper
1. A form of support placed between the rails and the ballast. Originally the rails rested on stone blocks and later longitudinal wooden sleepers were used. Transverse creosoted softwood sleepers then became general for many years but iron, steel, hardwood and concrete transverse sleepers have all been tried; the latter are now becoming general in Britain.
2. (RS) The second driver in the cab of a diesel or electric loco/train.
3. A berth in a sleeping car, a sleeping car, or a complete sleeping car train.

Sleeper track
A section of tramway (3), usually away from public roads, or on reservations at the side or in the centre of roads, in which rly type track is used. *See also* Private right of way/track; Reserved track.

Sleeping partner (RS)
Second man (qv).

Sleet car (LTRS)
Electric sleet loco (ESL).

SLEP
A BR convertible sleeping car, i.e. adaptable for either class, with single or double berth compartments. For Mark 3 stock this code was used to designate a SLE (qv) fitted with a pantry.

Slew, to (sometimes spelled slue)
To move track back to its correct alignment or a short distance from its original position.

SLF
BR Sleeping Car, First class, with single berth compartments.

Slim Jims (RS)
BR class 33 diesel electric locos built with narrow bodies for use on the formerly substandard loading gauge line between Tonbridge and Hastings.

Slim Lines (RS)
Slim Jims (qv).

Slip car (USRS)
A loaded banana van.

Slip coach (obs)
A coach capable of being detached from the rear of a moving train. Controlled by its special guard, it was 'slipped' to travel under its own momentum until braked at the platform of its destination station, thus eliminating the delay entailed in stopping the main train. Some expresses included up to three slip coaches. Slip coach operation in Britain ceased (at Bicester) in 1960. The reverse process defied the ingenuity of inventors.

Slipper boy (obs)
A youth employed to unhook horses from vehicles when these were used for shunting.

Slips
Short connections between two sets of rails crossing over one another. *See also* Double slips.

Slip working
The parking of an unpowered MGR (qv) train ready to be loaded at a later time.

SLM
Swiss Locomotive & Machine Works, Winterthur.

SLO
BR Second/Standard class open coach with centre gangway (3 + 2 seating) and lavatory in the centre.

SLOA
Steam Locomotive Operators' Association. An organization concerned with the operation of

preserved steam locos on BR and other lines.

Slotted post (obs)
A design of semaphore signal which had three aspects – arm at horizontal = danger; 45° downward = caution; arm dropped vertically and hidden inside the post = clear.

Slotted signals
Two signals on one post (home and distant or starter and distant) each worked by a signalman in separate, closely-spaced boxes. Mechanical or electrical slotting equipment prevents one signalman changing his signal to 'off' unless the other has withdrawn his slot, thus ensuring that a train does not move forward into the next block section until the signalman in charge of that section has allowed it to do so. Either signalman can put both signals to danger at any time.

Slough, in the (RS)
Derailed at catch points.

Slovakia
A service between Moscow and Vienna via Košice and Bratislava.

Slow & Dirty
Nickname for the S&DJR.

Slow, Dirty and Jerky
Nickname for the S&DJR.

Slow, Easy & Comfortable
Nickname for the SE&CR.

Slow, Mouldy and Jolting
Nickname for the S&MJR.

Slow order
A written instruction to drivers requiring a speed restriction to be observed at a particular location.

SLR
South Leicestershire Rly, Nuneaton and Hinckley, inc 1859 as N&HR, name changed to SLR 1860, opened 1862, worked by L&NWR. Vested in L&NWR 1867.

SLS
Stephenson Locomotive Society, formed 1909 as the Stephenson Society, a splinter group from RC (*1*) (qv) comprising those members whose interest lay mainly in steam locos. Renamed the SLS 1911. A pioneer in preservation, the SLS purchased the LB&SCR 0–4–2 *Gladstone* in 1927.

SLSTP
BR sleeping car, Second/Standard class, with pantry.

Slug (USRS)
A poor fire in a loco.

SLW
Single Line Working.

SM
Stationmaster, and more recently, Station Manager. Now obs on BR.

Smalls (obs)
Traffic conveyed at small consignments scale of charges, later combined with sundries (qv).

SM&AR
Swindon, Marlborough & Andover Rly, inc 1873, opened 1881, 1882, 1883, amalgamated with S&CER (qv) as M&SWJR (*2*) (qv), 1884.

Smash board (USRS)
A semaphore signal.

Smash 'em and turn 'em over
Nickname for the LC&DR.

SMI (LT)(obs)
Station Manager's Instructions – a duty in which the crew worked according to instructions issued by a SM.

SMJR
Scottish Midland Junction Rly, inc 1845, Perth to Forfar, opened 1848, merged with Aberdeen Rly to form SNER, 1856. *See also* S&MJR.

Smoke/Smoke agent (USRS)
A loco fireman.

Smokebox
The front section of a steam loco,

forming an extension of the boiler and containing the main steam pipes to the cylinders, the blastpipe and the chimney.

Smoke deflectors
Metal plates fixed either side of the smokebox or either side of the loco chimney to deflect the smoke upwards and prevent it from blowing down over the cab and restricting the engine crew's vision of the line ahead.

Smoke orders (USRS)(obs)
Running on a single line without train orders, relying only on visual indication of any opposing train (qv).

Smoker (USRS)
A steam loco; also the firebox.

Smokestack (US)
Term for loco chimney. 'The term locomotive chimney seems weak and effeminate to an American.' — *Railway Mechanical Engineer*, USA, 1938.

Smoking 'em (USRS)(obs)
Taking a chance, completing a run in less than the scheduled time. From smoking in (qv).

Smoking in (USRS)(obs)
Moving cautiously along a single line, without a train order, looking out for the smoke of any opposing train (qv).

SMR
1. Snaefell Mountain Rly: *see* MER.
2. South Manchuria Rly. Built by the Chinese Eastern Rly Co. in 1900–1 to connect the Chinese rly system with the Trans-Siberian Rly. Following the Russo-Japanese war, the rly was ceded by Russia to Japan in 1905. The Japanese converted it from 5 ft/1,524 mm gauge, first to 3 ft 6 in/1,067 mm and then to standard gauge, reopening it with the latter as the SMR in 1907.

SMT
Snowdon Mountain Tramroad/Rly, Llanberis to Snowdon summit, 2 ft 7½ in/800 mm gauge, Abt rack system, inc 1894, opened 1896.

Smudge/Smudger (RS)(obs)
A loco cleaner.

Snagger (RS)(obs)
An inspector of finished work in a main works.

Snake
1. GWR TC for passenger brake van (five types).
2. (LTRS) Insulated, ribbed multi-core cable. From its appearance.
3. (USRS) A shunter. From his movements when busy.

Snakehead (USRS)(obs)
A rail worked loose from the track, rising up to penetrate the floor of a wagon or coach.

Snap (RS)
Packed food, hence snap tin, to snap off (to take a break for a snack). From the snap fastening of box lid.

Snapper (RS)
1. A ticket collector.
2. An assisting loco.

SNAT
Société Nouvelle d'Armaments Trans-Manche. Formerly the French arm of Sealink (qv).

SNCB
Société Nationale des Chemins de Fer Belges; Belgian National Rlys, formed 1926. Also expressed in Flemish and abbreviated *NMBS*.

SNCF
Société Nationale des Chemins de Fer Français; French National Rlys, the nationalized system, formed 1938 from all main line rly undertakings, state and company-operated, existing at that time.

SNCV
Société Nationale des Chemins de Fer

Vicinaux; National Local Railways Company, formed 1885, grew into an extensive undertaking, operating light rlys and some tramways (*3*) throughout Belgium. The Flemish title was abbreviated *NMVB*. In 1991 it became *VVM* (qv) and *SRWT* (qv).

SNDM
Special Non-Driving Motor Car in an LT emu set (with guard's position).

SNER
Scottish North Eastern Rly, formed by amalgamation of Aberdeen Rly and SMJR (line Perth–Forfar–Aberdeen). Part of CR (1) from 1866.

Snifting valve (obs)
This device, mounted on the smokebox behind the chimney, admitted air to cool the superheater elements of a steam loco when the steam was shut off during running. Later designs of superheaters were able to stand intense heat and the sv was rendered superfluous.

Snip (RS)
A ticket collector.

Snipe (USRS)
A track worker.

Snip turn (LTRS)
An easy duty.

Snoozer (USRS)
A sleeping car.

Snowdonian
A summer service Rhyl/Llandudno to Llanberis (for Snowdon mountain), operated 1956–62. Name used for a London (Euston)–Pwllheli summer service introduced 1987.

Snow dozer (USRS)
Snow plough.

Snowflaker (USRS)
A newly-recruited worker.

Snow shed
A roofed structure (usually wooden) erected over tracks to prevent accumulation of snow on the line; normally sited on hill or mountain sides.

Snuff dipper (USRS)
A steam loco burning lignite. From its snuff-coloured stain.

SO
1. Saturdays Only.
2. BR Second/Standard class Open coach with centre gangway and 2 + 1 or 2 + 2 seating, no gangway connections.

Soap & towel (RS)
Bread and cheese.

SOCRATE
Système Offrant à la Clientele la Reservation d'Affaires et de Tourisme en Europe; a Europe-wide computer-based seat reservation, ticket sales, hotel booking and general information service introduced by the *SNCF* in 1992.

Soda jerker (USRS)
A loco fireman.

SOE
Simplon–Orient Express (qv).

Soft belly (USRS)
A wooden-framed wagon or coach. Easily damaged in an accident.

Soft class
On certain overseas rlys, notably those of Russia and China, this accommodation, with its fully-upholstered seats, is the superior class. *See also* Hard class.

Soft plug
A fusible plug in the crown sheet of a steam loco.

Sole bars
Longitudinal members of coach or wagon frame, formerly of wood, but nowadays of steel, to which are fixed the horn plates or axle guards.

Solent & Wessex
NSE brand name (1990) for the Hampshire and Dorset services.

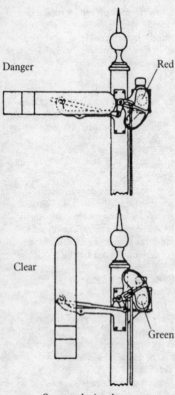

Somersault signal

Somersault signal
A form of semaphore signal with a balanced centrally-pivoted arm which is connected through a linkage to the light spectacle casing, which is also pivoted to the outside of the post. The arrangement eliminates the possibility of ice or snow falsely holding down the semaphore arm to give a spurious 'off' aspect. This problem was highlighted by the Abbots Ripton accident of 1876, which caused the GNR to adopt the somersault design, a few examples of which still survived on BR in 1991.

Soo Line
Minneapolis, St Paul and Sault Ste Marie Rly Co., a subsidiary of the CPR. From an approximation of the French pronunciation of Sault. From 1961 the Co. merged with the Duluth, South Shore & Atlantic RR and the Wisconsin Central RR to form the Soo Line RR Co. in which Canadian Pacific held 56 per cent of ownership.

Sorting carriage
Coach in which mail is sorted during the journey.

Sorting sidings
A group of sidings for the principal sorting of wagons and their assembly into trains, forming the major part of the main yard in a marshalling yard.

Sorting tender (obs)
The term for a sorting carriage (qv) until 1909.

Sorting yard
see Marshalling yard; Sorting sidings.

South American
A boat train between London (Waterloo) and Southampton Docks, connecting with Royal Mail Line sailings, introduced 1953. Ceased 1969.

Southbound
see Eastbound.

Solent Link
NSE brand name for the electric services introduced in 1990 between Portsmouth and Southampton and between Portsmouth and Eastleigh.

Sole plate
A component fixed on the sleeper under the rails at facing points to hold the rails to gauge. The point locking mechanism is fixed to it.

Solid car, a (USRS)
A fully-loaded wagon.

Solum
Scottish term for formation (*1*) (qv).

South Eastern, The
SER (2) (qv).

Southern Belle
A Pullman service between London
(Victoria) and Brighton, introduced
1908. Ceased 1916, re-introduced
1919. All-Pullman from 1921.
Renamed Brighton Belle (qv) 1934.

Southern Crescent
see Crescent Limited.

Southerner
An express between Christchurch
(NZ), Dunedin and Invercargill,
introduced 1970. 10 h in 1989.

Southern Pacific (US)
A steam loco with 4–10–2 wheel
arrangement, The first one was
supplied to that rly.

South Hams
South Hams Light Rly, Yealmpton to
Newton Ferrers and Noss Mayo;
construction begun 1906, never
completed,

South London Line
London (Victoria), Clapham, Peckham
Rye and London Bridge. First section
of the LB&SCR to be electrified,
known as 'The South London
Elevated Electric' on its introduction
in 1909 and for some years afterwards.
See also Atlantic Line.

South London Link
Brand name for South London Line
(qv) from 1991.

Southpaw, The (US)
Nickname for the Chicago & Northwestern RR, the only rly in the US to
adopt left-hand running (southpaw is
US (S) for a left-handed person).

South Staffordshire Line
see SSR.

South Tynedale
South Tynedale Rly, a 2 ft/609 mm
gauge tourist line on part of the
former BR Alston branch, first section
reopened 1984.

South Wales & Bristol Direct
Wootton Bassett–Patchway, opened by
GWR 1903.

South Wales Pullman
Service between London (Paddington)
and Swansea, introduced 1955; dmu
'Blue Pullman' sets used from 1961,
ceased 1973.

South Western Lines
NSE brand name for former L&SWR
suburban area services.

Southwold
Southwold Rly, 3 ft/914 mm gauge,
Halesworth GER to Southwold, inc
1876, opened 1879, closed 1929.

South Yorkshireman
An express between London
(Marylebone) and Bradford
(Exchange) introduced 1948. Ceased
1960.

South Yorkshire Supertram
Light rail transit scheme for Sheffield
area, opened from 1993.

Sou'West (RS)
The G&SWR (and that company's
lines from 1923).

Soviet (US)
A steam loco with 4–14–4 wheel
arrangement.

SP
1. Signalmen's code for 'urgent and
   important'.
2. (US) Southern Pacific RR, now SP
   Lines. Absorbed D&RGW from
   1988.

Space ships (RS)
BR standard 9F 2–10–0 steam locos.

SPAD
Signal(s) Passed At Danger.

Spam cans (RS)
SR Bulleid Pacific locos, Merchant
Navy, West Country and Battle of
Britain classes. From their streamlined
outer casing.

Spar (USRS)(obs)
A shunting pole.

Spark/sparker/sparkler (RS)
An emu (qv).

Sparks (USRS)(obs)
A rly telegrapher.

Sparks effect
The additional traffic, not abstracted from other services, or arising from any other identifiable cause, which usually follows the electrification of a rly. A term coined by BR in the 1960s.

Spa Valley Line
A preserved rly based on the former BR Tunbridge Wells (West)–Groombridge–Eridge line. Opened 1992. *See also* TWERPS.

Special duties (LTRS)
Unofficial evasion of work.

Special stop order
A written instruction (usually authorized by Control) to the driver of a train to stop at one or more stations at which his train is not scheduled to call, e.g. when other trains have been cancelled or service has been temporarily interrupted.

Special train
A train hired, often at short notice, for the convenience of one individual or a private party.

Special work
Points and crossings.

Spectacle plate
The motion plate beneath the boiler of a steam loco through which the connecting rods pass. Also the weatherboard, i.e. the front of the loco cab, containing the spectacle windows through which the enginemen may view the line ahead. Purists accept only the first of these definitions.

Spectacles
The frame on a semaphore signal which moves in front of the lamp. It contains the coloured glasses which give the signal indications at night.

Speed boards
Lineside indicators showing the maximum speed which may be used on the section ahead.

Speeder (USRS)
A light motorized inspection trolley used by track workers.

Speedfreight (obs)
1. BR overnight express freight service carrying 10-ton containers between London and Manchester, introduced 1963. The prototype Freightliner (qv) working.
2. A wagon load freight service (registered wagon system), introduced by BR (M) 1969–70.

Speedlink
A BR term for its air-braked wagon-load freight network combined with TOPS (qv) computer control, introduced 1977, merged with Freightliner (qv) as Railfreight Distribution (qv), 1988. Speedlink services were generally withdrawn by BR in 1991.

Speed whiskers (RS)(obs)
Painted curved lines on the front of early BR dmus.

Speedy (USRS)(obs)
A call boy (qv).

Speller Amendment [Legislation]
A 1981 amendment to the 1962 Transport Act (moved by an MP called Speller) which allows BR to reopen a line experimentally for passenger traffic without the burden of going through the statutory closure procedures should it prove a failure.

Spen Valley Line
Huddersfield–Bradley–Gomersal–Farnley–Leeds.

Sperry car
A track recording railcar manufactured by Sperry Rail Service Inc, USA.

Speyside Line
Craigellachie–Boat of Garten.

Spider (RS)

1. Signal apparatus between the rails.
2. The metal component, reminiscent of the shape of a spider which slides between the two steel horizontals of the crosshead of a steam loco motion.

Spike

The heavy nail of square section which holds a flat-bottomed rail to a sleeper. Screw spikes with threads are also used, and, in recent years, patented clips (e.g. the Pandrol (qv) clip).

Spill (USRS)

A station.

Spinners (RS)

Midland Rly Johnson 4–2–2 locos. From a propensity to suffer from wheel slip.

Spirit of Capricorn

An electric (ICE = Inter-City Electric) service between Brisbane and Rockhampton, introduced 1989, with speeds up to 75 m.p.h. on 3 ft 6 in gauge.

Spiv days/spiv turn (RS)

Rest days. From (S) spiv = a person who does not like hard work but lives by craftiness.

Spiv link (RS)

Rest day relief drivers' link. *See also* Spiv days/spiv turn.

Splash, to give it/her a (LTRS)

To apply the air brake.

Splice bar (US)

Term for fishplates (qv).

Splits/Split turns

A very unpopular arrangement in which duties are broken into two sessions, separated by two or more hours, e.g. 5 h in morning and 3 h in the evening.

Splitting distants

Normally only one distant signal is provided in the rear of a junction, worked only for the direct route, but

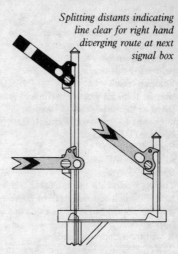

Splitting distants indicating line clear for right hand diverging route at next signal box

in some cases where the speeds are the same on more than one route, distants are arranged in bracket form to correspond with junction stop signals. They are then called splitting distants.

Spoornet

Brand name for South African Rlys, introduced 1990. *See also* Transnet.

SPORTIS

A portable version of APTIS (qv), developed from PORTIS (qv).

Sports Centre (LTRS)

Signal Engineer's Report Centre.

Spot, to

1. (US) To shunt; to place a wagon in its designated position.
2. (RS) To see a specific loco/traction unit/vehicle for the very first time. *See also* Train spotter.

Spotter

1. (RS) *see* Train spotter (qv).
2. (USRS) A company checker or inspector.

Sprag (RS)(obs)

A freight train guard. From sprags (qv).

Sprags (obs)
Pieces of wood placed between the spokes of wagons to prevent or slow down movement; also the men who performed this operation.

Sprague trains (obs)
Generic term for electric multiple unit trains in the early years of their use, after their US inventor, Frank Julian Sprague (1857–1934).

Sprat & Winkle
see Crab and Winkle (qv).

Spring
The place at which the moveable and tapered switch or tongue rail of points ends up against the stock or side rail.

Springbok
A boat train between London (Waterloo) and Southampton Docks in connection with Union Castle Line sailings to South Africa. Introduced as Union Castle Express 1953, renamed 1957. Name dropped *c*. 1971.

Spring points
Unworked trailing points which return to the normal position under spring load after the passage of a train.

Sprinters
1. NS two-car emu type SGM of 1974–7, With high acceleration, capable of making many intermediate stops without delaying long distance trains.
2. BR diesel railcars, classes 150, 151, 152, 154, 155, 156 and 158.

SPT
A Signal Post Telephone.

Spudler (RS)
A person who causes trouble indirectly.

Spur
Very short section of line branching off another, hence shunting spur.

Sputnik (LTRS)(obs)
An all-motor car (and therefore fast-running) six-car COP stock train.

Named after the first man-made satellite, launched by the USSR in 1957.

Square wheels (RS)
Wheels worn unevenly, i.e. with 'flats'.

Squeezer (USRS)
A wagon retarder. From its action.

Squirrel, to (USRS)
To climb up a wagon.

Squirter (RS)
An injector on a steam loco.

SR
1. Southern Rly, formed 1923, a grouping of the L&SWR, LB&SCR, and the SE&CR. Part of BR from 1948.
2. Stourbridge Rly, inc 1860, 1861, first section, Stourbridge–Cradley Heath opened 1863, amalgamated with GWR 1872.
3. Stratford-upon-Avon Rly, inc 1857, Hatton to Stratford-upon-Avon opened 1860. Part of GWR 1883.
4. Strathspey Rly, Dufftown to Craigellachie, inc 1861, opened 1863, part of GNofSR 1866.
5. (US) Southern Rly System.
6. Southern Rly [of India], formed 1951
7. Sudan Rlys.
See also Southwold; Stocksbridge.

SRPS
Scottish Railway Preservation Society, founded 1961.

SRT
State Rlys of Thailand.

SRWT
Société Regionale Wallonne du Transport; Wallonne Regional Transport Co., the Wallonne section of the former *SNCV* (qv), independently managed from 1991. *See also* VVM.

SSI
Solid State Interlocking, in which

signalling and points interlocking is carried out centrally by one or more micro computer interlockings, their number depending on the size and complexity of the control area.

SSM&WCR
South Shields, Marsden & Whitburn Colliery Rly, opened by Whitburn Colliery Co. 1879, passenger service from 1888. Operated by Harton Coal Co. from 1891, vested in National Coal Board 1947, passenger service ceased 1953, closed 1968.

SSR
South Staffordshire Rly, Wichnor Junction (with Birmingham & Derby Rly, later Midland Rly) to Lichfield, Walsall and Dudley, inc 1846, opened 1847, 1849, 1850, 1854, worked by L&NWR from 1852, leased by L&NWR 1861, vested in L&NWR 1867.

ST
Saddle Tank (qv).

Stab (USRS)
A delay faced by a train.

Stable, to
To put a train away in its shed, depot, sidings etc. after work.

Stack music (USRS)
The sound of a steam loco working full out.

Stack of rust (USRS)(obs)
A steam loco in an advanced state of neglect.

Stadtbahn (Ger)
City rly; usually operated as an independent entity by a local transport undertaking and normally of conventional underground/ elevated/ surface rly type as distinct from light rapid transit. The Vienna *Stadtbahn* is, however, a unique hybrid of an underground rly and an electric tramway (*3*). Not to be confused with *S-bahn* (qv).

Staff
see Train staff/tablet/token and ticket.

Staff of ignorance (USRS)(obs)
A brake club (qv).

Staggered platforms
A station arrangement in which the side platforms serving the 'Up' and 'Down' lines are not placed opposite one another but with one end of one somewhat set apart from the opposite end of the other, thus virtually doubling the length of the station site. Its adoption often reflects site considerations: the physical difficulty (and therefore extra expense) of building platforms to the conventional plan; the position of sidings and level crossings; or the site of the passenger exit. Also, by placing the platforms either side of a road crossing on the level, obstruction to road traffic could be minimized. Some nineteenth-century engineers apparently considered staggering would save the cost of footbridges and subways since passengers could cross on the level in relative safety, using the clear space which could always be maintained between the ends of two trains standing at the staggered 'Up' and 'Down' platforms. This argument, however, is flawed, since it overlooks the possibility of a train passing through the station in the opposite direction without stopping while passengers are still moving between a train and the exit.

Stainmore Line, The
Darlington–Barnard Castle–Kirkby Stephen–Tebay/Penrith, passing over Stainmore summit.

Stairway to the stars (RS)
The ladder up a signal post.

Stake (USRS)(obs)
A pole attached to a wagon in front of a loco and used for shunting.

Stake driver (USRS)
A surveyor or civil engineer's employee.

Stall (USRS)
A compartment in a van.

Standard class
Former BR Second class (qv), so renamed 1987.

Standard gauge
The most widely-used rail gauge, 4 ft 8½ in/1,435 mm. In Britain, the choice was determined by a Royal Commission in 1845–6.

Standedge Line, The
Leeds–Manchester via Huddersfield and Stalybridge, through Standedge Tunnel.

ST&MJR
Stratford-upon-Avon, Towcester & Midland Junction Rly, Towcester to Ravenstone Wood Junc and spur to L&NWR at Roade, inc 1879, opened 1891. Part of S&MJR 1909.

Standseilbahn (Ger)
A funicular rly.

Stanhopes (obs)
Box-like open wagons, often without seats, provided for the lowest class of passenger traffic in the early days of rlys. Rather unfairly they took the name from the light open road vehicles called after the Hon. and Revd Fitzroy Stanhope (1787–1854), for whom these were first made.

Stanier Black
see Black Stanier.

Stanislas
TEE Paris–Nancy–Strasbourg (3 h 47 min), introduced 1971. Lost *TEE* status 1982.

Stargazer (USRS)
A brakeman failing to attend to his duties.

Star guard (LTRS)
Guard-motorman, i.e. one trained to perform both guard's and driver's jobs.

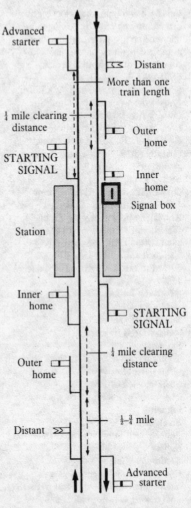

Starting signal

Starlight Specials
Very cheap-fare summer weekend night services between London (St Pancras) and Glasgow (St Enoch) and between London (Marylebone) and Edinburgh (Waverley), introduced 1953 to counter road coach competition. Ceased in 1962.

Star of Egypt Express
CIWL sleeping car service between Cairo, Luxor and Aswan, introduced 1929.

Starter
Starting signal (qv).

Starting Signal
A stop signal (qv) placed in advance of a signal box and the home signal, usually at the front end of a station platform, controlling the entrance to a block section. On the LM&SR and BR (M) known as Home no.3. *See also* Advanced starter.

Starved/ing lion (RS)(obs)
A facetious term for the BR emblem adopted in 1949.

State room (obs)
A segregated section of a US Pullman sleeping car, usually with three berths and lavatory en suite, affording privacy and obtainable by payment of a supplementary fare.

Statesman
A boat train between London (Waterloo) and Southampton Docks in connection with sailings of SS *United States*, introduced 1952. Ceased 1969.

Station limits
Section between the outermost stop signal (qv) of one box and the last stop signal under control of the same box, containing a station. Within these limits, the signalman is able to make some train movements without referring to the adjacent boxes and there can be more than one train within them if the appropriate signals

exist. Where an intermediate block signal is controlled from the box, station limits cease at the last stop signal in the rear of the intermediate stop signal; the space in advance from that point to that signal is known as the intermediate block section. Where power boxes (qv) exist, station limits are defined as being the section of line between two specified stop signals.

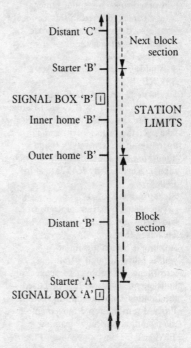

Station traffic (obs)
Traffic conveyed by rail to and from stations without collection and delivery by rly road vehicles at each end.

Station trucks (obs)
1. Two-wheeled hand barrows for goods, or four-wheeled trucks for

passengers' luggage and large items. Now generally superseded by BRUTES (qv).

2. On the GWR, a 'station truck' was a rly wagon carrying small quantities of freight, usually over branch lines, picking up and delivering at each station as required, when there was insufficient traffic for a wagon to be worked to each station. Other companies referred to this variously as a road box, road truck, road van, or road wagon.

Statutes, railway
see Railway Acts; Transport Acts.

STCRP
Société des Transports en Commun de la Région Parisienne; Paris Region Public Transport Company, formed 1921 to take over the management and operation of all tramways (*3*) and motorbuses in and around the French capital. Replaced by *RATP* (qv) in 1948.

Steam Banana (obs)
A van heated by steam pipes to ripen bananas while in transit.

Steaming (S)
A crime in which a gang of youths move through a train, terrorizing and robbing passengers at knife-point. This was first practised on the London Underground in the 1960s. From the rapid movement of the operation (cf. 'in a steaming hurry').

Steam keys
Shut-off valves for the main steam manifold of a loco.

Steam Navvy (obs)
A steam-powered digger or steam shovel, invented in the US *c*. 1840 but not adopted in Britain for rly construction until *c*. 1880. *See also* American devils.

Steam pig (RS)(obs)
A person or thing which cannot be easily identified or defined.

Steamroller (LTRS)
Line Controller (rhyming S).

Steam rollers (RS)
L&SWR Adams small-wheeled 4-4-0 locos of 1879. From their solid-wheeled bogies.

Steamtown
Steamtown Rly centre; a depot and maintenance centre for preserved steam locos based on former BR mpd at Carnforth, Lancs, established 1969.

Steel gang (USRS)
A rail-laying gang.

Steeple cab
A centrally-placed cab, enabling a loco to be driven without difficulty in either direction without reversal.

Steiermark Express
A service between Ostend, Graz and Rijeka, introduced 1955. Replaced by Dalmatia Express (qv).

Stem (USRS)
A rly right of way, trackage.

Stem winder (USRS)
1. Car fitted with nothing but a screw-down handbrake.
2. Climax geared loco.

Stendhal
A Paris–Turin–Milan sleeping car service, introduced 1983.

Stephensons
Robert Stephenson & Co. Ltd, loco builders, founded in Newcastle 1823, works transferred to Darlington, 1902. Merged with Hawthorn, Leslie to form Robert Stephenson & Hawthorns Ltd, 1937. Part of EE (qv) from 1955.

Stephenson valve gear
A form of steam loco valve gear or link motion with two eccentrics for each valve fitted to the crank axle to give a reciprocating motion through eccentric rods to a slotted expansion link.

Stepping up/back (LTRS)

Obtaining quick turnrounds at termini in peak hours by requiring the driver and guard of an arriving train to 'drop back' and take over the next arriving train, assuming the correct positions on the platform ready to take up their posts as soon as it arrives, instead of 'changing ends' on the same train.

Step-plate junction

A trumpet or cone-shaped junction of two tube (qv) lines made by using circular linings of increasingly larger diameters from the normal running tunnel size to one large enough to accommodate two tracks.

Stevens

Stevens & Sons, Southwark, London, manufacturers of signalling equipment from the 1840s until *c.* 1901.

Stick

1. (RS) A signal.
2. (USRS) A train staff (qv).

Stick to stick running (RS)

Stopping at all signals.

Stick trouble (RS)

Defective working of signals.

Sticky door (RS)

Air doors not closing properly.

Stinger (USRS)

A brakeman.

Stink bombs (RS)(obs)

Capsules placed in the hollow crank pin of the middle big ends of certain L&NER locos, designed to evaporate when the bearing was running hot, releasing a strong smell to warn the enginemen to take appropriate action.

Stink buggy (USRS) (obs)

Rlymen's contemptuous term for a motor bus or coach. Also used of petrol- or diesel-powered railcars.

Stinker

1. (RS)(obs) A wagon much delayed, and held in a yard. From the smell of decaying perishables therein.

2. (USRS) A hot box (qv).

Stock car (US)

Cattle wagon.

Stockholder (USRS)

1. A rly employee who is always overly conscientious, always concerned to work for the company's interests.
2. Anyone riding on a free pass or at reduced rates.

Stock pen (USRS)

A yard office.

Stock rails

The lengths of running rail against which point blades bear.

Stocksbridge

Stocksbridge Rly, inc 1874, opened 1876, remained independent until closed in 1988.

Stock train (US)

Term for a train composed entirely of cattle wagons.

Stoker (obs)

A steam loco fireman.

Stood down (RS)

Suspended from duty.

Stoot/stute (RS)

Institute (qv).

Stop and proceed [rule] (LT)

Rule G 7 enables a driver to pass a defective automatic signal at danger after re-setting a tripcock arm which has been knocked off by the related train stop. The train may then be moved very slowly, with its driver ready to stop at any obstruction, not resuming normal speed until a clear signal is reached. *See also* Apply the rule, to.

Stop order

see Special stop order.

Stopper puller (USRS)

A brakeman or shunter.

Stopping the job (LTRS)

Interrupting the train service. *See also* Job.

Stop signal
Any type of signal capable of displaying danger ('on') and clear ('off') indications, and which must not be passed when 'on'.

Stores train (obs)
A train running regularly over a rly system, distributing requisitioned stores of all kinds to stations, signal boxes, yards etc.

Storno (LTRS)
Driver to controller telephones. From the name of the suppliers, Storno Ltd.

S to S (obs)
Station to Station rate of charge for freight (coal, bricks and other low class traffic) or parcels brought in by the sender and collected by the consignee.

Stour Valley
Birmingham (New St.)–Dudley Port–Wolverhampton (HL)–Bushbury; orginally promoted in 1846 by the Birmingham, Wolverhampton & Stour Valley Rly.

Stove piping (USRS)
Shop talk among rly workers.

Strapontin (Fr)
A tip-up seat, usually located in the vestibule area of rly car and available if not too many passengers are standing.

Strappers (obs)
Rly employees whose duty it was to strap luggage on to the roofs of passenger coaches.

Strap rails (obs)
Wooden rails with iron strips laid on top to reduce wear.

Strassenbahn (Ger)
Tramway (*3*).

Strata-Domes (US)
Vistadomes (qv) equipped with powerful searchlights to sweep the night scenery, introduced in 1952 by the Baltimore & Ohio RR.

Strathearn Express
Service between Glasgow and Crieff, introduced 1911.

Strathspey Railway
Preserved rly on former BR line between Aviemore and Boat of Garten, on the former BR Aviemore–Forres line. First section opened 1978.

Strawberry patch (USRS)
The rear end of a train, with red lights shining in the night, also a yard at night with many red signal lamps visible.

Straw boss (USRS)
Foreman of a track gang.

Straw hat (USRS)
A rlyman not inclined to work in extreme climatic conditions.

Streaker (RS)
A fast train.

Streak of rust (USRS)
Rly tracks.

Streaks (RS)(obs)
Streamlined locos, mainly the LM&SR and L&NER 4–6–2s.

Streetcar/street car (US)
Tramcar (qv).

Street railway (US)
Tramway (*3*) (qv).

Stretch 'em out, to (USRS)
To take out the slack in the drawbars and couplings of a train.

Stretcher
The bar which connects the two tongue rails or switch blades of points and holds them in the required position in relation to the stock rail and the track gauge.

String (USRS)
A cut (qv) of wagons or cars.

Stripping the road
Removal of old track and ballast in preparation for relaying.

Strip tickets (obs)
Tickets covering up to six or more journeys, issued at a single transaction, often at a discount.

Strong arm (USRS)(obs)
A steam loco not equipped with mechanical stoker.

Stub
Any short dead-end siding or line.

Stub switch
Points without tongue rails (blades) which secure the change in direction simply by lateral movement of the running rails. Used in early rly practice and still to be seen on portable rlys.

SU
BR (S) Single [electric, motor brake] Unit.

SUB
SR and BR (S) SUBurban emu sets of 1941, 1944, 1945, and 1946–51. Early examples were compartment stock, but in subsequent production open saloon design predominated, 3-SUB, 4-SUB. *See also* Queen of Shebas.

Sub (RS)
A substation (qv).

Sub, The
South Suburban Loop Line, Edinburgh.

Subscriber's ticket (obs)
Season ticket (qv).

Substation
A building containing the machinery (originally rotary converters but later rectifiers and transformers) which converts the industrial electricity supply to low voltage direct current for traction purposes.

Subsurface lines
see Surface lines.

Subway (US)
Any type of urban underground rly, apparently picked up from the use of this term in the early (1868–87) legislation for London tube rlys (*see* Tube (*1*)) which, for convenience, was sometimes vague as to what would be put in the 'subway' after it was built.

In Britain, this rather specialized application of the word had ceased by the end of the nineteenth century.

Sud Express
CIWL service Calais/Paris, Bordeaux, Biarritz, Irun and Madrid and Lisbon, introduced 1887 (with a change of trains at Irun owing to gauge difference). Daily from 1900. Revived after the First World War, all-Pullman from 1926. Ceased 1939. Revived 1946 as Paris–Lisbon/Madrid, but no longer all-Pullman. Pullman cars withdrawn 1971. Madrid portion withdrawn, 1973.

Sugar (USRS)
Sand.

Suicide pits
Pits placed between the running rails for the full length of the platforms at London tube tunnel stations to frustrate suicide attempts and afford some measure of protection from serious injury to anyone falling on to the track. Installed from the 1930s onwards following the extreme difficulty encountered in extricating from beneath trains the bodies of those committing or attempting suicide at such stations.

Suisse–Arlberg–Vienne Express
A *CIWL* service introduced 1924.

Sulzers (RS)
BR diesel locos, class 26/27, equipped with Sulzer diesel engines.

Sunbuckle (USRS)
Rails distorted by the heat of the sun.

Sunday Pullman Limited
A LB&SCR service between London (Victoria) and Brighton, introduced 1898. A description rather than a train title.

Sunday Scotsman
The Sunday version of Flying Scotsman (qv) until 1939.

Sundries [traffic] (obs)
Consignments of less than one ton

which did not require exclusive use of a wagon and were carried at the lower rates charged for freight train transport.

Sunny South Express

A service between Liverpool (Lime St.)/Manchester (London Rd) and Brighton/Eastbourne/Ramsgate, so named 1927. Name dropped 1939.

Sunny South Sam

SR (*1*) publicity figure, a smiling, smartly-uniformed, idealized passenger guard, 'always at your service', conceived by the SR publicity department in 1930 and featured in posters and press advertisements etc.

Sunset Limited

Southern Pacific RR express between New Orleans, Los Angeles and San Francisco, introduced on a weekly basis with a 75 h journey time in 1894. The longest through passenger working in the US (2,480 m) in 1911. Daily service started in 1913. Restored by Amtrak but between Los Angeles and New Orleans only.

Sunset Route, The

Slogan of the Southern Pacific RR.

Sunshine Express

Winter season *CIWL* Pullman service between Cairo and Luxor, introduced 1928, ceased 1939.

SuO

Sundays Only.

Super Chief

The flagship of the AT&SF RR, the first high speed diesel-hauled service between Chicago and the Pacific Coast (Los Angeles), introduced in May 1936, 2,228 m in 39 h 45 min. Conveyed Los Angeles sleepers from New York off the Twentieth Century Limited and the Broadway Limited, with similar facilities eastbound. In 1936 it was the world's fastest train, covering the 202.4 m La Junta–Dodge City in 145 min (average 83.7 m.p.h.). Operated from 1937 with streamlined diesel sets, the first diesel-powered all-Pullman streamlined sets. Revived by Amtrak in 1971, 2,222 m in 40 h, name dropped 1974, now called the South West Chief.

Super Clauds

GER Claud (qv) locos, with Belpaire firebox.

Super-Continental

A CNR service between Toronto, Montreal and Vancouver, introduced in 1955 with a schedule of 72 h 5 min eastbound.

Super-elevation

The difference in height between the outer and inner rails on curves to counteract the effect of centrifugal force. The amount of difference is known as the degree of cant; negative cant is when the inner rail is higher than the outer.

Superheater

An apparatus which raises the temperature and volume of the steam leaving the boiler of a loco.

Superliners

Amtrak double-deck coaches introduced on long-distance services in 1979.

Super Mountain (US)

A steam loco with 4–10–2 wheel arrangement.

Superpointe (Fr)

A weekend which coincides with a public holiday, causing a major traffic peak.

Super-rapido (It)

A high speed emu train with supplementary fare.

Supertram

South Yorkshire Supertram (qv).

Surface lines

Term used by LT to distinguish the Metropolitan, Hammersmith & City,

Circle, District, and East London lines, with their 'full size' loading gauge from the smaller deep level tube lines. Sometimes also referred to as the sub-surface lines.

Surfaceman
A track maintenance worker, repairing and checking the permanent way.

Surface Raiders (RS)
BR Southern Region emus. From the initials.

Surfing (S)
A 'thrill game' in which juveniles and adolescents ride on the roofs of trains standing upright and dodging overhead wires and structures. Originated in Rio de Janeiro in the 1980s.

Susie Q
see Suzy Q.

Suspended joint
A connection between the ends of two rails by fishplates when they project beyond the ends of the last supporting chairs.

Sussex Scot
A BR service between Glasgow and Brighton via Reading, introduced in 1988.

Suzy Q (US)
Nickname of the New York, Susquehanna & Western RR.

SV
BR IC 225 coach (Service Vehicle), with kitchen, and buffet/bar/dining area.

SVR
1. Swansea Valley Rly, inc 1847, opened Swansea–Glais 1852, renamed Swansea Vale Rly 1855, opened Swansea–Pontardarwe 1860, leased by Midland Rly 1874, part of Midland Rly 1876.
2. Severn Valley Rly (qv).

SW (on a lineside board)
Instruction to drivers to sound whistle.

Swammies (RS)
L&NWR four-cylinder compound 0–8–0 locos, also L&NER large-boilered 2–8–0s (Big Swammies).

Swanage Rly
Swanage Rly Co., a preserved line using the former BR Wareham–Swanage branch, first section reopened 1979.

Swan necks (RS)
L&SWR Beattie 2–4–0T. From their tall slim chimneys.

Swansea District Line
Neath–Felin Fran–Llandeilo Junc.

Swansea Pullman
A service introduced in 1967 between London (Paddington) and Swansea, using Midland Pullman (qv) mu sets. Ceased 1973.

SWB wagon
A Short Wheelbase (four-wheel) wagon.

Sweat box (RS)
A slewing or aligning jack requiring much muscular effort.

Swedey/Sweedie (RS)(obs)
The GER, its trains, its locos, or its staff.

Swellhead (USRS)
A conductor (*3*). Fully in charge of the train, and therefore often apt to put on airs.

Swift & Delightful
Nickname for S&DJR.

Swing (USRS)
1. A brakeman stationed in the middle of a train.
2. Additional staff allocated to very long trains or other difficult workings.

Swing a bug, to (USRS)
To brake.

Swing bolster
A bolster (qv) able to swing laterally in relation to the bogie/truck to reduce lateral blows and shocks transmitted to the body of the vehicle and also to

cushion the body momentum action on the truck frames and the wheel flanges.

Swinger

1. (RS) An additional coach on a train.
2. (RS) Any vehicle (usually unbraked) at the back of a fully-fitted train.
3. (LTRS) A collector shoe of a car when out of alignment.
4. (LTRS) The bracket supporting cables, suspended from the lineside compressed air main on open air sections.
5. (LTRS) An unbraked unit on a train following a defect.
6. (RS)(obs) A heavy and long loose-coupled train.

Swinging window (LTRS)
A hinged car window not correctly seated in its catch.

Swing link
Part of the suspension system of many types of truck/bogie, consisting of a metal bar, pivoted at each end.

Switches
Another term for points, hence switchman; universally used in US, interchangable in UK.

Switch, to (US)
To shunt.

Switchback

1. A rly in mountainous area laid out in zigzag pattern to minimize gradients. At the end of each gradient is a 'reversing station' where the train is 'switched back' or reversed in direction ready to tackle the next gradient.
2. A rly constructed with alternate steep ascents and descents so that momentum achieved in descents provides enough, or almost enough, power to negotiate the ascents.

Switch engine/switcher (US)
A shunting loco.

Switch heel
see Heel.

Switch hog (USRS)
A yardmaster.

Switching (US)
Shunting. Hence switching yard.

Switching company (US)
An undertaking principally or solely engaged in providing shunting or terminal facilities.

Switching out
Linking block instruments either side of a signal box and closing it down. More than one box may be switched out at the same time to provide a very long block section between the two boxes remaining open.

Switch line/railroad
Switching company (qv).

Switchman (US)
A yard brakeman.

Switch monkey (USRS)
A shunter or switchman.

Switch toe
see Toe/switch toe.

Switzerland Express
A *CIWL* service Calais–Lucerne, introduced 1890.

SWMR
South Wales Mineral Rly, inc 1853, Glyncorrwg to Briton Ferry, opened 1860–2, worked by GWR from 1908, part of GWR 1923.

SWR

1. South Wales Rly, Grange Court Junction near Gloucester to Cardiff, Swansea, Carmarthen and Neyland, inc 1845, first section opened 1850. Amalgamated with GWR 1863.
2. Saffron Walden Rly, inc 1861, 1863, Audley End–Saffron Walden–Bartlow, opened 1865, 1866. Part of the GER, 1877.

SX

Saturdays excepted. Not always understood by passengers reading station time sheets; rly officials are sometimes asked 'Where is platform 3 SX?'.

SYD&GR

South Yorkshire, Doncaster & Goole Rly, inc 1847, 1848, Barnsley–Swinton–Doncaster and branches. Opened 1849, Swinton to Doncaster and Mexborough to Elsecar, 1850. Retitled SYR&RDN (qv) 1850.

SYJR

1. South Yorkshire Junction Rly, inc 1890, Conisborough to Wrangbrook Junc (with H&BR), opened 1894, worked by H&BR. Part of L&NER 1924.

2. South Yorkshire Joint Rly, Kirk Sandall Junc (with GCR)–Tickhill–Dinnington/Firbeck Colliery. Inc 1903, opened 1909, 1926, 1929. Passenger service (Shireoaks–Doncaster) 1910–29. GCR, L&YR, GNR from 1909, LM&SR & L&NER from 1923–47.

Sykes

see Syx.

Sykes' lock and block

see Lock and block.

Syphons (RS)

BR class 37 diesel-electric locos.

SYR

South Yorkshire Rly: *see* SYD&GR; SYR&RDN.

SYR&RDN

South Yorkshire Rly and River Dun [Don] Navigation, inc 1850, new title of SYD&GR (qv). Extended to Barnsley 1851, to Thorne 1856 and to Keadby 1859. Operated by and leased to MS&LR 1864. Part of MS&LR 1874.

Syx

Trade mark of W.R. Sykes' Interlocking Signal Co. Ltd, Clapham, London, manufacturers of rly signalling equipment, founded by W.R. Sykes, 1899.

SZD

USSR Rlys.

T

T
1. Trailer car.
2. Tank engine.

T2
CIWL sleeping car containing small two-berth compartments on two levels.

T3
CIWL sleeping car containing three-berth (upper, middle and lower) compartments.

TA
Training Allowance.

TAA (Fr)
Train Autos Accompagnés; equivalent of day Motorail (qv) services, introduced 1957. *See also TAC; TAJ.*

Table
A turntable (qv).

TAC (Fr)
Train Auto Couchettes; Motorail type service with sleeping accommodation. *See also TAA; TAJ.*

Tackhead (USRS)
A yard clerk.

TACV (obs)
Tracked Air Cushion Vehicle; developed by THL (qv).

Tadpole
1. GWR TC for open fish truck.
2. (RS)(obs) BR (S) demu sets made up from DMB and TC of the narrow Hastings line conformation, and DTS of standard width, the whole giving the appearance of a tadpole.

TAF (Sp)(obs)
Tren Automoteur Fiat; express diesel railcar sets used in Spain and Portugal in the 1950s and 1960s.

Taff Bargoed Joint
Inc 1867, opened 1875, 1876, Nelson & Llancaiach to Dowlais, GWR and Rhymney, part of GWR 1922.

Taff Vale Judgement
When its employee members of the ASRS were on strike in 1900, the TVR was granted an injunction against the Union, which was reversed by the Court of Appeal but upheld by the House of Lords in 1901. This established that a trade union could be sued and legally restrained from picketing and offering violence to those employees who remained at work. As a result, the TVR recovered £24,000 damages from the ASRS. The law was subsequently altered.

Taffy
Nickname for the L&NWR.

Tag, The (US)
Nickname for Tennesee, Alabama & Georgia RR (formerly the Chattanooga System). From the initials.

Tail end Charlie (RS)(obs)
Freight train guard.

Tail lamp
Invariably carried on the last vehicle of a train, day and night, to indicate the train is complete.

Tail over her back (USRS)(obs)
A full head of steam, with a plume of steam blowing back like a tail from the safety valve.

Tail rope (obs)
A rope with hook at each end used for moving wagons when the shunting engine was working on a parallel track; also called a tow rope/chain. The term was also used to denote the lower rope of a counterbalance incline or funicular when the winding equipment was at the lower end of the line.

Tail wag (RS)
Sideways motion at the rear of a train.

TAJ (Fr)
Train Auto Jour; day Motorail (qv) type trains, introduced 1967, now *TAA* (qv). *See also TAA; TAC.*

Taj Express
A day service New Delhi–Agra–Gwalior.

Take the dolly, to (RS)
To make a movement authorized by a shunt signal.

Take the rubber out [of them], to (USRS)
To pull out or disconnect brake air hoses.

Take minutes, to (USRS)
To stop for lunch.

TALGO (Sp)
Tren Articulado Ligero Goicoechea–Oriol. An ultra-lightweight articulated train design with short and low-slung car bodies, each body resting on a single pair of independent steered half-axles, the other end carried on the axles of the adjoining car. Invented by an army engineer, Alejandro Goicoechea, and sponsored by Sr Oriol. Prototype tested in Spain in 1941. ACF (qv) built the first complete trains in the US in 1949 and these ran regularly in service between Irun and Madrid from summer 1950. In 1969, *TALGO* trains began to run internationally in Europe, following the development of devices to facilitate gauge change at the Spanish frontier.

See also Barcelona TALGO; Catalan TALGO; Pablo Casals; *Paris–Madrid TALGO*.

Talisman
An express between London (Kings Cross) and Edinburgh, introduced 1956 to replace the Coronation (qv). Pullman cars included until 1965. Name dropped 1968, revived 1972.

Tallowpot (USRS)(obs)
A steam loco fireman. It was one of the fireman's duties to draw and use a supply of tallow for cleaning and lubricating purposes.

Talyllyn
Talyllyn Rly, 2 ft 3 in/686 mm gauge, Tywyn to Abergynolwyn and Nant Gwernol, inc 1865, opened 1866 principally for slate but also carrying passenger traffic. Closed 1950 at end of summer season, reopened 1951 as Britain's first preserved line.

Tamp, to
To compact ballast under the sleepers, hence tamping machine.

Tanat Valley
Porthywaen Junction to Blodwell Junction and Llangynog, LRO 1898, opened 1904, worked by Cambrian, part of GWR from 1922.

T&BR
Tenbury & Bewdley Rly, inc 1860, opened 1864, worked by GWR, part of GWR from 1869.

T&CLR
Timoleague & Courtmacsherry Light Rly, Ireland, Ballinascarthy to Courtmacsherry, inc 1888, opened 1890, 1891, 5 ft 3 in/1,600 mm gauge, part of GSR from 1924, CIE 1945, regular passenger services ceased 1947, closed 1961.

T&DLR
Tralee & Dingle Light Rly, Ireland, 3 ft/914 mm gauge, inc 1888, Tralee to Dingle and branch to Castlegregory.

Opened 1891, part of GSR 1925, CIE 1945. Closed to passengers 1939, closed entirely 1953.

Tandem working

Two locos coupled together with power applied separately, a driver in each, both drivers able to apply brakes throughout the train. *See also* Multiple working.

T&FGR

Tottenham & Forest Gate Rly, inc 1890, South Tottenham (T&HJR) to Woodgrange Park (LT&SR), jointly owned by Midland and LT&SR, opened 1894. Midland from 1912, LM&SR 1923.

T&HJR

Tottenham & Hampstead Junction Rly, inc 1862, Tottenham North Junction (GER) to Highgate Road and Gospel Oak (HJR), opened 1868. Jointly vested in Midland and GER 1902, LM&SR/L&NER 1923–47.

T&NDR

Tiverton & North Devon Rly, Tiverton to Morebath Junc, inc 1875, opened 1884, part of GWR from 1894.

T&RSMD

Traction and Rolling Stock Maintenance Depot, BR.

T&RW

Tramway & Railway World, founded as *Railway World* 1892, and soon renamed T&RW. Renamed *Transport World* 1934. Mainly concerned with tramways (*3*), and trolleybuses and (in later years) motor buses.

T&TM

Transport & Travel Monthly, a renaming of R&TM (qv) in 1920, merged with RM (qv) from January 1923.

Tanfield Waggonway

Opened 1725, horse-hauled over wooden rails, to carry coal from Tanfield collieries to Dunston staithes on the river Tyne at Gateshead. Converted to a rly by 1839 including inclines operated by steam winding engines and self-acting rope inclines. Part of NER, 1854. Sunniside to Causey Arch section operated as a preserved line from 1977.

Tangos (RS)

GNR 2–8–0 locos of 1914 (L&NER 01/02). From the contemporary dance craze.

Tank

1. (US) A loco with 4–6–6 wheel arrangement.

2. (USRS) Loco tender.

Tank, The (RS)(obs)

The GCR Works at Gorton, Manchester. From a high water tank which was a prominent feature.

Tank engine

A steam loco carrying its water supply in tanks placed around the boiler and with a small supply of coal in a bunker behind the footplate, rather than in a separate hauled tender. Designated T in Whyte notation (qv). *See also* Pannier tank; Saddle tank; Side tank; Well tank; Wing tank.

Tanker (US)

Tank wagon (qv).

Tank stock (LTRS)

MDR 'F' stock trains.

Tank town (USRS)

A community built around a point where steam locos could take on water.

Tank transporter

A wagon adapted to carry army tanks.

Tank wagon

A vehicle with a large container for carrying liquids or gases.

Tanner-oner (RS)

A GWR 2–6–2T of the 61XX series.

Tanzam

3 ft 6 in/1,067 mm gauge line between Kapiri Mposhi, Zambia, and Dar-es-

Salaam, Tanzania (1,154 m/1,857 km).
Opened 1975. Also known as the
Great Uhuru (Freedom) Rly or the
TZR. Administered by TAZARA
(qv).

Tap line (US)
Alternative term for a short line (qv);
it 'taps' a main line, giving access
between it and industrial, military etc.
complexes.

Tapper (RS)(obs)
A C&W examiner. From wheel tapper
(qv).

TAR
Trans-Australian Rly; Port Augusta–
Kalgoorlie.

Target (US)
A device giving a visual indication of
the direction in which a pair of points
has been set.

Tarka line
BR brand name for Exeter–Barnstaple
line, 1989.

Tartan Arrow
A road haulage firm which began to
operate company trains of containers
and parcels traffic between London
and Glasgow in 1967, constructing
special depots at Kentish Town and
Bridgeton, Glasgow. Road journey
times were cut by half. The
operation was nationalized into the
THC (qv) in 1967 and became part of
NFC (qv) in 1969. The service ceased
in 1976.

Tasmanian Government Rlys
see TGR.

Tauern Express
A service between Ostend (connecting
with sailings to and from UK),
Munich, Klagenfurt and Ljubljana,
with through portion to Belgrade,
introduced 1950. Ceased 1987.

Tauern Line
[Salzburg]–Schwarzach–St Veit–
Spittal–[Villach–Trieste–Belgrade].

Tauern Orient Express
A service between Munich and
Belgrade, with through coach to
Istanbul. Ceased 1979.

Taurus/Toros Express
A *CIWL* restaurant and sleeping car
service between Istanbul
(Haydarpasa), Aleppo and Baghdad/
Cairo. Introduced 1930, as an
extension of the Simplon–Orient
express, using road and air transport
to cover rail gaps in the Middle East.
Re-routed via Ankara, 1935. All-rail
service to and from Mosul, 1939; to
and from Baghdad, 1940. Revived
after the Second World War,
Istanbul–Baghdad, connecting at
Istanbul with the Paris service (Simplon
Orient, (qv)). Subsequently confined to
Turkish territory owing to political
disputes. *See also* Baghdad Rly.

Taw Valley
see NDR.

Taxis (RS)
GWR 0–6–2T class 66XX.

TAZARA
Tanzania–Zambia Rly Authority. *See
also* Tanzam.

TBCF
see TCF.

TBF
BR Trailer Brake First class, brake
coach with some First class seating.

TBS
1. BR Trailer Brake Second/Standard
   class, passenger brake coach in a
   dmu set with some Second/
   Standard class seating.
2. Transmission-based Signalling, in
   which a micro-processor on the
   train communicates with a central
   computer, registering the train's
   position and speed. 'Advice' is then
   signalled back to the train
   regarding its continuing progress
   within the margins of its safety.

TBSL
TBS (*1*) (qv) with Lavatory.

TC
1. Trailer Composite –BR dmu trailer with First and Second/Standard class seating.
2. Traffic Circular: LT equivalent of Working Notice (qv). Originally called Joint [Weekly] Circular.
3. BR (S) control trailer corridor sets for Bournemouth electrification, two driving trailer Second/Standard class and one brake coach Second/Standard class, 3-TC; also the same plus a First class trailer car, 4-TC; also six-car trailer corridor units formed of 4-COR cars – two driving brake Second/Standard class, three trailer cars Second/Standard class and one trailer composite car, 6-TC.

TCC
Traffic Control Centre. A refinement of CTC (qv), introduced in US *c*. 1957, allowing one man to control signalling on up to 100 m of single track line. By pressing the appropriate buttons, the controller makes all the necessary point and signal movements at chosen locations.

TCDD
Türkiye Cumhuriyeti Devlet Demiryollari Isletmesi; Turkish State Rlys.

TCF
To be Called For; parcels consigned to be collected by consignee at destination station.

TCFD
Tyne Central Freight Depot.

TCL
TC (*1*) (qv) with Lavatory.

TCV
BR Tiered Car Van; an end-door car carrier with space for two motor cars in the well between the bogies and up to four on an intermediate hydraulically-raised floor.

TDM
Time Division Multiplex; a control system for the remote working of traction power units in push/pull formations, introduced by BR in 1979. Also used in mu operation of locos.

Tea kettle (USRS)
An elderly loco.

TEB
Telephone Enquiry Bureau (BR).

TEC
Transports Européens Combinés; European container services operated under the auspices of Intercontainer (qv).

Teddy Bears (RS)
GNR 0–6–2T, introduced 1907. After the children's teddy bears which first appeared in that year. Also BR class 14 diesel-hydraulic locos, eventually sold to the NCB.

TEE
Trans-Europ Express. A network of supplementary fare, all-First Class luxury trains, with on-board customs and immigration facilities, introduced in 1957 to run in and between France, Belgium, Luxembourg, Italy, West Germany, Switzerland and Holland. Conceived by F.Q. den Hollander, president of NS (*1*). Managed by *SNCF*, *SNCB*, *CFL*, *SBB* and NS (*1*) (and *RENFE* when Spanish workings were added from 1969). In decline from 1982–5, virtually abandoned with the cessation of the last international workings in 1988. Replaced by the EC network (qv).

TEEM
Trans-Europ Express Marchandises; fast international freight services, introduced 1961.

Tees–Thames Express
A service between Saltburn and

London (Kings Cross), calling at principal stations to York, introduced 1959, replacing Tees–Thames Link (Middlesbrough–Doncaster (connection to London)), an 'Up' dmu headboarded train introduced earlier in the year. Name very soon discarded.

Tees–Tyne Pullman
An all-Pullman train between London (Kings Cross) and Newcastle, introduced 1948, ceased 1976. Relaunched as a 3 h 12 min HST service in 1985.

Teifi Valley
Pencader–Newcastle Emlyn, former BR branch partly reopened as 2 ft/609 mm gauge tourist/pleasure line, 1986.

Teign Valley Line
Heathfield–Christow–Exeter (City Basin Junc). *See also* TVR (2).

Telescoping
The manner in which a rly coach was apt to force itself into the adjoining one in a serious collision, resembling the action of closing a telescope. Eliminated by modern methods of coach construction.

Télésiège (Fr)
Chairlift.

Telltales (USRS)
Strips of material hung in front of bridges and tunnel mouths etc. to warn men on the roofs of wagons.

TEN
Trans-Euro Nacht/Nuit/Night; name used from 1980 for the pool of *DSG* and *CIWL* sleeping cars leased to West German, French, Swiss, Italian, Belgian, Dutch, Austrian, Danish and Luxemburg rlys for international services. The pool, which is financed by the rly administrations involved and Eurofima (qv), was formed in 1971–2; the first services were operated in 1974 and new stock was added subsequently.

Tenbury
Tenbury Rly, Wooferton Junction to Tenbury Junction, inc 1859, opened 1861, worked by S&H, transferred to L&NWR and GWR 1869, LM&SR and GWR from 1923–47.

Tenby & Carmarthen Bay Express
Summer service between London (Paddington), Tenby and Pembroke Dock, introduced 1928.

Tender dip (obs)
The pick-up scoop used for raising water from water troughs (qv).

Tender engine
A steam loco hauling its supply of coal and water in a separate vehicle (tender).

Tender first
A steam tender loco running backwards, with its tender in front.

Tenderlok[omotive] (Ger)
A tank engine.

Ten foot, The (RS)
The space between parallel sets of double tracks, which is approximately this width.

Tennants (RS)
NER 2–4–0 locos of 1884–5 built when the co. was temporarily without a loco superintendent and the general manager, Henry Tennant, was in charge of the loco department.

Ten wheeler (US)
Term for a steam loco with 4–6–0 wheel arrangement.

TER
1. (Fr) *Transport Express Régional*; co-ordinated *SNCF* rail or road local services sponsored by the Departmental or Regional Authority. Identifiable by distinctive liveries and logos. *See also Métrolor.*
2. (Sp) *Tren Español Rapido*; express diesel railcars, successors to *TAF* (qv).

Terminal company (US)
Switching company (qv).

Termite
GWR TC for a Third class coach
(nine types).

Terra firma, on (RS)
A derailment at catch points.

Terriers (RS)
LB&SCR Stroudley 0–6–0T,
introduced 1872. *See also* Rooters.

Tevan
GWR TC for Mica (qv) converted to
carry tea traffic.

Texas (US)
Term for a steam loco with 2–10–4
wheel arangement. The first was built
for the Texas & Pacific RR.

Texas Eagle
A St Louis–Dallas–San Antonio
service of the Missouri Pacific RR,
introduced 1948. Renamed Aztec
Eagle 1958 and extended to El Paso
with through cars St Louis–Mexico
City from 1962 until 1969. Now Texas
Eagle again and operated by Amtrak
between Chicago, Dallas and El Paso.

TF
Trailer First; a First class trailer in a
BR diesel-hauled set; side-corridor,
compartments.

TGR
Tasmanian Government Rlys, formed
1872, part of ANR (qv), 1976. 3 ft
6 in/1,067 mm (and originally also
2 ft/609 mm) gauge. Part of ANR (qv)
1975. All regular passenger services
ceased 1978.

TGS
Trailer Guard Second class; a HST
trailer car with guard's accommodation
and Second/Standard class seats.

TGV
Trains à Grand Vitesse; the *SNCF*'s
very high speed electric trains,
travelling for the greater part of their
run over purpose-built rlys.

Introduced 1981. *TGV–PSE* = Paris–
Lyon; *TGV–A* (Atlantique) = Paris–le
Mans/Tours; *TGV–Nord* = Paris–
Channel Tunnel/Brussels. Extensions
to Marseille and Nice etc. in progress.

Thames
NSE brand name introduced 1989 for
services between Paddington–
Reading–Oxford/ Bedwyn; branches
Henley, Marlow, Bourne End; and
Oxford–Bicester/Banbury.

Thames–Clyde Express
A service between London (St
Pancras) and Glasgow (St Enoch)
introduced 1927. Restored 1949.
Name dropped 1975 when it ceased to
run from and to London.

Thames–Forth Express
A service between London (St
Pancras), Leeds and Edinburgh
(Waverley), introduced 1927. Ceased
1939. *See also* Waverley.

Thameslink
Brand name for dual-voltage emu
services linking stations north and
south of London (Bedford/Luton–
Brighton/Sevenoaks/Guildford etc.)
using the reopened Farringdon–
Blackfriars line, introduced from 1988.

Thameslink 2000
Expansion of Thameslink services
including a new tunnel at Kings Cross to
serve Hertford, Welwyn Garden City,
Stevenage etc., first proposed in 1988.

Thames Valley Rly/Line
Strawberry Hill–Shepperton, inc 1862
as Metropolitan & Thames Valley Rly,
opened 1864, part of L&SWR from
1865.

Thanet Belle
An all-Pullman summer service
between London (Victoria), Margate
and Ramsgate, introduced 1948,
renamed Kentish Belle (qv) 1951.

Thanet Pullman Limited
An all-Pullman First Class only

Sunday service London (Victoria), Margate, Broadstairs and Ramsgate, introduced 1921. As an independent train, it ran in summer only and ceased in 1928.

THC
Transport Holding Company; a statutory company set up under the Transport Act, 1962 to own and manage all transport investments of the former BTC except those transferred to BRB, LTB, BTDB and British Waterways Board. Following the Transport Act 1968, its bus businesses were vested in the National Bus Co. or the Scottish Transport Group, and its road haulage and shipping interests in the NFC. The residue of travel and tourism interests were subsequently also sold off, including Thomas Cook & Son Ltd (in 1972). The residual BR activities of the BTA (qv) became a wholly-owned subsidiary of the BRB, retaining the name BTA Ltd.

Theatre type indicator
Indicator used in conjunction with

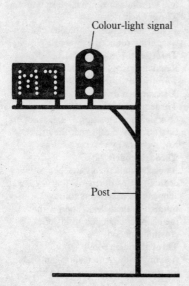

Colour-light signal

Post

colour-light signals, showing the platform, line number or letter designation of the route set up by the signalman (e.g. ML = Main Line). From the device placed by the stage of a theatre to indicate the number of the scene or turn in progress.

Thick as a bag (RS)
Very foggy.

Thin oil engine (RS)(obs)
A diesel loco.

Thin red line (RS)(obs)
The marking on loco steam pressure dials indicating a full head of steam.

Third class
In Britain, the cheapest class of passenger accommodation. Renamed Second class, 1956, further renamed Standard class, 1987. Third class was withdrawn on west European rlys (except in Portugal and Spain) in 1956; in Portugal in 1963; and in Spain between 1965 and 1973.

Third rail
The conductor rail carrying the positive dc traction current. Usually placed to one side of and slightly above the running rails. The loco/train collector shoe may make its contact with the top (most usually), side or lower surface of this rail. The latter two methods provide reliability in ice and snow.

Thirty (USRS)(obs)
The end of a telegraphed message.

Thirty one order
A US train order (qv) which requires a signature to acknowledge that it is received and understood, and therefore causes the train to stop.

THL
Tracked Hovercraft Ltd; a subsidiary of the National Research Development Corporation which, with government financial support, undertook trials of a high speed magnetically-levitated

vehicle propelled by a linear motor on an experimental track at Earith, Cambridgeshire between 1970 and 1973.

Thomas Cook
Thomas Cook & Son Ltd, formed in 1924 to take over the travel agency founded by Thomas Cook (1808–92) in 1841. Controlled by CIWL from 1928. Taken over by the four British main line rly companies in 1942 after the CIWL had become 'enemy property'. On the nationalization of the British rlys in 1948, the ownership of Thomas Cook was vested in the BTC. With the dissolution of the BTC imminent, it became part of the THC in 1962. In 1972 the undertaking was sold to a consortium of the Midland Bank, Trust Houses Forte and the Automobile Association. *See also* Cook's Timetable.

Thomas the Tank Engine
A blue-painted Hudswell–Clarke 1945 0–6–0T of the British Sugar Corporation, Peterborough, bought in 1973 by the Nene Valley Rly and adopted as a character in the highly popular children's rly stories written by the Revd W. Awdry.

Thousand-miler (USRS)
A very dark-coloured working shirt which can allegedly be worn by engine and train crews for 1,000 m before requiring re-laundering.

THR
Tendring Hundred Rly, inc 1859, Hythe (Colchester)–Wivenhoe, opened 1863, worked by GER; extended to Colchester (St Botolph's) 1866, and to Walton-on-the-Naze 1867. Part of the GER, 1883.

Three-bagger (USRS)
Three locos on a train.

Three Counties Line
BR brand name for Bletchley–Bedford services from 1990.

Three-phase
A system of electric traction using high voltage alternating current and two overhead wires per track, the asynchronous induction or constant speed motors on the locos and trains taking power directly from the generating station or via transformer substations and usually operating at line voltage. Regenerative braking (qv) is possible. First used on certain Swiss mountain rlys but employed on main lines, principally in northern Italy, from 1902 until 1972. Still survives on some mountain rlys. *See also* Single phase.

Three-throw points
Points working three sets of rails diverging at the same place.

Three valve sets (RS)
SR 2–6–0 locos (N1 and U1). From the popular contemporary radio sets.

Throat
The complex tracks at the approaches to a terminus or other large station.

Thrombosis (RS)
Traffic apprentice – 'a bloody clot wandering round the system'.

Throttle, throttle lever (US)
Regulator, regulator handle.

Throttle artist/jerker/puller (USRS)
A steam loco driver.

Through, [to go] (LTRS)
Overshooting a platform, e.g. 'two cars through' means that the driver has overshot by two car lengths.

Through coach (obs)
A coach shunted and attached to two or more trains during its journey, allowing its passengers to travel through to their destination without the chore of changing trains or crossing London.

Through siding (obs)
A siding without signalling but usable for through movements under the

control of a shunter or other authorized person.

Throw-off points
Catch points (qv).

Thumpers (RS)
BR class 205 demus. From their characteristic sound.

TI
Trains Illustrated, founded 1946, and at first largely directed at juvenile train spotters (qv); monthly publication from February 1950. Gradually altered to cater for professional as well as amateur rly interests and covering all aspects of contemporary rly engineering, operation, administration and politics; accordingly renamed MR (qv) from January 1962.

TIA
Traitement Intégrale Armand; an invention of Louis Armand, one time president of the *SNCF*, a device for the chemical processing of steam locomotive feed water to neutralize those ingredients which encourage scaling and boiler and firebox corrosion.

Tichies (RS)
GWR 0–4–2T and 2–4–0T. From children's (S) for small.

Ticino Express
TEE Zurich–Milan, introduced 1961. Ceased 1974.

Ticket agent
A person/firm selling passenger tickets on behalf of rly companies/BR. Also current in US.

Ticket grabber (USRS)
A conductor (*3*).

Ticket office (US)
Term for booking office, now generally adopted in UK.

Ticket platform (obs)
Special platforms erected outside large stations, at which ticket collectors took up tickets from passengers on incoming trains, and used for no other purpose. Some conveniently-sited public stations with very light traffic (e.g. Holloway for Kings Cross) were also mainly given over to this role.

Ticket snapper (RS)
A ticket collector.

Tickhill
Tickhill Light Rly, Bawtry–Haxey, LRO 1901, part of GNR 1907, opened 1912.

Tiddly Dike Rly
Nickname for M&SWJR (*1*).

Tie (US)
Sleeper. Sometimes expressed as a cross tie (i.e. transverse sleeper), as distinguished from a switch tie (supporting points) or a bridge tie.

Tie bar/rod
A metal bar placed across the roadbed to keep rails to gauge at places where side pressure is high, or when rails are laid on a flat concrete base, e.g. in a roadway.

Tie ['em] down, to (RS)(obs)
To set handbrakes.

Tie ['em] off, to (RS)
To uncouple.

Tie on, to (RS)
To couple up.

Tie up, to (USRS)
To pause for sleep or eating.

Tilbury, The
LT&SR (qv).

Tilt bar
A bar or rod placed above the centre of a wagon from end to end to carry a canvas cover.

Time and Time (RS)
Punctual arrival and departure of a train.

Time bill (US)
A poster-size timetable.

Time freight (USRS)
A fast freight train.

Time interval system
A crude method of signalling in which
a train is allowed sufficient time to
clear a section ahead after which a
second train is admitted to the section.
In general use in the early days of
rlys.

Timkenised (USRS)
A wagon or car equipped with
(Timken) roller bearings.

Tingalairy (RS)
A manually-operated auger.

Tinies (RS)
1. L&YR Aspinall 4–4–2 locos.
2. GCR 0–8–0 locos (L&NER class
   Q4).

Tin lizard/lizzie (USRS)(obs)
A streamlined train or loco.

Tin opener (LTRS)
A device erected in LT depots to
remove snow from roofs of cars stored
in the open. So called because it has
occasionally begun to remove the car
roofs as well .

Tinsel string (USRS)(obs)
A circus train (qv).

Tin tabs/tabernacles (RS)(obs)
L&YR iron-sided brake vans. From
the corrugated iron chapels and
churches, known as tin tabernacles.

Tinto Express
A 1911 renaming of the Upper Ward
Express (qv).

Tip (RS)
1. A tippler wagon.
2. Advice passed by hand signals to a
   pointsman.

Tip-out, tipping 'em out (LTRS)
Detraining passengers, especially when
a defective train has to be taken out of
service.

TIS (obs)
Three-car set of former LT tube stock
refurbished in 1967 for working the
BR Ryde Pier–Shanklin service,
3-TIS. Operated with the associated

four-car VEC (qv) sets, combining as
VECTIS, the Roman name for the Isle
of Wight.

Tishies (RS)
L&NWR Prince of Wales inside
cylinder 4–6–0s fitted with outside
Walschaerts valve gear. From a
racehorse named Tishy which had a
reputation for getting its legs crossed.

Tissue (USRS)
A train order (qv).

TLV
Trailer Luggage Van (gangwayed),
BR (S).

TM&WER
Tooting, Merton & Wimbledon
Extension Rly, inc 1864, vested in
L&SWR and LB&SCR 1865, opened
1868, Streatham Junction to
Wimbledon, part of SR from 1923.

TMD
Traction Maintenance Depot (BR).

TML
Trans-Manche Link. The consortium
of contractors responsible for building
the Channel Tunnel.

TMS
Tramway Museum Society, founded
1955. It owns and operates the
National Tramway Museum, Crich,
Derbyshire, opened with horse
operation 1963, electric working from
1964.

TMST
Trans-Manche Super Trains; designed
to work the first Channel Tunnel
services between Britain and France
etc., 1993.

TO
Tourist Open coach (BR).

Toad
1. GWR TC for freight brake van
   with large balcony at one end only.
2. BR TC for any type of freight
   brake van.
3. (USRS) A rolling stock repair man.

4. (USRS) A derailing device.

Toadfit

BR TC for a fitted freight brake van.

Toastrack

An unroofed tramcar with open body sides and crossbench seating entered from the footboards at the sides. From its vague resemblance to its namesake.

TOC

Train Operating Centres; sited at Wembley, Crewe and Doncaster and designed for marshalling freight trains using the Channel Tunnel.

TOD

Tourist Open Disabled coach. BR IC 225 coach with wheelchair space and lavatory designed for use by the disabled. Marshalled next to a catering vehicle.

TOE

Tourist Open End. BR IC 225 coach, marshalled next to the loco.

Toe/switch toe

The tapered end of a switch or tongue rail, fitting against the stock rail (qv).

Toe boards (USRS)

Walkway on roofs of freight wagons.

Toe path (USRS)

1. The running board of a loco.

2. Toe boards (qv).

3. The cess (qv).

TOFC (US)

Trailer On Flat Cars. *See also* Piggy-back.

Toffee apples (RS)

1. (obs) Casks of asphalt or pitch.

2. BR diesel locos class 31/0. From the shape of the control handles.

Tokenless block

Block instrument, with electrical interlocking, suitable for single lines, giving the same safety as train staffs, tablets or tokens (qv); introduced on BR in 1965. After a train has been accepted by the box in advance, signals at both boxes are released to allow it to pass through the single line section. A further release can only be obtained when it arrives at the entrance to the passing place in advance, actuating a track circuit and an electric treadle. *See also* Non-token lock and block.

Token working

see Train staff/tablet/token and ticket.

Tolstoi

A Helsinki–Moscow service, so named 1982.

Tommy (RS)

A ground disc signal.

Tommy Dodd (RS)

A calling-on or ground disc signal.

Tongue rails/switch blades/rails

The moveable rails in a turnout (qv) which incorporate the 'sharp' end to guide the wheels of a train.

Tonk (USRS)

Carriage and wagon fitter (i.e. a carman (qv)).

Ton-mile

A unit measuring the movement of one ton of freight over one mile.

Tonnage hound (USRS)

An official who loads up trains to the point of straining their motive power.

Tool train (USRS)

A breakdown train with re-railing equipment.

Toonerville [trolley] (USRS)

A very small (i.e. with approximately one to five short routes) electric tramway (*3*) system in US. After a comic strip, *The Toonerville Trolley that meets all the Trains*, by Fontaine Fox, begun in 1908 and syndicated in newspapers throughout the US.

Toothpaste (RS)(obs)

NSE's initial red, white and blue livery.

Top (RS)

The top of the track formation; rail level.

Top, to (RS)
To double-head a train.

Top and tail (RS)
A train with a loco at each end.

Top dresser drawer (USRS)
The upper bunk or berth in a caboose or a sleeping car.

Toplight
The openable section at the top of a coach window, or a small window above main light, often in a door, to allow a standing passenger to see out.

Top link
see Link.

Topo, el (Sp)
The Mole; name for the line between Hendaye and San Sebastian with its numerous tunnels.

Topping the road (RS)
Correcting rail height by packing.

TOPS
BR computer-based Total Operations Processing System of freight information and transit control, introduced 1973–5 and copied from that used by the SP (qv). Every event concerning freight traffic is transmitted, as it happens, to a central computer to form a comprehensive and up-to-the-minute picture of the freight traffic situation over the whole of BR. Details of the deployment of all freight rolling stock, locos, services, depots and yards are stored on the central computer.

Tops gen (RS)
Information gained from the TOPS (qv) computer printouts or screen displays.

Top Shed (RS)(obs)
Kings Cross Loco Depot.

Torbay Express/Limited
A service between London (Paddington), Torquay and Paignton (to Kingswear in summer), introduced 1923, restored 1946, name dropped

1968. Relaunched 1984 as a summer service to Paignton only.

Torbay–Tyne
An express between Paignton, Torquay and Newcastle, introduced 1970; ran that year only.

Toros Express
see Taurus/Toros Express.

Torpedo (USRS)
A detonator.

Torpedo wagons (RS)
Wagons designed to carry molten steel. From their shape.

Torquay Pullman Limited
A service between London (Paddington), Torquay and Paignton, the first all-Pullman service on GWR, introduced 1929, ceased after 1930.

Tortillard (Fr)
Popular name for train on a secondary line, or the line itself; literally 'twister' or 'shuffler'.

Torville & Deans (RS)
BR class 141 dmus. From their propensity to skid, like the ice skaters, Torville & Dean.

TOT
Train–Omnibus–Tram. Title of the staff magazine of the London Underground Group of companies, 1913–33. Also the name of the through road–rail tickets issued by the Underground Group.

Totem
GWR TC for twelve-wheel wagons to carry 45-ton loads, originally designed to carry armour plating.

Touch, to get a (LTRS)
To receive an electric shock from a live rail.

Tourist, The
Summer through service between Ventnor and Freshwater, Isle of Wight, introduced 1934, revived 1951. Ceased 1953 with closure of Freshwater branch.

Tourist car (obs)
An inferior type of US Pullman sleeping car available at half the normal Pullman fare.

Tourn
GWR TC for 36-ft bogie open truck to carry 25-ton loads.

Touropa (Ger)
A holiday tour company owning couchette cars (*Liegewagen*).

Tower (US)
Signal box or the control cabin in a marshalling yard.

Tower buff (USRS)
A rly enthusiast.

Tower Subway
A deep level tube tunnel beneath the Thames from Tower Hill to Tooley Street, inc 1868, opened 1870. Since it briefly contained a 2 ft 6 in/762 mm gauge cable-worked rly, it was in effect the first passenger tube (qv). However, rail service lasted only a few months although the subway remained open for pedestrians until 1896.

Town Halls (RS)
BR standard class 5 4–6–0 locos. From the prominent steps at the front of the frame.

Towns Line (RS)
The GNR direct line between Doncaster and London via Grantham and Newark.

Toy rly (obs)
Used up to *c.* 1940 to describe any UK passenger-carrying narrow gauge or miniature rly.

Toy trains (LTRS)
Name given by Metropolitan Line crews to the (small size) tube stock running to Stanmore.

TPH
Trains Per Hour; a unit of frequency on intensive services.

TPO
Travelling Post Office; a train exclusively devoted to the carriage of Royal Mail, in which letters are sorted during the journey to save time. This system, introduced in 1838, still continues today but the lineside apparatus which enabled mail to be taken up into the train or dropped from it at speed was finally taken out of use in 1971.

Track
1. The running lines and sidings etc. of a rly or tramway.
2. (RS) A track circuit [section] (qv); hence 'track failure', which is not what it may seem to the untutored when announced as a cause of train delays.
3. (US) Station platform (usually with the associated numeral).

Trackage rights (US)
Running powers (qv).

Track basher (RS)
One who indulges in track bashing (qv).

Track bashing (RS)
Travel by gricers (qv) and others over rarely-used or unusual stretches of line, difficult or impossible to cover in ordinary passenger trains, with special emphasis on travelling to the very limits of such lines ('buffer-kissing'); also the pursuit of an ambition to travel over *all* lines in use in the UK or in some other defined area.

Track chargeman
The leader of a track maintenance team.

Track circuit [operating] clips
Two metal spring clips connected by a wire band, carried in all BR driving cabs for use in emergency. Clipped to the running rails, they close the track circuit in the same way as the train, putting all automatic signals to danger to prevent any train running into a derailment or incident affecting the parallel track.

Track circuits
A valuable safety device invented by the American William Robinson in 1872. It involves the passing of a low voltage electric current through one of the running rails of a section of line (the rails have to be bonded and insulated joints made at each end of the section), then via a track relay and back through the other rail, thus completing the circuit. Should a train or part of a train be on the line, however, this signal current will take the shorter path through its wheels and axles, thus demagnetizing (de-energizing) the track relay. Should there be an electrical failure or accidental short circuit, the relay is also de-energized, thus 'failing safe'. By this means signalmen can be informed on track diagrams of the presence and progress of a train on any section, and if track circuiting is continuous, automatic signalling is made possible, since signals in the rear of a train can be made to remain 'on' by the opening of the track relay while a train is in the section in advance. Track circuits also enable points to be secured against movement under or in front of an approaching train and, where manual signalling is in use, permit signals or block instruments to be locked or controlled so that signals cannot be moved to 'off' while a train (or part of it) is on the section and closing the circuit in the rear of the relay. The introduction of track circuits in the UK was much delayed by the widespread use of Mansell (qv) wheels but the device was universally adopted for London's Underground from the early 1900s, both on new tube lines and on existing lines when these were electrified. The system is now widely used on BR. *See also* Overlap track circuit.

Tracked hovercraft
see THL.
Track failure
see Track (2).
Track man/woman
A member of a track maintenance team.
Track miles
The total mileage of single track, i.e. the geographical miles of route of a rly multiplied by the number of parallel tracks, together with the mileage of track in sidings, depots etc.
Track pans/troughs (US)(obs)
Water troughs (qv).
Track 29
A profit centre of BR Parcels Group (qv) specializing in the heavier consignments. From a line in the song *Chatanooga Choo Choo* referring to the track (platform) from which that train departs.
Track walker
A track man/woman who walks along the line (usually daily) to check for defects and adjustments needed.
Traction pole/standard
Steel poles at the side of a rly, interurban or tramway (3) which are used to suspend the overhead traction current wiring.
Tractive effort
The maximum force developed at any given time at the rim of a loco's driving wheels while working itself and its train. Its value always exactly balances the net resistance forces met by the train and it is not by itself a measure of power. *See also* Drawbar pull; Rail tractive effort.
Tractors (RS)
BR diesel-electric locos, class 37.
Traffic apprentices (obs)
A scheme in which promising youngsters were selected and trained for management positions on the rly, originally adopted by the NER by the

initiative of Sir G.S. Gibb in 1897.
Superseded by the BR Management
Training Scheme.
Traffic Circular
see TC.
Traffic Regulation
Control exercised over the movement
of traffic for a particular destination or
consignee in circumstances where
conditions demand a departure from
normal planned movements. *See also*
Regulation [of passenger traffic].
Traffic Regulator
A supervisor employed in large signal
boxes to decide local priorities in train
working and give directions to the
signalmen. The TR is not concerned
with 'traffic regulation' (qv).
Trafford Park
Rlys in the Trafford Park Industrial
Estate, Manchester, opened 1900.
Trail boss (RS)(obs)
A stationmaster.
Trailer
Any passenger vehicle without a power
unit of its own, usually those in dmu
or emu sets. Also any non-powered
unit hauled by a tramcar or dummy
(*1*) and (*2*) (qv).
Trailing load
The gross weight of passengers and
freight and the rolling stock pulled by
the power unit, expressed in tons.
Trailing points
Points where lines converge in the
direction of running, passed over by
the train from the heel to the toe of
the switch; the opposite of facing
points (qv).

TRAIN
Acronym for Telerail Automated
Information Network, a computerized
freight car information system
operated in the US, Mexico and
Canada by the AAR (qv). Introduced
1971, 1974.
Train Bleu, le
see Blue Train.
Train call (obs)
A notice posted in a theatre to inform
a touring company of actors of the
details of their rail journey to the next
engagement.
Train captain
An employee in charge of an
automatically-operated train on the
DLR (qv). The duties include
checking tickets and taking over
manual control when normal working
is interrupted or inexpedient.
Train car (US)(obs)
An early term for caboose (qv).
Train control
Supervision of train running exercised
by Control (qv). Not to be confused
with traffic regulation (qv).
Train de luxe (Fr)(obs)
A First class only luxury train.
Train de neige (Fr)
A special train for winter sports traffic.
Train describer/indicator
An apparatus by which descriptions of
a train (type and route) are passed
from one signalbox to the next or
provided on a panel on power box
track diagrams. The term 'train
indicator' was used for the early forms
of electrically-operated apparatus
serving this purpose. With the
development of computers and
electronics, train describers have been
adapted to trigger route-setting,
together with associated signal and
point movements and also to operate
indicators (now normally vdus) to

show passengers the destinations etc.
and sequence of trains due to arrive at
a station.

Train dispatcher/runner
see Train order.

Train doors (US)
The doors at each end of a car which
give access via step flaps to the next
car. Also in use on LT.

Train Ex
A term first used in 1969 for
exhibition trains (qv). Title of a
limited company formed in 1973, with
BR participation, to provide a
complete service for design,
construction, management and
operation of trains for travelling
exhibition purposes.

Train express (Fr)(obs)
A fast train with all three classes of
accommodation.

Train ferry
A purpose-built ship fitted with rly
tracks, which, in combination with
suitable ramps on shore, enable rail
vehicles, including complete trains, to
be moved across water gaps. Among
the through passenger and freight rail
services operated by this means are
those between Germany, Denmark
and Sweden; between European and
Asiatic Turkey at Istanbul; and (until
the opening of the Channel Tunnel)
between Britain and France. *See also*
Night Ferry.

Train graph
A graphical representation of train
movements over a section of line in
terms of time and distance. Used in
planning timetables etc.

Train indicator
see Train describer/indicator.

Train length limit
The maximum number of vehicles
which may be formed into a train
passing over a given section of rly.

Train line
The complete system of brake pipes
through a train.

Trainload
The formation of a train, taking into
account train load and length limits.

Trainload Freight
A separate BR business sector formed
in 1990 to manage the bulk load
freight business. Subdivided into
Trainload Coal [solid fuels and nuclear
flasks], Trainload Construction
[aggregates, cement and refuse],
Trainload Petroleum [oils and petrol],
and Trainload Metals [steel and
aluminium]. All other rail freight
activity remained a responsibility of
Railfreight Distribution (qv).

Trainload limit
The maximum tonnage which may be
conveyed by a given class of train
and/or hauled by a loco over a route.

Train mile
A measurement representing the
movement of one train over one mile.

Train omnibus (Fr)(obs)
A train stopping at most but not
necessarily all stations on its route. *See
also* Tramway, train.

Train order
Telegraphed instructions given by a
train dispatcher as to the exact
operation of trains over long
unsignalled and lightly-used sections
of single line in the US and elsewhere
outside the British Isles. These orders
give details of locations and times for
the train to cross others coming in the
opposite direction etc. Responsibility
for observing a train order is shared
by the conductor and the engineer,
who both have to sign for restrictive
train orders. In theory, written train
orders are only necessary for extra
trains or when late running is
occurring, since trains otherwise

proceed according to the planned
timetables and recognized running
priorities, but with the dispatcher
always in overall control.

Train pipe
The pipe through a train with flexible
connections between wagons or
coaches used in connection with
automatic air and vacuum brake
systems. *See also* Train line.

Train protection bar
A locking bar to prevent a signalman
taking off a home signal while a train
remains in the station.

Train Régional (Fr)
A term used in France and Switzerland
to denote a local stopping train.

Train register
The written record kept in a signalbox
of the actual times when the approach
of a train is advised; when it passes;
when it is warned on to the next box;
the minutes it is late or early, and any
unusual state such as open door, tail
light not visible etc. The primary
purpose of the register is to remind
the signalman of the position of the
trains he is dealing with at any given
time. *See also* Booking lad.

Train regulation
The work of control (qv) or of a traffic
regulator (qv).

Train regulator (LT)
An operator stationed in a signalling
control centre, who continually
supervises the working of a whole line,
aided by mimic diagrams, vdus etc.,
intervening to manage local regulation
and make minor adjustments of the
train service as required.

Train runner
Train dispatcher: *see* Train order.

Train shed
An overall roof covering all tracks and
platforms at a through or terminal
station.

Trains Illustrated
see TI.

Train spotter
A term introduced *c.* 1945 for a breed
that had existed for at least seventy
years without a name – those (mostly
juvenile and male) addicted to lineside
or station observation for the purpose
of recording in a notebook ('copping')
the numbers of locos when first seen.
The word 'spotter' was borrowed from
the rather more purposeful aircraft
spotters of the Second World War,
and the Ian Allan 'Spotters' Club' was
formed in 1945; its name was changed
to 'Ian Allan Locospotters' Club' in
1948. The term was subsequently
adopted by media hacks and others as
a mildly derogatory label for anyone
interested in rlys.

Train staff/tablet/token and ticket
Train staffs are a visible token of a
driver's authority to enter a single line
section between crossing places.
Before a train can enter, this staff
must be held by the driver, and since
only one exists for each section,
working is thus restricted to alternate
trains moving in opposite directions. A
refinement is the *train staff and ticket*
system in which drivers of the first
trains through the section are shown
the staff (to demonstrate the section
ahead is clear) and given a paper form
or metal ticket. These tickets are kept
in signal cabins or booking offices in
boxes which can only be opened and
closed by use of the key in the train
staff. Removal of the staff relocks the
box. By this means two or more trains
can pass through the section in the
same direction, only the last of the
group carrying the staff. No trains can
pass in the opposite direction until the
staff has arrived at the other end of the
section. Normal block working

applies. A further refinement is the *electric token or tablet* system, in which the 'visible authority' (staffs,tokens or tablets, unique to their section) is contained in electrically-controlled and interlocked instruments which allow only one to be released at a time. When this authority is placed in the instrument at the other end of the section, a second staff/tablet can be taken from the instrument at the beginning of the section, allowing a second train to pass through and so on. Tokens or tablets are usually placed in a leather pouch attached to a metal hoop to facilitate exchange between signalman and train crews.

Train station (US)
Term for a rly station, adopted by the UK media and others from the 1980s. Until then, in the UK, the word 'station' had, for around 150 years, always been taken to denote a rly station, the other types (police station, bus station, coach station, petrol station etc.) being distinguished by their full title.

Train Stop
A device at the trackside, usually at a signal, which automatically stops a train attempting to pass the signal when it is at danger since, when that

Trip handle

Signal at green, Train Stop arm lying down

Signal at red, Train Stop arm, sticking up, knocks back trip handle on train, so applying brakes

is the case, its arm is raised and held vertically in a position in which it knocks open the trip cock (qv) on the offending train or loco.

Train tramway (Fr)(obs)
see Tramway, train.

Tram
1. (obs) Any vehicle, but usually a wagon, used on a tramroad (*1*) (qv).
2. A shortened form of tramcar (qv).
3. (RS) A mildly derogatory term for an electric train, which was more widely current when steam trains were ubiquitous and provided a much more interesting object for the activities of the average train spotter (qv).

Tram basher (RS)
A fanatical type of enthusiast who indulges in haulage bashing (qv) on electric rlys. *See also* Undergricing.

Tramcar
Used from *c.* 1860 for vehicles working over tramways (*3*), usually passenger-carrying, and since *c.* 1898 (earlier in the US), usually electrically-powered. Often abbreviated to tram and, until *c.* 1950, to 'car'.

Tram engine (obs)
A steam tank engine with enclosed motion suitable for running on tramways (*3*) and (*4*), or on sections of rly laid in the roadway. *See also* Dummy.

Tramlink
A light rail transit system for south London [Wimbledon–Croydon–New Addington/Elmers End/Beckenham] planned to open in 1994–5.

Trammie (S)
A tramway (*3*) driver or conductor.

Tram pinch
Wording of a road sign warning motorists that tramway (*3*) track swerves close to the edge of the roadway ahead.

Tramroad

1. The earliest form of rly, lightly laid, with stone, wooden, metal-stripped wooden, or iron plate L-section rails, carrying vehicles pushed manually or hauled by horses or mules, and wholly or mainly used for carriage of freight between mines, quarries, mills etc. and ports and navigable water. The word was first used *c.* 1800 replacing the earlier 'dram road'. *See also* Plateway; Tramway (*1*); Waggon road/way.

2. A term used occasionally in the late nineteenth and early twentieth centuries in the formal titles of undertakings operating tramways (*3*). By that time few tramways (*1*) existed and the word was a convenient way of distinguishing lines or systems which included sections not laid on public roads.

Tram walloper (S)

A pickpocket specializing in the tramcar side of the business.

Tramway

1. A term used in the early nineteenth century for the earliest forms of conventional rly. *See also* Tramroad (*1*) with which, in this sense, it was virtually synonymous.

2. A portable or lightly-laid industrial rly.

3. A term used in Britain from *c.* 1860 to describe a tracked system, wholly or mainly used for the carriage of passengers within urban and suburban areas, or linking up such areas within a conurbation, its tracks mostly laid along the centre or at the side of streets and roads but possibly with some sections segregated on a central or side reservation, on private right of way off roads, or in shallow subways. Originally animal,

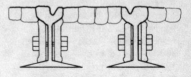

Cross section of track for tramway (3)

cable and steam traction were the main forms of motive power, but since *c.* 1898 (*c.* 1888 in the US), virtually all such systems have been electrically-worked, usually with traction current taken from an overhead line by trolley wheel, skid, bow, or pantograph. *See also* Light rail [transit]; Light rly.

4. (obs) A form of light rly, usually alongside or on public roads, connecting two or more towns, a town and nearest rly station, or a city with a satellite community. Usually worked initially with steam tram engines or steam tramcars and carrying freight as well as passengers.

5. (US) An aerial cable rly with suspended cars (aerial tramway).

Tramway & Railway World
see T&RW.

Tramway Museum Society
see TMS.

Tramway, train (Fr)(obs)
A local stopping train not conveying heavy luggage or parcels traffic.

Transalpin
An express emu service between Vienna and Zurich, introduced 1958, became an EC 1987.

Transalpino
A limited company, formed in 1952 to

organize discount fare rail travel for adults under twenty-five. Ceased to function in 1989.

Trans-Andine

Rly from Buenos Aires to Valparaiso, completed 1910. Destroyed by floodwaters in 1934, rebuilt and reopened 1944. Journey time about 36 h. Closed again by a landslide, 1984. Service at present interrupted.

Transatlantique, trains (Fr)(obs)

Boat trains between Paris (St Lazare) and Le Havre (Gare Maritime) in connection with Transatlantic liner sailings.

Trans-Australia Express

Service between Port Pirie and Kalgoorlie with connections at these break of gauge points, to provide a Perth–Melbourne journey. The timing in 1938 was 29–30 h. The connecting Perth–Kalgoorlie service (The Westland) was timed at approx 15 h and the Port Pirie–Melbourne connection at 17 h 5 min. At this period, the 2,690 m from Perth to Sydney could be covered in 85 h 45 min westbound and 88 h 15 min eastbound. The line is now standard gauge throughout and the Sydney–Perth journey has been reduced to about 64 h, travelled in the same train. *See also* Indian Pacific.

Trans-Canada Limited

CPR all-sleeper service between Montreal, Toronto and Vancouver, introduced 1919, 93 h 30 min westbound, 92 h 15 min eastbound.

Trans-Europ Express

see TEE.

Transfer

1. A method of applying inscriptions, coats of arms and other insignia, logos etc. after the completion of coach painting.
2. (obs) A type of ticket issued on some tramways (*3*) which allowed the holder to transfer at specified points to cars on other lines to reach a specified destination.

Transfer Agent (US)(obs)

Term for an official who walked through long distance trains as they approached major stations, undertaking the delivery of passengers' luggage and giving receipts in exchange for the baggage checks. Transfer Agents also undertook delivery of luggage to rly stations and its transfer between stations in the large centres. *See also* Baggage master; Check system; Parmalee transfer.

Transfers (RS)(obs)

Wagons to be exchanged between sidings, lines or companies.

Transfer table (US)

Traverser (qv).

TRANSFESA (Sp)

Transportes Ferroviarios Especiales SA; Special Railway Transport Co. Formed 1943 to facilitate the operation of through running freight cars between Spain and other European countries.

Tranships (obs)

Freight loaded into one wagon for various destinations when traffic to these is insufficient to justify a through wagon. Hence tranship wagon/van. *See also* Station trucks.

Trans-Maghreb Express

A service between Tunis and Algiers, introduced 1975. Political disputes have prevented its planned extension to serve Casablanca.

Trans-Manchurian Express

A *CIWL* service Harbin and Changchun, introduced 1906. Restored after the First World War, ceased 1935.

Transmark

Transportation Systems & Market

Research Ltd, BR subsidiary advising and assisting overseas authorities on rly matters. Formed 1969, began trading 1970.

Transnet Ltd
The private operators of South African Rlys from 1990.

Trans-Pennine
BR dmu services between Liverpool (Lime St.) and Leeds/Hull, introduced 1961, name dropped 1969. The title survived tenuously as a general brand name for services Liverpool/ Manchester to Leeds/Hull/ Newcastle for another twenty years until their integration into the new Provincial Sector Express services.

Transport Acts
A general title adopted for legislation affecting BR, LT and other public transport operations, beginning with the 1947 Act, which nationalized public transport and set up the BTC (qv). Further structural and policy changes were made by the Transport Acts of 1953, 1962, 1968, 1969 (London), 1980, 1981, 1983 and 1985.

Transport & Travel Monthly
see T&TM.

Transport 2000
An organization formed in 1973 to bring together all groups concerned about the future of public transport services. It calls for a co-ordinated national policy to avoid wastage of rail and other public transport assets, the improvement and modernization of these assets, and control of the increasing environmental damage caused by the relentless growth of road transport.

Transport World
see T&RW.

Trans-Siberian Express
A *CIWL* service between Moscow and Irkutsk, introduced 1898 as Siberia Express, extended to Harbin

(Kharbin) and Vladivostok 1904 and so named. *See also* Rossiya.

Trans-Siberian Rly
Connects Moscow and Vladivostok; completed 1891–1904. An all-Russian route via Khabarovsk was completed in 1916, and the line was laid with double track throughout from 1928. Now electrified throughout.

Trap points
Safety points provided in a line to prevent unauthorized movements on to another line.

Traps (RS)
Guard's equipment, or any equipment normally carried on duty by any rlyman.

Travel agent
A private individual or firm selling rly passenger tickets on behalf of BR in return for a commission.

Travel card
A ticket allowing unlimited travel by rail, underground and buses in a closely defined urban area for periods of one day or longer.

Travel centres
Offices established at principal BR stations in the 1960s and 1970s to advise passengers on BR travel facilities and sell tickets and seat reservations for journeys to any destination. The name had an earlier origin: the BR London Travel Centre in Lower Regent St. was opened in June 1953, serving a similar function and replacing several smaller ticket and enquiry offices in central London.

Travelers' Aid
A US social agency formed in 1907, to give assistance to travellers in difficulties, notably children, immigrants and old people. TA staff man booths or desks at rly stations which are marked by a blue and white globe.

Traveling card (US)
A card issued by a trade union (brotherhood) to a member in search of rly employment.

Travellers-Fare
Brand name for BR catering outlets, adopted 1973. Separated from BTH (qv) as a free-standing division of BRB, 1982. Sold to management 1988, BR retaining freehold of station sites.

Travelling College
A BR train of thirteen coaches, including sleeping accommodation, shop, meeting room and classrooms, launched 1989. Ceased trading 1991.

Travelling crane
A crane mounted on a truck, used for minor breakdowns and accidents and also for loading and unloading in sidings etc. where no fixed crane exists. The term is also used for workshop cranes moving along fixed overhead tracks.

Travelling porter (obs)
A man who rode on a hooded seat at the back of loco tender to observe the train, ensuring that all was well. The practice lasted from 1847 until 1861.

Travel on one's basket, to (obs)
Free travel in the guard's van for minor or junior members of a theatrical party sitting on the basket containing their personal gear. An unofficial but apparently tolerated extension of free trucking (qv).

Traverser
A powered platform with a short section of rly track, running across the ends of depot etc. tracks and used to transfer vehicles or locos one at a time to and from parallel roads. Also a feature of tramcar depots.

Traversias (Sp)
Track sleepers.

Traversing jacks
Pairs of jacks, linked by a crossbeam containing a screw thread and used for re-railing vehicles.

TRB
BR Trailer Buffet.

TRBF
BR Trailer Buffet First class.

TRBFL
BR TRBF (qv) with Lavatory.

TRBS
BR Trailer Buffet Second/Standard class.

TRBSL
BR TRBS (qv) with Lavatory.

Treacle toffee (RS)(obs)
Welsh coal.

Treadle
A device attached to a rail in which electrical contacts are operated by the passage of a train. Used for example to prove that a train has left a block section.

Treenail or Trenail
A hardwood plug used with track spikes for fastening chairs to sleepers.

Tren de Sierra
A service between Lima and Huancayo over the world's highest main line rly, reaching 15,694 ft/ 4,783.5 metres above sea level.

Trent Valley Line
Rugby–Tamworth–Stafford.

Triangle
An arrangement of facing and trailing points leading into and out of a spur which enables loco to be turned without use of a turntable.

Trick (USRS)
A shift or duty.

Tricomposite/compo (obs)
A coach with seating for First, Second and Third class passengers.

Trimmer (USRS)
A shunting loco assigned to recovering misdirected wagons in a hump yard.

Trip

1. A local train movement of a small
lift of freight wagons or vans
between freight terminals/private
sidings/marshalling yards etc.,
hence tripping, trip engine, trip
working.

2. (LTRS) A tripcock (qv).

3. (RS)(obs) The annual holiday
outing of employees at Swindon
Works.

Tripcock/trip handle

A valve attached to a train or
locomotive which, if activated by an
erect train stop arm (qv), releases
compressed air from the train pipe,
causing an immediate emergency
brake application.

Trip past, to (LTRS)

Apply the rule, to (qv).

Triple crown (RS)

A loco exhibiting three headlamps.

Tripped, to be (LTRS)

A train brought to a halt by the action
of a train stop (qv) and tripcock (qv).

Tri-Rail (US)

An organization formed in 1989 and
sponsored by three counties to operate
a passenger rail service between West
Palm Beach and Miami, southern
Florida.

TRM

A Track Relaying Machine, BR.

Trolley

The current collection gear of an
electric tramcar or other simple
electric rail vehicle, consisting of
trolley pole, trolley head, grooved
trolley wheel or skid, and base.

Trolley [line/system] (US)

Term for a tramway (*3*) operated by
electric cars; hence trolley car,
sometimes shortened to 'trolley'.

Trolley freight (US)

Term for any freight service operated
by electric locos or cars powered

through an overhead line and trolley
(qv), interurban or otherwise.

Trouble card (LTRS)

A form provided in driving cabs for
reporting train defects.

TRS

Temporary Restriction of Speed. *See
also* TSR.

TRSB

Trailer in a BR HST set with Second/
Standard class Buffet.

TRT

Turn-Round Time:

1. The time allowed at the terminus
or end of a working to turn a train
or loco round, service it as
necessary and start the next run,
possibly including a rest period for
the crew.

2. (obs) The time from the start of
one loaded journey of a freight
wagon to its next.

TRUB

Trailer Unclassed Buffet/restaurant car
with kitchen in a BR HST set.

Truck

1. Any open wagon.

2. A fixed, rigid undercarriage to a
rail vehicle, incorporating axles and
wheels and, in electrically-powered
cars, the motors.

3. A four- or six-wheeled
undercarriage attached to a loco or
vehicle by means of a king-pin or
pivot, thus allowing an easier
passage round curves than is
afforded by (*2*) and also permitting
a vehicle of greater length. In electric
vehicles the trucks incorporate the
traction motors. This type of truck
has long been known in the UK as a
'bogie' (except in the case of
tramcars and some electric rly cars)
but the word truck is also used, as it
has always been used in the US, for
both (*2*) and (*3*).

TRUK
Trailer Restaurant Unclassed [with] Kitchen in a BR HST set.

Trumpet (LTRS)
A loud hailer.

Trunk haul (obs)
The main part of a freight transit, usually from the initial to the final marshalling point.

Trunk line
A rly system serving an extensive area.

TRUST
Train Running System; a BR computer system.

TS
Trailer Second/Standard class in a BR dmu or HST set.

TSDB
Train Service Data Base. A computer system holding details of all BR scheduled passenger services. Based at York.

TSG
Transport Supplementary Grant. A central government grant paid to local authorities in respect of public transport expenditure carried on local budgets.

TSL
BR TS (qv) with Lavatory.

TSO
Tourist Open Second/Standard class coach, BR, with 2 + 2 seating.

TSR
Temporary Speed Restriction. Also TRS (qv).

TSSA
The Transport Salaried Staff Association; founded 1897 as Railway Clerks' Association and so renamed after the formation of the BTC.

TT
1. The Transport Tribunal.
   Established under the Railway Act, 1921 as the Railway Rates Tribunal and so renamed by the Transport Act, 1947 which conferred upon it jurisdiction over rates and charges for public transport facilities.
2. The Transport Trust, a registered charity founded in 1964–5 to encourage the permanent preservation through affiliated organizations, or directly, of representative items of the UK transport heritage, land, sea and air. The Trust gives financial assistance and advice to transport preservation projects, and maintains a register of such projects.

TTI
Travelling Ticket Inspector.

Tub (RS)
A brake.

Tube
1. Strictly an underground rly using tunnels driven at deep level by means of a tunnelling shield, or the trains which operate on such lines, notably in London, thus, the tube, tube rlys, tube stations, tube trains etc. The word 'tube' was first used c. 1885 to describe the special type of tunnel, but by 1890 the expression 'tube rly' was current. The special meaning was maintained for over sixty years and is respected in this dictionary, but since about 1950 loose journalistic use ('Tube Chaos' made a snappy headline) has increasingly led to its being employed to describe *any* type of underground rly, particularly in London, whether of tube or cut and cover construction. Sadly, since c. 1978 London Transport has given this sloppy custom its official blessing by misusing the word in its own publications, notably in the title of

its newspaper for Underground staff, *Tube Line*, first issued in 1986.

2. (obs) A booking office ticket container for Edmondson (qv) card tickets.

Tubes, loco
The horizontal pipes carrying smoke and burning gases from the firebox to the smokebox, heating the boiler water which surrounds them and thus producing the steam.

TUCC
Transport Users' Consultative Committees. *See also* CTCC.

Tumblehome
A contraction in body width of a rly coach or tramcar below the waistline.

Tunnel
A rly tunnel is defined by BR civil engineers as any structure that carries the rly through or under a *natural* obstruction. Anything else is a 'bridge', or 'covered way' and some passages beneath or through man-made obstructions are longer than short tunnels.

Tunnel miners
Specialist labourers employed on the construction of tube rlys and similar tunnels.

Tunnel motor (RS)
GWR 0–6–0 PT loco fitted with condensing gear for working over the Metropolitan and Circle lines of the London Underground.

Tunnel rats (LTRS)
Trainmen working on London tube rlys.

Tunnel tigers
Nickname for tunnel miners (qv).

Tuppenny Tube
Nickname bestowed on the CLR by a journalist. When opened in 1900, it had a uniform 2d fare for all journeys.

Turbomotive
LM&SR 4–6–0 built in 1935 to the designs of W.A. Stanier and equipped with a turbine drive instead of the usual cylinders. Rebuilt as a conventional steam loco in 1952, it was destroyed in the serious accident at Harrow & Wealdstone later that year.

Turbotrain (obs)
A French gas turbine train design, usually with auxiliary diesel engines, exported to Egypt, Iran, USA and Canada. *See also* ETG; RTG.

Turin–Nice–Cannes Pullman
A *CIWL* service, ran summer 1927 only.

Turin–Venice Pullman
A *CIWL* service, ran summer 1928 only.

Turksib
A major Russian rail project of the period between the two world wars, connecting the Trans-Siberian line (qv) with Turkestan in the far south. Opened 1931, and the subject of a film of this title.

Turn
The daily duty or shift for uniformed and ticket office staff.

Turnback link (obs)
The link (qv) of enginemen which relieved incoming crews at the end of a journey, taking the loco to the depot and preparing it for the return run.

Turner, engine (obs)
An employee at an engine shed whose duties were to move locos around the yard and turn them on the turntable.

Turnout
The total assembly of trackwork involved in 'turning out' one line from another by means of a pair of switches, a crossing and a reverse curve running in the direction of the second line, with or without an

intermediate section of straight line. Strictly *not* synonymous with points, but often so used.

Turnover working
An arrangement in which the loco of the previous train is attached to the rear of the next arrival at a terminus to secure a rapid turnround.

Turnplate (obs)
A small turntable for moving wagons and short coaches from one line to another.

Turn-Round Time
see TRT.

Turntable
A revolving table fitted with a section of line, used to turn a loco around or move it from one line to another.

TUT (obs)
Terminal Utilization Time; the time between the arrival of a particular wagon at a depot until its despatch, loaded or empty.

TV
Trent Valley (qv), Tanat Valley (qv). *See also* TVR.

TVLR
see Tanat Valley.

TVR
1. Taff Vale Rly, Cardiff to Merthyr/ Aberdare/Maerdy/Treherbert etc., inc 1836, first section opened 1840. 124 route miles by 1914. Part of GWR from 1922.
2. Teign Valley Rly, Christow– Heathfield, inc 1863, opened 1882, worked by GWR. Part of GWR from 1923.
3. Tees Valley Rly, inc 1865, from near Barnard Castle to Middleton-in-Teesdale, opened 1868, worked by NER, part of NER 1882.

Twelve wheel loco (US)
A loco with 4–8–0 wheel arrangement.

Twentieth/20th Century Limited
An overnight NYC express between

New York and Chicago, introduced 1902 with a time of 20 h. Affectionately known as 'The Century', it had become 'a national institution' by 1926. Journey time reduced to 18 h in 1932. Timing became 16 h in 1938, with new stock, and all sleeping accommodation in rooms. The 16 h schedule was resumed in 1946, and had been reduced to 15 h 30 min by 1954. The consist remained all-Pullman until 1957. Ceased to run on 2 December 1967.

Twenty-four hour clock
A system in which p.m. times are distinguished by adding 12, e.g. 3 p.m. = 15.00. Adopted by Indian rlys 1864–70; Italian rlys *c.* 1890; Belgian and Spanish rlys in the 1900s; French and Portugese rlys in 1912; the British Army in 1918; Cook's Timetables (qv) in 1919, and by most European rlys other than those mentioned in the 1920s. BR moved to the system in 1965; LT in 1964–5.

TWERPS
Tunbridge Wells–Eridge Railway Preservation Society, responsible for the reopening of this former BR line as a preserved rly and also as a public service operation. *See also* Spa Valley Line.

Twin Rover (obs)
A ticket formerly available for one day's unlimited travel on most of London Underground and central area buses and trolleybuses on Saturdays, Sundays and Bank Holidays, introduced 1958.

Twirly (RS)
A pensioner using a concession ticket/ free pass, or the ticket itself. Usage of these facilities is normally restricted to the period after the morning peak and the origin of the term is

the question frequently asked by holders uncertain whether the hour for its use had been reached: 'Am I *too early*?'.

Twist
A change of cant.

Twisters (USRS)
Hand brakes.

Two crows for a banker (RS)(obs)
The whistle code exchanged between train engine and banker when ready to move.

Two labour gains (RS)
see Labour gain[s].

Twopenny Tube
see Tuppenny Tube.

Two rooms and a bath
A colloquialism for an articulated tramcar set in which two cars are connected by a small flexible central entrance section in which the conductor is seated.

Two-two-two (RS)(obs)
222 Marylebone Road, London, the former headquarters of the RE (*3*), BRB and BTC.

Two Woodbines and an aspirin (RS)(obs)
The engine driver's breakfast; Woodbines were a very cheap cigarette.

Tyne & Wear Metro
The prototype British light rail transit system (qv), largely based on former BR tracks in the Newcastle area and serving Whitley Bay, Gateshead, Jarrow and South Shields. First sections opened 1980.

Tynesider
A sleeping car express between London (Kings Cross) and Newcastle, so named 1950. Name dropped 1968.

Tyne Valley Line
Newcastle to Hexham and Carlisle.

Tyre (US = tire)
The flange and tread profile of rly/tramway wheel.

Tyrol Express
A *CIWL* service [Calais] Paris–Zurich–Innsbruck–Salzburg, introduced 1932.

TZR
Tanzania–Zambia Rly: *see* Tanzam.

U

U
Unclassed vehicle, BR.

U-Bahn (Ger)
Untergrundbahn; underground rly, not part of main German rly system; synonymous with metro (qv).

U-boats (RS)
SR 2-6-0 locos.

UCC
Union Construction Company; the manufacturing subsidiary of the UERL (qv), registered 1901. Reconstituted as Union Construction & Finance Co. Ltd, 1929. Built and rebuilt tramcars and tube cars at Feltham, Middlesex, 1925-32. Wound up in 1933 following the formation of the LPTB.

UEC
United Electric Car Co. Ltd, Preston, rly and tramway vehicle builders. Inc 1898 as ER & TCW (qv), a subsidiary of DK (qv); renamed UEC 1905, after purchase of the assets of the BEC (qv) and Milnes (qv). Became part of EE (qv), 1919.

UERL
Underground Electric Railways Company of London Ltd. Popularly known as the Underground Company or, with its subsidiaries, as the Underground Group. Also known (mainly among politicians) as the London Traffic Combine. Formed in 1902 to take over the MDET (qv), and held a controlling interest in the MDR (qv) and the three tube rlys which became the LER (qv). Absorbed the London General Omnibus Co. in 1912, and the CLR (*1*) (qv) and the C&SLR (qv) in 1913. Also acquired control of the company-owned tramways in the London area and the North Metropolitan Electric Power Supply Co. Its transport interests became part of LPTB from 1933. 'The mysterious American Corporation' — RM 1906.

UIC
Union Internationale des Chemins de Fer; International Union of Railways, formed 1922 to standardize and improve rly equipment and operating methods, with special regard to international traffic. Since 1950 the UIC has been responsible for ensuring co-ordination and unity of action in international rly organizations including the CIT (*3*), *EFK*, *EWP*, *RIC* and *RIV*.

UITP
Union Internationale des Transports Publics; International Union of Public Transport, founded 1885 to pool the experience of urban and interurban public transport undertakings for joint study and research and promotion of the technical and economic development of the industry.

Ukeleles (RS)
Class J39 0-6-0 locos L&NER.

UKRAS
United Kingdom Railway Advisory Service; formed in 1959 to provide an

advisory and consultancy service to
rlys overseas and to sponsor the
training of overseas rly staff on BR.
Reconstituted as UKRAS Consultants
Ltd, 1966. Wound up 1969 and
superseded by Transmark (qv).

Ulster Express
A service between London (Euston)
and Fleetwood connecting with Belfast
sailings, name introduced 1927,
diverted to Heysham 1928. Name re-
introduced 1949; service ceased 1975
with the withdrawal of the Heysham–
Belfast service.

UMLER
Acronym for Universal Machine
Language Equipment Register; a
computerized inventory of US rly
rolling stock.

UN
Underground News. The monthly
publication (since December 1961) of
the LURS (qv). From 1961 to
December 1974 it was known as
UndergrounD; *The Journal of
the London Underground Railway
Society*.

Unbalanced working
A duty without provision for return to
depot or other starting point.

Unclassed/unclassified
BR terms for a coach available for use
by both First and Second/Standard
class passengers.

Uncle Sam (USRS)
A Post Office employee working on a
mail train.

Underbridge
A bridge carrying line over a road,
canal, river or another rly, i.e. an
underline bridge.

Underframe
A wood or metal framework carrying
the main body structure of a vehicle.

Undergricing (RS)
Track bashing (qv) on underground

rlys. Also undergricer, one who
indulges in undergricing.

Underground [the]
The brand name since 1908 for all
London underground rlys, deep tube
and subsurface, including those not
controlled by the UERL (qv) but
excepting the W&CR. Often displayed
on signs and publicity as U-N-D-E-R-
G-R-O-U-N-D. Use of the term persisted
through and beyond the LPTB era but
in more recent years it has to some
extent given way to 'tube' (qv).

Underground hog (USRS)
1. A senior driver.
2. Chief engineer in charge of track
   maintenance.

Undermen (obs)
Men working on track under a ganger
(qv).

Under the arm (RS)
Not up to standard.

Under the hammer (RS)
A train accepted at caution by a
signalman.

Under the wire(s) (RS)
Travelling over an electrified line
equipped with overhead catenary.

UNDM
Uncoupling Non-Driving Motor car in
a mu set.

Undums (LTRS)
Colloquialism for UNDM (qv).

Unimog
A four-wheel drive diesel-engined
vehicle capable of operating on roads,
across country or using rly tracks,
developed by Mercedes-Benz in the
1960s.

Union Castle Express
see Springbok.

Union Express/Limited
A boat train service between
Johannesburg and Capetown, First
Class only, connecting with Union
Castle Line sailings; 956 m in 28 h

23 min on 3 ft 6 in gauge in 1926.
Superseded by the Blue Train (2) (qv).
Union Pacific (US)
A steam loco with 4–12–2 wheel
arrangement. The first was ordered by
the UP.
Union station (US)(obs)
Term for large rly station shared by
two or more companies. At St Louis
(Missouri), no less that twenty-one
companies used the Union station.
Union switch[er] (US)
Term for a steam loco with 0–10–2
wheel arrangement.
Unit train (US)
A high tonnage train chartered for
carrying a single bulk product, not
requiring any marshalling between
departure and destination points.
Unload, to (USRS)
To jump from a moving train.
Unterpflasterstrassenbahn (Ger)
U-strab (qv).
UP (US)
Union Pacific RR; absorbed Mopac,
1982, and MKT, 1988.
Up
1. The running line to or in the
   general direction of London, or
   (less usually) of the company's
   headquarters, or, for lines wholly
   in Scotland, of Edinburgh, the
   other direction being known as
   'Down'. These terms were taken
   over from road coaching and in the
   London area and other urban
   locations have to some extent given
   way (notably on LT Rlys) to the
   more readily-comprehensible US
   terms, eastbound, northbound,
   southbound and westbound. *See
   also* Down (*1*).
2. (RS) Used of a train running early,
   e.g. 'four up', meaning four
   minutes early against the timetable.
   See also Down (*2*).

UP&SS
United Pointsmen's & Signalmen's
Society, founded 1880, amalgamated
1913 with the ASRS and GRWU to
form the NUR.
Uplift [tickets], to (USRS)
To collect tickets. *See also* Lift
[tickets], to.
Uplighters
Lighting columns placed between
escalators or in circulating areas which
directed their illumination towards the
ceiling, producing a soft and even
reflected glow. Used widely in the
1930s architecture of the London
Underground but subsequently mostly
displaced by less atmospheric
fluorescent tube lighting.
Upper quadrant
A semaphore signal with an arm
which moves into the upper quadrant
when 'off'. Adopted from US practice
and used on some British lines,
particularly the Underground,
LM&SR and L&NER. Early types
incorporated three positions
horizontal (red light) = danger; 45°
(yellow light) = caution; vertical
(green light) = clear/proceed, *or* two
positions, horizontal = danger;

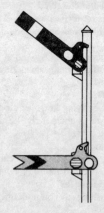

45/50° = clear/proceed. The latter
became general.
Upper Ward Express
A service between Glasgow and
Moffat, introduced 1904, renamed
Tinto Express 1911.
Ups and downs (RS)(obs)
GWR men used this term for
ECS (qv) workings in and out of
Paddington, London and
the associated light engine
runs.
Up siding
A siding trailing off an 'Up' (qv) line.
Up the hole (LTRS)
In a tube tunnel dead end siding.
Up the madhouse (RS)(SR)
London.
Up the road, to go (LTRS)
To see a manager regarding a
misdemeanour.
UR
1. Ulster Rly, inc 1836, Belfast to
   Armagh, first section opened 1839,
   6 ft 2 in/1,879.6 mm gauge,
   converted to 5 ft 3 in/1,600 mm,
   1849, part of GNR (I) from 1876.
2. Uganda Rly. *See also* EAR.
USRA
1. United States Railroad
   Administration; formed in 1917 by
   the US government to operate the
   main rly systems in wartime.
   USRA functioned in this role from
   1 January 1918 until 1 March 1920.
   There was no similar state takeover

in the Second World War in the
US.
2. United States Railway Association;
   a federal agency, formed in 1973 to
   plan and direct the reorganization
   of bankrupt private rly companies.
   See also Conrail.
U-strab (Ger)
Subways used by tramways (*3*).
U-Strassenbahn (Ger)
Subways used by tramways (*3*); also
Unterpflasterstrassenbahn or *U-strab*
(qv).
UTA
Ulster Transport Authority; formed
1948, a merger of the Northern
Ireland Road Transport Board, the
NCC and the B&CDR. Took over
GNR(I) (qv) from GNR Board in
1958, became UTR 1966.
UTM
Urgent Train Message; a written
communication sent by passenger
train.
UTR
Ulster Transport Rlys; took over the
rlys formerly operated by UTA (qv),
1966, became NIR (qv) 1967.
UTS
Underground Ticket Scheme. A
system of ticket-checking entry gates,
self-service automatic machines issuing
magnetic-coded tickets and secure wall
ticket and enquiry offices for staff,
installed at all London Underground
stations 1987–90.

V

Vacuum brakes
A braking system in which the brakes are held off by maintaining a vacuum in an operating cylinder on each vehicle and applied by partially destroying the vacuum by controlled admission of air. Normally arranged as continuous brakes (qv).

VAL (Fr)
Véhicule Automatique Légère; light automatic vehicle. A light rapid transit system (qv) developed by the firm of Matra, using automated rubber-tyred driverless trains running along concrete tracks and guided by horizontal rubber wheels bearing on concrete guideways. Introduced in Lille, 1983.

Valencia Express
A summer service between Paris and Port Bou, introduced 1966, with connecting service to and from Valencia from 1968. Name dropped after 1976.

Vale of Clwyd
Inc 1856, Foryd–Denbigh, opened 1858, worked and managed by L&NWR, part of L&NWR, 1868.

Vale of Glamorgan
Barry to Bridgend, inc 1889, opened 1897, worked by Barry Rly, part of GWR 1922.

Vale of Llangollen
Ruabon to Llangollen, inc 1859, opened 1861, 1862, worked by GWR, amalgamated with GWR 1896.

Vale of Neath
Neath to Aberdare/Merthyr/ Cwmamman, inc 1846, first section opened 1851, amalgamated with GWR 1865.

Vale of Rheidol
Vale of Rheidol Light Rly, Aberystwyth–Devil's Bridge, 1 ft 11½ in/597 mm gauge. Inc 1897, opened 1902, absorbed by Cambrian Rlys 1913, part of GWR 1922, closed 1939, reopened 1945. Part of BR 1948, sold in 1989 to Brecon Mountain Railway Ltd.

Vale of Teifi
Vale of Teifi Narrow Gauge Rly, 2 ft/ 609 mm gauge tourist/pleasure line over part of the former BR Newcastle Emlyn branch, opened 1985.

Vale of Towy
Llandovery Junction to Llandeilo. Inc 1854, opened 1858, vested in L&NWR 1884 but Llanelly Rly & Dock Co. (absorbed by GWR 1889) had power to lease. GWR & L&NWR Joint 1889–1922, GWR & L&MSR joint 1923–47.

Valleys Lines
see Cardiff Valleys [Lines].

Valve gear
The apparatus for controlling the steam distribution valve in the cylinder steam chest of a loco.

Van Beethoven
TEE Amsterdam–Bonn, introduced 1972, replacing *Rhein–Main* (qv),

extended to Frankfurt 1976. Lost *TEE* status 1979.

Vangölü Express

A service between Istanbul (Haydarpasa) and Tehran introduced 1971 using train ferry on Lake Van.

Varnish, the (USRS)(obs)

A passenger train; strictly applicable only to old wooden stock. Also string of varnish, varnished boxes, varnished job, varnished shot, varnished wagons.

VEC (obs)

Four-car emu set of LT tube stock refurbished 1967 for BR service between Ryde Pierhead and Shanklin, 4-VEC; ran with TIS (qv), making VECTIS (the Roman name for the Isle of Wight).

VEG (obs)

BR (S) four-car emu sets Vestibule, Electro-pneumatic brakes Gatwick, converted for Gatwick Airport–London (Victoria) service, 1978, 4-VEG.

Vente ambulante (Fr)

A *CIWL* facility providing drinks and light refreshments from a trolley moved along the corridors and gangways of a train.

VEP

BR (S) four-car corridor emu sets of 1967–74, Vestibule, Electro-Pneumatic brakes; two driving trailer composites (compartments only in the First class), one motor brake Second/Standard class coach and one trailer Second/Standard, all seating in open cars 2 + 3, 4-VEP.

Versailles

A Paris–Geneva *TGV* service, introduced 1983.

Vestibuled [train/coach]

A train or coach with vestibules and gangways enabling passengers to move between one coach and another. The term originated in the US in 1887. *See also* Corridor.

Vesuvio

TEE Milan–Naples 1973, lost *TEE* status 1986.

VFIL (Fr)

Compagnie Générale des Voies Ferrées d'Intérêt Local; a grouping of French secondary rlys.

VFR

Visiting Friends and Relatives; term used by BR to describe this class of passenger traffic. Adopted from air lines and travel trade usage.

VGR

Victorian Government Rlys (Australia).

VIA Rail

A Canadian organization formed in 1977 (CNR had used VIA as a brand name from 1976) to take over the CPR and CNR passenger service marketing functions. From 1978 VIA became an independent corporation contracting with the federal government to manage all rail passenger services, acquiring the CPR and CNR passenger rolling stock and locos.

Vic (LTRS)

Victoria Line, London Transport (qv).

Vichy Pullman Express

see London/Londres–Vichy Pullman.

Vicinal/Vicinaux

see SNCV.

Vickers

see MCW; Metro–Cammell; MV.

Victoria Line

LT Tube rly from Walthamstow to Brixton via Oxford Circus and Victoria, connecting with most other Underground lines. The first of London's second generation of tube rlys, opened in sections 1968–71.

Victory

A London (Waterloo)–Portsmouth express, so named 1989.

Vie du Rail, la

The title assumed by the *SNCF*

magazine in 1952 , formerly *Notre Métier* (qv). A unique blend of well-illustrated and authoritative historical, technical and news items covering not only French rlys and tramways but those of the whole world, together with television, film, fashion and other pages for the family.

Vienna-Tyrol–Cannes Express
A *CIWL* service introduced in 1913.

View finder (RS)
Second man (qv).

Vigilance device
Any arrangement which requires a driver to take positive action at frequent intervals to prevent the train from coming to a halt.

Vignoles rail
Flat-bottomed rail, introduced 1837 by the engineer Charles Blacker Vignoles (1793–1875).

Viking Express
A service between Stockholm, Copenhagen and Hamburg, introduced 1968. Name subsequently dropped, then revived for a service between Paris and Stockholm (24 h) introduced 1986, incorporating sleeping cars between Paris and Helsingør, which replaced the Paris coaches of the Nord express (qv).

Village, the
A two-storey office block completed in 1920 between platforms 15 and 16 at London (Waterloo). Demolished 1991 in connection·with the construction of the London Channel Tunnel Terminal.

Vindobona
An express between Berlin, Prague and Vienna, introduced 1957.

Virgil
GWR TC for 30-ton bogie freight van.

Vistadome
An observation saloon occupying part of a passenger coach roof space, introduced on the Burlington RR (US), 1945. Full length dome cars followed in 1953.

VofGR
see Vale of Glamorgan.

VofLR
see Vale of Llangollen.

VofNR
see Vale of Neath.

VofRR
see Vale of Rheidol.

VofTR
see Vale of Towy.

Volk's Rly
see VR (*1*).

Voltaire
A Paris–Geneva *TGV* service, introduced 1983.

Vomit Special (RS)
Any late night train patronized by inebriates.

VR
1. Volk's Rly, along Brighton seafront, opened by Magnus Volk (1851–1937), the electrical engineering pioneer, with electric traction in 1883, 2 ft gauge, converted to 2 ft 9 in gauge 1884, then to 2 ft 8½ in about 1886. Still operating in the summer season.

2. *Vaultionrautatiet*; Finnish State Rlys.

VS&PR

Victoria Station & Pimlico Rly, inc 1858, opened 1860, absorbed into SR 1923.

VSOE

Venice Simplon–Orient Express; a luxury tourist train operation, using restored traditional British Pullman Co. stock between London (Victoria) and Folkestone and restored *CIWL* restaurant, sleeping and Pullman cars between Boulogne, Paris and Venice, introduced 1982. Later also ran to Vienna in summer. Some runs made to Budapest from 1991. The British cars are also used for day luxury excursions under the same brand name, mostly in south-east England. Owned by Sea Containers Ltd.

Vulcan

1. Vulcan Foundry Co. Ltd, Newton-le-Willows, Warrington, loco builders, founded 1830. Part of EE, 1955.

2. (US) Vulcan, a loco building firm, based at Wilkes Barre; no connection with (*1*).

Vulcans

LB&SCR 0–6–0 goods locos built by the Vulcan Foundry Co.

Vulkan (Ger)

A loco building firm, at Stettin. No connection with Vulcan (*1*) or (*2*).

Vulnerables

Traffic vulnerable to theft (wines and spirits, tobacco, clothing etc).

Vulture (LTRS)

A retirement pensioner travelling free or at concessionary fares.

VVM

Vlaamsevervoer Mij; Flemish Transport Company. The Flemish section of the former *SNCV/NMVB* (qv), independently-managed from 1991. *See also Lijn, de*; *SRWT*.

W

Wabash (US)
Wabash, St Louis & Pacific Rly, latterly known officially as the Wabash Rly Co.

Wabash, to (USRS)
To drive a train with skill and speed. Also (sarcastically) to corner (qv). The Wabash was a company famed for its high standards of training.

Waggon road/way (obs)
Seventeenth- and eighteenth-century term for tramroad (*1*) or tramway (*1*).

Wagner Palace Cars
Pullman type cars operated by the 1882 Wagner Palace Car Company, owned by Webster Wagner and the Vanderbilts. The WPC Co., which originated in 1865 as the New York Central Sleeping Car Co., was acquired by the Pullman Co. (qv) in 1899.

Wagon
Generic term for any freight vehicle. On British rlys, after *c.* 1830, so spelled, i.e. *not* 'waggon', and universally used instead of 'truck'.

Wagon chaser (RS)(obs)
A brakesman or shunter in a shunting or marshalling yard. The duties included running after a moving wagon to pin down its brakes.

Wagon hoist (obs)
Machinery for lifting a rly wagon vertically between two levels, in a freight depot etc., both the hoist and each level being provided with tracks.

Wagon length (obs)
The length of track which will accommodate a four-wheeled wagon. Used as a rough measurement for sidings etc.

Wagon-lit (Fr)
A sleeping car. *See also CIWL*; *Couchette*.

Wagon load (obs)
A consignment of one ton or more, charged at wagon load rates.

Wagon teller
see Number takers (qv).

WAGR
Western Australian Government Rlys.

Waist
The widest part of the body of a rly or tramway vehicle.

Wakers (RS)(obs)
Facetious term used by GWR and BR (W) employees for sleeping car trains.

Walk against the gun, to (USRS)(obs)
To drive a steam loco up a steep gradient with the injector on.

Walker
Walker Brothers (Wigan) Ltd, manufacturers of diesel-mechanical railcars and power bogies.

Walking the length (RS)
The daily track inspection.

Walk-on rly/service
A rly service arranged so that passengers may rely on turning up at a station without reservation, with a good chance of finding a seat either immediately or after a short interval of standing. In Britain, this was

traditionally the case until the 1980s, with a reserve of rolling stock maintained to meet peak demands, but from that time, with increasing financial pressures imposed by central government, some parts of BR, and InterCity in particular, could no longer be regarded as offering a walk-on service.

Walk the dog, to (USRS)
To drive a freight train so fast that the high wagons sway violently from side to side.

Wall of Death, the (RS)
The steeply-graded line between Wimbledon and Sutton (particularly at the Sutton end), built in 1929 to be operated by electric rather than steam trains. From the fairground sideshow in which motor cyclists ride round the inside of a circular wall.

Wall Street notch (USRS)
see Company notch. From Wall Street, New York City, where rly shares are traded.

Walrus
TC for civil engineer's 40-ton ballast wagon.

Walschaert's valve gear
A very widely-adopted form of steam locomotive valve gear, in which movement is generated both from the piston crosshead and a single eccentric or return crank. Invented in 1844 by the Belgian engineer Egide Walschaert (1820–1901).

Waltzing Matilda (RS)
Track tamping machine; it appears to be dancing when in use.

W&B (RS)
Works and Bricks [the building department] (qv).

W&B Joint
Whitechapel & Bow Rly, London; Whitechapel MDR to Bow (Campbell Road Junction with LT&SR), inc

1897, opened 1902, joint MDR (LPTB from 1933) and LT&SR (LM&SR from 1923), part of LTE from 1948.

W&CIR
see W&KR.

W&CR
Waterloo & City Rly, an isolated electric tube rly from Waterloo station, London, to the Bank without an intermediate station. Inc 1893, opened 1898, part of L&SWR from 1907, SR from 1923, part of BR (S) since 1948.

W&KR
Waterford & Kilkenny Rly (Ire), inc 1845, first section opened 1848, renamed Waterford & Central Ireland Rly 1868, part of G&SWR from 1900.

W&LLR
Welshpool & Llanfair Light Rly, Welshpool–Llanfair Caereinion, 2 ft 6 in/762 mm gauge, LROs 1899, 1901, opened 1903. Constructed and worked by Cambrian Rlys; part of GWR 1923, BR (W) 1948. Passenger service ceased 1931, freight 1956. Restored and reopened as preserved line from 1963.

W&MER
Wrexham & Minera Extension Rly, Brymbo to near Llanfynydd. Inc 1865, opened 1872, vested jointly in GWR and L&NWR 1866, GWR and LM&SR 1923, BR 1948.

W&MR
Wrexham & Minera Rly, Wrexham to Brymbo. Inc 1861, opened 1862, vested in GWR 1871.

W&PR
Weymouth and Portland Rly. Inc 1862, opened 1865, leased to and worked by GWR and L&SWR, GWR & SR 1923–47, BR (W) 1948.

W&SCR
Woodside & South Croydon Rly, Woodside SER to Selsdon Road Junction. Inc 1880, jointly vested in

SER and LB&SCR 1882, opened
1885.

W&SJR
Wellington & Severn Junction Rly, inc
1853, 1854, Wellington (Salop)–
Ketley–Coalbrookdale–Lightmoor,
opened 1857, part of GWR 1892.

W&SS
Wolverton & Stony Stratford:
originally promoted as the Stony
Stratford & District Tramways Co.; a
steam tramway (*4*), 3 ft 6 in/1,067 mm
gauge, inc 1883, name changed to
WSS and District Light Rlys Co.
1886. Opened 1887, freight traffic
begun 1888, extended from SS to
Deanshanger 1888. Name changed to
W&SS District Tramroads Co. 1889,
closed 1889. W to SS reopened 1891,
name changed to W&SS District New
Tramway Co. 1893. Purchased by
L&NWR 1919, part of LM&SR 1923,
closed 1926.

W&TR
Waterford & Tramore Rly (Ire), 5 ft
3 in/1,600 mm gauge. Inc 1851,
opened 1853, GSR 1924, CIE 1945,
closed 1960. Not physically connected
to the rest of the Irish rly system.

W&UT
Wisbech & Upwell Tramway. Inc by
GER Act of 1881, steam tramway (*4*),
opened 1883, 1884, owned and
worked by GER, L&NER and BR.
Passenger service ceased 1927,
completely closed 1966.

Wankers (RS)
LB&SCR Marsh 4–4–2T, rebuilt by
Mansell.

Wantage
Wantage Tramway, steam tramway (*4*)
between Wantage town and Wantage
Road station GWR, with physical
connection to GWR. Inc 1873, opened
1875, passenger service ceased 1925,
completely closed 1945.

Warflats
Bogie flat wagons used for Ministry of
Defence traffic.

Warning boards
1. Boards exhibiting stripe or bar
    markings to warn drivers they are
    approaching a distant signal. First
    used in Belgium in 1907, also
    adopted in Germany and France.
    Copied by the British MoT/DTp to
    warn road traffic to slow down at
    the approach to a traffic
    roundabout etc.
2. Yellow boards illuminated at night
    and during fog or falling snow,
    installed on the lineside at a
    minimum of half a mile before a
    temporary speed restriction. *See
    also* C&T indicators.

Warnkreuze (Ger)
A fixed red and white warning signal
in the form of a cross installed at the
road approaches to level crossings,
widely used in Europe.

WARS
1. Waterloo Area Resignalling
    Scheme; completed 1991 and
    controlled from Wimbledon.
2. Initials of the PKP sleeping and
    restaurant car organization.

War well (obs)
TC for 50-ton bogie well wagon built
in the Second World War for the
Ministry of Supply.

Wash (LTRS)
Train washing machine.

Washing machines (RS)(obs)
Signal box frames made by Ransomes
& Rapier.

Wasps (RS)
People wearing high visibility jackets
seen walking on the track.

Water boiler (RS)(obs)
A steam loco fireman.

Waterburys (RS)
NER Worsdell 2–4–0 locos class G of

1887–8, converted into 4–4–0s from 1900 onwards From the name of a watch.

Water crane
A lineside appliance fed from a water tank or cistern and fitted with flexible hose (or bag) for filling steam loco water tanks. Usually located at the forward end of a station platform.

Watercress Line
Brand name adopted by the preserved rly using the Alton–Alresford section of the former BR Alton–Winchester line. First section opened 1977.

Water Level Route
The New York Central RR's name for its main line between New York and Chicago via Cleveland.

Water scoop
see Scoop (2).

Water troughs (obs)
Narrow and lengthy troughs placed between the rails from which water could be scooped up into the tender tanks of steam locos travelling at speed (optimum uptake was achieved at around 40 m.p.h.). Invented by John Ramsbottom, loco superintendent of the L&NWR and first installed on that rly in 1860.

Watford tanks (RS)
L&NWR 0–6–2T.

Wath Daisies (RS)
see Daisies.

Watteau
TEE Paris–Tourcoing, introduced 1978. With *Faidherbe* (qv), the last of the *TEE*s.

Wattman (Fr)(obs)
A tramcar or electric train driver.

Waveney Valley
see WVR.

Waverley
An express between London (St Pancras) and Edinburgh, so named 1957, ceased 1964, re-introduced as summer-only service 1965, renamed Waverley Express 1968, ceased 1968.

Waverley route
Carlisle–Hawick–Galashiels–Edinburgh.

Way car (US)(obs)
Early term for a caboose (qv).

Way freight (US)(obs)
A pick-up goods (qv).

Way switching (US)
Shunting operations carried out en route.

Way train (US)(obs)
A slow or local train.

WBR
The Wansbeck Valley Rly, Reedsmouth–Morpeth. Inc 1859, first section opened 1862, part of NBR, 1863.

WC (obs)
Wagon Control.

WC&ER
Whitehaven, Cleator & Egremont Junction Rly, Morehouse Junction, near Whitehaven to Moor Row, Rowrah and Marron Junction; Ullock–Parton; Moor Row–Egremont–Sellafield. Inc 1854, first section opened 1857. Paid a 15 per cent dividend in 1863, becoming one of the most prosperous rlys in Britain. Leased to L&NWR and FR 1879, part of LM&SR 1923, BR 1948, last section closed 1980.

WC&PR
Weston, Clevedon & Portishead Tramways Co. Inc 1885, opened 1897, 1907. By act of 1899 status changed from a steam tramway to a light rly, and name changed to WC&P Light Railways Co. Closed 1940.

WCJS
West Coast Joint Stock; rolling stock for WCML services jointly owned by L&NWR and Caledonian Rly.

WCML
West Coast Main Line, London
(Euston)–Crewe–Carlisle–Carstairs–
Glasgow.

WCR
1. West Clare Rly (Ire), Ennis to
Kilrush/Kilkee, 3 ft/914 mm gauge,
opened 1887 to Miltown Malbay,
extension to Kilrush/Kilkee
constructed by South Clare Rlys
Co., inc 1884, opened 1892,
worked by WCR. Part of GSR
1925, closed 1961. Subject of a
song by Percy French, *Are Ye
Right There, Michael, Are Ye Right?*
2. West Cornwall Rly, Truro to
Penzance etc., inc 1846, first
section opened 1852, leased to
GWR, B&ER and SDR 1865, part
of GWR from 1878.
3. West Cheshire Rly, inc 1861,
Northwich–Helsby, part of CLC
1867 opened 1869, 1870.

WDR
West Durham Rly, from collieries
near Crook to Hunwick/ Burnhouse
Junc (Bishop Auckland–Spennymoor
line). Inc 1839, first section opened
1840, part of NER from 1870.

Wear [the] blue, to (USRS)
To be delayed by a wagon, coach or
loco fault. From the blue flag
displayed on parts of trains on which
men are working. *See also* Blue light/
flag.

Weardale/Wear Valley Line
The Wearhead branch, NER.
Originally the Wear Valley Rly, inc
1845, first section opened 1847, leased
to S&DR 1847, purchased by S&DR
1858. Wear Valley Extension
Rly (Stanhope to Wearhead) inc
1892, absorbed by NER 1894, opened
1895.

Wear [the] green, to (USRS)
To run a train in more than one

section. From the colour of the flags
and lamps shown on such trains.

Weasel
1. (LTRS) A dmu.
2. (RS) A tip from a passenger. *See
also* Weasel, to/weaseling.

Weasel, to/weaseling (RS)(obs)
To race along an arriving train,
seeking out passengers wanting their
luggage carried to the cab/taxi rank; to
go all out for tips; to deprive another
porter of his tip by getting in first.
Probably from the weasel's alleged
ability to suck out the contents of an
egg without breaking the shell.

Weather board (obs)
The screen around the back of the
firebox of steam locos originally
forming the only weather protection
for the enginemen.

Web [of a rail]
That part between the head and the
base.

Wedglock coupler
A type of centre coupling which gives
an instantaneous linkage between cars
of all electrical and mechanical
connections.

Wee bogies (RS)
G&SWR Smellie 119 class 4–4–0
locos.

Weir Committee
A government committee on main line
electrification, chaired by Lord Weir.
It reported to the Minister of
Transport in March 1931.

WEL&CPR
West End of London & Crystal Palace
Rly. Inc 1853, opened 1856, Crystal
Palace to Wandsworth Common,
worked by LB&SCR, extended to
Pimlico terminus on south bank at
Battersea Bridge 1858 and to Bromley
(now Shortlands) in 1857 and
1858. The Crystal Palace–Battersea
section became part of the LB&SCR

in 1859, remainder passed to LC&DR 1860.

Wells Fargo
Express freight (qv) operation using rlys, founded in 1851 by William G. Fargo, Henry Wells and others. Purchased the Overland Mail Co. (formed in 1857 by Fargo and others to carry US mails) in 1861.

Wells Fargo (RS)
Old style Pullman cars with US features.

Well tank
A type of steam loco in which the water is stored in a tank slung between the frames, often under the footplate, providing a useful low centre of gravity, increasing stability on light or poorly-laid track.

Well wagon
A bogie wagon with a dip in the central section between the bogies which enables high loads to be carried without fouling the loading gauge.

Welsh Chieftain
see Land cruise.

Welsh Dragon
A summer service between Rhyl and Llandudno introduced 1950; 17¼ m, with a pull and push set, in 31–9 min. Dmu sets were used from *c.* 1960 and it ceased soon afterwards. Name revived for London (Euston) to Holyhead service introduced 1987 (journey time 4 h 34 min).

Welsh Land Cruise
see Land cruise.

Welshman
A summer service between London (Euston), Prestatyn (first stop), Llandudno, Bangor/Holyhead, and Pwllheli/ Portmadoc. Introduced 1927, revived 1949. Ceased 1966. Name revived 1987 for a Holyhead–Cardiff service, name dropped 1988.

Welwyn Control
A signalling modification widely adopted after the Welwyn accident of 1935, in which track circuits in the rear and in advance of a home signal were interlocked with the block instruments, thus preventing the signalman from accepting a following train until all the track circuits were cleared.

Wensleydale Line
Hawes to Northallerton.

WES
BR (S) class 442 emu sets for the Weymouth electrification of 1988, 5-WES. An abbreviation of Wessex.

Wessex Electrics
NSE brand name introduced 1989 for London (Waterloo)–Southampton–Bournemouth–Weymouth and Southampton/Eastleigh–Portsmouth electric services.

Wessex Line
BR brand name for Portsmouth–Bristol–Cardiff service.

Wessex Scot
A service between Poole and Glasgow/ Edinburgh via Oxford, introduced 1986.

Wessie/ey (RS)(obs)
The L&NWR, or its locos or employees.

Westbound
see Eastbound.

West Coast Corridor Express
With the introduction of corridor stock and dining cars in 1892 this became the unofficial name for the afternoon express between London (Euston) and Glasgow (Central) with coaches for Knutsford, Whitehaven, Edinburgh and Aberdeen, which had been introduced in 1889. The 1909 journey time was 8 h 20 min. *See also* Midday Scot.

West Coast Postal
The unofficial name for North
Western Night TPO Down, Euston–
Aberdeen.

West Coast Route, the
WCML (qv).

West Country Pullman
A London (Paddington) to Paignton
service, introduced 1988.

Westerns (RS)
BR class 52 diesel-hydraulic locos.
From their names which were all
prefixed 'Western'.

Western Valleys
see Eastern & Western Valleys Lines.

West Highlander
BR IC land cruise train from London
to Oban, Fort William and Mallaig.

West Highland Rly/Line
Craigendoran to Fort William and
Mallaig. Inc 1889, 1896, opened 1894
to Fort William, 1901 to Mallaig,
worked by NBR. Part of L&NER
1923.

Westinghouse
Westinghouse Electric Co. of London,
formed 1889, became British
Westinghouse Electric &
Manufacturing Co. Ltd, 1899 with
works at Trafford Park, Manchester.
Manufacturers of electric traction
equipment for rlys and tramways.
Became MV (qv), 1919. *See also*
Westinghouse brake.

Westinghouse brake
A compressed air automatic braking
system invented by the US engineer
George Westinghouse (1846–1914) in
1872–3. Much improved in 1886–7,
and subsequently adopted by the
Caledonian Rly, GER, LB&SCR,
NBR and NER. A works to
manufacture this brake was established
at Kings Cross, London in 1879
(rebuilt 1889) and the English
Westinghouse Brake Co. Ltd was inc

in 1881. Amalgamated with McKenzie
& Holland (qv) *c*. 1907 to form the
McKenzie, Holland & Westinghouse
Power Signalling Co. Name changed
to Westinghouse Brake & Saxby
Signal Co., 1920, after control had
passed to the Consolidated Signal Co.
(qv) and its Chippenham works. Name
changed to Westinghouse Brake &
Signal Co., 1935. Part of Hawker
Siddeley Group, 1979. *See also* Air
brake.

West Line, The
Newcastle–Hexham–Carlisle.

West London Line
Willesden Junc–Kensington (Olympia)
–Clapham Junc. *See also* WLR.

West Midlands Executive
An express between London (Euston)
and Shrewsbury, introduced 1987.
Name dropped 1988.

West Riding Limited
Supplementary fare streamlined steam-
hauled express between London
(Kings Cross), Leeds (Central) and
Bradford (Exchange), introduced
1937. Re-introduced as West Riding,
1949 but without streamlined stock.
Ceased *c*. 1963.

West Riding Pullman
An all-Pullman service between
London (Kings Cross), Wakefield,
Leeds, Bradford and Halifax, so
named 1927, renamed Yorkshire
Pullman (qv) 1935.

West Somerset
West Somerset Rly, Norton
Fitzwarren to Watchet. Inc 1857,
opened 1862, leased and worked
by B&ER, part of GWR from 1922.
Name adopted for the preserved
line between Minehead and
Norton Fitzwarren (former BR
Minehead branch), first section
restored 1976. *See also*
WSMR.

West Sussex Rly
see Hundred of Manhood.

West Yorkshire Executive
A service between London (Kings
Cross) and Leeds, so named 1984.
Name dropped 1989.

Wet mole in the firebox, a
(USRS)(obs)
A condition arising from incompetent
firing of a steam loco.

WEZ (Ger)
West Europäische Zeit; West European
Time.

Whack (USRS)
A carman (qv).

Whale body (USRS)
A wagon with a bottom hopper.

Wheel, to (USRS)
To drive a train at high speed.

Wheel arrangement
A method of identifying locomotive
types by the arrangement of the
driving and other wheels: *see*
Continental notation [steam locos];
Notation [of electric and diesel locos];
Whyte's notation [steam locos].

Wheelbase
The distance between the points at
each end of a vehicle where the tyres
of the wheels rest on the rail. If the
vehicle has trucks/bogies, the *overall or
outer wheelbase* is the distance between
the resting points of the outermost
wheels. The measurement from the
centre of one truck to the centre of the
other is known as *distance between
truck centres*, or in Fr, *l'entr'axe des
boggies*.

Wheel monkey (USRS)
A carriage & wagon inspector.

Wheel set
A pair of wheels mounted on their
axle.

Wheel tapper (obs)
A C&W examiner specifically
employed to check the wheels and
axleboxes of trains in service when
they stopped at the larger stations.
From the tapping of the hammer used
to confirm there were no defects in the
wheels.

Whelley Line
Bamfurlong Junc–Standish Junc,
avoiding Wigan.

WHH&R
West Hartlepool Harbour & Rly Co.
Inc 1852, an amalgamation of the WH
Harbour & Dock Co. with Stockton &
Hartlepool Rly and Clarence Rly. Part
of NER 1865.

Whipsnade
Whipsnade & Umfolozi Rly, 2 ft 6 in/
762 mm gauge, Whipsnade Park Zoo,
Bedfordshire, opened 1970.

Whirlybird (RS)
A Matisa ballast tamper.

Whiskers
1. (RS) Exhaust pipes bent up over
the cab ends of BR diesel railcars
(class 122 etc.). *See also* Speed
whiskers.
2. (USRS) A very senior rlyman;
seniority.

Whispering baritone (RS)
A garrulous, noisy person, a barrack-
room lawyer.

Whispering death (RS)
A dmu. From its quiet approach to
anyone on the track.

Whistle off, to (USRS)
To give two short blasts on the whistle
as a warning the train is about to
move.

Whistle out a flag, to (USRS)
To give one long and three short
blasts on the whistle, indicating that
the brakeman must protect the rear of
the halted train with a flag or lamp.
Or to give three short and one long
blast, indicating that the brakeman
must protect the head of the halted
train with a flag or lamp.

Whistle pig (USRS)
A loco driver.
Whistlers (RS)
1. BR diesel locos class 40. From the sound emitted when starting.
2. BR Class 312 emus. From the aerodynamic noise when in motion.
Whistle stop
A very minor station which trains approach with a whistle signal, not calling unless a flag or lamp is displayed. *See also* Flag stop (qv).
Whistle stop tour
A full scale tour of the US by presidential candidates, in a train using private cars (qv), during which stops were made at many small communities (whistle stops (qv)) for the candidate to address the crowd from the platform of the rear car. Harry S. Truman was the last presidential candidate to undertake a full whistle stop tour, in 1948. Some others have undertaken abbreviated tours subseqently, e.g. Jimmy Carter in 1976.
Whistling post (US)
A white post at the trackside warning that a level crossing is ahead and a whistle should be sounded.
White feather (USRS)(obs)
A plume of steam over the safety valve of a steam loco. Hence to carry a white feather, to run with a full head of steam.
White period
A period of total occupation by the civil engineers, when no trains of any kind are allowed on a section of line.
White ribbon (USRS)
A white flag carried by an extra train.
White Rose
An express between London (Kings Cross), Leeds (Central) and Bradford (Exchange), introduced 1949, later Leeds only, name dropped 1964.
White Rose Pullman
An all-Pullman train between London

(Kings Cross), Leeds (Central), Bradford and Harrogate, introduced 1964. Ceased 1967. Name re-introduced 1991 for a First class Pullman express between York and London (Kings Cross).
White shirt (USRS)
A rly officer or manager. Sufficiently remote from manual labour to be able to wear a white shirt.
Whitewash coach/van (obs)
A vehicle equipped with a device which deposited whitewash on the track at any point where defects were sensed, to mark them for subsequent investigation.
Whizzers (RS)
BR class 52 diesel-hydraulic locos.
WHR
Welsh Highland Rly, Portmadoc–Dinas Junction, 1 ft 11½ in/597 mm gauge, LROs 1922, 1923, acquired NWNGR and PB&SSR. Opened 1922, 1923, leased by FR 1934–42, closed to passengers 1936, to freight 1937. Partially reopened as preserved line from 1980.
Whyte's notation
A method of classifying steam locos,

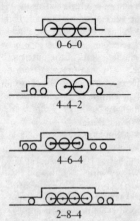

0–6–0

4–4–2

4–6–4

2–8–4

invented by F.M. Whyte (1865–1941); one time general mechanical engineer, NYC RR. The notation enunciates from left to right the total number of *wheels*, the central number(s) referring to the coupled driving wheels and the first and last to the leading and trailing uncoupled wheels. Thus 0–6–0 indicates three pairs of driving wheels and no others, 4–4–2, a four-wheeled leading truck, two pairs of coupled driving wheels and a two-wheeled trailing truck. The suffix T, e.g. 0–6–0T, indicates a tank loco: PT, a pannier tank; WT, a well tank; ST, a saddle tank. *See also* Continental notation.

Wicket gate
A gate at a level crossing which can be locked from the signal box to prevent pedestrians from crossing the line when a train is approaching.

Wickham
D. Wickham & Co. Ltd, Ware, manufacturers of railcars, mu diesel sets and powered rail trolleys.

Wide gauge
The US term for broad gauge (qv).

Widen, to (USRS)
To open the throttle of a steam loco to increase speed.

Widened Lines
City Widened lines (qv).

Widows and Orphans (RS)
A term used to describe the unsafe practice of walking along a running line with one's back to approaching traffic.

Wiener Walzer
A night service between Basle and Vienna, introduced 1959, extended to Bucharest 1962 (Budapest in winter).

Wiggly wire
1. (RS) A wavy band of stainless steel set in the top of the running rails to assist the conductivity of low tension current on little-used sections of track-circuited lines.
2. A system of AWS (qv) with a cab display showing the indication of the last signal passed.

Wig-wag (USRS)
A signal at a level crossing. From the action of its swinging arms.

Wild cat (USRS)
A loco moving without a driver on board.

William Shakespeare
Summer express between London (Paddington) and Wolverhampton/ Stratford-upon-Avon, so named 1951; ran that summer only.

William Tell Express
A summer service (two and sometimes three trains each way) between Boulogne and Lucerne (also Lugano, when traffic warranted), with all seats reserved for British travel agencies, introduced by CTAC (qv) in 1934. Connecting trains were also chartered by CTAC to carry clients between London and Folkestone/ Dover.

Willie (USRS)
Waybill for a loaded wagon.

Willmott Group
Harry Willmott and his son, Russell, who took up interests in unsuccessful railways, managed them and sought to improve their fortunes. Their achievements were much lauded in the Edwardian RM. At various times they managed or controlled the E&WJR, IofWCR, LD&ECR, Sheffield District, SDR (2), S&MJR, Edge Hill Light, and N&BJR.

Wimbling (RS)
1. Any drilling operation by track maintenance staff.
2. The use of a manually-operated auger.

WIMR
see LMR.

Wind (USRS)
Brake air/air brakes.
Windcutters (RS)(obs)
An early term for streamlined locos;
(Fr) = *coupe-vent. See also*
Windsplitters.
Windjammer
1. (RS) A blocked airpipe on a diesel
   engine.
2. (USRS) An air compressor used in
   a rly brake system.
Windowhang, to (RS)
To lean out of a window of a moving
train for a protracted period.
Window music (USRS)
Attractive scenery.
Windsor Lines
The westernmost pair of tracks from
London (Waterloo) to Clapham
Junction, Barnes etc.
Windsplitters (obs)
US term for streamlined locos and
diesel sets.
Wind up, to (LTRS)
To move the handle of the master
controller of a train from the off
position to a motoring position.
Wing her, to (USRS)
To set the hand brakes on a moving
train.
Wing rails
Guide rails at the open spaces in
crossings, which prevent derailment.
Wing tank
A design of industrial tank loco in
which the main water tank forms
a cradle for the boiler and
smokebox.
Wiper (USRS)
A loco cleaner.
Wipe the clock, to (USRS)
To make an emergency brake
application (qv), sending the needle
right round the dial.
Wire tapper (USRS)
A rly telegraph operator.

Wirral
see WR
Wirral lines
Liverpool (Central LL) to New
Brighton/West Kirby.
Wisdom box (USRS)
A facetious description of a
yardmaster's office.
Wise guy (USRS)
A station agent.
Wissington
Wissington Light Rly, an agricultural
system connected to the GER Stoke
Ferry branch at Abbey & West
Dereham, first section opened 1905,
latterly operated by the British Sugar
Corporation, closed 1982.
Withered Arm
A name coined in 1967 by the late
T.W.E. Roche for the former
L&SWR/SR lines west of Exeter after
Beeching (qv) had done his work.
WL&WR
Waterford, Limerick & Western Rly
(Ire), Waterford–Limerick–Sligo with
branches to Killaloe, Foynes, Tralee
and Thurles, inc as Waterford &
Limerick Rly 1846, first section
(Limerick–Tipperary) opened 1848.
Renamed WL&WR 1895. Part of
GS&WR from 1901.
WLER
West London Extension Rly, from a
point just south of the present
Kensington (Olympia) station to
Longhedge and Clapham Junctions
with the L&SWR, LC&DR and
LB&SCR. Inc 1859, opened 1863.
GWR, L&NWR, L&SWR and
LB&SCR Joint; GWR,SR and
LM&SR joint from 1923. BR from
1948.
WLR
1. West London Rly, from North Pole
   Junction (with GWR and
   L&NWR), near Old Oak Common,

to near the present Kensington (Olympia) station. Inc as Birmingham, Bristol & Thames Junction Rly 1836, name changed to WLR 1840, opened 1844, vested in GWR and L&NWR, 1854; GWR and LM&SR 1923, BR 1948.

2. West Lancashire Rly, Southport to Preston, inc 1871, first section opened 1878, part of L&YR from 1897.

WM&CQJR

Wrexham, Mold & Connah's Quay Junction Rly, inc 1862, opened 1866. Purchased by GCR 1905.

WMR

1. West Midland Rly; an 1860 amalgamation of the OW&WR, the Worcester & Hereford Rly and the Newport, Abergavenny & Hereford Rly. Part of GWR from 1863.

2. Woolmer Military Rly: *see* LMR.

WNJR

West Norfolk Junction Rly, Heacham-Wells, inc 1864, opened 1866, worked by GER, merged with Lynn & Hunstanton Rly to become Hunstanton & West Norfolk Rly, 1874. Part of GER 1890.

WO (obs)

Waiting orders, goods on hand awaiting the consignor's instructions.

Wolds [Coast] Line

Brand name for BR Hull–Scarborough line and services.

Wolf (USRS)

See Lone Wolf.

Wolves (RS)

GNR large Stirling 0-4-4T. From their distinctive bark.

Womble (LTRS)

An elderly person, especially one travelling on a concessionary or free ticket.

Womming (RS)

Rail turning.

Woodhead Line/Route

The former GCR Manchester to Sheffield line via Guide Bridge, Woodhead Tunnel and Penistone. Closed to through passenger trains, 1970, to freight, 1981.

Wood Line (LTRS)

The Metropolitan line from Baker Street to Uxbridge/Watford/Chesham and Amersham. From the name of the original section, the Metropolitan & St Johns *Wood* Rly.

Woolworths (RS)

2-6-0 locos built in the early 1920s at Royal Arsenal, Woolwich, or 2-6-0 locos assembled from parts made there.

Work a car, to (USRS)

To unload freight from a wagon.

Work(s) cars/work equipment

Rolling stock designed specifically for rly and tramway (3) construction and maintenance or used solely for those purposes, hence 'work trains'.

Working Notice

The weekly bulletin covering all engineering and signalling work, signalling changes and other occurrences affecting the operation of the rly (or sections of it) and also including other important information for train crews and operating staff.

Working timetable

The timetable produced for the use of rly staff showing all the trains on each line, passenger, freight, light engine movements, etc, their order of running, lines they shall use and also the exact time to the nearest half minute of passing, stopping and departure at stations etc. Paths for trains run 'as required' are also shown. The times of passenger trains printed in the working timetable may differ from those given in the public timetables. Also known as the Service Time Book.

Workmen's fares and trains (obs)
Cheap tickets for those travelling daily to and from work in the early morning, only available by stipulated trains or at stipulated times for travel from specified stations. They were required by various private railway acts, beginning with the LC&DR Metropolitan Extensions Lines Act, 1860. This act fixed the times such trains were to be run and the fares to be charged (the lines concerned were opened from 1865). The Metropolitan Railway had however voluntarily offered such facilities from May 1864. General and obligatory introduction of workmen's fares dates from the Cheap Trains Act of 1883. The workmen's facilities were replaced by 'Early Morning Fares' in 1950 but these were withdrawn after 1961.

Works and Bricks (LTRS)
LT Works and Buildings Department and its staff.

Work the yards, to (USRS)
To shunt.

Work through, to (LTRS)
To work through the middle of a split turn (qv).

Work train
A train carrying materials to lay or repair track or trtack formation, to repair or erect bridges etc.

Worsborough branch
Wombwell-Worsborough-Silkstone.

Worth Valley
Keighley-Oxenhope. *See also* K&WVR.

WP (US)
Western Pacific RR.

WR
1. Wirral Rly, West Kirby to Liverpool ferry terminal at Seacombe and to Birkenhead Park/

New Brighton, inc 1863 as Hoylake Rly and opened Hoylake to Birkenhead Docks 1866, closed 1870. Reopened by Hoylake Rail & Tramway Company from 1872, renamed Seacombe, Hoylake & Deeside Rly 1881. Wirral Rly Company inc 1883, opened Birkenhead Docks to Birkenhead Park 1881. Reconstituted and amalgamated with Seacombe, Hoylake & Deeside Rly Co as the Wirral Rly, 1891. Part of LM&SR from 1923.

2. Wycombe Rly, Maidenhead to High Wycombe and Aylesbury also Princes Risborough to Thame and Kennington Junction (Oxford), inc 1846 (Maidenhead to High Wycombe), opened 1854, 1862, 1863, 1864, part of GWR from 1867.

3. Wenlock Rly, inc 1861, opened Coalbrookdale-Presthorpe 1864, to Craven Arms 1867. Worked by GWR. Part of GWR 1896.

4. Witney Rly, inc 1859 Yarnton to Witney, opened 1861, part of GWR 1890.

5. Woodstock Rly, inc 1886, Kidlington to Blenheim & Woodstock, opened 1890, worked by GWR. Part of GWR 1897.

6. Wigtownshire Rly, inc 1872, Newton Stewart-Whithorn and branch to Garliestown, first section opened 1875–6. Amalgamated with PR (*1*) to form P&WR (qv), 1885.

7. Western Region of BR.

8. Western Rly [of India], formed 1951.

WR&GJC
West Riding & Grimsby Joint Rly, Wakefield-Stainforth/ Doncaster, inc 1862, opened 1866, vested in MS&LR & GNR 1866 as WR&G Joint Rly, L&NER from 1923.

Wreck crew (USRS)
Breakdown gang.
Wreck train (USRS)
A breakdown train (qv).
Wrington Vale
Wrington Vale Light Rly,
Congresbury Junction to Blagdon,
LRO 1898, opened 1901. Constructed,
worked and financed by the GWR.
Wrong iron (USRS)
Wrong line/road (qv).
Wrong line/road
A reversal of the normal direction of
working on a rly. *See also* Wrong line
working; Wrong line orders.
Wrong line orders
Forms authorizing movement of a
train over the wrong line (qv) during
emergencies. Four types of form exist
to be completed, according to the
circumstances: guard to signalman;
driver to signalman; guard to driver;
and signalman to driver. Each move
requires a separate form. *See also*
Wrong line working.
Wrong line working
When one line of a double track
section is obstructed or under
maintenance, and there is no system of
bi-directional signalling, locos and
trains may be allowed to proceed
wrong line (qv), by the introduction of
single or wrong line working, using a
pilotman (qv) between one signalbox
and the next, as arranged by a station
manager, district inspector or other
responsible official who completes
special single line working forms
addressed to the pilotman, signalmen
and station managers in the area
affected. *See also* Wrong line orders.
Wrong one off (LTRS)
A signal cleared to the off mode, but
for an incorrect route.
WRUR
West Riding Union Rly, inc 1846, an

amalgamation of the WYR and the
Leeds & West Riding Junction Rly,
part of L&YR 1846. Bradford–
Halifax–Sowerby Bridge; first section
opened 1850.
WS&WR
Wiltshire, Somerset & Weymouth Rly,
Salisbury–Westbury–Thingley
Junction/Bathampton/Devizes,
Westbury–Weymouth, Frome–
Radstock. Inc 1845, opened 1848,
1850, 1851, 1854, 1856, 1857, part of
GWR from 1851.
WSMR
West Somerset Mineral Rly, Watchet
to Gupworthy and Brendon Hills iron
ore workings, inc 1855, opened 1859,
passenger service 1865 (officially to
Combe Row only). Closed 1898.
Partially reopened 1907, closed 1909.
WSR
West Somerset Rly (qv).
WT
1. Wotton Tramway, also known as
   the Brill Tramroad or Tramway;
   Quainton Road to Brill, with
   branch from Wotton Underwood to
   Kingswood Lane Wharf; opened
   without parliamentary sanction
   1871, 1872. Horses used initially,
   steam locos later. Passengers and
   freight carried. Leased and worked
   by Metropolitan Rly 1899 (Met
   & GC Joint Committee from
   1906), under a 'temporary'
   arrangement. Closed 1935. *See also*
   O&AT.
2. A well tank locomotive (qv).
3. Initials used by GEC (qv) (Witton
   Works) to avoid confusion with GE
   (2) (qv).
WTT
Working timetable (qv).
WVER
Wear Valley Extension Rly: *see*
Weardale/Wear Valley Line.

WVLR
Wrington Vale Light Rly: *see*
Wrington Vale.

WVR
1. Waveney Valley Rly, Tivetsthall-
   Beccles, inc 1851, 1853, first
   section opened 1855, worked by
   ECR. Part of GER, 1863.
2. Wear Valley Rly: *see* Weardale/
   Wear Valley Line.
3. Wye Valley Rly: *see* Wye
   Valley.

WWW&DR
Waterford, Wexford, Wicklow &
Dublin Rly: *see* D&SER.

Wye (US)
A triangle (qv). From its 'Y' shape.

Wye Valley
Wye Valley Rly, Chepstow to Monmouth,
inc 1866, opened 1876, worked by GWR,
part of GWR from 1905.

WYPTE
West Yorkshire Passenger Transport
Executive.

WYR
West Yorkshire Rly, title assumed in
1863 by Bradford, Wakefield & Leeds
Rly (Wakefield–Leeds, worked by
GNR from its opening in 1857). Part
of GNR 1865. *See also* MJR.

X

X (USRS)
An empty wagon.

Xmundifier (obs)
Maltese term for rly, a corruption of the Fr *chemin de fer*. The Maltese also called their rly *il vapur* = the steamer.

XPT
An Australian high speed train with diesel power units at each end, a version of BR IC125 trains adapted to Australian conditions, the first of which entered service in New South Wales in 1982.

XP 64 (obs)
Prototype BR express passenger coaches in blue and grey livery introduced on the Talisman (qv) in 1964.

Y

Y
An abbreviation for a wye (qv).

Yam-yams (RS)
Diesel multiple units. From the noise made by the engines when idling.

Y&NMR
York & North Midland Rly, York to Castleford and junctions with NMR, inc 1836, first section opened 1839. Later extended to serve Harrogate, Scarborough, Filey, Bridlington, Pickering, Market Weighton and Knottingley etc. Part of NER from 1854.

Y&NNR
Yarmouth & North Norfolk [Light] Rly, Great Yarmouth–Stalham. Inc 1876, first section opened 1877 as Great Yarmouth & Stalham Light Rly. Renamed Y&NNLR 1878 (authorized to extend to North Walsham, which was reached in 1881), Y&NNR 1881. Part of E&MR (qv) 1883.

Yankees (RS)
Highland Rly 'P' class 4–4–0T, originally built by Dübs & Co. for use in Uruguay, which someone must have thought was in the USA; also used of others built to the same design.

Yanks (RS)
General Motors diesel locos of the IE.

Yard (LTRS)
A car depot.

Yard geese (USRS)
Shunters; always moving hither and thither round the rly yards.

Yard goat (USRS)
A small shunting loco.

Yardmaster/yard manager
The official responsible for the control of all operations within a shunting or marshalling yard and its effective working, directing inspectors, foremen, shunters, goods porters, checkers etc.

Yardmen (US)
Shunters.

YDR
Yorkshire Dales Rly (qv).

Yellow Engine
see Red engine.

Yellow eye (USRS)
A signal showing the caution indication.

Yellow Perils (RS)
Special printed notices, similar to TC (*2*) (qv), regarding signalling arrangements (especially on LT) or (generally) any operating notices issued to staff and printed (or originally printed) on yellow paper. From yellow peril, a fear raised in the 1890s/1900s in Europe that the Chinese and Japanese would before long terrorize and over-run the white races and their civilization.

Yellowstone (US)
A Mallet (qv) steam loco with 2–8–8–4 wheel arrangement.

Yellow whisker (RS)(obs)
Speed whiskers (qv).

Yerkes Tubes
Those London tube rlys (Bakerloo,

Piccadilly and Charing Cross, Euston
& Hampstead) originally built and
controlled by the syndicate headed by
the US financier Charles Tyson Yerkes
(1837–1905).

YM
Yardmaster/manager (qv).

York, the (RS)(obs)
No. 9 platform in the old London
(Euston) terminus, originally provided
for trains to the Midlands and York.

Yorkie (RS)
A nickname for GNR, its employees
or its locos.

Yorkshire
Yorkshire Engine Co. Ltd,
Meadowhall Works, Sheffield, loco
builders, inc 1865. Acquired by
United Steel Companies 1945–8.
Diesel loco manufacture started 1949.
Last steam locos produced 1956.
Taken over by Rolls Royce Ltd 1965
and loco production transferred to that
company's Sentinel (qv) works.

Yorkshire Dales Rly
1. Skipton to Grassington, inc 1897,
   opened 1902, worked by Midland
   Rly, part of LM&SR from 1923.
2. Original name of ESR (5) (qv).

Yorkshireman
An express between London (St
Pancras), Sheffield and Bradford
(Exchange), so named 1927. 4 h 1 min
timing in 1937.

Yorkshire Pullman
A renaming in 1935 of the West Riding
Pullman (qv). All-Pullman service in
three sections running between London
(Kings Cross), Hull/Harrogate/
Bradford (Exchange) and Halifax.
Restored 1946, separate Kings Cross–
Hull section, using Midland Pullman
diesel units, 1966. Ceased to run as a
Pullman service in 1978 and name
dropped. Revived 1985 as a London
(Kings Cross)–Leeds/Bradford service
with a 1 h 59 min journey time
London–Leeds in 1990.

Z

Zahnradbahn (Ger)
A rack or cog-wheel rly.

Zero point
The point from which the mileage of a rly is measured.

Zone ticket
A ticket allowing unlimited journeys in a specified area for a short period, usually a week.

Zoo box (RS)
A mess van used by gangs working on the line.

Zoo keeper (RS)
A rlyman or woman checking tickets etc. at station barriers.

Zulu
1. (obs) The unofficial name for the 15.00 express from London (Paddington) to Plymouth and the corresponding return working, introduced in 1879 (during the Zulu War). The usage was current until around 1914.
2. (USRS)(obs) An immigrant rail passenger on US/Canadian rlys on the way to settling in his new home. Hence Zulu train and to travel Zulu style, i.e. with all portable household possessions and farm equipment.